THE ART OF SEXUAL ECSTASY

There are no holy places and no holy people –
only holy moments.

In the end these things
matter most :
  How well did you love ?
How fully did you live ?
How deeply did you learn
to let go ?

Things to do today:
  Inhale, exhale
  inhale, exhale

Those who are awake live in
a state of constant
      Amazement.

J Kornfield

Other books by the author:

L'Univers des Hippies
Le Chemin de L'Extase
Tantra weg der Ekstase

THE ART OF
SEXUAL ECSTASY

THE PATH OF SACRED SEXUALITY
FOR WESTERN LOVERS

❦

MARGO ANAND

ILLUSTRATED BY LEANDRA HUSSEY

A Jeremy P. Tarcher/Putnam Book
published by
G. P. PUTNAM'S SONS
New York

A Jeremy P. Tarcher/Putnam Book
Published by G. P. Putnam's Sons
Publishers Since 1838
200 Madison Avenue
New York, NY 10016

Library of Congress Cataloging in Publication Data

Anand, Margo
   The art of sexual ecstasy : the tantric path of sacred sexuality for western lovers /
Margo Anand (a.k.a. M. E. Naslednikov).
      p.   cm.
   Includes index.
   1. Sex instruction.   2. Tantrism.   I. Title.
HQ64.N37   1989
613.9'6—dc20   89-35137
                                                                       CIP

ISBN 0-87477-540-X (hardcover)
ISBN 0-87477-581-7 (paperback)

Jeremy P. Tarcher, Inc.
5858 Wilshire Blvd., Ste. 200
Los Angeles, CA 90036

Design by Tanya Maiboroda
Cover design by Deborah Daly
Cover illustration by Gustav Klimt, Detail, The Kiss (1907)
Illustrations by Leandra Hussey
Jacket illustration: detail, *The Kiss*, (1907–1908) by Gustav Klimt. Reprinted with
permission, Osterreichische Galerie, Vienna.

Manufactured in the United States of America

     14 15 16 17 18 19

To the Master within and without
To the Goddess within and without
To Gaia, our planet, our mother.

❦

CONTENTS

The Way In   1
> This opening section describes my personal exploration of the various traditions of ecstatic sexuality, and my subsequent development of a systematic training in the art of sexual ecstasy, The Love and Ecstasy Training, which this book presents in an easy, step-by-step approach.

How To Use This Book   9
> Here you learn what you need to know in order to receive optimum benefit from the training. Each practice builds up to the next, integrating the previous steps.

1. HIGH SEX AND THE TANTRA VISION   27
> This chapter challenges the sexual myths that prevent us from fully developing our potential as ecstatic lovers. It offers a vision of sacred sexuality, giving the underlying principles of High Sex to help you create a supportive context for the practices that follow.

2. AWAKENING YOUR INNER LOVER   47
> The practical training in sexual ecstasy starts here. This section answers the question *How do I begin?* It introduces you to your Inner Lover and emphasizes the importance of loving yourself before you can love another.

CONTENTS

Conscious Breathing: Following the Breath   52
Awakening Your Inner Lover   55
The Heart Salutation   59

3. OPENING TO TRUST   65

A heart-to-heart connection with your partner is established so that you can feel safe and protected before engaging in High Sex. Together you learn how to create the haven of a sacred space around you, and to reduce any fears that may inhibit further exploration.

Creating Your Sacred Space   71
The Melting Hug   78
Moving Beyond Resistance   82

4. SKILLS FOR ENHANCING INTIMACY   93

Partners learn the delicate art of seduction and of awakening the five senses. Then they express their vision of the god or goddess within as they dance for each other. They develop humor and playfulness in love, and harmonize their energies in a soul-to-soul communion.

The Sensory Awakening Ritual   96
The Dancing Gods   105
The Inner Smile   114
Soul Gazing   116

5. HONORING THE BODY ECSTATIC   123

Preparations are made for the body to welcome and contain the high energy of ecstasy. This section deals with rediscovering the body as a friend and as a temple for the spirit of love.

The Ritual of Purification   132
The Basic Stance   134
The Ceremony of Recognition of the Body   136
The Art of Erotic Touching   139
    Feathering   140
    Fingertip Stroking   142
    Slipping and Sliding   144

CONTENTS

The Square Stretch	146
Squatting Together	148
The Pelvic Curl	152
The Opening Lotus	159

6. OPENING THE INNER FLUTE   163

Here you open a hidden channel called the Inner Flute
that connects the body's seven energy centers. This
prepares you for an orgasm of the whole body. You
learn how to expand and contain sexual energy and to
channel it upward to other energy centers.

The PC Pump	175
Sexual Breathing	179
Pelvic Rocking	184
Dual Pelvic Rocking	188

7. SELF-PLEASURING RITUALS   193

As you integrate the previous exercises of the book,
you now apply them in the sexual context. You learn
the art of loving and pleasuring yourself, discovering
what arouses you sexually, and developing a deeper
understanding of your attitude toward your genitals.
You give pleasure to yourself and to your partner.

The Self-Pleasuring Ritual	200
The Sexual Dialogue	214
Self-Pleasuring Under the Eyes of Your Beloved	219
Self-Pleasuring in Front of Each Other	223
Coming Together: Pleasuring Each Other	224

8. HARMONIZING YOUR INNER MAN AND
INNER WOMAN   237

In High Sex, harmonious relationships are based on
equal partnership and start with the recognition and
balancing of the Inner Man and Inner Woman within
each partner. You enact gender roles, move beyond
them, and then balance your masculine and feminine
polarities through developing the art of giving and
receiving blissful surprises.

Visualizing Your Inner Man and Inner Woman   247
Role-Playing Each Other   253
The Yin-Yang Game   257

9. AWAKENING THE ECSTATIC RESPONSE   271

The key to awakening the ecstatic response within yourself is the art of relaxing in high states of arousal. You learn how to generate excitement, contain it, and relax into it. You discover how to awaken the orgasmic reflex independent of the sexual context.

Shaking Loose   276
The Streaming Process   279
The Butterfly   286
The Bonding Relaxation   290
The Sexual Bonding Relaxation   295

10. EXPANDING ORGASM   301

Unhappy sexual experiences leave tensions in the genital area that need to be healed. This chapter teaches you sexual healing so that you may develop the capacity to enjoy a fully satisfying genital orgasm.

Healing the Yoni   323
Healing the Vajra   332
The Anal Healing Massage   336

11. FROM ORGASM TO ECSTASY   347

Here you learn to contain genital orgasm, using advanced techniques to move it up through the body to the brain. This creates a variety of ecstatic states and a sense of expanding your energy beyond the body.

Riding the Tiger Alone   354
Riding the Tiger Together   365
Shooting to the Crown Together   370
Charging Other Areas of the Body   374
The Valley Orgasm: Level One   375
The Valley Orgasm: Level Two   379

12. RIDING THE WAVE OF BLISS   383

This is the highlight of the training: a seven-step process through which you can integrate all that you have learned so far and experience sexual ecstasy. You begin with a playful exploration of the basic postures of lovemaking, preparing your body for the ultimate practice in High Sex—Riding the Wave of Bliss.

The Basic Postures of Love	387
The Man on Top	389
Morning and Evening Tuning	390
The Rolling Tickle	392
The Push-Pull	393
The Woman on Top, or Shakti	393
Swooping Shakti	394
Erotic Shakti	396
The Scissors Position	397
The Spoon Position	397
Hiding in the Crevice	398
The Piercing Tiger	398
The Standing Shiva	399
Oral Loving	400
Riding the Wave of Bliss	403
Step One: Pelvic Rocking	411
Step Two: Cultivating Arousal	411
Step Three: Opening the Inner Flute Together	411
Step Four: The Playful Wave	412
Step Five: Connecting Breath to Breath	415
Step Six: Opening to Your Inner Light	416
Step Seven: The Infinite Cycle	418
The Advanced Infinite Cycle	421
Integrating High Sex in Your Daily Life	424
Appendix I: Safe Sex	429
Appendix II: Musical Selections	437
Appendix III: Resources	441
Acknowledgments	443
Index	445

❧

THE WAY IN

W hile making love or just afterward, have you ever wondered, *Isn't there more to sex than this?* Most of us have.

Have you ever felt incomplete during sex because your partner has already "landed" before you have even had a chance to "take off"?

Have you ever felt bored with sex in a long-term relationship and found yourself wishing you could recapture the passion that used to make sex between you so exciting?

Have you ever wished to be touched at the core of your being, yet felt afraid to open yourself up and be vulnerable?

Have you ever glimpsed an ecstatic moment in love and later felt that you didn't know the way back?

If you have answered yes to any of these questions, you sense intuitively the value of peak experiences in lovemaking—those special moments, either preceding or during orgasm, when you feel transported beyond the limitations of your personal problems and preoccupations. Suddenly you are flying; you feel gloriously alive, filled with light and laughter, at home in a moment that seems to go on forever, in a space that fills you with awe. It is these rare, intense, often unexpected experiences that awaken fresh energies and inspire feelings of closeness and gratitude between you and your partner.

As a psychologist specializing in enhancing sexuality, I have worked with thousands of people around the world who have come to me because they want more out of their love lives. Most either have had peak experiences through sex or feel intuitively that they are achievable.

Because we know such moments are possible, each time we enter into lovemaking, we secretly hope that this time we will enjoy them again. We hold the vision of a deeply fulfilling and joyful embrace, in which the vibrant pleasure of the body encompasses the delight of the heart, the meeting of minds, and the mutual recognition of kindred spirits.

Such moments are often described as "a sense of flow." When you let yourself relax into a flow, your body knows what to do before your mind thinks about it. You forget everything else; you are totally absorbed. Time seems either to stand still or to move very fast. Your perceptions are expanded. The touch of your lover's hand can send ripples of delight all the way down to your toes. In the embrace of a loved one, you feel floated out of self and time. Naturally, easily, you move into the state of relaxed awareness comparable to meditation.

Such peak moments leave unforgettable memories, and most of us yearn to find this ecstatic sense of flow again. Yet normally we are unable to do so because we lack the cultural context in which to understand it and the personal skills with which to cultivate it.

My first peak sexual experience took place in Paris, France, my hometown, when I was 18 and set me off on a course of study and teaching that I have pursued ever since. At the time I was very much in love with a young American artist named Robert. He certainly fit the all-American male image: tall, strong, good-looking, and more than capable of sweeping me off my feet. Sex between us was raw, primal, and wild, fulfilling my adolescent dreams of how a "real man" should behave with his woman. I was studying yoga at the time, however, and was beginning to experience some subtle dimensions of feeling—quiet, meditative, serene moods—and soon I began to wonder what it would be like to integrate these states into my sex life.

I spoke about my feelings one evening during our lovemaking. We were having sex in the usual energetic way, when I said, "Robert, please slow down; let's try something new." We stopped and simply relaxed, staying bonded together with Robert still inside me. I was lying on top. I felt excited because I had initiated something new, removing his responsibility for making something happen. There was a subtle switch of roles, and I felt him shift into a more feminine, receptive attitude. We remained like that for many minutes, relaxed while at the same time feeling the excitement of sexual arousal in our bodies. I soon felt a kind of warm, glowing energy beginning to diffuse itself through my whole pelvic area.

We wanted to maintain sexual arousal, so when the excitement began to fade, we returned to our usual style of active lovemaking. Then, just before the peak of orgasmic release, we stopped, relaxed, and became still once more. We repeated this pattern several times, and then something totally unexpected happened. Suddenly we both seemed to be floating in an unbounded space filled with warmth and light. The boundaries between our bodies dissolved and, along with them, the distinctions between man and woman. We were one. The experience became timeless, and we seemed to remain like this forever. There was no need to have an orgasm. There was no need even to "make love." There was nothing to do, nothing to achieve. We were in ecstasy.

After that extraordinary experience I tried many times to recapture the ecstasy in our lovemaking but without success. Robert quickly forgot about it, but I began to feel that ordinary genital orgasm was not the only desirable state to which lovemaking could lead. Like many others, I felt the frustration of loving at 10 percent of my potential. I recognized that the pleasure of routine or recreational sex was not the ultimate pleasure; indeed, it was just a beginning. How would it be, I wondered, if during lovemaking one could consistently re-create the conditions that led to bliss? I decided to search for ways to cultivate ecstatic states in conjunction with the sexual experience.

For the next 15 years, I explored the great traditions of ecstatic sexuality. What I discovered and developed is a unique path to sexual esctasy that I call High Sex. It is this path that I teach as a complete practice in this book. It emerged gradually through my study of various traditional and innovative sexual practices in the East and in the West, on three continents. Far from being complex and esoteric, High Sex is a simple, step-by-step process that is accessible to anyone who wants to find a gentle and conscious way of bringing the spirit back into sex, of honoring sexual union as a bridge between body and soul.

High Sex takes the experience of orgasm to a new dimension—a dimension in which genital orgasm is only the beginning. It inspires you to explore the full capacity of orgasm, culminating in ecstatic body-to-body and soul-to-soul communion. It is an experience of the whole body, the whole being. The path of High Sex helps your body to be free of tensions, your heart to be trusting and open, and your mind to develop such psychic skills as visualization, imagination, and meditation. When this integration has taken place, you are ready for a new, qualitatively higher sexual experience in which physical pleasure becomes a delight of the heart and an ecstasy of the spirit.

The course on sexual ecstasy that I have developed teaches you how to contain the energy charge that erotic arousal generates, which is normally concentrated in the genitals, and to consciously redirect it through the body using subtle channels that are comparable to the meridians in acupuncture. When this energy reaches the heart and head, a whole

Sexuality is not a leisure or part-time activity. It is a way of being.

—Alexander Lowen
Love and Orgasm

3

range of peak experiences becomes available. Orgasm is experienced as ecstasy, pleasure floods through every pore of your body, your heart dances with delight, you feel contentment and peace, and your energy is expanded beyond the boundaries of your body.

This experience is not, as many people believe, beyond the reach of ordinary human beings. Ecstasy is a state as natural as sleeping or breathing. It is our birthright. As children we are born ecstatic. The world is a place of wonder. We are not separate from things but intuitively and profoundly connected to what is around us. In growing up, we lose this sense of unity as we adapt to the cultures that surround us and separate ourselves from the fullness of life. According to R. D. Laing, a psychiatrist who has given much attention to ecstatic states, "To adapt to this world, the child abdicates its ecstasy." We simply forget.

By emphasizing ecstasy, High Sex distances itself from the so-called sexual revolution that began in the 1960s. That revolution was about access. It was a rebellion against the puritanical attitude that made sex forbidden outside the context of marriage. Instead, sex was freely explored for its own sake. Through the sexual revolution, more people felt better about having more intercourse with more partners in more ways. Thousands of books and articles told us to have more intense orgasms, to multiply their number, to coordinate them between partners, and to extend them.

For many people those goals were accomplished, but as psychologists, sociologists, and others have pointed out, this access to orgasm has not brought about long-term satisfaction, physically or emotionally. Somehow, "having" sex, as one "has" other things, seems to be self-limiting. Using sex for relief, entertainment, or reassurance that one is attractive appeals to needs generated by the ego but diverts attention from our real sexual potential.

Today the issue no longer is access to sex, but a transformation of sex; it is no longer transitory pleasure for its own sake, but a recovery of our ecstatic self in love. We need to bring the spirit—the inspiration to manifest our highest potential—back into sex. We can discover erotic bliss not by separating sex from other higher purposes and treating it as recreation only, but by cultivating the art of sexual ecstasy to reach higher states of consciousness and in this way deepening our intimacy with our loved ones.

To bring High Sex into perspective, let me tell you a little bit about my personal quest for a coherent approach to sexual ecstasy.

Promethean ecstasy strikes like a divine lightning that destroys all the limitations and obstructions and provides entirely unexpected solutions. The individual is flooded by light of supernatural beauty and experiences a state of divine epiphany. He or she has a deep sense of emotional, intellectual and spiritual liberation and gains access to breathtaking realms of cosmic inspiration and insight.

—Stanislav Grof
Beyond the Brain

At the time of my Parisian love affair with Robert, I was studying for my M.A. in psychology and philosophy at the Sorbonne. I soon realized I could not find the answers I sought in the dark recesses of the Sorbonne's lecture halls. The knowledge offered there was much too theoretical and abstract. I wanted answers that I could taste, experience, and embody. After completing my degree, I was pleased to discover more concrete methods of self-understanding in a variety of bodywork therapies and self-development groups—bioenergetics, encounter, rolfing, Gestalt. I traveled between London, New York, and California, working with the leading practitioners in each field. Because my taste of ecstasy with Robert had resembled the state of meditation I had experienced in yoga, I also spent three years studying integral yoga with Swami Satchitananda.

In 1974, I met the South American mystic Oscar Ichazo and joined the spiritual school that he founded, the Arica Institute in New York, which blended martial arts, Sufism, the teachings of Gurdjieff, and other spiritual traditions. With Arica I began to understand the basic principles of how energy functions in the human body, learning how to activate specific energy centers through light, color, chanting sacred sounds, and the visual impact of symbols and images.

During this time I discovered Tantra, an ancient Eastern science of spiritual enlightenment. I felt intrigued immediately because unlike most mystical paths, Tantra included sexuality as a doorway to ecstasy and enlightenment. Tantra was born in India around 5000 B.C., through the cult of the Hindu god Shiva and his consort, the goddess Shakti. Shiva was worshiped as the embodiment of pure consciousness in its most ecstatic state, and Shakti as the embodiment of pure energy. The Hindus believed that through uniting spiritually and sexually with Shiva, Shakti gave form to his spirit and created the universe. Tantra, therefore, views the creation of the world as an erotic act of love. The joyful dance between Shiva and Shakti is reflected in all living beings and manifests itself as pleasure, beauty, and happiness. This, in Tantra, is the nature of the divine, the root of all that exists.

Tantra originally developed as a rebellion against the repressive, moralistic codes of organized religions and the ascetic practices of the Brahmins—the Hindu priesthood—particularly against the widespread belief that sexuality had to be denied in order to attain enlightenment. *Tantra* means "weaving," in the sense of unifying the many and often contradictory aspects of the self into one harmonious whole. *Tantra* also

The schism that has taken place in the West between spirit and matter, between the transcendent and the secular, between the male and the female, and between the body and the mind, is healed in Tantra. For Tantra brings together the seemingly irreconcilable, polarized fragmented opposites into a coherent whole, as wholism is one of the paths and goals in Tantra.

—Azul
Shiva Nataraj

means "expansion," in the sense that once our own energies are understood and unified, we grow and expand into joy. Always a rebellious and nonconformist approach that challenged taboos and belief systems, Tantra branched out and influenced not only the Hindu but also the Taoist and Buddhist traditions. Tantra influenced Western religious history through the ecstatic cult of the Greek god Dionysius around 2000 B.C.

The great mystics of the Tantric tradition scandalized mainstream society and were often condemned and persecuted. The style of their teaching is characterized by what the Tibetan Tantric tradition calls "crazy wisdom," a process in which the teacher uses paradoxical stories, seemingly absurd questions, and unexpected behavior to tease, jolt, startle, and provoke people to drop conventional attitudes and embrace the whole spectrum of life, with no contradiction between the sacred and the profane, the spiritual and the sexual.

One of the most extraordinary Tantric mystics was Saraha, who lived in India around the ninth century. Respected in his day as a great scholar and philosopher, he shocked everybody, so the legend goes, by becoming the consort of an enlightened Tantric woman teacher. They lived together in a cemetery, dancing and singing with such contagious ecstasy that everybody who arrived sadly to bury the dead became enraptured and enlightened. Through him, it is said, the king and queen of the land became enlightened, and eventually the whole kingdom entered a period of great joy and peace.

Other heroes of the Tantric tradition include the legendary teachers Marpa and Milarepa, who lived in Tibet around the tenth century; Drukpa Kinley, who was born in Tibet around 1455; and Yeshe Tsoguel, an enlightened woman called in her day the Sky Dancer and the Female Buddha. She was the consort of the Buddha Padmasambhava in eighth-century Tibet.

I was fascinated by the stories in the Tantric scriptures. I wanted to find teachers who personified the Tantric spirit and lived by it. During the next few years I continued to investigate a wide variety of spiritual disciplines. While traveling and learning, I absorbed many methods of self-development and found that I possessed a natural gift for distilling their essential truths and weaving them together in a practical course from which others could benefit. In 1973, I started teaching seminars in Europe and the U.S., focusing on integrating physical, mental, and emotional balance.

I continued to travel through Asia, Europe, and the U.S., much

The experiences or behavior of shamans, Indian yogis and sadhus, or spiritual seekers in other cultures would be more than sufficient for a diagnosis of psychosis by Western psychiatric standards. Conversely, the insatiable ambitions, irrational compensatory drives, obsession with technology, the modern arms race, internecine wars, or revolutions and riots that pass for normal in the West would be seen as symptoms of utter insanity by an East Indian sage.

—Stanislav Grof
Beyond the Brain

like an anthropologist on a field trip looking for clues to a forgotten culture in which sex and spirituality might be compatible. I met extraordinary teachers, shamans, mystics, and saints—men and women alike. I was fortunate to receive personal guidance from some of them in Europe, the U.S., and India. In the course of these intensive trainings I learned how to integrate sexuality, love, and meditation. During this time, I had profound experiences that revealed to me how meditation can become very ecstatic, comparable to the experience of orgasm without sex.

Gradually, I incorporated much of what I had learned into my own seminars, taught in Europe and California. Out of these seminars I created a year-long training called *The Love and Ecstasy Training,* to guide people step-by-step toward sexual ecstasy, helping them to integrate the Tantric perspective into their daily lives. The training consists of three ten-day seminars held over a year-long period in which participants meet as a group to learn various practices that can heal their sexuality and bring joy to their lives. In the time between the seminars, they practice what they have learned and prepare for the next cycle. For many people in many countries, this training has opened the door to their personal and direct experience of ecstasy in love. This book presents the practices that I offer in the one-year course.

Let me explain now what I mean when I refer to Tantra in this book. Because the science of Tantra was developed thousands of years ago, it offered methods that were suited to the culture of people at that time. Having to some degree been trained in classical Tantric methods and studied the scriptures, I feel that many of the techniques are not relevant to the needs of the contemporary Western lover. For example, I see no need for the repetition of long Sanskrit mantras, the prolonged use of uncomfortable postures of meditation, the construction of complex mandalas, or the strict ritualization of lovemaking. In studying the traditions, I realized that they are not only incredibly complex but often contradictory, offering a jungle of conflicting teachings in which the Western lover would soon get hopelessly lost.

So while I have retained the Tantric goal of sexual ecstasy, I've developed new approaches to make this experience accessible to people today. High Sex weaves together the disciplines of sexology and humanistic and transpersonal psychology in order to give Western lovers the experience of sexual ecstasy that was taught by Tantra, but using new and contemporary tools. What makes this training so powerful as a system is not one technique, but the combined, synergistic effect of these various methods. The training awakens highly positive emotions, vitality, and the hidden powers of the brain, allowing it to access ecstatic states and integrate them into the sexual experience.

The methods I propose in this book are not, therefore, the heritage of any one specific Tantric tradition, school, or scripture. They are approaches that I developed through direct experience rather than scholarship, through teaching rather than reading and discussion. I did not learn Tantra in a university, because the *experience* of Tantra cannot be found there. It is for this reason that I choose to call my training High Sex, not Tantra. The training offered in this book does not depend on adopting any particular religious belief, such as Hinduism, yoga, or Buddhism. It is compatible with any view of the world that includes a positive response to the sexual experience.

In this book you will have the opportunity to discover many methods that people of all ages, from teenagers to the young-at-heart in their sixties, have practiced successfully. In my experience as a teacher, everyone who learns them can feel the deeply healing nature of ecstasy. I have seen ecstatic experiences—especially when they are linked with sex—ease or remedy compulsive jealousy, low self-esteem, stress, ailing marriages, timidity, drug dependency, and even bulimia. I also have seen relationships between couples who had become bored—not only with sex but with each other—suddenly blossom into entirely new love affairs, with open, heart-to-heart communication; renewed sexual intimacy; and an underlying spiritual connection that gave their lives together new meaning and fulfillment.

Ecstasy works. Yet for a long time it has been underemployed. The time has come to rediscover it. One moment of ecstasy can transform your life.

HOW TO USE THIS BOOK

The following chapter-by-chapter outline will help give you an overview of the training that this book offers.

High Sex and the Tantra Vision

In the first chapter I invite you to examine your ideas and assumptions about sexuality, challenging the ready-made attitudes and myths with which our culture has surrounded this taboo-laden subject. In addition, I propose a new vision that offers a viable alternative to the sexual guilt and limitations that these myths perpetrate. Chapter 1 creates the context and understanding that are essential for you to derive the maximum benefit from the practices that follow.

Awakening Your Inner Lover

The training in the art of sexual ecstasy begins here. Chapter 2 addresses the reality that love begins at home—with yourself. The more you learn to appreciate yourself, the more you realize that you, not your partner, are the source of your own orgasm. Through an exercise that I call Awakening Your Inner Lover, you discover yourself to be a lovable person and open yourself up to new feelings of relaxation, self-acceptance, and self-esteem. You also learn a simple breathing technique that enhances mental clarity and a Heart Salutation that honors both yourself and your partner. This salutation is used to mark the beginning and end of each practice in the book.

Opening to Trust

In order to feel protected and supported in your endeavor to transform your sexuality, you need to create a Sacred Space, and chapter 3 shows you how. Once you have established this sanctuary, you begin to open clear lines of communication between yourself and your partner, establishing mutual trust; moving beyond resistances; sharing expectations, fears, needs, and fantasies; and relating past peak sexual experiences as a way to discover what elements can help re-create these experiences today.

Skills for Enhancing Intimacy

In a spirit of playfulness and theatrical ingenuity, you discover in chapter 4 how to abolish any sense of dullness or familiarity between yourself and your partner, promoting intimacy and your willingness to explore High Sex together. The Sensory Awakening Ritual provides a delightful method for you to introduce a partner who perhaps may be reluctant to High Sex. Then you will visualize your highest potential and express it through the Dancing Gods. Your sense of intimacy and your reverence for your partner are deepened further through the Soul-Gazing exercise, a way of attuning your hearts and minds beyond the limitations of the personality.

Honoring the Body Ecstatic

Next, in chapter 5, you prepare your body for ecstasy, awakening your sensuality and sense of reverence through the Ceremony of Recognition of the Body. This leads naturally into a playful exercise called The Art of Erotic Touching, which heightens your capacity to give and receive pleasure. Then you learn exercises to train your body to produce and maintain a higher energy charge, focusing on relaxing and opening the pelvic area. Finally, you learn a meditation position that will be an important ingredient in the advanced practices of lovemaking introduced in later chapters.

Opening the Inner Flute

In chapter 6 you develop specific tools for generating sexual arousal and channeling it from the genital area to other parts of the body. You learn how to open the Inner Flute, the secret channel that connects all the energy centers between your sex center and your brain. By using this channel, you begin to learn how to transform sexual energy from a localized, genital sensation into a longer-lasting, expanded whole-body orgasm.

Self-Pleasuring Rituals

At this point in the training, in chapter 7, you take all your newly learned skills and apply them in the sexual context of self-pleasuring. You learn to understand what pleases you sexually and how your body responds to stimulation. Then you progress to self-pleasuring with a partner, learning how to show and give pleasure to each other, moving beyond feelings of guilt and shame to the mutual enjoyment of erotic arousal.

Harmonizing Your Inner Man and Inner Woman

Chapter 8 is about love and relationship. Each partner will learn how to integrate the feminine, receptive side—the Inner Woman—with the active, dynamic side—the Inner Man of your nature. In the process you explore ways of escaping from the "gender trap" that identifies you exclusively as either masculine or feminine. You see how to play different roles—masculine and feminine, active and passive, giver and receiver—to establish a balanced partnership. Powerful exercises presented in the form of humorous games enable you to develop a spirit of adventure, spontaneity, and erotic creativity in your love life.

Awakening the Ecstatic Response

When the energy in both of your bodies has been tuned and your relationship with your partner has become intimate and harmonious, you are ready to welcome ecstasy. In chapter 9 you learn techniques that trigger the Streaming Reflex, which transforms your body into a stream of vibrating energy. First, in a nonsexual context, you learn to welcome different kinds of vibrations into different areas of your body, allowing these vibrations to cleanse your body of built-up tensions, transforming them into highly pleasurable sensations. By staying relaxed in states of high arousal, you permit orgasmic energy to flow uninterruptedly through your body. Then you practice the same method in a sexual union with your partner.

Expanding Orgasm

In chapter 10 you learn how to heal the sexual organs of past emotional and physical traumas and greatly increase sensations of pleasure in your genitals. You will be breaking old taboos: Through deep massage you will free your pelvis and sex organs from the lingering imprint of past experiences that deadened them and prevented you from enjoying their full potential for pleasure. Through this process you give life back to the genitals and experience the joy of uninhibited lovemaking.

From Orgasm to Ecstasy

When you have fully enjoyed your genital sexuality, you are ready to learn how to channel orgasmic energy up the Inner Flute toward the brain, where it can be experienced as ecstasy. Chapter 11 teaches you the beauty of changing from the explosive orgasm of genital release to the implosive orgasm of inner expansion. You experience how this kind of orgasm can go on for hours and can be expanded beyond the boundaries of the body into an ecstatic and meditative experience.

Riding the Wave of Bliss

Having learned the previous steps of the training, you are ready, in chapter 12, to approach High Sex at its highest level: Riding the Wave of Bliss, the ultimate art of sexual ecstasy. This is a subtle and internalized way of lovemaking, circulating the energy of arousal through the Inner Flute together with your partner, thus creating an infinite and ecstatic circle of orgasmic energy. Through an advanced posture of sexual union, you create a state of bliss that takes you beyond technique into pure ecstasy.

You may wonder why so much time is spent on preparations that create the right conditions for lovemaking before we come to the sexual dimension itself. The reason is this: the Tantric tradition of ecstatic sexuality stresses the importance of skillful preparation so that when you come to lovemaking, you feel whole, unified, and healed. You will then be ready to integrate these skills into your lovemaking and transform it into a great celebration.

How to Approach the Practice

To understand the spirit of the practices you will encounter on the following pages, I invite you to imagine that this book is a map of an enchanted garden and that you are an explorer with all the time in the world to enjoy each of the flowers you find there. Before you actually begin the training in High Sex, I suggest that like travelers planning an expedition, you read the book once from beginning to end so that you understand the territory you will be visiting and learn the special language that is spoken in this delightful garden.

For any traveler who wishes to record and remember his or her experience fully, a diary is an invaluable traveling companion. Let yours be a beautiful book, bound in attractive, sensual colors and materials, in which you can record observations, describe your experiences, make notes about the things that interest you most, or even compose erotic poems and paste in photographs that illustrate or symbolize the expanded perceptions you may experience during your training.

For example, you may start your "Ecstatic Diary" by dividing the page with a vertical line. On the left side, at the top, write the following question: "What do I want to change in my love life and my sexuality?" Then, underneath, list each aspect that needs transformation. When you have finished, review the book and on the right side list the exercises and practices in this book that address each issue and support your desire for transformation.

For instance:

1. I want my partner to do this training in High Sex with me.	Alone, then together, we will explore the awakening of the Inner Lover in chapter 2 and offer each other the Sensory Awakening Ritual in chapter 4.
2. I want to talk more clearly about what I feel and what I need in sex.	Alone, then together, we will go through the sequence of Moving beyond Resistance in chapter 3.
3. I want to be more daring in my sensuality and lovemaking.	Together we will go through the Dancing Gods in chapter 4, the Ceremony of Recognition of the Body in chapter 5, and the Self-Pleasuring Rituals in chapter 7.

When you have completed your list, you will see that this book is devised to respond to your basic wishes concerning sexual enhancement. Writing out your wishes and finding where they are addressed in the text will help you build up the kind of confidence and excitement that motivates you to begin your training in the art of Sexual Ecstasy.

In addition, you need not fear that the training in this book will require you to give up anything in your sex life. Instead, it offers new approaches as a complement to whatever you now enjoy sexually. To the extent that the new approach works for you and your partner, you can use it more often. There is no way to fail. You succeed in your own way, at your own pace, respecting your own experience.

Ultimately, I believe that one learns techniques only to go beyond them and relax into the self-acceptance of the heart. High Sex happens not through effort or conquest but through the acknowledgment that you already have what it takes to create pleasure and joy in your life. You can begin right now, from where you are.

Taking the Training in Sequence

Even though you have highlighted specific exercises that can motivate you to do the training, it is very important to complete the practices in the sequence in which they are laid out, step by step, chapter by chapter. If you have participated in other self-development programs, you may feel that some of these practices are familiar to you and simple in their approach. This is a positive sign for you because it means the practices will be easier to assimilate; however, don't skip any step along the way, because each is a preparation for the next, and their effects are cumulative. The sequential arrangement is done in a way that maximizes your chances of building your sexual energy and experiencing ecstasy.

You also may be tempted to modify the practices in this book to create your own blend. These techniques are very powerful and in the past were often guarded with secrecy because they were considered too intense for people to try without the direct guidance of a master teacher. Give them the respect they deserve, and do not try to create a different training until you have perfected this one.

To determine your progress, remember that the first step is practice, the second step is enjoyment, and the third step is integration. When you feel you are moving beyond the effort and concentration of practice into sheer enjoyment—when you are riding the crest of the energy that the exercise has generated—you will know that a particular exercise is working. Do not feel discouraged if a particular practice seems difficult at first. Like a passenger in a plane taking off on a foggy morning, you may not be able to see anything until you reach a certain altitude. Then suddenly you will break through the clouds to a blue sky where the sun is shining. Then you can integrate the particular method you have learned into your lovemaking, and it will become part of your ongoing style. When you feel you've reached this stage, you can move on to the next practice.

When you have completed the whole course, you can drop the sequencing and use this book as a treasure chest, choosing any method you require in a particular situation. For example, if you have a quarrel with your beloved, you can use the tools given in chapters 3 or 8 to help resolve it. If you wish to enhance your sensitivity in lovemaking further, you can repeat the practices given in chapter 10, and so on.

Learning the Instructions

Detailed instructions are given for each step along the way. Follow them carefully. At first, when a practice is unfamiliar, you may need to follow the guidelines slowly, step by step. There are several ways you can do this. If you are alone, you can record the instructions on a tape and practice while you listen to your own voice—a wonderfully efficient and persuasive way of proceeding. If you are with a partner, you can be each other's guides, one reading while the other practices. Then, as the exercise becomes more familiar, you may be able to reduce the instructions to your own form of mental shorthand or perhaps even to a series of mental images that avoid words.

You can compare the art of assimilating instructions to following a recipe. Initially the cook may repeat each step aloud: "First, I have to peel the potatoes, then boil them until they are soft, then mash them." As he or she comes to know the recipe by heart, the cook may simply say, "Peeling, boiling, mashing." Finally, he or she may say nothing at all, not even internally, but hold a mental image of the potatoes being peeled, boiled, and mashed. The same kind of process will develop as you repeat the practices and integrate them into your memory.

The Practice

In this book you're unlearning old habits and absorbing much that is new, so don't be in a hurry. Be patient with the material and with yourself. You will not be able to complete the training in a weekend or even a week. When I work intensively with a group, the Love and Ecstasy Training takes 30 days. Working individually or with a partner at your own pace is likely to take longer.

This book contains about 50 practices that last between 15 and 90 minutes, totaling about 75 hours. You will need to reschedule your daily life, setting aside quality time for practice, free of obligations, when you can focus on your own well-being and enjoyment. For example, you might make a commitment that you are going to set aside one evening a week for High Sex, starting at 6 P.M. so that you have ample time for preliminary preparations. Keep that appointment, even if you are the only person involved. Or you could set aside one weekend a month.

At the beginning of each session, create a clear vision of what you want to accomplish and of the strategies you will explore to foster an atmosphere of celebration and intimacy—with yourself and with your partner. Let the evening fill you with expectancy and excitement, as if you were about to reinvent your honeymoon. You can practice at home or away from home. It is the quality of the environment that counts more than its location.

The training offers you the opportunity to proceed gently while having a good time. It takes you through a series of stages that will revitalize your body, expand your breathing, and sharpen your mental imagery in a sexually creative and supportive way. Take time to read each chapter before you start. Then, moving at your own pace, enjoy each practice for its own sake, as you would enjoy each bite during a gourmet meal.

Be thorough. Unless you devote yourself wholeheartedly to practicing the exercises in this book, everything remains hearsay, theoretical, something borrowed from someone else. In my experience the best way to practice is with a spirit of adventure, saying to yourself, "I am going to discover something new." Like an explorer, you might say, "I will complete the whole journey and learn more about myself." Also try to maintain a quality of innocence, saying, "I will not compare myself to others or think that I know a particular exercise without bothering to experience it."

Only through practice can you generate and contain the new energy that this book will provide. Only through practice can you create the new pathways in your body through which this energy can travel and expand.

You may find yourself doing a certain exercise several times and thinking that nothing is happening. Then, a few days later, you may be involved in some activity completely unrelated to the training, or you may be cuddling your lover, and some transformation happens to you— you breathe more deeply without even thinking about it, you feel more turned on, your genitals feel more alive than ever before, new parts of your body become aroused, you relate to your partner with more patience, more humor. It is like weaving a tapestry—you concentrate on one stitch at a time, and the overall beauty of the pattern slowly reveals itself.

Practicing Alone

Many of the people who come to my training—especially women— believe it is of the utmost importance to have a partner. For this reason, they initially feel discouraged if they cannot find one. But it is possible to complete almost all the steps of this training by yourself. For example, in chapter 2, instead of doing the Heart Salutation to your partner, you can do it to yourself, in front of a mirror. In chapter 3, instead of answering questions in dialogue form, you can do it with a tape recorder or using a diary. You need a partner for the practices of chapters 8 and 10, but even the most advanced practices in chapters 11 and 12 can be done alone.

If you are looking for a partner, please do not adopt the attitude that you need to find Mr. Right or Ms. Wonderful in order to achieve the cosmic orgasm. These ideal partners tend to be a figment of the imagination. If you remain practical, reaching out, expressing warmth and enthusiasm to those whom you know and trust, you should be able to find a supportive friend with whom to share this adventure.

Practicing with a Partner

Even though you can approach it alone, the training offered in this book is particularly beneficial for couples. As you progress through the steps together, it is as if you are giving each other support to learn a new language, discovering a new and exciting vocabulary. In my experience people who are in loving relationships have an advantage in this training because they have already made a commitment to grow together.

When you come together for the purpose of practice, there is often a moment of trepidation or nervousness. You may wish to have a true heart-to-heart connection, yet it feels threatening. Resistance and tension may appear in the form of sudden back pains, exaggerated smiles, excuses that you have something urgent to attend to before you can be available. This is why I recommend that you relax together first. Meeting for the purpose of practice begins with a pause, taking a moment to make the transition from a busy schedule to relaxation and trust. Connecting from your center will make it a pleasurable experience, giving more depth to your meeting, more power to your practice.

Tuning yourself, you first seek to let go of any negative thoughts or tensions that may block the flow of energy between you. I often compare this inward tuning to what happens when you are about to dive into unknown waters. You do not just casually leap off the cliff. You first check the edge from which you will jump, then the general landscape, the currents, the color of the water, your breathing, and finally your inner commitment. This tuning brings you back to your center—a feeling of being relaxed and at home in yourself. Connecting with yourself allows you to connect with your partner. When your partner feels that you are in touch with yourself, he or she will feel confident that it is possible to open up and trust you.

As you experiment and play with your partner, you will feel moments of merging and deep communion. This is why at the beginning and at the end of each practice, I suggest that you re-collect your energy and return to your own center, so that you "remember yourself" rather than getting lost in the other. Doing the training in this way will emphasize self-empowerment and freedom from dependence on your partner.

Practicing with a Partner of the Same Sex

Even though I address myself in this book to heterosexual partners, I know from experience that these practices can be beneficial to partners of the same sex. As I will explain in more detail later on, the goal in High Sex is for each individual to explore both the masculine and feminine aspects of his or her nature, thereby greatly expanding the range of experiences that are available in lovemaking. From the Tantric perspective, this expansion—especially in the beginning of the practice—can take place more easily when the male and female polarities are present in the form of a man and a woman. Any relationship in which male and female qualities are consciously developed, however, can create support for exploring High Sex. For example, in a sexual relationship between two men, there is likely to be one man in whom the male qualities are more dominant and one who is more feminine. The same is true of most sexual relationships between women. This training will help partners of the same sex to expand their awareness of both polarities within themselves, thereby giving them a wider range of roles to explore with each other. It will also, I hope, offer them a supportive context for their practice beyond moralistic judgments about what is "acceptable" in the way genders relate. In the ancient Hindu and Greek traditions of sacred sexuality, as well as in many other cultures, there were no such judgments about loving a person of the same gender.

Wooing a Reluctant Partner

This training also teaches you the art of wooing and seducing a reluctant partner into the delights of High Sex. If your partner does not want to get involved, do not complain, get discouraged, or try to insist, which is likely to make him or her even more resistant. Instead, look upon your partner's resistance as a challenge for you to develop the art of seduction. This, too, is part of your training in the art of sexual ecstasy. Be positive and supportive, noncritical and nondemanding. Try the practices for yourself. As I have said, many of them can be done alone. By applying your newly learned skills to your lovemaking, without necessarily telling your partner about it, you can greatly enhance your experience. Your improved ability to enjoy yourself may prove to be a far more powerful attraction to High Sex than anything you can say.

Then you might suggest attractive surprises, like a weekend in the country or a special evening for relaxation and lovemaking. During this time offer to perform one of the practices that you feel is most appropriate to the situation, perhaps without mentioning that it comes from this book. You will discover that the book contains many ideal practices, such as the Sensory Awakening Ritual in chapter 4. Use these practices to introduce your partner to the pleasures that are available on the road to High Sex.

Giving to your partner in this sensual way is, however, only half the story. In order to become involved in the training, he or she must also learn the art of reciprocating. So after you have pleasured your partner, explain that you would like to exchange the roles and receive a gift. Specify your needs. It may be a massage or an intimate conversation concerning your lovemaking.

Safe Sex

The emphasis in High Sex is on creating a healthier, more whole, and happier love life, so clearly there is no place in this vision for behavior that promotes the transmission of diseases. To make sure that you enjoy healthy sex, not only while experimenting with the practices in this book but also in your daily life, I encourage you to read the appendix on safe sex at the back of this book before beginning the practices and to follow my recommendations carefully.

Staying in the Present Moment

The secret is all in the way you approach the matter of time. Since earliest childhood, most of us have been taught to direct our attention to the past and to the future. Those are nice places to visit—necessary, in fact, for survival and success. But they are not where pleasure resides. If you're really interested in finding pleasure, start by directing your attention to the present.

—George Leonard

The key to experiencing sexual ecstasy, whether alone or with a partner, is to allow yourself to be fully engaged in what you are doing here and now, in this moment, and maintaining that attitude every step of the way. This means not thinking about what you have to do next, not worrying about how well you are doing, not comparing the experience you are having with the one that you had yesterday.

You may know enough about meditation to appreciate the concept of being present in each moment, but an intellectual understanding is not the same as doing it. The moment is elusive. Our goal-oriented culture tells us that happiness is rarely now, but just around the corner, and as a result, we focus our minds mostly on future events. It takes mental alertness to break this habit and to realize that the present moment is the only *real* moment—the only reality that you can actually feel, experience, and learn from. Sexual ecstasy happens when you are so completely absorbed by the fullness of the present moment that nothing else exists. Therefore, throughout the book, I will be providing you with ways of remaining focused on the present moment.

Overcoming a "Problem" Orientation

At first you may be skeptical about the idea of ecstasy combined with sex. Many people feel there are serious problems to solve before they can even think about ecstasy. For example, some may feel that they can't satisfy their partners, or that they ejaculate too soon, are not attractive enough, or don't feel anything. I have experienced many such problems myself and have resolved them through the training presented in this book.

The secret of High Sex is to celebrate and tap into the inherent perfection of your ecstatic nature, learning how to enjoy your sexuality—and, indeed, your life—as a dance in which your spontaneous, sensual, vibrant aspects can be discovered and find expression. This may sound wildly implausible ("Listen, don't talk to me about celebration; I have a *serious* sexual problem to sort out"), but time and time again, experience has shown me that focusing on feeling good about yourself and on what *does* work in your life is far more helpful than paying obsessive attention to apparently insoluble difficulties. When a client complains to me about being shy or about having erection difficulties or other basic impediments, I always say, "Okay, let's forget about that for now and concentrate on all the ways you can feel good about yourself through positive thinking and self-empowering exercises."

This book is not offering a therapy or cure for sexual dysfunctions. It is based on the assumption that sexual healing as well as personal growth can happen through pleasure and delight much more easily than they can through "working" on a problem. You will be focusing on what I believe is the basic solution to almost all sexual difficulties—a new approach that assumes that you as an individual are already whole and healthy and naturally capable of great enjoyment. All you may need is a shift in perspective and some encouragement to claim your potential for unlimited pleasure.

Overcoming Your Resistance

At times you may confront resistance or have the impression that you are not feeling anything, or the fear that "it won't work." Or during a practice your vital energy may build up to a level of intensity to which you are not accustomed, as when a jogger runs to the point where he feels his lungs might burst—a subjective impression rather than actual fact.

When this happens, you may be tempted to break off the practice. I encourage my clients to become aware of these behavior patterns and to continue the practice so that they can, in their own time, overcome the resistance and discover that such breakthroughs are exhilarating and fun. If you find yourself wanting to take a hiatus when the energy builds too high, you are free to do so. But then come back to the practice and try to move through the point of resistance.

Look upon each episode of resistance as an occasion to learn about your own innate wisdom. You will be going through major changes, confronting old patterns, challenging the beliefs you grew up with. We have not been trained for sexual ecstasy. Our sexuality has been kept within well-defined boundaries of behavior that are measured, analyzed, and compartmentalized. Order and predictability separate the good from the bad, the sacred from the profane, the acceptable from the forbidden.

High Sex is a calling to cross these boundaries. At first you may feel as though you are entering unchartered territory. It may feel dangerous. You are leaving the old; you have not yet experienced the new. Now is the time to ask yourself, "Do I have a satisfying love life? And if not, what am I willing to do to change it?" Reading this book, taking this training, is a big jump. If you are committed to doing it, I commend you for your courage. Together we are going to transform the attitudes and strategies that have kept you away from your deepest, most innate, and natural state of being: ecstasy.

In these explorations you not only will be learning new approaches and practices but also dropping habits and patterns that limit you and replacing them with more satisfying forms. You are opening yourself up to skills and states of consciousness that you already have within you, that you need to recognize, remember, or rediscover.

Fritz Perls once said the only difference between a wise man and a fool is that the wise man knows he's playing.

—Bernard Günther
Dying for Enlightenment

As you progress through the exercises, I will offer suggestions and guidance drawn from several different cultures and traditions, offering alternative ways to reach your goal so that you are building a complex assembly of skills. At each stage I will encourage you to assimilate these skills in a *playful* manner, without effort. Focus your full attention on each exercise. You will find that the skills you have already practiced and absorbed will return by themselves as required. You will integrate these skills into your own style of lovemaking and your own way of enjoying life naturally because you will remember that they feel good.

In case you feel challenged beyond your limits, remember that thousands of people, young and old, who have taken the training felt as you do, yet successfully moved beyond their hesitation. Trust the process enough to stretch yourself a little further.

At times you also may feel that this book is presenting you with unusual or unfamiliar perspectives, or that I am suggesting that you do something that may seem foreign to you. On those occasions I ask you, as I ask my clients, to suspend your current beliefs and, as it is said in the Zen tradition, to "empty your cup" so that you can assimilate new information in a spirit of curiosity and innocence. Sometimes I will precede the instructions with the words *You will find that.* When you see that phrase, I ask you to trust my years of experience as a teacher, and the easiest way to do that is to behave as if the suggestions offered in this book will work for you. By adopting this simple strategy, you will discover how to stop acting in ways that prevent ecstasy.

A wise teacher once asked me to answer a question. My subconscious resisted. I couldn't reply and said so. "Well, if you did know the answer, what would it be?" he asked, supportingly. My resistance simply disappeared. I knew what to say.

In the same way, if you hesitate in this training, imagine my saying to you, as your friendly guide, "Well, if you did want to take the next step, what would you do?" Then you will know the answer.

What to Do When You Doubt

Doubt does not have to be a problem as long as you do not chastise yourself for doubting. If self-doubt assails you—if, for example, you say to yourself, "I am too clumsy to manage"—remember to retain your sense of humor. Say instead, "Okay, I am clumsy—so what? I can still roll around and have a good time." In moments of doubt, try not to fight with your own resistance. You can stay relaxed by accepting it, yet still continue with the practice. Here are four steps to help you continue.

- ☐ Remember you are not alone. Not a single person who has completed the training has not complained at some point that it doesn't work.
- ☐ Go to the source of the resistance. Try to understand where it comes from. The source may be a deep-seated fear within yourself. Fear makes you feel like contracting, holding back, and giving up because at a deep level you do not wish to experience the discomfort

or pain of growth that results from disturbing the old, traumatic memories that have inhibited your sexuality.

☐ Identify the fear. Name it. Write about it in your diary, or discuss it with your partner. If you do not shrink away but persevere with the practice, you will probably have a direct experience of the fear that has been aroused—for example, fear of being touched in a particular way or in a particular place. There are practices in this book during which this is especially likely to happen, and I describe in detail how to handle these situations.

☐ Move through it. Express it, feel it, allow it. Interestingly, the oldest meaning of the word *fear* signifies "to pass through," so if you follow that meaning, you will understand that it is part of your growth process to move through the fear instead of withdrawing at the very point at which the fear manifests itself. When you move through the fear, you will experience a release of blocked energy, followed by enhanced pleasure. Then you will realize that fear is a good teacher.

I don't mean by this approach that you have to disregard your limits, however. If you come to a place where you feel that the challenge is too great, trust yourself and break off the exercise gracefully in ways that are suggested in the book. Try not to end a practice session on a negative note or sudden interruption, however, because it will be counterproductive to the overall process of expansion, relaxation, and trust.

Be Playful and Lighthearted

Playfulness is an expression of the innocent child we all carry within ourselves. It means that while you are sincere in your intention to explore the methods leading to High Sex, you also want to enjoy yourself. Calling on your sense of humor can enhance a sense of flow and self-acceptance. The playful attitude takes you beyond a sense of self-importance—"I must have it the way I want it," or "No other way can work," or "I must succeed, or she'll think I'm a wimp." If you look upon learning as playful, the training will not only be easier but more effective.

Throughout this book I will be asking you to play, to pretend, to act "as if," to experience the practices without judging or worrying about the outcome. Try to just play along.

The Enchantment of Sound

Music is such an effective mood enhancer that it can augment the effect of these exercises tremendously. According to its tempo, tone, and harmonics, music can slow down or quicken the rhythm of blood circulation, stimulate or soothe the nervous system, and improve your intuitive faculties. Using the specific music that I have indicated in the appendix will magnify the effect of your practices, but you need not limit yourself to my suggestions. Create your own library of sound so that you can, at the touch of a button, feel that you are walking into a magnificent cathedral where angelic voices are singing, or participating in a rhythmic African tribal dance, or floating dreamily on a cloud, or standing by the ocean. Used in this way, music can create exquisite environments for lovemaking and pleasure.

A Word about Language

I have tried as much as possible to avoid terms from Eastern spiritual practices that may be unfamiliar or open to misinterpretation. Instead I have used Western concepts whenever possible or created and explained my own teaching terminology. For example, instead of talking about awakening Kundalini energy, I talk about awakening the Ecstatic Response. To me this seems to be a more practical and pragmatic approach, congruent with my wish to make Tantra available to Western lovers who have not studied the ecstatic traditions of the East.

I have, however, retained a few terms that may seem foreign to you. For instance, instead of the words *penis* and *vagina,* which I find cold, clinical, and ill-suited for the romance and poetry of certain practices in this course, I have sometimes used the Tibetan word *Vajra* for penis, and the Indian word *Yoni* for vagina. These and other terms will be defined and explained in the text.

If for any reason you find them awkward to use, choose the English word for which I have made the substitution. But please try my phrases first. Experience has shown me that they help to break through language-based habit patterns. Old words are loaded with connotations that are often unconscious and negative. New words offer a new world.

Now you are about to begin the training. Chapter 1, The Tantra Vision, will challenge current cultural and individual attitudes about sex and offer the alternative of the Tantric attitude.

❦

HIGH SEX AND THE TANTRA VISION

The first time I discovered ecstasy without a partner was in 1978, during an experiment in sensory deprivation that was part of a psychological research project. I was in isolation for seven days and seven nights, wearing earplugs and a blindfold in a darkened room, cut off from external stimuli. I progressively discovered how to relax deeply and focus my attention inside on my feelings, thoughts, and sensations. After a period of restlessness, I felt a growing peace, a transparency, as if the "I" of ordinary consciousness—the ego that defines each of us as separate from the world—no longer existed. I felt at one with everything within and without, as a wave is part of the ocean. Yet I had a sense of great power and wisdom, as if in that moment I had the answers to all the questions I had ever wanted to ask. And I heard my own voice saying, "Do not look for ecstasy outside yourself. It is already within you."

This experience happened simply as a result of letting go of distractions. Afterward I had to laugh at the paradox. I had searched around the world for teachings that could open me up to ecstasy, and although that search had helped me immensely, in the final analysis there was no need to go anywhere. From this experiment I had discovered that ecstasy is only to be found within. It confirmed what the Tantric masters had always said: Your true nature is blissful. If you close your eyes and go inside, if you give yourself a chance to go deep enough, past the chatter of everyday consciousness and outside distractions, you can discover that you already have ecstasy within you, 24 hours a day.

This insight gave me strength and security in working with others. I knew that no matter what problems and complaints they brought to

There is something within every human being that is . . . the very source of all our potential; it is the seed from which our lives grow. It is the origin of every experience we have ever had of love, truth or beauty. Its presence within can be intuited, deduced and read about, and it can be experienced directly . . . The biggest surprise in my search for the inner self was finding that it could be experienced by any human being whenever his desire for it was sufficiently sincere.

—Tim Galwey
The Inner Game of Tennis

me, I could stand in front of them, knowing that fundamentally they possessed an ecstatic potential equal to mine. Therefore, I could encourage them to explore and feel confident that they would succeed.

THE THREE-STEP PROCESS

The sensory deprivation experiment also confirmed my intuitive understanding that relaxation was an essential ingredient for the experience of ecstasy. I also understood, however, that relaxation by itself was not enough to trigger an ecstatic response. I saw that a special context was required in which the body was flooded with energy through intense events involving profound emotions and dynamic action that naturally open the way to deep relaxation.

This context can be provided through many different approaches, from ancient Tantric meditations to modern methods of working with the body. Through years of study and experimentation, I sought to create the best approach for generating ecstatic states and integrating them into the sexual experience. I arrived at a three-step process: Generating the Streaming Reflex, Awakening the Ecstatic Response, and Riding the Wave of Bliss.

Generating the Streaming Reflex

Sex is first of all a matter of energy. The more energy you have, the more blissful you can be, and the better sex becomes. In step one you learn to mobilize your energy and express it more fully until you experience orgasm as an "energy event" that can be learned and duplicated independent of the sexual context. In this process you experience the essential part of orgasm, which I call the streaming reflex.

As you experience the streaming reflex, you learn to welcome various kinds of vibrations and let them happen until they are felt as highly pleasurable. The result is a sense of being cleansed and relaxed. Once you have learned how to experience orgasm as an energy event outside the sexual context, you feel empowered to take responsibility for your own well-being in sex. You know that the true source of your pleasure lies not in your partner but within yourself.

Awakening the Ecstatic Response

Having learned how to trigger the streaming reflex, you then learn to contain the energy, relax into it, and expand it. This is the fundamental secret of High Sex: Ecstasy happens to you when you learn the art of staying relaxed and aware in high states of sexual or nonsexual arousal—a condition that I call the Ecstatic Response. You can experience this state with or without a partner, for long periods of time.

At first this may sound like a paradox. How can apparent opposites like relaxation and arousal be combined? You probably assume that you are either relaxed or aroused. In ordinary sex, relaxation occurs only *after* sexual excitement has climaxed in orgasm. The Ecstatic Response, however, combines the best effects of both: high energy and profound peacefulness. This is not, as one may experience in ordinary sex, an alternation between arousal and relaxation, but a simultaneous *resonance* between them. In the Ecstatic Response you allow the energy to rise to higher and higher levels while at the same time relaxing into the excitement, letting it spread through the body and containing it for longer and longer periods. This results in a blissful, regenerative experience.

Recent clinical studies confirm my own research, showing that when sexual orgasm is extended, the body's natural response is to relax. Dr. Alan Brauer, coauthor of the book *ESO* (Extended Sexual Orgasm), explains that after several minutes of extended orgasmic response, the body's level of arousal decreases—as measured by pulse, breathing rates, and blood pressure—even though the orgasmic contractions are continuing. Brauer states, "The subjective experience is one of continuous and increasing pleasure. The body responds as though it is going into a more relaxed state." As a professional in Western medicine, Brauer regards this result as "surprising." But the Tantric tradition has known about it for centuries.

In the Ecstatic Response you learn how to generate high levels of sexual arousal that are followed, just before the point of orgasmic release, by complete stillness of mind. At the same time, you relax certain muscles, breathe deeply and slowly, and apply other simple techniques that transform the nature of your orgasm. This prepares you for a full-body orgasm, which depends on the body's ability to vibrate beyond conscious control. Instead of a localized genital release, you experience a prolonged series of subtle, continuous, wavelike pulsations that spread through the body, resulting in the impression that you are melting into your partner.

I am the poet of the body,
And I am the poet of the soul.

The pleasures of heaven are with
me, and the pains of hell are
with me,
The first I graft and increase
upon myself. . . . the latter I
translate into a new tongue.

—Walt Whitman
Leaves of Grass

29

In this state the orgasmic sensations are no longer exclusively dependent on genital interaction but are often perceived as an altered state of consciousness. Unlike the short peak of genital orgasm, what you feel is not a reflex act that leads to a sudden and uncontrolled release of energy, but a deep letting-go that is reached through a consciously controlled practice. As the energy between your bodies melts and merges, sexual communion becomes an experience of deep intimacy.

In a sense, the ordinary genital experience is like rowing on a windy sea in a small boat—you bounce up and down. In contrast, the ecstatic state could be compared to the soft ripples of a quiet sea reflecting the sun. In High Sex you learn both to row more skillfully and to watch the sunlight on the ripples.

Riding the Wave of Bliss

In the final stage of the three-step process, you learn the ultimate form of Tantric lovemaking, which is gentle and slow and can transform the energy of sexual arousal into an experience of pure bliss. All other practices in the training have been preparations for this final stage— Riding the Wave of Bliss—which I teach in a seven-step sequence.

You begin by riding the wave of energy that has been released by the streaming reflex. This energy is consciously channeled from the genitals up through the body to the head. Orgasmic sensations then flood the brain, and you learn how to perpetuate the ecstatic experience, maintaining this state from 30 seconds to several minutes and, in the advanced stages, for up to an hour or more.

Most lovemaking is very dynamic. You move vigorously, and you breathe hard, building up sexual passion until you explode outward the energy in a final release. In contrast, the orgasm of the brain resembles the smooth, endless gliding of a kite in the wind. You enter effortlessly into a sense of floating, as if the boundaries of your body are expanding. From the Tantric perspective this "orgasm of the brain" greatly stimulates the brain cells and creates a bridge between the right and left hemispheres, fusing the intellect of the left hemisphere with the intuitive faculties of the right. It is this fusion that creates the experience of ecstasy, in which body, mind, heart, and spirit all participate.

Although Riding the Wave of Bliss was inspired in part by Tantric and Taoist approaches to love, it was not "transmitted" to me by a teacher. Instead it emerged from within me slowly, as the natural outcome of many different Western and Eastern practices. Far from being complex and esoteric, it is a clear, structured process that is accessible to anyone who wants to find a gentle and conscious way of "bringing the spirit back to sex," of honoring sexual union as a bridge between body and soul.

Why, you may wonder, haven't we heard of this kind of orgasm before? The reason is that our culture has lost the understanding that sexual energy is a physical expression of spiritual power. In truth, the desire to unite sexually with another human being is a reflection of an underlying spiritual need to experience wholeness and complete intimacy, transcending the individual's sense of separateness and isolation. It is a need to return to the original source of creation, to the oneness we

Here is Kabir's idea: as the river gives itself into the ocean, what is inside me moves inside you.

—Robert Bly
The Kabir Book

31

experienced in our mother's womb and, beyond that, to a oneness within the self. Sexual union without this sacred element, carried out only for the sake of pleasure, is commonly thought to be enough to satisfy our needs. But it rarely does, and then only fleetingly. With the sacred element added, it is possible for us to experience a connection with the life force itself, with our deepest creative impulses.

Yet when the sexual force is not understood as spiritual or sacred, sex is considered to be a purely physical, instinctual drive and as a result is not held in reverence. Rather, it is often misused as it becomes associated with personal power—the dominance of one gender over another—and conquest. Deprived of its sacred dimension, sexual energy is repressed and eventually directed against life itself. This, in turn, results in disrespect, disease, abuse, rape, and other forms of sexual violence.

Negative social conditioning about sex inevitably creates fear, and this fear is passed from generation to generation by well-intentioned agents such as parents, teachers, and religion. In early childhood most of us absorb condemnatory attitudes about sex without even becoming aware of the process. This conditioning cripples our spontaneity, our expression of sexual vitality, our pleasure, and our ability to love and honor one another. Fear, in this context, says, "Watch out—it will hurt if I open up to love and sex more fully."

Fear also inhibits communication in sex. Instead of being a deep communion between two people, lovemaking often becomes a tense encounter in which both partners are afraid to express their real needs. For example, many women believe that the only "adult" way of receiving tenderness and warmth is to be sexual with a man. They are unable to communicate their need for nongenital affection and contact and end up feeling used. Ann Landers, the syndicated advice columnist, asked her readers if they would prefer to be cuddled and held tenderly or to have sex. Of the 90,000 women who responded, some 64,000 replied that they would prefer to be cuddled and forget about intercourse. For them, sex does not convey the tenderness and intimacy they are seeking. Yet there is no inherent contradiction between sex, cuddling, and tenderness. It is simply lack of knowledge about the skills needed to create a wholly satisfying experience, a real communion, that makes them seem mutually exclusive.

The reduction of sex to a purely physical act also promotes an externalized view of intercourse, in which lovemaking is perceived as a performance. "Did you come yet?" asks the anxious lover to his mate.

As a result, we get caught up in efforts to improve our performance. We are always striving to be better than we are, wondering, *Am I doing this right?*, and thereby remaining contracted and stressed. This reliance on external guidelines, on the urge to "do it right" rather than trusting our own direct experiences, turns poor lovemaking into a self-fulfilling prophecy. Our beliefs limit our sexual potential.

This book offers an alternative based on sexual healing and the assumption that we have within us, naturally, the potential to experience wholeness and fulfillment in our love lives. It will, I hope, inspire you to look deep inside, not only at who you are but also at what you can become and what you really want out of your love life. My own answer to this line of inquiry is always the same: I want the best. This book shows you how to achieve it, step by step.

It is highly probable that sexual activity, indeed the frenetic preoccupation with sex that characterizes Western culture, is in many cases not the expression of a sexual interest at all, but rather a search for the satisfaction of the need for contact.

—Ashley Montagu
Touching

CHALLENGING SEXUAL MYTHS

Before we begin the practical aspect of this training, I would like to create the appropriate theoretical context. I begin by briefly challenging some of the prevailing sexual myths that inhibit the joyful exploration of our sexuality. As I have said, most of us have absorbed attitudes about sex that powerfully influence our behavior in unconscious ways. Unless we become aware of them, there is little chance of transforming the way we act in our sexual lives.

Sex Is for Procreation

According to the Christian perspective, sex is for creating children, not pleasure. As a result the inherent joy and feeling of being alive that sex can bring us is poisoned with guilt. Think for a minute how many times you will make love in your lifetime. A friend of mine, who is 43, came up with the figure 3000. But to create one child, you need to make love only once. So what are you going to do with the other 2,999 times?

The role of High Sex is to take care of these "other times," to shift the emphasis in lovemaking from procreation to ecstasy.

Sex Is Shameful

This condemning attitude stems from the Western religious tradition of separating the flesh from the spirit. Sex represents the libido, the instinc-

33

tual drive that cannot be controlled by the will; hence, it is regarded as dangerous. Even today, after the so-called sexual revolution of the sixties, these attitudes influence and cripple our feelings about sex. In my opinion, sexually transmitted diseases, AIDS, and pornography are a direct outcome of sexual condemnation. High Sex will teach you new ways of perceiving the erotic experience, ways in which sex is honored as a celebration, an act of creation, an art.

Sex Is Natural, So Don't Interfere with It

It often has been observed that "When you're hot, you're hot; when you're not, you're not." The idea this saying expresses is: Don't interfere with the natural flow of your libido; just "let it happen." Nature knows best. Consequently, some people take the view that the introduction of any formal practice into the realm of sex might interfere with their spontaneity.

I believe that the sexual urge as we experience it individually is not nearly as "natural" as it seems. It is continuously being influenced by cultural conditioning. For example, "gentlemen prefer blondes," "big breasts are better," and "bigger penises give better orgasms," are all beliefs that influence our sexual responses. We are the products of our culture, not just politically or in terms of diet or sports, but sexually as well. In my view the expression of sexual energy is both natural and cultural.

Much of sex is simply a set of learned responses. For instance, research has shown that bodily sensations are not experienced naturally, as they really are, but are interpreted by the brain according to past experiences, parental conditioning, and popular beliefs. The newly developed science of biofeedback, which monitors the brain's response to stimuli, has shown that people can learn to influence voluntarily many kinds of bodily responses, such as slowing down the heartbeat, controlling blood pressure, and responding to pain.

High Sex teaches you how to unlearn, transform, and recondition the body's responses during lovemaking. High Sex is not a formal practice but a preparation for lovemaking. It provides you with skills, enhances your sensitivity, broadens the range of possibilities open to you. When you have learned these practices, you will find that you can integrate them effortlessly into your love life without interfering with your spontaneity.

There Is a "Right" Way to Make Love

In Woody Allen's film *Manhattan,* a woman says, "After all these years I finally had an orgasm, and my doctor told me it was the wrong kind." All too often people—women especially—fall under the influence of "experts" who through scientific studies of sex have created a "norm" for lovemaking.

High Sex dissolves all these distinctions. In High Sex there is no wrong kind of orgasm or wrong way of lovemaking; there are only wrong attitudes. This book will inspire you to trust yourself and discover your own uniqueness in the realm of the erotic. It will teach you that orgasm is not just a sexual event but can be expanded to embrace the body, mind, heart, and spirit.

Sex Is Only a Genital Affair

Most people's understanding of sex is limited to the genitals. Pioneer feminist Germaine Greer once observed, "After all the porno flicks have been watched, all the vibrators and sexual techniques applied, sex has not changed that much. It still boils down to ejaculating seminal fluid into a vagina."

There is, however, another way. High Sex teaches you that the ordinary orgasm of release is not the only goal of sexual intimacy. The whole body can be transformed into an erogenous one, offering a multitude of erotic and sensual experiences that become increasingly subtle and ecstatic. Genital orgasm is the first step. Bliss is the last.

Intercourse Is the Only Meaningful Part of Sex

In our culture all sexuality is directed toward the goal of intercourse. Noncoital ways of enjoying sex have been condemned as preparation only, or as immoral and unhealthy. The very word *foreplay* implies that sensual pleasures such as touching, stroking, and kissing are relevant only within the context of sexual intercourse. As a result, by and large we follow a male-oriented model of hot, thrusting lovemaking that lasts a few minutes and ends abruptly. Included in this model is the myth that women want hard, aggressive, and fast sexual intercourse.

In High Sex you develop the art of prolonged noncoital eroticism to a highly refined degree, discovering that you can have full-body orgasms without penetration. High Sex opens up a more tender, feminine perspective of sexuality in which thrusting intercourse is seen as only a part of a much bigger picture that also includes relaxation in high states of arousal.

Arousal Follows a Set Pattern

Many men believe that as long as they kiss and stimulate a woman's breasts and clitoris for some minutes, she immediately will be ready to make love. Similarly, some women, when they kiss a man and stroke his penis, expect the proud erection of "Mr. Ever-Ready" within a few minutes. As a result, sexuality is centered in and limited to a few "hot" areas.

High Sex teaches you that the rest of the body—the hands, stomach, shoulders, neck, thighs, belly, even the feet—is equally sensitive and capable of orgasmic sensations. Any part of our body can become as fired up, sensitive, and open as the genitals, and the orgasmic pulsations experienced in those areas can be so satisfying that genital sex is temporarily forgotten. It also teaches that preparation for lovemaking is not merely a question of physical stimulation but a delicate harmonization between lovers that requires trust, openness, creativity, and many other mental, emotional, and spiritual qualities.

Your Sexual Pleasure Depends upon
Your Partner

The belief that you are dependent on a partner who is responsible for your sexual fulfillment is a widespread myth. It is based on the assumption that the source of your pleasure is not within you, but a result of what is done to you and how your lover does it.

High Sex teaches you that *you* are responsible for your own sexual pleasure and that this realization is the first step in learning the art of ecstasy. A person who has developed the ability to be orgasmic alone is naturally attractive to others, and more likely to find a mature partner for the further exploration of High Sex.

In Men, Orgasm Equals Ejaculation

As long as orgasm is thought to be the same as ejaculation, its biggest shortcoming will be the shortness of the act of coming—usually from four to ten seconds. Many people believe that the goal of lovemaking is to achieve the most intense possible release of sexual tension. This is particularly true for men, who are taught that sex without ejaculation is not worthwhile.

Through the training offered in this book, a man can gradually master his urge to ejaculate, so that he can decide when to release his semen instead of feeling it happen as an involuntary spasm. As they develop the Ecstatic Response, men discover that they do not even have to ejaculate to feel sexually fulfilled. They can, in fact, like some women, experience multiple orgasms when they separate orgasm from ejaculation. This enables men to prolong lovemaking with their partners almost indefinitely. It is possible for a man to have orgasms ranging from powerful genital vibrations to subtle streaming sensations through the whole body without emitting sperm. There is no sudden postejaculation cut-off point that is normally experienced when men have released their seed. High Sex stresses the importance of prolonging preejaculatory pleasure: a non-goal-oriented physical intimacy, enjoyed unhurriedly for its own sake, valuing exploration, intimacy, and sensitivity.

Tantra Requires Celibacy

When people think of Tantra, they often think of celibate monks and yogis and, therefore, the suppression of orgasm. This is a misconception, implying that the attainment of ecstasy is based on the denial of one of life's most enjoyable activities. In High Sex, lovemaking is cultivated and celebrated. Indeed, it is out of the seed of lovemaking that the flower of ecstasy grows. High Sex teaches that to be fully understood, lovemaking must be fully explored.

Tantra Condones Orgiastic Indulgence

Another popular view is that it resembles a sexual orgy and promotes hedonistic indulgences. Historically, the tendency of societies has been to swing continuously between sexual repression and indulgence. Indulging, you repeat habits in a mechanical way. Repressing, you never discover what sexuality can be.

Just as sexual energy has helped man out of his spiritual state into the body, so it can help him to return in full awareness to his divine primal state of wholeness.

—Elisabeth Haich
Sexual Energy and Yoga

Tantra is the middle path. It is neither indulgence nor repression. It teaches you to look directly into your sexuality so that you can understand, experience, and transform it rather than being either antagonistic or enslaved by sex. Tantra offers pragmatic answers to these basic questions: What is the ecstatic state? How can it be achieved in the context of sexual embrace? How can it happen in today's cultural context? How can it help us in our daily lives?

There are many more sexual myths propagated by our cultural heritage. As you go through this book, you will be challenged to unlearn many of the stereotypical ideas that have inhibited your sexuality, and you will be encouraged to develop skills that take you far beyond the normal limitations that have been imposed on pleasure. Each chapter will explore and challenge a particular sexual myth, then give you the experience of a constructive alternative through specific practices. I have found the most comprehensive and far-reaching perspectives on a modern approach to Tantra for western lovers in *The Tantra Vision* by Osho Rajneesh (published by the Rajneesh Foundation, India), a book I highly recommend. Because my own experience has been confirmed by his vision, I have incorporated some of Osho's teachings in the section that follows.

THE TANTRA VISION

The Tantra vision *accepts everything.* There is nothing forbidden in Tantra. Everything that a person experiences, regardless of whether it is usually judged as good or bad, is an opportunity for learning. For instance, a situation in which you feel sexually frustrated is not viewed negatively in Tantra, but as a teaching. It provides an opportunity to understand your motivations about going into sex. What does it mean to you? When have you repeated this pattern of behavior in the past? Why you are tolerating the situation? What opportunities for change are available to you? Through this questioning you can develop a sense of how to make your sex life work better. This vision can guide you as a blueprint for the kind of experiences that you wish to create for yourself.

In Tantra there is no division between what is good and what is bad, what is acceptable and what is unacceptable. For instance, Tantra, as I understand it, places no moral judgment on your sexual preferences. In Tantra the focus is not so much on with whom you do it but rather on how you do it. Hence, Tantra can be practiced by anyone.

"One who knows the male, yet cleaves to what is female, becomes like a ravine, receiving all things under heaven."

The Tantra vision is one of wholeness, of embracing everything, because every situation, whether pleasant or unpleasant, is an opportunity to become more aware about who you are and how you can expand your capacities. And this provides a great opportunity for integrating all aspects of yourself, including those parts that you may normally reject or hide. This vision also recognizes that within each adult human being there is a natural, unspoiled, childlike spirit who can openly and innocently explore unfamiliar territory. The innocence of this spirit remains intact and represents our natural capacity to enjoy life, to love, to play, and to be ecstatic. I call this aspect of the self the Ecstatic Self.

Because Tantra believes in wholeness, it embraces opposites, seeing them not as contradictions but as complements. The concepts of male and female therefore are not set apart, forever divided by a gender gap, but are viewed as two polarities that meet and merge in every human being. Tantra recognizes that each human being, whether man or woman, has both masculine and feminine qualities.

What this means is that by discarding our gender stereotypes, we can expand our sexual identities tremendously, honoring the polarity in

Tantra is a cult of ecstasy, a personal religion based on the mystical experience of joy rather than established dogma. Sex is holy to a Tantric. It is worship; it is energizing and life-giving. Tantric art, writings and religious rituals glorify sex. Tantrics are anti-ascetic; they affirm life. They teach the discovery of the divine through the exhaltation of the total human. They use all of the senses, the mind and the spirit to reach mystic peaks.

—Kamala Devi
The Eastern Way of Love

ourselves that until now has been largely ignored. In Tantra the man can be encouraged to explore his soft, receptive, vulnerable, feminine aspects. He can slip out from beneath the weight of his male responsibilities, stop performing, and relax, taking his time in sex, making love without a specific goal, allowing himself to receive while his partner initiates. For her part, the woman can explore her masculine dimension, recognizing that she is capable of dynamic leadership in lovemaking, taking the initiative, creating new ways of guiding, teaching, and giving herself and her partner pleasure. The man does not give up his masculinity, nor does the woman abandon her femininity. They simply expand their potential to include the other polarity.

In Tantra, when the male and female polarities merge, a new dimension becomes available—the sense of the sacred. When the sacredness of sexual union is felt, it is possible to experience your connection to the life force itself, the source of creation. This connection lifts your consciousness beyond the physical plane into a field of power and energy much greater than your own. Then you feel linked, through your partner, to everything that lives and loves. You feel that you are a part of the great dance of existence; you feel one with it.

Introducing a sacred dimension to sexual loving allows both partners to acknowledge that they possess divine qualities. By this I mean that they recognize their true potential as infinite and unlimited. In Tantra you discover that by honoring the god or goddess in your partner, you can see beyond the limitations of personality and, by seeing the divine in the other person, perceive the same potential in yourself. The other person becomes a reflection of your own godlike nature. That is why Tantric partners greet each other by saying, "I honor you as an aspect of myself." This means, "You are one with me, and your consciousness is a reflection of mine." This may seem farfetched to you now, but you may come to see it as an effective device for moving beyond the self-imposed and self-limiting images by which people tend to confine themselves.

Tantra views sexual union not only as sacred, but as an art. Interestingly, the Sanskrit root of the word *art* means "suitably united." To become Tantrikas, practitioners of Tantra, lovers were required to be versed in a multiplicity of skills, such as conversation, dance, ceremony, massage, flower arrangement, costumes and makeup, music, hygiene, breathing, and meditation, among others.

When we learn the erotic arts in this way, a deep healing of our sexuality takes place. The sex act is not a hurried and tense affair, fraught

Creation was for the purpose of lovemaking. As long as there was only one-ness, there was no delight. But when division occurred and afterwards they [man and woman] were connected with one another, this brought about great delight.

—Reb Hayim Haikel
eighteenth-century
Hasidic master

with the dangers of disease (transmitted by partners who do not take time for thorough preparations), but a safe and healthy exchange between partners who respect and know each other intellectually, emotionally, and sensually before they enter into sexual union. This is what is urgently needed today: a playful, loving, and comprehensive perspective on sex that makes it safe and ecstatic at the same time. A modern resurrection of Tantra can offer these alternatives, reducing the carelessness that contributes to sexually transmitted diseases.

According to Tantra, sex is first a matter of energy, and Tantra views energy as the movement of life. Within the human body, energy is continuously in motion. For example, the nucleus and electrons of an atom have characteristic vibratory movements and rhythms. The same goes for the molecules, cells, and organs of the human body. Each cell in the body pulsates rhythmically, and so do the heart, diaphragm, intestines, lungs, brain, and many other physiological components. The vibrations from these rhythmic movements generate bioelectrical currents that stream continuously through the whole body. They also generate energy fields that surround the body, and our moods and emotions generate specific vibrations that alter these energy fields as well.

Tantra sees each human being as an organism that is part of a larger whole—the surrounding environment, the planet Earth, nature itself—in which rhythm and vibration are the unifying factors. They are also the factors that influence the relationship of one person to another. So Tantra teaches lovers how to harmonize their energies and be on the same wavelength, creating a measurable resonance between their energy fields. In Tantra the art of creating such a resonance is equivalent to what we call foreplay.

One of the deepest insights of Tantra is that the human body is a single energy phenomenon. At one end of the spectrum, at the physical level, this energy is expressed as the sex drive. At the other end of the spectrum, at the level of the nervous system and the brain, energy is experienced as ecstasy. The sexual drive is instinctual, raw, unrefined energy. Through the practices in this book, you will discover that this same sexual drive can be transformed and refined into ecstasy. But it is one energy manifesting itself in different ways. Sexual energy is therefore to be accepted and respected as the raw material—the "crude oil"—from which the high-octane fuel of ecstasy is produced.

It is said that the earliest Eastern mystics obtained their first glimpses of spiritual enlightenment at the moment of orgasm. Indeed, many people

Sexual liberation implies the liberation of the whole being: body, mind and spirit. This holistic viewpoint is an essential ingredient to the understanding of the Sexual Secrets.

—Nik Douglas
Sexual Secrets

41

The secret of sexual energy, therefore, is not only that it is capable of begetting new generations, but that it has a second function of much greater importance for man: to lead his consciousness step by step up the great Jacob's ladder of consciousness to God.

—Elisabeth Haich
Sexual Energy and Yoga

know that orgasm can temporarily transport them to a state of rapture. For a few seconds the mind becomes devoid of thought, the egocentric view of life disappears, and we step outside of time into the timeless "now" of bliss. So sex, to the early mystics, was the very source of the religious experience, as it can still be today, given the right attitude and conditions.

THE TANTRIC ATTITUDE

I have outlined the essential cultural perspective of Tantra. Now I would like to offer you an individual perspective. In order to experience High Sex, you will need to understand what I call the Tantric attitude that pervades the teaching in this book. Understanding this attitude will greatly increase your ability to experience sexual ecstasy, providing a context in which the exercises will work best for you.

Learn Self-Love

Love begins at home, with loving yourself. By this I don't mean self-centered indulgence, but the ability to trust yourself and to listen to your inner voice—the intuitive guidance of your own heart. Loving yourself means that you realize that you deserve the experience of ecstasy; loving yourself also means that you are not willing to compromise or settle for less than you really want, especially in sex. Trying to love another when you do not love yourself does not work. You end up feeling possessive, jealous, and dependent. By contrast, when you really begin to love yourself, you become a magnet, attracting the love of others.

Yet you don't need the others to feel whole. Love becomes a state of being. Out of your own sense of abundance, you want to share and celebrate—you are grateful to receive and to give. This is freedom, the basis of true partnership. This is the goal of High Sex.

Through the practices in this book, you will come to experience the idea that sexual loving is a delicate cocreation between two equal partners. In High Sex you honor each other's differences, yet you move beyond them into a space of respect and devotion.

Tantra sees each human being
as an organism that is part of
the surrounding environment,
the planet Earth, nature itself.

Drop Guilt

Yes, it's true that the senses can lead you astray and the pursuit of pleasure can get you in trouble. Sensual pleasure needs the guidance of practical and ethical judgment. But you won't gain good health by repeatedly vetoing the vote of the senses and denigrating the wisdom of the body. Nature was neither capricious nor perverted in making sure that, other things being equal, *what feels good is good for you.*

—George Leonard

High Sex teaches you to drop your guilt about sex. You may think you have already done this, but guilt goes very deep, below our conscious thoughts. Why? Because for centuries organized religions have used guilt about sex as a subtle way of manipulating and exploiting people, and the recent liberalization of sexuality has not yet succeeded in erasing this cruel legacy. The practices in this book will help you root out guilt and allow you to experience sex as a healthy drive—a celebration of life that keeps you youthful and alive.

Enjoy Spontaneity

We have a tendency to trust experts, methods, and techniques while denying our own spontaneous feelings. You may be a victim of this attitude, which relies too much on external guidance and inhibits your ability to follow sudden changes in the way your energy is flowing. In High Sex you accept the idea that life is a great mystery. In addition to learning techniques, you give yourself the freedom to respond to the new and unfamiliar. This is not another "how-to" sex book. I teach from the perspective that if you are thoroughly prepared in all the areas—physical, mental, and emotional—then the "how-to" happens by itself, and you do not have to impose any borrowed techniques. I trust in your own originality. I teach you how to explore your own natural, original, unique way of making love.

Cultivate Pleasure

Our culture has trained us to believe that we don't really deserve pleasure, that cultivating pleasure is selfish, that giving it is more honorable than receiving it, and that having fun is wasting time—a distraction from more important matters. When we do allow ourselves to receive pleasure, we give ourselves conditions such as, "I should give him or her something in return for all this pleasure I am experiencing"; "I am taking too much of his or her time"; or "I shouldn't show how much I enjoy this, or he'll think I'm a whore!"

High Sex helps you to develop the precious ability to be totally and unconditionally receptive to pleasure. Through this training both men and women will have many opportunities to develop the ability to receive and welcome pleasure, giving themselves permission to close their eyes, lie back, relax, and let it happen.

Discover Meditation

You may wonder what meditation has to do with sensuality and love-making. In a nutshell, it provides clarity. Imagine a bottle filled with sand and water. Shake it, and you can't distinguish a thing. This is the way the human mind functions during most of our normal, daily, waking life. It is processing so many thoughts, perceptions, and pieces of information that is continuously "blurred." Often the circuits are jammed. But if you set the bottle down and leave it for a few minutes, the sand will arrange itself in harmonious layers on the bottom, and the water will become clear. In a way, meditation does the same.

By sitting in a position of relaxation and stillness, focusing your attention inside and deepening the rhythm of your breathing, the busy chatter of your thought processes gradually settles. As your mind quiets down, you will be able to direct more attention to your feelings and sensations, expanding your ability to experience pleasure. In High Sex, meditation helps you bring heightened awareness to the body, heart, and mind and to tune these three aspects of your being into a harmony that allows higher, more intense levels of pleasurable experience.

By meditation I do not mean that you have to master complex advanced methods of introspection. Rather, I mean a simple shift in focus—tuning in, turning within, relaxing, learning how to navigate beyond the chatter of the mind to expand your inner perceptions. Meditation in this sense is not an effort, but simply the conscious observation of what is happening inside.

The way to do is to be.

—Tao Te Ching

In long-term relationships there is a tendency for lovemaking to become routine, an automatic process, and this reduces the couple's capacity for enjoyment. By quieting the mind, meditation allows freshness and innocence to return to the act of lovemaking. In fact, meditation in High Sex can be seen as a process of deautomating sexuality.

Give Up Goal Orientation

Keep in mind the subtle distinction between doing these practices with a goal in mind and doing each one for its own sake—getting so absorbed in each exercise that it takes you over completely. This training is inspired by the orgasmic model: At first you are doing, doing, doing—using your will, using effort—then suddenly you come to a peak, you let go, and it starts happening to you. You are being swept off your feet. Most practices work in this way. I will ask you to put your whole effort into the practice and then to allow yourself to be taken over by its effects.

Remember, you cannot *will* the effect. The same is true for ecstasy. You can simply prepare the right conditions for ecstasy to happen to you. This is why so many Western lovers are frustrated in their attempts to experience ecstatic sex. They strive to achieve it through willpower and control, whereas it is actually a question of creating very intense experiences that are immediately followed by relaxing and letting go.

Allow Surrender

Surrender is an essential aspect of the learning process in Tantra. There is, however, a lot of confusion about what surrender means. People are suspicious of this term, which they equate with loss of free will and personal power. In fact they are confusing surrender with submission, which is a passive attitude that implies giving up responsibility for one's behavior—wanting someone else to do things for you. The word *surrender* has significant roots, in which *render* has the meaning "to melt," and *sur* means "super" or "highest." In other words, the true meaning of *surrender* is to melt into that which is higher than yourself.

In High Sex you give yourself voluntarily to the highest aspect of your potential so that you can begin to grow into it. Understanding the art of surrender will make the experience of High Sex much more available to you. True surrender is a conscious choice made from free will. It means opening your heart and trusting the person you are with, whether it is your beloved or your teacher. By surrendering to the practices in this book, you will allow yourself to be deeply touched by a new vision.

❧

In this chapter you examined the myths that surround sexuality, and you learned the positive vision of Tantra through which you can open yourself up to the new dimension of High Sex. You also learned the Tantric attitudes that will help you draw the maximum benefit from this book.

In chapter 2 you will begin the practices of High Sex, focusing on exploring your inner sensations, quieting your mind, and experiencing yourself as the source of your own pleasure.

CHAPTER 2

᭳

AWAKENING YOUR INNER LOVER

In launching yourself into this adventure of sexual discovery, your first question is likely to be "Where do I begin?" Many of my clients, when they come to work with me, assume that the answer is, "By finding the right partner." They believe that if only the right man or woman would come along, their lovemaking would be wonderful. Even if they have been through a number of such "right" partners, they still want to believe that the next may hold the magic. They don't realize that by searching outside themselves, they are relinquishing responsibility for their pleasure.

From the perspective of High Sex, the real answer to the question "Where do I begin?" is simpler and more direct: You begin with yourself as you are now. Think of yourself as a scientist who is interested in a new theory and who decides to test its validity in a practical experiment. The theory that you will be testing is: You are the principal source of your own pleasure. The poverty or richness of your sexual experience is ultimately up to you. No one can give you sexual ecstasy; it comes from within.

Your focus in this chapter will be to discover yourself as the lover within—that essential part of you that is already whole and capable of experiencing the fullness of sexual pleasure. Instead of looking outside for the right partner, you give to yourself *first* everything that you would give to your beloved. It is liberating and exciting to acknowledge that you hold your sexual destiny inside yourself. This is what I mean by awakening your Inner Lover.

Loving yourself in this way does not mean being self-absorbed or narcissistic, or disregarding others. Rather, it means welcoming yourself as the most honored guest in your own heart, a guest worthy of respect, a lovable companion. Your Inner Lover is not separate from yourself, nor

As we are about to become citizens in a universe richer by far than any we have ever known, we deeply need our archetype, our Beloved in the depth world, to partner us in this larger citizenship. Our Beloved knows the patterns, forms, and places where the vast latencies and psycho-spiritual knowings are coded. In this way love grows reality.

—Jean Houston
The Search for The Beloved

is he or she a dreamlike phenomenon. Your Inner Lover is more like a quality, a feeling, that you can recognize in moments of joy or stillness when, moving deeply inside yourself, you connect with a natural innocence, simplicity, and spontaneity. The Inner Lover is expressed in your ability simply to be as you are without trying to be other than you are.

The story of Naomi, an American ballet dancer in her thirties, illustrates the healing effect of self-love and its role in awakening the Inner Lover. Naomi came to one of my seminars with her husband, Louis, a prominent French surgeon. Both were obviously in love and looking forward to learning the art of High Sex. But Naomi soon told me of a problem that tormented her: Whenever she felt especially open and vulnerable and her husband gave her a look of deep affection, she would suddenly feel ugly and unworthy.

I helped Naomi explore the images and memories connected with her pain. After a while she regressed to a situation in her childhood. Describing the scene, she told me that she saw herself as a five-year-old girl cringing away from contact with an old aunt with the same name—"a cold, shriveled, and ugly spinster," as Naomi described her. As a little girl, the future ballet dancer had been appalled to discover that she had been given the same name as this aunt and concluded that her parents found her ugly.

Every day she looked in the mirror for signs of the same wrinkles that her aunt had. She grew up with the feeling that she had to hide the terrible secret of her ugliness from everyone. Even though she was stunningly pretty and her husband told her so and adored her, she subconsciously feared that Aunt Naomi and her wrinkles inhabited her body and could reappear if one so much as scratched the surface.

I told Naomi to meet her husband's tender gaze and sustain eye contact until the feeling of ugliness surfaced. When it did, I told her to breathe deeply, turn her head, and contemplate the image of herself reflected in a mirror that I held in readiness. As she did so, I asked her to give an exact account of what she saw. Hesitantly, reluctantly, she started describing precisely each part of her face until she had to admit that she was seeing the reflection of an exquisitely beautiful woman. Then I asked her to close her eyes and contemplate the image she had just observed in the mirror. "Hold that vision in your mind's eye as you resume looking at Louis," I suggested. "See that he is seeing you as the beautiful woman you just saw in the mirror. Every time you feel yourself wavering, turn your head, look again into the mirror, and describe what

The divine lovers, Shiva and Shakti, in union with the God in each other.

you see." By repeating this process many times, Naomi was able to gain a positive image of herself, not only feeling beautiful but being seen as beautiful. It was an important step on the way to awakening her Inner Lover.

The practice of Awakening Your Inner Lover has roots in the Tantric tradition, in which devotees were encouraged to visualize in great detail the form and qualities of a divine lover, such as the god Shiva and the goddess Shakti. Their aim was to focus with such devotion on the spiritual beloved that they ultimately attained union with the deity, thereby manifesting in themselves the divine qualities of the godhead.

In this chapter my goal is to inspire you to fall in love, not with a symbolic deity, but with yourself as the spiritual beloved. When you enter a loving relationship with yourself, you become both the lover—the one who gives love—and the beloved—the one who receives it.

In a sense we are alone, for our "inner freedom" means that a love relation can no longer fetter us; the other sex has lost its magic power over us, for we have come to know its essential traits in the depths of our own psyche. We shall not easily "fall in love," for we can no longer lose ourselves in someone else, but we shall be capable of a deeper love, a conscious devotion to the other.

—J. Jacobi
The Psychology of C. G. Jung

Through this self-directed love, you can experience yourself as a limitless being, in tune with the whole of existence.

The purpose of meeting your Inner Lover is rooted in the understanding that the more self-accepting you are, the more orgasmic you can become. Let me explain what I mean. When you criticize yourself, one part of you is fighting another part, and consequently your energy is in conflict. In a state of self-acceptance, your energy is unified. Only then can you enjoy pleasure and become fully orgasmic in love. Orgasm, by its very nature, requires your total participation. By connecting with your Inner Lover and experiencing self-acceptance, your potential to be orgasmic is greatly enhanced. This potential may not be immediately available to you. But throughout this book you will be taking one step after another toward an experience of your ecstatic nature, moving gently toward the source of your own being.

THE BREATH OF LIFE

The first step in the process of Awakening Your Inner Lover is to become aware of the way you breathe and of what breathing does to your body. Conscious Breathing helps you to connect with your physical sensations and to amplify them. It focuses your attention on the life energy that courses through your whole body. This is important because your ability to awaken your Inner Lover depends on your capacity to experience yourself and your sensations from within. You are going on an inner journey, using your breath as a vehicle.

As you become more sensitive to the flow of your breath, you will find that you can direct your attention to any part of your body, breathe into that part, create tingling sensations of warmth and aliveness, and then spread these sensations to the rest of the body.

To show you what I mean, let's conduct a simple experiment. Take a few minutes, close your eyes, relax, and imagine that a familiar hand comes to rest gently on your own hand. The hand feels good. Because you are relaxed, you are receptive to the touch. You find that you can "listen" to it, welcoming its warmth as if it were a subtle current of energy. Feel this sensation of warmth spreading through your hand. Inhaling deeply, feel as if you are drawing the warm energy from your hand into your arm and then to the rest of your body. With practice you can welcome the subtlest sensations, allowing them to be enhanced by

Imagine a hand resting on your hand.

deep breathing. This is how breathing can serve you as a vehicle for pleasure, eventually turning your whole body into an instrument—even a symphony—of pleasure. You will be practicing Conscious Breathing throughout this training.

Many forms of spiritual practice and methods of self-development place great emphasis on breathing. In the East teachers of meditation emphasize breathing in a slow and conscious way—that is to say, with attention fully focused on the inflow and outflow of breath. This constant awareness of breathing switches your attention away from the thought processes, an important step in quieting the mind. This creates an inner silence that allows sensory perceptions to be much sharper and more intense. In addition, some meditation schools teach certain techniques of breathing that fill the body with *prana,* the universal life force. The deeper you inhale, the more *prana* you can absorb.

In High Sex, deep breathing is what connects us to our sexual centers. The deeper we breathe, the more we come into contact with our sexual energy. Most of us, however, live on a beggar's ration of air. The average person inhales one pint of air per breath, while our lungs can actually contain seven pints when fully expanded. This is one of the reasons that the range and depth of our experiences—especially sexual sensations—disappoint our longings. We simply do not breathe well enough to reach our full orgasmic potential in love.

CONSCIOUS BREATHING: FOLLOWING THE BREATH

The smoke of my own breath,
Echos, ripples, and buzzed
whispers. . . . loveroot,
silkthread, crotch and vine,
My respiration and inspiration.
. . . the beating of my heart.
. . . the passing of blood and
air through my lungs,
The sniff of green leaves and dry
leaves, and of the shore and
darkcolored sea-rocks, and of
hay in the barn.

—Walt Whitman
Leaves of Grass

In lovemaking, thoughts often invade the territory of our senses. For instance, while making love, you may suddenly be distracted by an anxious thought—"What if he doesn't like the way I am responding to his caresses?" "What if she notices that I have a scar on my abdomen?" And so on. Conscious Breathing, the first practice in this chapter, provides an easy way to free yourself from unwelcome thoughts and reconnect yourself with your sensations. You can do it any time, and it is always available. It is almost impossible to follow your breath and think at the same time.

Purpose and Benefits

Doing this simple exercise regularly will expand your capacity to be sensual. You will begin to notice how you can receive more pleasure by increasing your sensitivity to what is naturally available, rather than by seeking experiences of increasing intensity. A radio receiver, for example, may have a loud volume without the ability to lock accurately onto the signal, amplify it clearly, or filter out extraneous noise. As a result, it may be able to blast out a heavy beat but not to discriminate among the finer harmonics of the music. To get good reception it needs to be finely tuned. In the same way, you need to be able to tune in, filter, and amplify your sensations to awaken your Inner Lover.

Preparations

Throughout this book you will be asked to create quality time for your practice. I would like to give you a few hints about how to do this, which you can then apply to the rest of the training.

Choose a space and a time that will allow you to remain alone and undisturbed for the duration of the practice. Make sure that you have privacy from telephones, television, visitors, children, and other distractions. It is important that all daily activities be put on hold so you can devote your full attention to the exercise. This is not only quality time; it is sacred time—time for yourself, time for your lover, time for ecstasy.

Come to the practice after having showered. Then take ten minutes to relax, creating a transition between your daily life and your practice time.

Make sure your clothing is loose and comfortable. Your chest and belly should be unrestricted.

It will help if the air in the room is fresh. You also can do this exercise outdoors, but you need to be warm enough to feel relaxed.

Allow ten minutes for the practice.

Practice

Sit comfortably and close your eyes. For one minute do nothing at all. Simply try to watch what's going on behind your closed eyes.

Unless you're an experienced meditator, your mind will be flooded with an abundance of thoughts. You may be thinking about your next business meeting, what to buy for dinner, what you really should have said to someone with whom you had a disagreement. Maybe you are daydreaming about some lover or pet project. Perhaps you are wondering whether it's time to open your eyes, or whether you are doing it "right."

Generally, thoughts preoccupy people so much that their breathing remains shallow, and they block out awareness of the other things that are going on—sensations in their bodies, the atmosphere in the room, the quality of another person's presence.

This first, quick experiment reveals our standard, everyday operating mode: We live in our minds, sustain ourselves on a minimal flow of air, and consequently operate at low levels of energy and awareness.

Now redo the experiment. Sit comfortably in your chair, and close your eyes. This time focus on your breathing rather than your mental state. As you inhale, feel the fresh air coming in through your nostrils. Follow it down into your chest and belly. As you exhale, feel the warm air coming out your nostrils. Note the gentle rise and fall of your stomach as you inhale and exhale.

Notice what happens each time you lose awareness of your breathing. Your mind moves away to some thought, and suddenly you realize that you have taken several breaths without being conscious of them. Your awareness shifts somewhere else, and your breathing switches back to being shallow and automatic.

Each time this happens, bring your awareness back to your breathing. Follow each breath down into your abdomen and then out again as you exhale. Be patient and easy on yourself. Moving out of your head and back into your body comes naturally as you follow the current of your breath, but it doesn't happen without practice. Count every moment

"Watching over the breath" consists in letting the breath come and go as it wants, without forcing it or clutching at it. In due course its rhythm automatically slows down, and it flows in and out so smoothly. This is both a symbol of and a positive aid to letting one's whole life come and go without grasping.

—Alan Watts
Nature, Man and Woman

that your awareness remains on the breath as successful and every time you return to conscious breathing after a lapse.

Do this exercise a few times until you begin to notice the difference between breathing that takes place while you are thinking and breathing with awareness.

At this point you may be wondering why I am trying to shift your attention away from the thought process. You may ask, "What's wrong with thoughts? Isn't the mind the noblest human faculty?" Perhaps it is, but it may also have a tendency to dominate your life in areas where it really has no useful contribution to make. Making love through your thoughts is a bit like trying to do differential calculus with your genitals.

Pointers

With this practice some people fall into the trap of concentrating too hard on trying to stop thinking. If this happens to you, be aware that it might create a conflict within your mind, and all you're likely to get out of it is a big headache. Thinking won't go away just because you decide you don't want to listen to it anymore. Let your mind think. Have a good chuckle each time you discover it has led you away into thinking about some past or future event, then bring your awareness back to the breathing—and to the present. That's all you can do, and it is enough.

Now that you have started traveling within, you can take the next step: combining your breathing with your imagination in order to take you to your Inner Lover.

AWAKENING YOUR INNER LOVER

In sex and love we have been deeply conditioned by the role models offered by the glamorous worlds of entertainment and fashion. We absorb romantic ideals from Hollywood and deep down long to be Supermen and Superwomen with perfect figures, perfect hair, and stunning good looks, casually assured in conversation and irresistible to the opposite sex.

What this means is that we long to be someone different from who we really are. Or we feel trapped into behaving in a certain way when really we are experiencing something quite different. For example, we might feel angry toward someone, yet want to appear compassionate and loving. Or we may want to be the best lover in the world, while in fact we do not feel aroused or excited. There is a conflict within us, and this has unfortunate consequences, for unless we start by accepting who we really are now, with our so-called imperfections, we will not experience the personal power needed to develop our true potential in the realm of sacred sexuality. High Sex depends on your willingness to awaken the real, authentic lover in you.

In the following practice you will be drawing on the power of your imagination—your ability to create pictures in your mind. We imagine in various ways. Some people see sharp images. Others feel it bodily. There is no right way to use the power of your imagination. As you progress in Awakening Your Inner Lover, you will find your natural method. Whatever happens most easily is right.

Purpose and Benefits

The purpose of this practice is to develop self-appreciation, which is the quickest way to connect with your Inner Lover. Loving yourself, you simply relax into the moment, accepting who you are, accepting even the fact that sometimes you don't accept yourself. This self-acceptance produces a deep relaxation in your being, allowing pleasure and delight to happen naturally.

Preparations

Settle yourself alone into a comfortable environment where you will be uninterrupted for 20 minutes. You can either sit or lie down.
　　Play soft, relaxing music. (See Appendix II).

Practice

Begin with the deep, relaxed breathing that you learned earlier, letting the breath flow deep into your chest and belly and then slowly out. Let it go as deep inside as possible without having to make an effort. Let the amplifying and cleansing power of the breath support the appreciation that you are about to give to yourself.
　　As you close your eyes and take a deep breath, let your hands rest on your heart. Imagine that you are entering into a relationship with yourself in which you are at once the lover and the beloved. Feel your heart beating. Follow the ebb and flow of air through the center of your chest, cleansing and relaxing it. Let the breath be easy and gentle. Watch it go in and out, not putting any effort into the breathing, just staying with it.
　　Then let a memory, an image, or feeling arise behind your closed eyes—a visualization of a time in your past when you felt totally loved and supported, cared for, and protected. Perhaps you remember being a little child cuddled in your mother's arms or feeling the enveloping embrace of a childhood friend or the affection and acceptance of a special teacher.
　　Feel the trust, gentleness, and vitality that blend with this feeling. Delight in your youthful innocence, vulnerability, and openness.
　　From there, gradually progress in time, recalling moments when again you felt totally loved, open, vulnerable, energized. Maybe you

were picking flowers in a garden flooded with sunshine, or perhaps you had a very deep and fulfilling sexual connection with someone you loved. As images come forth, do not censor or rush through them. Let them come forth as they will.

When you are immersed in one strong, rewarding image, breathe deeply as you contemplate it. At first remain a passive spectator, relaxed, receptive. Then settle into deep, rhythmic breathing, and participate more fully in the remembered scene, filling in as many details as possible. Let the particular colors, sounds, smells, texture, and taste come back to you: the coziness of your mother's embrace, the smell of her hair; the fragrance of the flowers; the softness of your lover's skin.

Now try to step into the picture and become the actor in the scene rather than a spectator of a vision. As you "warm up" through deep, conscious breathing, let the feelings of that time well up inside your heart. Welcome them. Amplify them. Feel them as intensely and directly as you can.

Immersing yourself even deeper, hold your hands to your heart, and allow the feelings connected to the experience to resonate within you. You may feel the joy you felt then, or the quickening of your heartbeat, or a sense of excitement, of being nurtured. As in the hand exercise mentioned in the previous practice, use your breathing to expand this feeling so as to experience it fully, vibrantly. Carry these sensations along the flow of your breath until they quicken the blood and bring the special thrill of the moment flooding back to you again. Let your consciousness be filled with the feeling that everything is easy, flowing, simple.

Find a word or a phrase that expresses the sense of well-being and personal appreciation that you are feeling right now. Whisper, "It feels good to love me," or "I really enjoy giving myself support." Repeat these positive statements until you feel the pleasure of hearing them, perhaps until you can comfortably say them aloud. You are accepting yourself, recognizing your uniqueness. You are beginning to hear the voice of your Inner Lover. As you say yes to this voice, you may be able to see that life is really on your side, willing to support you, teach you, and help you to grow if only you allow it to.

Then gradually return to the present, letting your breathing slow down. Release the images, memories, and feelings as you exhale, as if they are birds taking off in flight. Know that you have remembered who you really are—a lovable person. You have met your Inner Lover.

When you return to your normal waking state, review the moments in your life up to this day when you have felt the flavor of these deeper qualities. Spend some time writing down a list of these events. Then let your imagination loose, and envision which of these occasions you could re-create—moments in which you can let go and be childlike and playful. Make a list of them. Here are some examples from my own list:

☐ Receiving a long, long hug.
☐ Lying in a friend's arms, relaxing, listening to music, with no plans, no intentions.
☐ Getting a luxurious massage.

☐ Having a tickle session when I get too serious.
☐ Following and mimicking a child.
☐ Reading a comic book.
☐ Dancing and rolling around on the floor.

Pointers

What we have done in this practice of Awakening Your Inner Lover is an example of a very important strategy in High Sex: Whenever you find satisfaction, in whatever act, feel it, deepen it, become one with it, remember it. Drinking fresh water when you are extremely thirsty, meeting the one you love after a long absence, taking a walk along the beach during a beautiful sunset . . . cultivate your awareness of such moments, however small. This gives you the opportunity to expand the joy in your life and to break the habit of the mind to focus on problems rather than pleasure. It is a way to build up your potential for ecstasy.

THE HEART SALUTATION

Now that you have encountered yourself as the Inner Lover, you'll likely feel warmth and joy in your heart, or simply an overall sense that you're just fine exactly as you are. In my experience love always carries with it a spiritual dimension, a sense that you are part of the larger creation, an expression of the infinite.

When you have touched this dimension within, there is a natural instinct to want to share the gift with someone close to you. It may be a friend, a lover, or your life partner. In fact, you may find yourself looking at your partner with new eyes, recognizing in him or her the same divine lover, the same connection to the larger existence. Approaching your partner with the attitude that "I am lovable and so are you" immediately gives you a feeling of respect for each other.

As a tribute to this recognition and as a reminder of your mutual commitment to the expression of your higher selves through High Sex, you will now learn a ritual salutation. It is inspired by the traditional *namaste* greeting used in the East, signifying, "I honor the god within you."

Purpose and Benefits

The greeting ritual communicates that both of you are ready to enter into a sacred moment. You are saying to each other, "I recognize and honor you from my heart." Such practices that break us away from our normal behavior and attitudes are especially beneficial when, as is often the case in modern life, we come to lovemaking after spending the day focused mostly on hectic activities and business with others.

As you acknowledge this deep connection, you may wish to let go of any lingering resentments against each other. Through the Heart Salutation you are making the choice to honor each other's higher self and relate at a level that transcends whatever divides you.

The Heart Salutation ritual will become a regular part of the exercises throughout this book as a way of clearly demarcating the beginning and end of each practice. You also can do these salutations alone, directing your greeting to your own higher self. You are due honor and love as much as your partner is.

Preparations

Create a private space in your home or in some other attractive, quiet place where you can be insulated from distractions.

Allow five to ten minutes for this practice.

In this exercise I will assume that you are doing the Heart Salutation with a partner. If you do not have a partner, do the salutation to yourself in front of a mirror.

Practice

This practice may seem simple, but it is important to observe the body posture precisely. You will find that the proper gesture sets your energy moving in the most beneficial way, engendering a distinct feeling of respect and recognition of the Inner Lover in each other.

There are two forms of the Heart Salutation. For your practice you can choose the one that feels the most comfortable, or alternate between the two. The first involves a verbal greeting, while the second uses the sacred sound *Om* to give you the feeling of being centered in your heart.

Sit facing your partner for a few minutes, gazing gently into his or her eyes.

Heart Salutation.

As you inhale, bring the palms of your cupped hands together in front of you, and rest your thumbs against your chest. Note the feeling of availability and welcoming that this posture conveys.

Together with your partner, close your eyes. As you exhale, gently bend forward from the waist, keeping your back straight. Bend forward at a 45-degree angle, until your foreheads touch lightly. Hold this contact for a few moments, feeling the connection between you. Take in the full sense of honor and reverence that this mutual gesture conveys, letting go of all extraneous concerns while you focus your breathing and your awareness in your heart.

Inhaling, come up gently with your back straight, keeping your hands cupped together against your chest.

Sit up straight, open your eyes, look into your partner's eyes, and say, "[Your partner's name], I honor the Higher Self in you."

Or you can use other expressions that may more comfortably express your recognition of your partner's perfection and lovability, such as:

"[Your partner's name], I salute the [god/goddess] within you."

"I honor you, [your partner's name], as an aspect of the Divine."

When you are in love with someone, you do indeed see them as a divine being. Now, suppose that is what they truly are and that your eyes have by your beloved been opened. Through a tremendous outpouring of psychic energy in total devotion and worship for this other person, who is respectively god or goddess, you realize, by total fusion and contact, the divine center in them. At once it bounces back to you and you discover your own.

—Alan Watts
Play to Live

"I honor you, [your partner's name], as an aspect of myself."

As your partner reciprocates, you can receive and feel the profound meaning of this gesture. Appreciate the devotion and reverence this greeting conveys. See that you each embody the fullness of being and share in this spark of divinity, despite the differences between you.

The alternative to this spoken salutation is to make the sound "OOOMmm" as you each bend forward. In Eastern traditions, *Om* is regarded as the root of all sounds, the very "humming of being." You may find that chanting "Om" helps to focus your awareness within yourself. As you begin the *Om,* open your mouth wide, and make an O shape with your lips. Let the sound come from deep within your belly and emerge slowly with resonance. Toward the end of your exhalation, close your lips to hum the "Mmmmm" part of the sound.

When you sit up again and gaze into each other's eyes, you need not speak, but simply drink in the meaning of the salutation and feel the centering effect of the sound.

Pointers

As with the other practices in this book, you may need to repeat this one a few times before you can fully enjoy its effect.

Take a moment to contemplate how the simple practices in this chapter have affected you—whether you enjoyed them, whether there are any variations or adaptations that might suit you. For instance, you can do the Heart Salutation sitting on a chair or use another greeting phrase. Play, adapt, and create, but make sure you follow the sequence of the training.

❧

Through Conscious Breathing you learned how to dive within yourself. Through Awakening Your Inner Lover, you made a commitment to be supportive of yourself, and through the Heart Salutation you acknowledged the presence of an Inner Lover in your partner.

In these basic introductory exercises, you began to discover some of the fundamentals of High Sex. First, you learned that the source of sexual pleasure is within you and does not depend on connecting with an ideal partner. You also learned that full breathing energizes and centers you in your body, expanding physical sensations. Finally, you came to understand that visualizing yourself as a lovable, relaxed, open, playful person frees you from negative thinking that keeps you sexually limited.

In the next chapter you will learn how to create a Sacred Space, a sanctuary to assist you in developing the right conditions for High Sex. You will also discover how to communicate openly about the fear and resistance, the fantasies and peak experiences that arise in your love life so that you may develop trust in each other.

CHAPTER 3

❦

OPENING TO TRUST

High Sex requires a deep level of communication between you and your partner. When you feel a heart-to-heart connection with each other, communication becomes communion, and lovemaking can carry you into an experience of ecstasy. Yet the attempt to create this depth in a partnership is a challenge that often provokes fears. Some people try to ignore such fears and never mention them. Others spend a lot of time talking about them, focusing on communication through language, ideas, and concepts because they don't want to risk being open and emotionally vulnerable.

Yet love is such an opening experience that it often creates situations in which fears are aroused in spite of our attempts to rationalize them away. For example, frequently it is when we desire a lover most that we are most afraid to show our feelings, thinking, "What if I reveal my heart completely and he rejects me?" We believe that expressing fears or negative thoughts about a partner will create distance. Actually, speaking the truth is healing. And if we learned how to receive it, it creates intimacy rather than distance.

As you explore High Sex more deeply, it is also likely that feelings of insecurity or hurt will surface during the practices. In a way, these practices have the same effect as love: They open you to beautiful feelings, but in doing so they allow old, unexpressed resentments from difficult sexual experiences in the past to surface. For example, you may be primed up and ready to start a practice; yet shortly after you begin, you may be surprised to find yourself fearful. These feelings are normal. In fact, they are a healthy sign because their sudden reappearance shows that you are

Trust and its sister, surrender, are like a womb in which all of consciousness can gestate and mature.

—Richard Moss
The I That is We

65

allowing more energy into your system. You are making progress in breaking out of limiting patterns of behavior.

The ancient Greeks called these fears and resistance our "demons"; the Tibetans called them "monsters." Every spiritual tradition and method of inner growth has names for them and mythologies about them and offers various ways to deal with them. But all traditions agree on one point: If you know how to remain aware and centered in yourself when the demons appear, you can confront them, accept them, make friends with them so that they become your allies rather than your enemies, and you ultimately transcend them.

In this chapter you will learn exercises that teach you gradually to master these demons—to acknowledge your apprehension and to reveal it to your partner in a way that is healing for both of you. Then, when you have both talked openly about your fears, you may find that a bond of trust has begun to develop between you. You may start to feel that you can be more spontaneous, relaxed, and open with each other about matters concerning your love life. This calling to increasingly let down your guard is the challenge of High Sex because relating in an undefended way with your partner opens the door to sexual ecstasy.

But this is a risk that you can take only when you feel accepted by the other person. There is a kind of progression in opening yourself up to trust that, when verbalized, goes something like this: "The more you trust me, the more I feel accepted. The more I feel accepted, the more open and vulnerable I can be with you. The more open and vulnerable we are with each other, the more intimacy we can share. The more intimacy we share, the more our love will grow."

Trust is also a way of describing the friendship that can develop between two partners once the first rush of romance has passed, when they begin to see and confront differences—when one partner wishes to make love and the other does not, for example, or when one partner wishes to be touched in a certain way that the other partner finds unappealing. In this context trust means that beyond these contradictions, there is a bigger picture, a wider sense of commitment. You feel that you are on a common path and that the interaction between you is teaching both of you how to become more mature and understanding. In an atmosphere of trust, you do not blame your partner for not fulfilling your desires. You accept the fact that in some ways you are different, yet recognize that you both bring precious gifts to the relationship that can make it nourishing and rewarding.

It is always important for us to be aware of feelings. Our feelings exist for good reason and so deserve our attention and respect. Even uncomfortable feelings that we might prefer to avoid, such as anger and depression, may serve to preserve the dignity and integrity of the self.

—Harriet Goldhor Lerner
The Dance of Intimacy

66

Trust and openness in a relationship usually don't happen at the thump of a heartbeat. To let go of defenses, lovers need to feel protected and secure. In this chapter you will learn how to create your Sacred Space, a sanctuary that will help the atmosphere of mutual trust to develop between you and your partner. Here you can expose and "befriend" your fears in a safe and supportive atmosphere and thereby render them harmless. The Sacred Space is where you give yourself and your partner the opportunity to be transparent—to acknowledge who you are, what you feel, how you think and, perhaps most important, how you can become more deeply available to each other.

Chances are, the atmosphere in your living room and your bedroom—as they are now—does not convey the sense of a special, sacred space. They are probably too full of the sights and sounds of your everyday life to encourage exploration of another dimension of your being. But don't worry. The most unlikely rooms and spaces can readily be converted into magical environments.

Sometimes this can happen easily and unexpectedly. For example, two friends of mine, Suzanne and Eddy, were going on a short holiday together on the California coast, south of San Francisco. Although they had been in an intimate relationship for several years, they hadn't seen each other for a while and wanted their first night of lovemaking to be special. Eddy, in particular, had fantasies of making love in a wooden cabin somewhere near Big Sur, listening to the pounding surf of the Pacific Ocean below, with moonlight flooding through the pine trees outside the windows.

Through a series of delays and misadventures on the road, however, they were obliged to spend their first evening with a friend in a very ordinary suburban house, just outside San Francisco. Their host didn't have a spare bed, so she offered them a mattress on the floor in an empty room that she used for yoga and meditation. It was cold, the floor was tiled, and at first glance the room was quite unwelcoming. Eddy and Suzanne both decided to write off the evening, avoid sex, and reserve their special moment of bliss for the following night.

As Suzanne explains, "We both felt tired and disappointed and went to our room early. Eddy put some logs in the fireplace and started a fire. The room's central light was much too bright, so I turned it off and lit some candles that I had noticed around the room. There was a half-burned stick of incense, so I lit that, too.

"I saw a stereo system by the wall, loaded with a cassette. It was

The primary nature of every human being is to be open to life and love. Being guarded, armored, distrustful and enclosed is second nature in our culture. It is the means we adopt to protect ourselves against being hurt, but when such attitudes become characterological or structured in the personality, they constitute a more severe hurt and create a greater crippling than the one originally suffered.

—Alexander Lowen
Bioenergetics

something I'd never heard before, *Antarctica* by Vangelis. I switched it on but didn't pay much attention to the music because I was already heading for the shower. We washed and got ready for bed.

"When I walked back into the room, the atmosphere was totally transformed. The room was warm and aglow with soft, flickering light from the candles and the fire. The music was heavenly and so unfamiliar that I lost all sense of space and time. The incense lent an exotic quality. The room had silence, peace, a sacred quality. It felt magical.

"We were both thrilled—perhaps this night wasn't going to be wasted, after all. Excitedly, we hauled the mattress to the center of the room so that it wouldn't seem like a regular bed, covered it with fresh sheets, lay down, and enjoyed the most exquisite night of intimacy and lovemaking we had ever experienced."

You may already have had an experience of a special place, or sanctuary, even if you did not think of it in those terms—a dimly lit romantic restaurant, a secluded beach, a honeymoon hotel suite, or a religious setting of some kind.

A sanctuary protects you from the hubbub of the ordinary world. It lifts you up and out of ordinary reality. It possesses distinct qualities that set it apart: silence, beauty, elegance, sensual delight. It engenders feelings of confidence and harmony and sets the stage for moments of special grace, for being your best, for experiences of the highest quality.

Connecting with a partner in High Sex requires a special haven that is dedicated to lovemaking as a form of art. If you have a place that can be set side for that purpose, wonderful. If you do not, an everyday space can be transformed. In such a setting the TV is not glaring at you from the foot of the bed; telephones don't ring; alarms are shut off; children aren't knocking at the door or playing loud, raucous games immediately outside. And you don't feel as if you are squeezing sex in hurriedly between the last TV show and the first sleepy yawn.

This sanctuary should not only afford protection from the outside world, but positively contribute to extraordinary lovemaking. It should be your Persian garden of pleasure, your Tantric temple of sexual fulfillment, your Japanese teahouse of ultimate delight. This is your Sacred Space, a place designed to create the conditions for ecstatic lovemaking. It is an environment for bliss.

When lovers enter into a sexual connection without creating a special physical and psychological environment, they often find themselves physically close yet emotionally absent. For example, Ann, a client,

The transformed place becomes our paradise as well, and in that world we're welcomed home.

—Albert Pinkham Ryder

told me about an evening when she drew her partner, John, into lovemaking. "Even though I had the idea that I wanted to make love, I soon realized that our sexual energies were not really connecting," she explained. "It felt mechanical; our bodies were going through the motions, but the rest of us was not engaged."

John noticed this too and told her, "We're just not into it. Let's stop." I had already introduced Ann and John to the idea of creating a Sacred Space, so they decided to give it a try. They improvised, finding ways to make their familiar surroundings as exotic as possible and highlighting their ritual by bringing each other favorite objects as gifts. "I enjoy your well-rounded spirit," declared John as he gave Ann a crystal egg.

Ann gave him her flute and said seductively, "I enjoy feeling like the flute you play at night."

Ann told me, "We liked the ritual so much that we forgot about everything else. We kept going until we were surrounded by a heap of gifts—from Christmas tree decorations to old postcards. Soon afterward we began to make love. This time our spirits joined the party, and the longer we continued, the higher we went."

Now I invite you to enjoy creating your own special sanctuary.

Along about the time I decided to "re-think" the whole issue of sexual pleasure and satisfaction, I was also in a position to perceive what I was missing. I noticed that when my lover penetrated me physically, he didn't penetrate me energetically. The current of his excitement and aliveness remained within him. I felt untouched.

—Julie Henderson
The Lover Within

69

A ritual of giving gifts to show your love.

CREATING YOUR SACRED SPACE

You can create your Sacred Space together with your lover as a ritual that gives you both a heightened sense of collaboration and purpose. Some people feel awkward about rituals because they associate them with obsolete religious practices. Yet rituals pervade our daily life and give it a sense of ceremony and celebration. They range from the simple gesture of shaking hands, to the vows exchanged during a marriage, to the visit of Santa Claus at Christmas. In a ritual, through your own unique symbolic gestures, you mark an occasion as having out-of-the-ordinary importance and the participants as being special. In the same way, creating your sanctuary together will help you to transform your lovemaking into a special and sacred act.

Purpose and Benefits

The purpose of this exercise is to create a space in which the practices of High Sex can be explored in seclusion, without interruption, in a distinctly separate context from everyday concerns, and to add the dimension of ritual to the art of lovemaking. In addition, the simultaneous stimulation of the senses—through color, sound, texture, rhythms, shapes, and objects—will inspire you to bring all your enthusiasm and creativity to the art of learning High Sex.

You will be using your Sacred Space as the location for learning the rest of the practices in this book.

Preparations

Choose the room or area that you are going to transform into your Sacred Space. Give it a good cleaning, removing dust and dirt and taking away unnecessary furniture, ornaments, old newspapers, magazines, toys, ashtrays, and so on. The sanctuary should be uncluttered so that you can move around easily.

In this and the following exercises, I have assumed that you have set aside a room or space that is at least equal to the size of two large beds put next to each other—about 14 square feet. You will need such a space for later practices that include dancing and stretching. If, however, you are unable to create a space of this size, adapt the exercises and rituals

Create a sacred space for practicing High Sex.

to the configuration of your room. You can, for example, create a Sacred
Space around your bed, or temporarily transform your living room.

Decorate the space with fabrics, paintings, or photographs that give
it a mystical or romantic or aesthetic quality that particularly appeals to
you. You may wish to create a rich, tentlike atmosphere by draping fabric
on the walls, or the space may be enhanced best by being left almost
empty, with only a few large potted plants for decoration.

Creating this sacred environment should be great fun. Remember
how, as a child, you made special places in your parents' house, using the
simplest materials, yet imparting a magical significance? That magic is still
available to you. I encourage you to do the same thing now, to see how
your imagination can transform an ordinary space into something marvelous and special.

72

You can use flowers, candles, bells, incense, or your favorite art object, such as a beautiful painting, suggestive sculpture, poster, or a deeply personal memento. Some of my workshop participants like to purchase special "power objects"—a magician's wand, a quartz crystal, a Tibetan *Vajra Dorje* thunderbolt emblem, a Native American medicine man's peace pipe—which they feel can amplify and transmit their energy. Traditionally such objects have played a significant role in sacred rituals in many different cultures. If you can't find a wand or peace pipe, a variety of more readily available objects can convey a sense of personal power—for example, candles for purity of spirit, bells for clarity of mind, a special stone for grounding your energy to the earth, feathers for lightness of being, or crystals for self-empowerment. When your eyes rest on these objects or when you hold them during a ritual, you may feel your self-confidence reinforced.

The effectiveness of your Sacred Space will be greatly enhanced if you dress in a way that is markedly different from your daily attire. Before starting the ritual—and after taking a shower—dress yourself in sensual clothes or beautiful robes. Loose-fitting garments that cover yet reveal your body are perfect. Silk kimonos and velvet evening robes are wonderfully stimulating. Special makeup and headdresses can add to the erotic appeal of the occasion.

Lighting needs to be soft and indirect. Candles in attractive holders can help to create an atmosphere of mystery. An easy way to change the lighting is to drape a colored shawl over a lampshade. Just be careful the bulb doesn't burn a hole in your favorite garment or start a fire.

Think of sounds that bring you a pleasing sense of clarity and relaxation—bells, perhaps, or chimes or a Tibetan singing bowl. If you can't get hold of a bell or bowl, use a drum, a tambourine, a triangle, or any gongs with a pleasing sound. Another good instrument is a pair of special hardwood sticks that make a sharp "clack" sound. Recorded music, for which recommendations appear in the appendix, will suffice, but you will be more involved if you make some of the music yourself by clapping, singing, chanting, or drumming.

Scents created by heating or spraying oils extracted from certain plants can be very beneficial in creating the right atmosphere. Extensive research in the science of "aromatherapy" has found that the evaporation of pure plant essences in the atmosphere soothes the nervous system, clears the sinuses, enhances erotic feelings, sharpens one's mental focus, and revitalizes the body. All these delights are yours for the cost of a plant

Musical instruments and power objects.

sprayer filled with water mixed with ten drops of your favorite plant essences, such as oil of mint, eucalyptus, lemon, and ylang-ylang.

In this practice I have incorporated gestures and movements from rituals in other cultures that are particularly effective in creating a sacred atmosphere. At first they may seem awkward, unfamiliar, even childish. After being introduced to this exercise in my seminars, some skeptical people make remarks like, "Margo, this is silly!"

To them I usually reply, "Would you be here if you weren't willing to take a step beyond the known? This ritual is an opportunity to try something new. If you are able to cross this easy boundary, you will see that it brings you more humor, openness, and courage to go farther on the road to High Sex."

Creating your Sacred Space is designed to bring greater awareness to the way you think, feel, and act, so do not concern yourself with whether or not it seems strange. Do it sincerely, for the fun of it, and see how it transforms both the environment and your mood. I have done this ritual in groups with hundreds of people and also alone with my beloved. Through it I have always been able to create a wonderful space, plus a delightful sense of sharing a secret.

Allow 45 minutes for this practice.

You can do this ritual alone or with a partner. If you do it alone, be aware that you are doing it for the purpose of bringing yourself pleasure and a heightened sense of your potential. Do it as a gift to your Inner Lover. If you do it with your partner, go through the steps together.

Practice

Do everything slowly, consciously, meditatively, as if you are the master of a secret ceremony, or a shaman conducting a sacred rite.

Stand on the perimeter of what will become your Sacred Space, facing the center. With your partner, turn to your left and make three circles, walking counterclockwise around the space. This follows the pattern of ancient ceremonies in which participants moved counterclockwise to decrease the energy, dispelling negative forces from the environment.

As you walk, imagine you are removing negative energies from the room, in much the same way as you removed the dirt and dust. Sing, chant, or murmur the following affirmation: "Let negative energies, such as worry, fear, anger, greed, and impatience, leave this room. If they return, let them come as opportunities for transformation." Add other phrases that seem appropriate, such as "I now remove [whatever feeling or attitude you wish] from this space." Emphasize your affirmation by beating a drum or tambourine after each phrase.

At the end of the three circles, stand facing the special place that you have created, and take a few deep breaths.

Then turn to your right and make three circles, walking clockwise around the space. This follows the direction the sun appears to move in the sky, and in ancient times such circling was thought to draw in power from the sun and the natural elements, enhancing the level of energy and blessing the space.

As you walk, imagine that you are pouring healing energy and love from your heart into the space. Chant, sing, or proclaim the following affirmation: "May the love in my heart now fill this room and protect us."

At the end, stand facing the center. After a few deep breaths, hold hands and step into it together. Open your senses and your minds to new possibilities and new experiences in this environment. Put critical

Any ritual is an opportunity for transformation. To do ritual, you must be willing to be transformed in some way. That inner willingness is what makes the ritual come alive and have power.

—Starhawk

thoughts and judgments aside. You are inside your Sacred Space. Commit yourself to enjoying it and to returning here for practice sessions.

Next, together with your partner, choose a special spot inside the space that will be comfortable to lie on but also firm enough to sit on while doing exercises. This will be the base for your exploration of High Sex. It may be a bed or a mattress on the floor or a piece of foam or the center of a rug. Cover this place with a beautiful sheet or quilt, and surround it with plants, flowers, and candles.

Place four candles around the bed or quilt, one for each of the four directions—north, south, east, and west. As you do so, bow in each direction, invoking the inspiration and protection of the four natural elements that these directions represent:

North represents the element air and the associated qualities of knowledge and intelligence. Your invocation may sound like this: "I call forth the energies of the North, the great winds of change and transformation. May they bring us intelligence and discrimination."

South represents water—fluidity, trust, innocence. Try this invocation: "I call forth the energies of the South, the healing waters of the deep. May they cleanse our hearts and let our emotions flow with innocence and trust."

West represents earth—grounding, balance, strength, and introspection. Your invocation may follow this model: "I call forth the energies of the West, the transforming powers of the earth that make things grow. May they bring us renewal, health, and creative inspiration."

East represents fire—illumination, passion, clarity, beauty, and revelation. Repeat this invocation, or one similar to it: "I call forth the energies of the East, the cleansing fires of illumination. May they help our spirit to shine forth, bringing us wisdom and insight."

Through this invocation you are integrating qualities that you wish to bring into your lovemaking and, in accordance with the Tantric perspective, acknowledging that you are connected to the four universal forces—water, earth, air, and fire—of which your body is a reflection.

Next, select which of you is Partner A and which is Partner B. While Partner B sits in the Sacred Space, Partner A picks up the plant sprayer and walks slowly around the space, lightly misting the air with fragrant spray and chanting the following affirmation three times: "I purify this space, I purify my heart." End by pointing the nozzle upward above your partner's head, sending a light mist showering delicately down on his or her face. You'll be delighted to discover how revitalizing these mist showers can be.

Then Partner A gives the sprayer to Partner B, who repeats the exercise, first spraying the air, chanting the affirmation, then gently misting Partner A's face.

Set down the plant sprayer. Keeping your sense of ritual and, reflecting it in your movements, pick up the musical instruments. Walk clockwise three times around the quilt or sheet that you have placed in the center of your Sacred Space, softly ringing bells or playing sounds and chanting the affirmation, "I dedicate this space to love." If you are lucky enough to have a Tibetan singing bowl, you can hold it in the flat outstretched palm of your hand while tapping the rim with a round wooden stick. This produces a sharp sound that ripples forth in countless subtle echoes and harmonics. These temple sounds have a mysterious but unquestionable ability to heal the mind. As you listen to the sounds, your mind will become clear, and bothersome thoughts will float away. Gradually you will feel centered and peaceful.

Set down the musical instruments. Then take a moment to appreciate the gentle atmosphere you have created: the plants and flowers, soft lighting, scented mists in the air, and soothing sounds.

End the ceremony with a Heart Salutation to each other.

Pointers

From now on at the beginning of each practice, I will ask you to prepare the Sacred Space. This doesn't mean that you need to go through the

The spiritual manifests itself not only in invisible forms but also in physical forms. . . . one passes through a world of forms ascending from reality to abstraction. In this manner one approaches Spirit, or purity itself.

—Piet Mondrian

whole ritual of dedicating the space each time you begin an exercise. It will be very beneficial for you, however, to establish a shorter ritual that makes a distinct break from your daily life and to practice it each time you enter this space anew.

For example, it will be helpful to tidy up the room and light candles and incense—simple, small things that create a sense of reverence and ritual. Then you may choose to walk counterclockwise around the space three times, visualizing any negative energies being removed, and then clockwise three times, visualizing healing, positive energy pouring into the space. All this will inspire you to focus more fully on the practices of High Sex.

THE MELTING HUG

Having created the Sacred Space, you are now ready to use it. What better way is there to start than with a deep, long hug?

Purpose and Benefits

Although it may be natural and easy for you, I find that many people are self-conscious about hugging. Being held close is such a simple, deeply longed-for experience, yet it can evoke initial shyness and sometimes emotional responses. Who has not been asked by a partner, "Please, just hold me," and known that the loved one has spoken from a profound need to be reassured and comforted?

Hugging matters. Good hugs are therapeutic. They can restore the feeling of being cherished and protected—that primal, wordless sense of security and well-being that we innocently demanded as children but rarely allow ourselves to experience as adults. Instead, we usually surround ourselves with defenses and resistance that shield us against experiencing things too intensely. The more we enter into the practices and explorations of High Sex, the more such resistance may appear. Hugging provides us with a simple opening of the door to trust. And because it feels so good, it can also remind us that bliss is our true nature. It is always there within us as a most precious resource.

Preparations

When I introduce people to hugging in my trainings, they say they often learn more about each other in those few moments of close embrace than they normally do in days or months of verbal interaction. Some typical responses after this exercise are:

"I felt as if you wanted to grab me. It was too strong."

"You were gentle and receptive. I felt I could trust you."

"You felt tense, so I couldn't relax myself."

"You enveloped me like a gentle cloud, and I melted away."

As you enter this practice, be open to anything that may happen, and be prepared to share honestly what you experience with your partner.

Allow 15 minutes for this exercise.

Do this practice with your partner.

Practice

Start by exploring your feelings about an ordinary hug by going to your partner and exchanging a hug. Just be natural about it—don't try to make it anything special. Do it for three minutes. It may feel like a long time because hugs are usually about as quick as a handshake, but this will give you time to explore your responses.

Then gently separate yourself, close your eyes, and check how it felt. Note whether resistance came up. This resistance may signal limits you have set for yourself, either conscious or unconscious. Did you feel guarded or uneasy? Did you feel that any part of your body remained stiff? Did you hold your breath part of the time? If so, why? Does that express some fear of intimacy that you may want to explore?

What about your partner? Check how you felt about him or her, in the same way that you reviewed your own feelings.

Then sit down, facing each other.

Partner A, honestly share what you felt, both about yourself and your partner. Partner B, listen attentively, in a receptive frame of mind.

When Partner A has finished, Partner B should say how he or she felt about the hug.

Some partners begin by giving what I call the "Donald Duck Hug"—coming together like two cartoon ducks, with their pelvises tilted

Donald Duck Hug.

back and only the upper parts of their bodies touching. The exchange conveys the feeling, "Okay, let's be friendly, but let's not get too close."

In High Sex we want to have a delicious whole-body, wholehearted hug. I call it the Melting Hug. Here's how you do it:

Stand across the room from your partner. Begin with a standing Heart Salutation.

Then slowly walk toward each other, maintaining eye contact and remaining as relaxed as possible. Let your breathing be deep and full, yet effortless. When you come near each other, open your arms in a welcoming gesture, with the palms of your hands open to each other.

Melting Hug.

Touching, nest against each other's chests, and slowly wrap your arms gently around each other. Let your hands feel they are really holding flesh, bones, and muscles, without exerting pressure. The aim is not to squeeze each other—love is not measured in pounds per square inch—but to embrace the whole body fully.

Allow your pelvis to relax and move forward, touching the pelvis of your partner. Allow your thighs and your bellies to meet. Try keeping your knees slightly bent to enhance your sense of balance and groundedness. Let your bodies relax so that you can melt into each other, giving yourselves over to a trusting embrace, secure in the kind of letting-go that you felt as a child when your mother held you.

After a minute or two, notice your partner's breathing pattern. Let your own breathing harmonize with your partner's so that you softly inhale and exhale together. If this harmonized breathing comes easily, do it now for a few minutes; otherwise, you can wait until you have a little more experience and it comes naturally. You need not make any effort. This exercise is about welcoming, receiving, enjoying, and dissolving into each other. That is why I call it the Melting Hug.

End with a Heart Salutation.

Pointers

It may seem unnecessary to receive suggestions about hugging, but as you will discover when you have practiced the Melting Hug a few times, even this simple activity can be transformed into a skill for High Sex. Melting Hugs can be blissful and healing. Gradually you will find that a delicious energy flows between you and your partner. The boundaries between you will seem to melt away, and you may become a single, vibrating energy field. Such hugs can go on for a long time.

If you are alone, you can create the same feeling as a Melting Hug by curling up on a soft rug by the fire or on your bed, or by doing something that feels warm, cozy, and nourishing to you.

MOVING BEYOND RESISTANCE

You may be thinking at this point, *A Sacred Space, a Melting Hug, and the expectation of sexual ecstasy sound great. But how do I get there from where I am now? What about all my fears, doubts, shyness, hesitations? And what about those of my partner?*

We tend to think that there is little we can do about our "negative" emotions because we assume that for the most part feelings just come and go as they please and that we have little power to influence them. We hide those we dislike or want to deny, hoping they will go away, and show only those that are considered acceptable. In High Sex it is important to acknowledge our fears, projections, and fantasies and to let our partner know about them.

At this point in the book, you have begun to establish conditions for closeness. Now it is time to look inside to see whether there are any unspoken fears and anxieties that are preventing you from feeling safe and relaxed in each other's presence. Now that you have tasted a heart-to-heart connection through the Melting Hug, it is time to communicate verbally at a deeper level; otherwise these unspoken problems will keep you restricted, tense, and unable to trust each other fully. A word of encouragement—before you expose your concerns, it may seem a very difficult thing to do, but afterward it will seem simple and natural.

Remember this key: Hiding gives strength to negative feelings; sharing in an atmosphere of sincerity and trust dissipates their power. Moreover, when you connect with a partner who is truthfully expressing deep feelings, more energy becomes available as a bond of authenticity develops between you.

Sexual ecstasy is incompatible with hiding your feelings because concealment creates a split in you—preventing you from wholeheartedly participating in lovemaking—whereas the ultimate goal in High Sex is to penetrate experience as deeply as possible. The process of exposing and sharing negative feelings presents a great opportunity to expand not only your lovemaking abilities, but your entire relationship with your lover.

I often work with couples who do not understand why they no longer feel sexually attracted to each other, even though they profess to love each other. After a few sessions it becomes apparent that they harbor resentments that have accumulated over time. When the partners come near each other, they feel emotionally choked and consequently sexually turned off. They are afraid to tell the truth about their feelings because they fear they will hurt the other person, or that the relationship will suffer as a result.

In the context of High Sex, a large number of our negative emotions fall under the category of "sexual fears." These fears are taboos and attitudes passed on from generation to generation by well-intentioned parents, teachers, and clergy. They choke off spontaneity, energy, and

For some, sex leads to sainthood; for others it is the road to hell . . . all depends on one's point of view.

—Henry Miller
The World of Sex

pleasure. Such fears contain all sorts of false images about what it is going to be like to experience lovemaking more fully or to open up and express what is really happening inside. Fear can create the worry that you may be hurt or look ridiculous or disappoint your partner.

You will want to undo this conditioning, and the easiest way is to identify and express the sexual fears you inherited.

The greatest resistance to sexual surrender is in the mind. When people have trouble letting themselves go sexually, often it has to do with interference from mental instructions . . .

—Stella Resnick

Purpose and Benefits

This practice helps you to acknowledge and release negative attitudes, freeing your sexual energy and promoting trust and intimacy with your partner. It is a simple communication exercise in three parts: expressing sexual fears, describing sexual fantasies, and describing a peak sexual experience.

Although you can do each part separately, I suggest you do all three in one session. Each succeeding part complements the previous one and in my experience corresponds to a gradual rise in mood from fearful to joyful.

Preparations

Prepare and enter the Sacred Space.

Allow 15 to 20 minutes for each stage of this three-part practice.

This is a verbal exercise, so it is best to avoid music or other distractions. You need to give your total attention to each other. When you are the partner who is listening, you should not interrupt while your partner is speaking unless you do not understand what is being said. Then you can ask for clarification.

If you are doing this exercise alone, use a tape recorder so that you can play back and listen to the responses you make, or write them in your diary.

Choose who is going to be Partner A, and who is going to be Partner B.

Practice

Begin with a Heart Salutation and Melting Hug. If you are alone, make a Heart Salutation to yourself.

Think of one sexual fear that you feel ready to discuss with your partner. Here are some common male fears from my seminar members: "I'm not big enough"; "I'm not doing it the way she wants me to"; "I'll ejaculate too soon"; "If I tell her my fantasies, she'll reject me."

Here are some typical female fears: "My body is not attractive to him"; "He won't touch me the way I want"; "I won't have an orgasm."

Sit comfortably, face to face, without touching. Maintain eye contact throughout the exercise.

Partner B gently asks Partner A, "Tell me, what are you afraid of in sex?"

Partner A has five to seven minutes in which to answer; Partner B keeps time. See if you can define the fear in one or two sentences. Then give a brief life story that illustrates your most recent experience of this fear.

For example, Partner A, a woman, might say, "What I am most afraid of is to pleasure myself in front of you. I guess it's the old belief that if I'm with someone, sexual pleasure should only come through intercourse; otherwise, if I do it myself, you might feel you are not good enough."

Then Partner A may move on to this story: "Two days ago we made love. I felt you penetrated me a little too early. My clitoris was very aroused, and I desired intensely that it be caressed. Actually I had a great desire to do that myself. I fantasized about doing that in front of you, but I've never dared to do that in front of anyone. It's too scary."

Partner B, give your full attention to Partner A, and listen without interrupting. Help yourself to stay centered and calm by breathing deeply and slowly in a relaxed manner. Watching your breathing helps you to remain more of a neutral observer of what your partner is saying rather than being personally involved in it. If you feel criticized—and you probably will, even if no critical words are directed at you—resist the temptation to protest or defend yourself. You may see things entirely differently, but the purpose of this practice is not to decide what is true or false, but to help your partner to dissipate fears that block sexual ecstasy. You are just a facilitator. Your silent and sympathetic observing is healing for Partner A, who is courageously exposing her fears.

If Partner A finishes talking before the time is up, Partner B can help by asking, "Tell me, what else are you afraid of in sex?" Partner A may then be able to speak about a second fear.

After seven minutes, Partner A should stop talking. Close your eyes and breathe deeply. Partner B then asks Partner A, "Are you willing to go beyond the limits you have set for yourself?"

Partner A, if the answer is yes, take the time to visualize a positive, supportive scenario in which your lovemaking unfolds without the fears you have mentioned. Feel fulfilled in the fantasy. You are getting what you need, and everything unfolds in a pleasurable and loving way. If the answer is no, say so, and acknowledge that you still need boundaries to protect yourself. The very fact that you have acknowledged these boundaries is the first step toward moving beyond them. Relax in the understanding that you may need to do this exercise a number of times before you can move forward.

Then exchange roles. Partner A asks the question, "Tell me, what are you afraid of in sex?"

Partner B answers, using the same structure—first defining the fear, then giving an illustration, and finally telling Partner A whether he or she is willing to transform the restrictive pattern.

Partner B, as you talk, resist any temptation to "answer" Partner A's speech. This exercise is not about reacting to your partner's feelings or justifying yourself. Focus on your *own* reality, your own fears, whether they are related to your partner or not. While Partner B is speaking, Partner A should act as timekeeper.

After seven minutes, stop. The point is not to provide an exhaustive catalog of fears, but to experience sharing one or two of them with your partner.

End with a Heart Salutation and Melting Hug.

Describing Sexual Fantasies

Move on to the next stage of this practice, in which you will describe one sexual fantasy. Think of a sexual fantasy that you are willing to discuss with your partner.

When I ask people in my seminars how they feel about sharing sexual fantasies, I hear nervous laughter and suggestions about doing it later. Many people feel ashamed about such fantasies, especially if they occur during sex. As little girls, many women were told not to think about such things. And partners often feel threatened by sexual fantasies, worrying, "Why does my lover need a fantasy when I am here in the flesh? Am I inadequate?"

In the Tantric tradition there is a different attitude that calls for

Sex is composed of friction and fantasies.

—Helen Singer Kaplan
The New Sex Therapy

the acceptance of everything that we are—including those things that we normally repress or keep secret. From this perspective you may discover that sharing sexual fantasies is a healing experience and even something that can be actively enjoyed, bringing more excitement into your sex life.

Give yourself permission to accept your sexual fantasies and to share at least one of them. Sharing does not imply any demand or need to act out a particular fantasy. Just as you have thought about it without saying it, you can also say it without doing it. You are free to do whatever you want about it. But give each other support, and don't be afraid to go into elaborate detail when your turn comes. There is a great feeling of relief—and often humor—that comes with sharing the most bizarre and explicit fantasies and dreams. Besides, it is often an indirect way of teaching your partner how you would like to be loved.

Some people do not have sexual dreams or fantasies. When they are sexually involved, they experience bodily sensations so deeply that they become lost in the feelings, the breathing, the touch. The mind or imagination is not visually involved. If such is the case, encourage your partner to describe these sensations.

Begin with a Heart Salutation and Melting Hug.

Sit comfortably, facing each other without touching, and maintain eye contact.

This time, Partner A can begin the exchange, asking Partner B, "Tell me a sexual dream or fantasy you have had."

Partner B then shares the fantasy in vivid detail, in five to seven minutes.

Partner A keeps time and gives his or her undivided attention and support. If Partner B can't find anything to say, Partner A can help by gently asking such questions as, "What dreams, visions, or imaginings have you had recently concerning your love life?" Or, "Recall the time when you were a teenager, or when you had no sex for a long time. Did you fantasize then? How did you imagine sex, and with whom did you imagine it?" Even if your partner remains silent, be supportive. The process is happening anyway, on the inside, in its own way. Use this exercise as an opportunity to be gracious, patient, and appreciative of the fact that you are ready to do such deeply revealing work together.

When Partner B has finished speaking, Partner A says, "Thank you for telling me your dream or fantasy."

Change roles. Partner B now asks Partner A to share a sexual fantasy.

Fantasy can be the poetry of sex . . .

—Sheila Kitzinger
Woman's Experience of Sex

End with a Heart Salutation and Melting Hug.

When you are ready, begin the third and last section of this practice.

Describing a Peak Sexual Experience

In this section you will describe a peak sexual experience. This is not only healing, but it is also a way to teach yourself and your partner what works best for you in lovemaking. The point is not to brag or show off. You are simply examining a particularly beautiful experience—how it worked and why it worked—as a way of seeing how you can create similar conditions within the present context. Your best experience may or may not have involved sexual intercourse. If you don't have a best sexual experience to tell, then choose a best sensual experience instead.

If you are in a committed relationship, my advice is to describe the best peak experience that you have had within this relationship. This will be a positive way to end the exercise and also to remind each other of the elements that enhance your lovemaking. Having done this, if you choose to repeat this practice at a later date, you may feel comfortable about sharing a peak experience that you had with a previous lover.

Before you begin, take a short break. Stand up, stretch, move around the room, make sounds, shake your shoulders, loosen yourself up. If the atmosphere has become too heavy and serious, run around, jump up and down, or kid each other.

Begin with a Heart Salutation and Melting Hug.

Then sit face to face, comfortably, holding hands. Close your eyes for a minute, and breathe slowly and deeply. Take the time to come back to yourself.

Partner B addresses Partner A by name and says, "Tell me about a peak sexual experience you have had."

Partner A, as you relate the experience, refer to the following points: what happened, the unusual and pleasurable aspects of what happened, why you think it was so pleasurable, and what the ingredients of the experience were that were common to other experiences.

Recall every detail of the experience, such as being relaxed before you began, feeling highly aroused, allowing yourself to trust, taking the time to play, putting everything else aside for a while, and so forth. Once you recognize these features, you can begin to explore concretely what is likely to make such a pleasurable experience happen again.

While listening attentively, Partner B should keep track of the

In a real conversation, a real lesson, a real embrace . . . in all these, what is essential takes place between them in a dimension which is accessible only to them both. . . . If I and another "happen" to one other, the sum does not exactly divide. There is a remainder somewhere, where the souls end and the world has not yet begun.

—Martin Buber

time—five to seven minutes—making no comment, asking questions only to help clarify specific details.

Then reverse roles, with Partner A asking the question and Partner B answering.

End the exercise with a Melting Hug and a Heart Salutation. Tell each other of your wish to give support and be supported in pleasuring yourselves in the ways you like.

Pointers

For many people communication about these matters is not a usual part of their daily life, so it requires sensitive handling. If you feel very shy with each other, it is easier to begin the practice by not facing each other. The partner whose turn it is to speak can lie down and close his or her eyes, while the partner who is listening sits close by.

If you are working with a partner who is somewhat reluctant to explore High Sex, while you are enthusiastic, this exercise provides a good opportunity to draw your partner into the process by way of your own example. If you can remain open and supportive in your communication, even at times when your partner does not know what to say, he or she will be touched by your positive attitude and, over time, will respond in a similar manner. It may take a number of sessions, during which your partner may say little or nothing that is truly revealing, but if you are able to become increasingly open yourself, the love and enthusiasm that you express will inspire your beloved.

When you have completed the three stages of this practice, wait at least an hour and preferably until the following day before you discuss your reactions to these exchanges with your partner. Give yourself time to integrate the information and to lessen any negative emotional charge that the words may have had.

If you feel the need to discuss what happened, focus on the following points: What was the most difficult moment for you in this exchange? And what did you learn that can improve and enrich your relationship? Make sure that in this exchange, one partner listens while the other speaks. Do not interrupt each other.

It is likely that many delicate areas will have been touched upon and many emotions stirred up by these three practices. Some feelings may be hurt. For example, you may feel upset because your partner recounted either a fantasy or a peak sexual experience that did not take place with you. Do not try to deny or repress the fact that you are upset, but refrain from accusations. For the sake of your relationship, allow yourself to be supportive, open, and constructive. You have been given precious information about how your partner can best experience the heights of sexual pleasure. It would be a pity to throw away this chance to learn how to be a better lover out of hurt pride or a wounded ego.

On the other hand, you may both be feeling highly stimulated by all that has occurred, eager to act out a particular sexual fantasy or to experiment with ways of lovemaking that in the past triggered peak sexual experiences. In this case, just relax, enjoy, and let it happen.

One more thing—some fantasies are more palatable than others. For example, what should you do if your partner fantasizes, "I am making love to your best friend"? Your first reaction is likely to be one of distress or unworthiness. Recognize, however, that everyone has sexual fantasies. Men especially are prone to fantasizing about almost every attractive woman they meet. Psychologists say that men think about sex every three seconds, while women think about it slightly less—every six seconds! The important thing to understand is that your partner's truthfulness is actually evidence of his or her commitment to your growth together; otherwise you would not be hearing about this very personal fantasy. Resist the temptation to make a big drama out of what may be a harmless daydream. Perhaps you can see that no one man or woman can possess all the qualities that are attractive to the opposite sex. This may be an opportunity, however, for you to learn certain attributes that you can easily highlight or develop in yourself.

If you follow the basic rules of this exercise, you will avoid the pitfall of reproach and experience a liberation from fears and fantasies that until now may have inhibited your ability to be spontaneous and open in lovemaking. In my experience truth is erotic. There is nothing more stimulating, refreshing, and exciting than to be faced with the challenge of truth. It reveals your deepest emotions and requires the expression of your authentic being. So by sharing your fears, fantasies, and peak experiences, you have taken a major step toward opening yourselves up to the experience of High Sex. You have rooted the vision of your Inner Lover in the humanness that you share together. You may have also learned to develop a sense of empathy and humor with your partner that will make the next steps on the path toward sacred sexuality easier and more enjoyable.

You know that jealousy is unreasonable. And you know that you can't possibly have all of another person's time and affection. . . . You know your lover needs other friends, other interests, and time to be alone. You know that jealousy makes you ugly and weak. But the monster accepts no reasons—except the ones that feed your suspicions.

—Deborah Phillips
Sexual Confidence

❧

In this chapter you learned how to create an inspiring environment—the Sacred Space—weaving together the right conditions for closeness, honesty, and respect. You experienced the nourishing benefits of the Melting Hug, establishing a heart-to-heart connection with your partner. Then you explored moving beyond the resistance created by your sexual fears and fantasies and described your peak experiences. Now you are ready to proceed with a renewed sense of trust and openness.

In the next chapter you will develop the skills needed to enhance intimacy with your lover, as a way of exploring lovemaking more deeply together. You will initiate your partner into the art of Sensory Awakening. After giving and receiving this subtle gift, you will be inspired to dance and celebrate the goddess and the god within; this will introduce humor and laughter into your love life. Finally, you will draw this expanded energy back into yourself and discover the art of fine-tuning your energies through Soul Gazing.

❧

SKILLS FOR ENHANCING INTIMACY

One of the deepest longings we experience when we relate to another human being is the desire for intimacy. By intimacy I mean closeness, empathy, the fine-tuning of a relationship that allows increasingly subtle levels of feeling to be explored and shared. In the context of High Sex, intimacy means that just as you learned in chapter 2 to welcome yourself into your own heart as your most beloved guest, you now welcome your partner with the same acceptance and love.

From this perspective intimacy does not mean falling in love in the conventional sense of romantic infatuation, but rising in love by under-standing what can make you and your partner expand and grow together. Nor does intimacy simply mean togetherness. It requires a delicate balance between aloneness and connectedness—alone, feeling that you are in the intimate company of yourself, your Inner Lover; together, feeling that you can maintain your freedom and independence even when you are deeply connected.

Intimacy can include:

□ Being natural and childlike together, rolling around on the bed, tickling each other like five-year-olds.
□ Feeling safe enough to show your soft spots—your sadness, your hurt, your need—and knowing that your partner will respond with warmth and kindness rather than criticism.
□ Tucking your partner into bed and telling him or her bedtime stories.

To love is to return to a home we never left, to remember who we are.

—Sam Keen
The Passionate Life

Many people believe that sex is the quickest way to open the door to intimacy, and they feel frustrated when, after sexual intercourse, they find that intimacy still has not happened, that the other person has remained distant. This is because in reality it is not sex that opens the door to intimacy, but intimacy that opens the door to good lovemaking. This is especially true in High Sex. In this chapter I introduce intimacy as a subtle set of skills, an art that has to be developed before sexual union should be considered. From this perspective sex happens as the crowning act of intimacy.

You may already have developed your own ways of helping intimacy to flower. If you have given your partner a massage when he or she is tired, found ways to be humorous and supportive when your partner is depressed, or told the truth about your feelings in a supportive way, then you have been exploring and expanding the intimacy between you.

I now invite you to expand your repertoire, using four of the most loving and sensual skills of intimacy that have been developed in High Sex.

First, in the sensual approach, you can learn to awaken your lover's senses in a very gentle, tender, and delicate way, using the art of sensory stimulation as an expression of the love that you feel in your heart. You will practice this in the Sensory Awakening Ritual.

Second, in the seductive approach, you can enjoy expressing the sensuality and radiance of your Inner Lover to your partner through movement and dance. You will do this as you learn to become the Dancing God and Goddess for each other.

Third, in the supportive approach, you can share with your partner, through direct, nonverbal methods, a sense of enjoyment, humor, and playfulness, slipping out of any fixed ways of relating. This you will learn through the Inner Smile.

Fourth, in the soul-to-soul approach, you will recognize the essential spirit of your partner, feeling that you are mirroring each other's innermost consciousness. This is done through the Soul-Gazing exercise, in which you share a meditative moment together and tune into each other's subtle energy.

These practices can be done separately, each one in its own time and setting. You also can consider them as a flowing continuum, however, each one leading to the next in a natural way. From the subtle sensuality of the Sensory Awakening Ritual, you can move easily into the celebration of the Dancing Gods. From there you can rejoice, laugh, and smile together before moving into a quiet, meditative Soul Gazing, drawing the awakened energy back to your own still center.

The sequence creates a distinct energy pattern. From the devotion and slow sensual receptivity required in the Sensory Awakening Ritual, you move into the high-energy games of the Dancing Gods and Skills of Playfulness. After dancing and laughing, you can dwell naturally in the stillness and resonance of Soul Gazing. In High Sex I often use high-energy practices before periods of stillness in order to create an *alive stillness*—a quiet that pulsates with energy. As you will see in later chapters, aliveness combined with tranquillity forms an essential part of High Sex.

Once you have gone through the practices in this chapter, you will be able to integrate them spontaneously into your love life in any circumstances. You should not look upon these skills of intimacy merely as a set of techniques. They go much deeper, requiring the development of three corresponding attitudes:

☐ *Remaining focused on the highest outcome.* For example, in the practice of the Dancing Gods, you may encounter moments when you doubt your ability to express fully the divine qualities within you. By holding before you the vision toward which you are moving, namely, your heartfelt desire to express the idea, "I am the goddess or god within," you can take the practice as a discipline, a challenge, moving through uncomfortable moments and resisting the temptation to give up.

☐ *Observing yourself closely, remaining aware of your feelings, desires, and responses at any moment in any situation.* It is only from this point of awareness that you can positively transform a problematic situation. For instance, in the Soul-Gazing practice, you may at some point feel that nothing is happening. A common response would be just to sit there, feeling insecure yet pretending that everything is okay. Pretending, however, cuts you off from your sensations. You need to pay close attention to how you are really feeling and then seek immediate remedies—for example, to breathe more deeply, shift your position, or discuss with your partner what changes can be made in the ritual. All observations of this nature teach you to feel and experience more deeply.

☐ *Cultivating an open attitude toward the paradoxical aspects of High Sex.* For example, you might think that practicing the Inner Smile has nothing to do with mastering the art of ecstatic sexuality, and as a result you may do the Inner Smile meditation half-heartedly. But these methods work in subtle ways that our rational minds cannot always follow. With an openness to paradox, you can learn to stay relaxed yet push yourself beyond old limits, to concentrate on the present moment yet move toward a goal. Now let us leave theory behind and step directly into the delicate awakening of the senses.

THE SENSORY AWAKENING RITUAL

Recall a magical day in your life—a great birthday or Christmas or your wedding, graduation, or bar mitzvah—a day when you were showered with love, attention, and presents. Remember the excitement of the occasion, the feeling of delight and elation from beginning to end, the sweet anticipation of gifts, the abundance of special food and drink, the warmth and solidarity you felt with your loved ones. This is the kind of event you will plan for your lover in the Sensory Awakening Ritual.

Purpose and Benefits

In this ritual each partner introduces the other to a whole range of surprising and intoxicating sensory experiences that are beyond the scope of ordinary perception. In this practice the simple act of eating a grape can become as intense and all-consuming as a king's banquet. Suddenly you are flooded with new sensory impressions; the round, soft texture of the grape and the sweetness of its juice occupy your whole being and become an erotic, almost orgasmic experience.

This ceremony also can be very helpful if one partner is enthusiastic about exploring the realms of High Sex while the other is more reluctant. It gives the enthusiastic partner a chance to seduce the other playfully into a world of sensual delight that will encourage him or her to explore it further.

Over the years many of my clients have felt particularly attracted to this ritual because it is easy to perform, fun, and adaptable to almost

I believe in the flesh and the appetites,
Seeing hearing and feeling are miracles, and each part and tag of me is a miracle.

—Walt Whitman
Leaves of Grass

any circumstance. For example, I once began an important business dinner with a modified version of the Sensory Awakening Ritual. Other people have performed the ritual for their parents, still others for their children at Christmas. In every case, the adventure succeeded in bringing people closer together.

Ordinarily we take our five senses for granted. We may notice for a moment the whiff of a woman's perfume as she passes by, or the smell of new-mown grass on a summer day. Occasionally we are enchanted by a bird's song, by the furry softness of a kitten, or by the erotic beauty of a naked body. But mostly we dull our sensory responses by not paying focused attention to them. We listen to music while talking on the phone; we eat while reading the paper; or we forget to notice nature's beauty on a Sunday stroll because we are discussing world politics. As a result, we feel very little; everything that comes to us through our senses seems muted and weak. But that's also why awakening the senses through this ceremony can be so magical. The experience of really tasting, smelling, seeing, feeling, and hearing comes as a wonderful surprise. As William Blake said, "If the doors of perception were cleansed, everything would appear as it is, infinite."

Preparations

Partner A is active, Partner B receptive. The receptive partner will be blindfolded because this makes it easier to focus on each sensation as it is presented, eliminating distractions that would otherwise dilute the experience. Surprise is a key element; the receptive partner must not know what to expect.

If you are the active partner—the one who is going to present the experiences—your first step will be to envision everything that can make this ceremony exquisite and unforgettable. Carefully plan the kind of atmosphere you want to create for your partner. For inspiration you might call up the image of a magic garden such as the one we find in Persian mythology, in which lovers dressed in silk robes are surrounded by flowering almond trees and aromatic fruit trees. A peacock fans out its glory; the sounds of sweet music can be heard above the splash of a fountain; and banners of silk ripple overhead, caressed by a breeze. A pitcher of nectar awaits as the lovers, whispering tender words, delicately feed and touch each other. You may have seen such pictures.

Now focus on your own environment. As you prepare the room for the ritual, keep in mind the idea that you are taking your partner on a fantasy ride. You should prepare the space specifically as a sensual feast for your lover. Make sure the air is sweet and fresh. You may wish to perfume the air with special incense because such fragrances can create vivid impressions of faraway places. Arrange soft lighting and set up some candles, and proceed as you did in creating your Sacred Space in the previous chapter.

Music is also very important. Find music that supports each sensory experience, and use a minute of silence to mark a transitional period between each of the five senses. At specific points in this ritual, I will, for precision's sake, mention particular musical pieces that I find very supportive for the kinds of sensations that you are seeking to awaken in your partner. (In most other exercises I will refer you to the appendix.) If the musical arrangement seems too complicated, find one piece that you like, and use that throughout, but retain the minute of silence between each phase of your presentation; otherwise your partner's perception of the different senses will not be as sharp.

In the center of the Sacred Space, facing your partner, place trays on which you will keep the following items:

☐ A sprayer with scented water, as in the Sacred Space preparations
☐ A choice of essential oils that are attractive to your partner—peppermint or eucalyptus essence is good to start with because these clear the lungs. After that, you can use sweeter and more mysterious scents such as ylang-ylang and gardenia.
☐ Musical instruments such as bells, cymbals, flutes, maracas, harmonicas, or Tibetan singing bowls
☐ Several items for sensual touching, such as a piece of fur and a feather. I like peacock feathers because they are so long, flexible, and soft.
☐ Sensuous food such as seedless grapes, lychees, or small chunks of fresh pineapple, along with toothpicks, a glass with a small amount of a favorite liqueur, and some chocolate mints

Avoid doing this ritual after a meal. It is best done on an empty stomach so that Partner B can perceive tastes more acutely.

The ritual itself should last about an hour. Make sure you have no appointments afterward. The last thing you want to do is hurry this beautiful experience.

Partner B, the receptive partner, will be sitting for a long time while Partner A presents these experiences, so make sure that Partner B is comfortably seated, either in a chair or on a cushion on the floor.

For this practice description I will assume that Partner B is a man receiving the ritual, and Partner A is a woman administering it, but you are free to choose who goes first. Later you will reverse the roles.

Practice

Partner A, when you are ready to begin, light the candles and the incense, start the music, and put the food tray in the center, where the other tools are gathered.

In the next room gently blindfold Partner B with a silk scarf. Explain that from now on there is no need to talk.

Softly tell Partner B, "Just relax and enjoy the ride. Remember to breathe deeply throughout, especially when you experience something new. Trust me and be open to whatever happens. I am taking you on a journey to an ancient Tantric temple, far away, in another time, another space. You will have nothing to do but breathe deeply, relax, enjoy, and receive."

Gently lead Partner B through the door into the sanctuary. Pause every two or three steps and breathe deeply, close to your partner's ear, to encourage him to breathe more fully.

Now you can begin to awaken each sense.

SMELLING. Once you have seated Partner B, bring a bottle of peppermint oil close to his nostrils, making sure it does not touch the skin—it is strong and could burn. Let him smell the scent deeply. This will cleanse the sinuses and bring a pleasant "zing" to the brain.

Slowly pass other scents under his nostrils, never touching his face directly, so that he can inhale deeply and enjoy each one. Allow one or two minutes between scents; during this time you can play various types of music. This will increase your partner's anticipation of the next event, and also his sensitivity.

Now expand the qualities of smell to include a more general feeling of being cleansed and purified. Play music that incorporates the sound of running water or the splash of waves. Point the nozzle of the sprayer above your partner's head, and let the delicate spray fall on his face a few times. The scented mist will have an immediately refreshing effect. Again, if need be, encourage your partner to breathe more deeply. Allow a minute of silence to mark the next transition.

HEARING. Now take your beloved on a journey into resonant sound. Begin by introducing just one sound. Ring a bell, play a Tibetan singing bowl, or sing one note. Let the sound be steady and continuous. Tibetan singing bowls, certain bells, and Japanese gongs have a deeply quieting yet stimulating effect on the brain. The sound begins with a strong impact and then continues as a faint, ever-diminishing tone that engages the listener's attention. By "riding" on the vibration of each sound, the mind is at once sharpened and relaxed.

Add more sounds as you go along. I favor bells or Tibetan bowls because you can move them in circles and spirals around your partner as you play them. As you play the various instruments, also play *Tibetan Bells* by Henry Wolfe and Nancy Hennings, from Celestial Harmonies (see Appendix II). This tape provides good support for the sounds you can make with your own bells.

Immersed in sounds, your partner will feel lighter, as if he is being lifted off the ground and is flying into space in an ever-expanding circle. If you lack access to bells and bowls, the tape alone will do.

At the end of this sequence, you should again use silence to mark a transition to the next surprise. By now your partner is most likely smiling and relaxed, ready and eager for the next experience. Watch how even the toughest resistance begins to fade away under the impact of delicate perfumes, scented mists, and floating sounds.

TASTING. Next you are going to initiate your partner into the sensory delights of taste. First, change the music to a piece suggesting sensuality, such as selections by Andreas Vollenweider or Vangelis. Then take the bowl containing the grapes. Put one on a toothpick, and dip it in the liqueur. Bring it close to your partner's nostrils. Watch and enjoy how your partner receives this new sensory signal—smelling the liqueur, trying to guess the flavor, eager to sample it. Often you can see a shudder run through his entire body as he registers the "taste" of this "smell."

After a moment caress his lips with the grape, offering the soft roundness to his mouth and leaving a trail of the liqueur's sweet, burning taste. Watch his eagerness to capture this tender morsel, and allow yourself to tease him seductively with it. Finally press the grape onto his lips until they part, and allow the fruit to go in ever so slowly. Then dip your finger into the liqueur and caress your partner's lips with it. Take your time.

Listen to a minute or two of music, then continue by giving your partner a chocolate mint. Wait a few moments for him to experience this new taste, as the chocolate melts in his mouth. Allow a few moments of silence and stillness before moving to the next phase.

TOUCHING. Next you will awaken the sense of touch. Hesitantly, almost imperceptibly, begin to touch your partner with various textures, such as a soft, old-fashioned shaving brush, a piece of silk, a feather, or a piece of fur. Let your imagination create a theater of touch. Move a peacock feather across his cheeks, neck, and arms; inside his elbows; along his ankles and the soles of his feet. Tickle the insides of his hands and behind his ears. Move the feather inside his robe or shirt to tickle his nipples until he can no longer hold back his laughter. Allow a sense of insistent, wicked seductiveness to be conveyed through the feather.

After a moment of silence, change the music to sounds that awaken the heart. For example, Donna Summers's "I Love to Love You, Baby," or Sande Hershman's *Shine* and *Journey into Love.* Sit behind your partner's back, or maybe to the side. With utmost gentleness, as if you had never touched him before, let your hand rest on his heart. Let your heart touch his heart through your hand. A moment later, let your other hand rest on his lower back, giving a sense of caring and support. Allow your hands to radiate warmth, tenderness, and love.

After a while whisper your partner's name in his ear, adding, "You are beautiful; I love you," or any sentence that feels good. Move to the right side and then the left. Whisper randomly in each ear so that your actions remain unexpected. Maintain this loving contact for at least five minutes to allow your partner to relax into it.

Then stop the music, go to the center of the room, and say, "Now, beloved, put your hands on your heart. Feel the life throbbing there. Feel how it relaxes you and brings you joy and self-acceptance. Feel how you can give yourself the love you so often give to others."

Next, play a beautiful piece of music for the heart—my favorite is "Listen to My Heart Song" from the cassette *On Wings of Song: Many Blessings*. Often at this point, a deep sob of relief wells up through people's hearts during the group rituals. Tears may come as the heart overflows with feelings. Let the music continue for 3 to 5 minutes. Allow a moment of silence.

Then play another piece of music for the heart, perhaps your favorite love song. Sit in front of your partner, and carefully take his hand in yours. Slowly explore the contact of your fingers, touching as delicately as you would touch the petals of a rose. Move from his hand to his arm. Go very, very slowly.

Move into a deep and satisfying hug, breathing together. Feel your hearts beating together. Enjoy the bond of the closeness between you. Feel the gratitude that comes from giving such a gift and being able to receive it. Stay bonded for a few minutes, then allow a moment of silence.

SEEING. Finally, you will convey the experience of enhanced sight. Gently take the blindfold off your partner's head. Avoid talking. Look into each other's eyes for a while, in silence. For most people, this experience is very deep. Being introduced again to sight and light in this magic way allows the recipient to perceive a glow around his or her partner's face, a radiance that expands and blends into the environment. Encourage your partner to look around the room with fresh eyes—to see the flowers, the crystals, the instruments on the trays in the center, the artwork you hung on the walls, the glow of the candles and, finally, yourself. Just sit facing each other in silence for a while, as if born anew. Then share a Melting Hug.

After a while Partner B may wish to share his impressions of the journey on which you guided him. Words help to anchor these experiences in the memory. From there you may wish to share a night of gentle and sensuous lovemaking. Notice that the way you touch, smell, see, and hear each other is fresher and more all-encompassing because you have allowed yourselves to be open and vulnerable to each other.

Pointers

Eventually you will exchange roles. The partner who acted as guide becomes receptive, and the one who was receiver creates a magical world for his partner. But don't try to arrange two Sensory Awakening Rituals on the same day, because the second journey is likely to be less stimulating than the first. Leave time for "ordinary reality" to return. This will provide the contrast that makes the journey so rich and rewarding. It also allows time for each active partner to plan and prepare the ritual carefully.

THE DANCING GODS

The next skill to be developed for enhancing intimacy is imagination. It is the ability to create in your mind's eye a vision of what is possible so that you can mobilize your talents to actualize it.

The power of imagination is operating all around us. Many athletes, for instance, visualize precisely how they are going to achieve optimum performance. "Once you dare to imagine your goal, you are flooded with ideas about how to realize that image," says Olympic athlete Marilyn King. Recalling her training as a high jumper, she says that before each jump she runs through every step in her mind.

"I stand on the lift-off, inhale, exhale, center, and run a mental movie," she says, "imagining myself as I take my first step, second step, accelerate through the curve, plant my foot; then my body rises up over, my body arches backward. . . ." Instead of simply thinking, *I'm going to jump higher than I ever have,* she imagines exactly how she's going to achieve that goal. This precision is an essential step in learning the art of sexual ecstasy, particularly when you are about to become the Dancing Gods. When you try new approaches, there are bound to be missed cues, false starts, and disappointing moves. But the more you can imagine exactly how to create the right move or situation, the easier it will be to enjoy the practices of this book and to integrate them into your love life.

Imagination is not the same as fantasy. Fantasizing is pretending that something is happening that you don't expect could ever happen, whereas imagination enables you to act as if something were actually true. For example, it is pure fantasy to expect that you will win the lottery and thereby solve all your financial problems. But imagining the fulfillment of your fondest sexual dreams can be empowering because the realization of your sexual potential is well within your grasp. Imagination reveals not only limits that prevent us from changing and growing but also ways to explore and transcend them. It bridges the gap between what we are and what we may be.

Purpose and Benefits

In this ceremony you are once again invited to experience your intrinsic beauty and self-worth. But here you also express these qualities with your partner through dance. The act of showing yourself at a deep level also brings your Inner Lover alive, not just for your partner but for yourself, adding flesh and vitality to the feelings that you contacted in chapter 2. This way of embodying the Inner Lover has a powerfully transforming effect on the way you look at yourself, giving you a strong and positive self-image.

This practice is inspired by ancient Tantric practices. For example, in some rituals the devotees of the goddess Shakti, renowned for her beauty and femininity, symbolically transformed themselves into the goddess, thereby embodying the entire spectrum of female qualities. In other rituals devotees of the god Shiva, also known as "the Lord of the Dance," participated in ecstatic dancing in order to evoke and acquire the magical powers of the god.

In this practice you are literally encouraged to express, in your own unique way, the playful energy of Shakti and the creative power of Shiva and to treat each other as if you are a god and goddess. To Westerners who are not accustomed to such imagery, this may seem pretentious. But if you think of the gods of Greek, Egyptian, or Hindu mythology, you will recall that these supernatural beings all have very human qualities— they are not as far above you as they may seem. They too suffer from

Shakti is the Power that creates and destroys, the womb from which all things proceed and to which all return. . . . Shakti is spontaneous vibration, the fullness of her blissful state and the outbursting of her joy compelling her toward self-unfolding.

—Ajit Mookerjee
Kali

jealousy, anger, passion, and other human emotions, yet they convey the grace and magnificence of those who dare to go to the limits of what is possible. Whatever they do, they do totally. They mirror our superhuman potential. Once you allow yourself to express your inner beauty, you will discover a flavor of these qualities within yourself. Like a good actor, put aside any skepticism, and throw yourself wholeheartedly into the role. Skilled actors act "as if" they are the characters and do this so completely that they become the role they are playing and feel the emotions they are representing. You may feel that the very idea of acting like a god or goddess is nonsensical, but if you let go of this attitude and simply try it, you will have taken the first step toward the experience of feeling godlike.

Many people feel awkward about dancing, because they have a stereotypical idea about how it should be done. You don't have to be Nijinsky, Isadora Duncan, Fred Astaire, or Ginger Rogers. Simply open yourself up to your body's natural ability to express itself, and any sense of awkwardness will gradually disappear. Your body already knows how it likes to dance.

Through this dance you are acknowledging the goddess or god in yourself. Let it be a sacred ritual but also a game in which the art of seduction plays a major role. To me, seduction happens when you have a strong sense of your personal beauty and you then seek ways to give it expression, enticing your partner with graceful sensuality into a mood where he or she can experience the beauty you are feeling. It is an invitation to share sensual intimacy.

In this dance everything is permitted, and no particular goal is to be achieved other than the joyous expression of your spirit. Dance is the language of the spirit.

Preparations

Prepare your Sacred Space. Make sure the area is uncluttered, so you have lots of room to move around. Create indirect lighting so that it shines on the walls and floors rather than directly on the dancer. This will give a sense of softness to your gestures and skin tone. Place votive candles in small glass containers around the room. The flickering light will enhance the atmosphere of mystery and celebration. Both partners should have their favorite music ready to play. Pick pieces that will last a total of 15 to 20 minutes. Wear something sensual and comfortable in which you can dance and feel beautiful. My favorite is a Tahitian *pareo* wrapped around my hips, a flower in my hair and nothing else.

A word to the spectator: Give your partner your full attention and unconditional support. Watch with a loving and accepting attitude. Keep in mind the fact that your partner is courageously revealing his or her innermost qualities, and let your eyes show your appreciation of this special revelation.

Practice

In this exercise one partner dances while the other watches. The spectator should sit alone in the Sacred Space, leaving a "stage" area free for the performance, while the dancer gets ready in another room.

I usually encourage women to start the dance, because they are more accustomed to moving flowingly and seductively. So I begin this practice section with the dance of the woman, which I call "The Dance of Shakti."

THE DANCE OF SHAKTI. Walk gracefully into the room, and pause in front of your partner. Look into his eyes. Standing, do the Heart Salutation as a way of saying to him, "I thank you for the gift of your presence." The spectator can return the salutation from the sitting position.

Start the music and come to "center stage." Close your eyes, tune into your feelings, and let your breathing be deep. Forget the person who is watching; forget everything except your breathing. You are alone with yourself. For a moment go back to the practice of Awakening Your Inner Lover, and reconnect with the feeling that you are lovable and beautiful, with the infinite capacity of a goddess to change roles and forms.

Bend your knees slightly, and focus your awareness in the area of your navel, letting your breathing go all the way down to it. This is your gravity center, your anchor, your power point. The more you can move from this center, the more power and balance you will feel.

Feel the music and how it echoes inside your body. Let yourself gently respond to the rhythm. Let your body guide you into the flow of the music until you begin to dance spontaneously, without deciding in advance what movements you are going to make.

Move every part of your body, including your head and neck. Keeping your neck and head stiff allows your mind to stay in control and doesn't allow the spirit of the dance to take over. Let each movement flow

The Dance of Shakti.

through your whole body. You'll notice how a movement of the hip can ripple up to your neck, and a movement of your arm can be extended down to your foot—like waves in an ocean of movement.

Let your breathing be deep, and let it carry you through the movements. Find the style of dancing that you really enjoy. It does not matter which one you choose—the pelvic thrust of the African dancer, the fluid movements of the belly dancer, or the dynamic jumping of rock and roll. You are not performing in the usual sense, as a way of pleasing the audience. That is a by-product. You are dancing primarily for your own enjoyment.

You may be feeling shy. This is natural. It's risky to show yourself in this way. But take courage and stay with your dancing. Creativity is a venture into the unknown. There is a risk in leaving the familiar behind, but the rewards ahead are great. This is the moment to tune into the goddess, the dancing goddess within.

Amplify your breathing and your movements. Let your voice animate your dancing with whatever sounds come naturally—sighs, growls, songs, chants. Let yourself go, and let the dance take over. Feel beautiful, loved, fulfilled. Stay connected with your Inner Lover—you are this lover now, a goddess manifesting joy, harmony, assurance.

Let this goddess energy grow within you. You are Shakti, the ultimate woman, the personification of attraction and seduction. When you feel connected to the Shakti within, open your eyes, and show this goddess to your lover. Let your eyes express her vitality; let your smile express the radiance of one who loves herself; let your body express her grace, her playfulness, her spontaneity. Let your breathing and your voice exhibit her power.

Become this goddess, and let her presence fill the room. See how it feels to watch your partner as you show this power, this radiance. Go beyond the ordinary limits of your shyness, and enjoy your own beauty under another's gaze. Remember, you are not looking for approval. Stay within yourself. If you experience doubts and shyness, close your eyes again for a moment, breathe deeply and strongly, and remain focused on the movements of your body and the sounds of your voice in order to stay centered. The more you relax under your partner's gaze, the more you can enjoy the power that another's undivided attention and love gives you.

Explore the different aspects of your goddess energy—the fluidity of water, the explosiveness of fire, the lightness of air, the strength of the earth, the grace of a panther, the seductive slinking of a snake. As you give free rein to the many dimensions of your being, realize that they are all within you, waiting to come out. You do in fact have the creative potential and playful freedom of the goddess whom you imagine yourself to be—free of concerns and preoccupations, transcending the inhibitions of habit and culture.

Keep dancing in this way for 15 to 20 minutes, or until you feel that the end has come. Then stand still in front of your partner and exchange a Heart Salutation.

When you have had time to catch your breath and "come back to yourself," your partner can address you as the goddess that he has now discovered in you: "Beautiful Shakti [or, if he prefers, your own name], you are my delight. I honor you as the embodiment of the creative energy that fills us with life." Then he can tell you what he especially enjoyed in your dance.

End the exchange with a Melting Hug. Then let the partner who has been watching become the dancer.

THE DANCE OF SHIVA. As the male partner, you can follow exactly the same steps as above. But, of course, your dance will emphasize the male aspects of the godhead, personified in Shiva, the Hindu deity who can assume myriad forms—the magician, creator, warrior, clown, destroyer, seducer.

The Dance of Shiva.

You will prepare yourself in another room and enter the Sacred Space to dance before your "Shakti." As a man, it is especially important for you to feel grounded and rooted to the earth and to feel your own power. So in the beginning be sure to take time to close your eyes and center yourself—relaxing your belly, thighs, and knees, with your feet planted firmly on the floor and your knees slightly bent.

You are the god Shiva—the god who, in the Tantric tradition, infuses matter with spirit as he unites with Shakti, creating the numerous forms of reality. Become rooted in this experience of your own divinity—think it, feel it, believe it—before opening your eyes and looking at your partner.

Remember the Inner Lover and plunge deeply into the spirit of the dance. Find the male within, and proudly show his godlike qualities to your partner.

As you get carried away by the dancing, explore the whole range of masculine qualities available to you. Beat your chest like a male gorilla facing his adversary; feel the power of the bull, the courage of the lion, the nobility of the warrior, the stealth of the hunter, the grace of an athlete. Dance with the total commitment of a tribal medicine man.

If it helps, think about the qualities of men you have met in your life and who have inspired you. Visualize their strength, courage, or sex appeal. As you dance, imagine that you embody these qualities, and give expression to them.

When you finish your dance, stand still in front of your partner and exchange a Heart Salutation. Then your female partner will tell you, "Beautiful Shiva [or your own name], you are my delight, and I honor the boundless spirit expressed in your dance." She will tell you what she most enjoyed in seeing you express the power and energy, the strength and grace, of the Shiva within you.

End the exchange with a Melting Hug.

THE DANCE OF SHAKTI AND SHIVA. You can conclude this session by dancing together, as Shakti and Shiva, exploring how you interact from your inner power. Stay centered in the awareness of the goddess and god within. Move close together, and keep your eyes riveted on each other.

Mirror each other's movements; explore the flight of the eagle or the fluidity of the snake. Then try sensual spoon dancing, with one partner's front against the other's back. Dance back to back, then nose to nose, forehead to forehead. Enjoy making wild sounds, animal sounds, seductive sounds.

When you've played out all the possibilities to your heart's content, end the dance by facing each other, with the fronts of your bodies touching and your knees slightly bent. Feel the subtle movements of energy streaming through your bodies. Be aware of each other's breathing patterns.

Be still. You have come to a point of balance between the male and female principles. In this equilibrium you can move gently together in a very slow, effortless dance, in which no one "pushes" or "does" anything. Thus poised, note where your center of gravity is—neither in you nor in the other, but somewhere between your bellies and chests, where your two energies meet. Enjoy the feeling of having come to a middle point, of being a part of each other yet centered in yourself.

Pointers

In my seminars many people experience major breakthroughs when they are able to remain relaxed and spontaneous as a goddess or a god in front of others. They realize that this dance is not about becoming someone else—some archetypal model—but about becoming more profoundly who they really are.

It takes courage to show yourself to others. Don't worry about not being good enough. Whatever your movement, it is perfect as it is because it shows your uniqueness. Even if you feel vulnerable and insecure, your willingness to give yourself to another in dance deepens your shared sense of intimacy, trust, and playfulness.

After watching the dance of your partner, when you give your comments, avoid criticism, as this tends to dampen spontaneity and enthusiasm. Instead reinforce what pleases you through sincere praise.

Create a balance. The outer and the inner are not opposed. They are movements of the same energy, two banks of the same river, and the river cannot flow with only one bank.

—Bhagwan Shree Rajneesh

SKILLS OF PLAYFULNESS

After developing your sensory awareness and imagination, you are ready to explore the next essential skill in High Sex: playfulness—the art of smiling at yourself and your partner and of laughing wholeheartedly together. The playful attitude gives you a sense of what is new and unexpected, and a chance to turn seriousness and possible conflict into creativity. For example, when you are with your lover and there is some difficulty in relating, there are two basic ways to proceed. You can either become serious, blaming the other person or becoming critical of your-

To play is to be unfettered and unconditioned, to perform actions that are intrinsically satisfying: to sing, dance, and laugh. To play is to step out of the ordinary world of the humdrum, to enter a special, magical world where one can revel in the superfluous. To play is to display oneself aimlessly and gracefully. As players, then, the gods are revealed to be delightful, joyful, graceful beings whose actions are completely spontaneous, unconditioned, and expressive of their transcendent completeness and freedom.

—David R. Kinsley
The Sword and the Flute

self, or you can put some distance on the problem by not taking it too seriously and introducing humor and creative playfulness. These qualities can help you to transcend self-importance. You perceive yourself as a clown or joker slipping on a banana peel, an amusing performance in the great arena of life's possibilities.

In High Sex the ability to see humor in tense situations, such as sexual situations, is highly valued. Laughter immediately breaks down barriers and resistance, lightens the mood to one of play, and turns a sexual encounter into a spirited game. It has been said that the sure sign of cosmic sex is "an orgasm accompanied by uncontrollable laughter," and I fully agree with the observation.

You can begin to develop this playful attitude through the Inner Smile before moving on to Soul Gazing.

THE INNER SMILE

The Inner Smile meditation was first devised by the Taoists, who believed in sending a daily smile to their internal organs to keep them in good health. In elaborate exercises they would smile at the heart, at the kidneys, at the liver, and so on.

Purpose and Benefits

This is a simple yet effective way to help you relax and to discover a smile inside that can be shared with another. For this exercise it's enough to take ten to fifteen minutes to stop everything, become centered, and smile at yourself and then at your partner.

Practice

Create the Sacred Space, then sit facing your partner. Begin with a Heart Salutation.

Close your eyes, and look inside. Is your mind occupied by thoughts about various projects and plans, or concerns about your relationships with others? Allow yourself to put such distracting thoughts aside, and focus your awareness on your breathing. Without making an effort, let it become deep and slow. Let your tongue float inside your mouth. Relax the muscles around your eyes. As you focus on these internal sensations, notice how the day's tensions start to dissolve. Bring your awareness back to your breathing each time you notice that it has slipped away.

After a few minutes see what happens when you perform the simple act of smiling at yourself. Lift the corners of your mouth a little. See how this smile starts to change your mood.

Think of a statue of the Buddha and the subtle, easy smile on his face, or the radiant yet discrete smile you see on the painting of the Mona Lisa. Feel the radiance of the Mona Lisa's smile within yourself. Think how wonderful you feel when someone looks at you and smiles. There is no better sign of love and acceptance, of friendliness and welcome. Invoke these feelings, and let them grow inside you. Accept the possibility that this may be the right moment to feel good about yourself.

Reconnect with your Inner Lover in your heart and the god or goddess who was dancing within you. See how this fills you with the feeling that you are beautiful, the knowledge that at the source of your being there are no contradictions and everything can be okay. This is the smile of compassion and understanding.

Let this inner radiance flower on your face, and when you feel it clearly, open your eyes and share it with your partner. If your partner's eyes are still closed, continue to look, feeling that you are expanding your radiance. Wait for his or her eyes to open.

Now you can both look at each other from behind this shared smile. See how wonderful it is to acknowledge the other person in this way and to receive the his or her radiance directed toward you. Let yourselves experience the smile for as long as it lasts naturally, then close your eyes again.

End with a Heart Salutation and a Melting Hug.

Pointers

You can also practice this exercise alone, looking at yourself in a mirror. Take time to smile at yourself whenever you wish to experience its transforming and healing effect.

SOUL GAZING

After the previous intense exchanges, you may feel ready to connect more quietly and deeply with your partner through Soul Gazing. You are about to dive into the deeper meaning of feeling godlike, reaching a sense of peace and emptiness together that is beyond the familiar boundaries of the personality.

This meditation is based on a technique developed by Oscar Ichazo, founder of the Arica school, which I have adapted to the Tantric perspective.

Purpose and Benefits

When you are together with the Beloved, this union and partnership extends you into the depth world and helps bring the depth world into time.

—Jean Houston
The Search for The Beloved

One of the great benefits of Soul Gazing is that it harmonizes people's energy fields. Like tuning musical instruments before a concert, it produces optimum conditions for a compatible, pleasing resonance between two partners.

In the Tantric tradition the art of gazing is developed by focusing one's eyes on a *yantra*—a geometric form symbolizing a certain energy pattern—or on the image of a deity that symbolizes a particular virtue, such as compassion or courage. Gazing at the *yantra,* becoming one with the form, the practitioner experiences the force behind it. In the same way, by gazing at the form of your beloved, the form can disappear, and you can become one with the energy the form represents. You experience the other person as part of yourself.

Soul Gazing is a delicate art. Normally people are shy about looking directly into someone else's eyes or letting someone gaze into theirs. They allow a casual glance for a few seconds, then turn away. Being looked at for too long feels like an intrusion. Through the eyes you can glimpse a person's secrets—hidden shyness, anger, fear, or impatience. So in the Soul-Gazing meditation, you may be confronted with places in yourself that do not feel comfortable. You may feel exposed, thinking, for example, *He can see that I don't like myself today. He's going to judge me for it.* During Soul Gazing, as you simply observe such resistance without feeling that you have to do anything about it, the impression of discomfort gradually dissolves, and you experience inner calm and emptiness. This will give you a deeper sense of self-worth and more distance from self-criticism.

Soul Gazing.

Preparations

Create the Sacred Space.

The period devoted to gazing should be no more than five minutes daily, for five consecutive days. Then you can gradually increase the time to ten, fifteen, and twenty minutes. Give yourself plenty of time to integrate what happens.

You also can practice Soul Gazing alone, in front of a mirror. Here again, you should undertake no more than five minutes of gazing at first, with special emphasis on deep, slow breathing to help you stay centered and energized.

Practice

With your partner loosen up by stretching your neck from side to side, then shaking your head and your shoulders while breathing deeply.

Then sit facing each other, either in chairs or crossed-legged on the floor or kneeling. If you are on the floor, sit on a thick pillow to keep your spine straight while your back is relaxed.

Begin with a Heart Salutation.

Touch each other in a way that feels relaxing, such as lightly holding hands.

Let your breathing be deep and slow, so you can feel the air flowing all the way down to your belly. Close your eyes, and go on a journey inside your mind and body, as if you were exploring your house and making a detailed inventory of the rooms and the furniture in them. Scan your body within to notice if there are any tensions—a tight muscle or a tense stomach, or perhaps a sense of strength and fullness. Allow yourself simply to accept whatever is there. At first it may seem difficult to be motionless when you encounter tensions in parts of your body. It is possible to acknowledge and accept them, however, while continuing with the meditation. For example, say to yourself, "I've got an itch on my left eyebrow and some tightness in my neck, but I can accept them for right now."

Check the area of your chest and heart—your feelings. Are you sad or distrustful? Do you feel joyful? Is everything okay? If not, can you accept for right now that it's okay *not* to feel okay?

Notice what is happening inside your mind. Watch the thoughts that arise. Are you deciding that something is wrong or judging that something is bad? Do you think your partner is okay? What about yourself? Note any conversations or monologues going on in your head. Accept these thoughts without being identified with them. Watch them pass, like clouds in the sky.

When you feel quiet, send a little signal to your partner—a gentle squeeze of the hand, perhaps—and wait for the return signal. Open your eyes and allow your gaze to connect with that of your partner. Keeping your eyes relaxed, look into the left eye of your partner. This is considered to be the "receptive" eye, which allows the energy of the other person in, reflecting the Taoist perception that the left side of the body is Yin, feminine, receptive, while the right side is Yang, masculine, active.

Direct your complete attention to your gaze, and allow yourself to be drawn completely into the present moment. Let the newness, innocence, and freshness flood you with a sense of expectancy and openness. See how it feels to be connected to another while staying aware of your breathing, centered in yourself.

Silently say to yourselves, "You love me," or, if you prefer, "We are one." As you repeat this to yourself, feel open to receiving your partner's love and appreciation. Let your eyes be the windows to your soul. Normally we project energy out through our eyes as we look at the people and things around us. In doing so we identify with the objects of our attention and forget ourselves. This way of seeing tends to drain our energy. Now reverse this tendency, using your eyes to attract energy and love toward you like a magnet.

The stillness of your gaze will gradually quiet your mind, and you will be able to reach a place of emptiness, the emptiness of a mirror that can reflect anything, yet itself contains nothing. In this moment of stillness, you cease to identify with your body, mind, and thoughts and become aware of what meditators call "the witness state"—the observing, centered self that quietly, dispassionately watches all you do. As you progress, enjoy the discovery that you can integrate seeing, thinking, and breathing.

Here, beyond individual personalities, you can recognize the essential humanness in your partner that is equally present in yourself. Enjoy recognizing the other person beyond any sense of ego, as you come together in a flow of breathing, looking, and simply being—without any goal, totally present in the here and now, experiencing yourselves moment to moment.

If your partner is a man, see in him all the men you have ever known. If your partner is a woman, see in her all the women you have ever known.

Notice the rhythm of your breath and that of your partner. Without effort, see if you can gradually harmonize your breathing until you are inhaling and exhaling together. Let the breathing be simple and subtle. As much as possible, avoid using words. Take your time.

Address your partner internally or aloud, saying, "I recognize you and honor you as an aspect of myself." Enjoy the feeling of devotion and reverence that this recognition brings. As you acknowledge this, you may feel it is possible to forgive your partner for any wounds that you have been secretly holding onto. If not, just accept that imperfection, too, is part of the universal dance.

End with a Heart Salutation.

Pointers

If you want to sit cross-legged on the floor but experience discomfort in doing so, try using several pillows so that you can sit higher off the

Lover divine and perfect
*   Comrade,*
Waiting content, invisible yet,
*   but certain,*
Be thou my God.
Thou, thou, the Ideal Man,
Fair, able, beautiful, content and
*   loving,*
Complete in body and dilate in
*   spirit,*
Be thou my God.

—Walt Whitman

floor with your knees pointing down, thereby relieving tension in your leg muscles. Or you can place a cushion under each knee so that it remains at the same height as your buttocks. You can also try kneeling on the floor, Japanese-style, straddling a big cushion between your legs.

While looking at your partner in Soul Gazing, you may suddenly have the impression that his or her "normal" face has disappeared and has been replaced by a procession of different masks and faces. In this procession you may see your partner at different ages, from childhood to old age, or in different moods, from wrathful to seductive to serene. You may even believe that you see faces from your partner's "past lives"—as a Mongol warrior, perhaps, or an Egyptian dancer.

Again, your attitude will determine the outcome of the practice. You can reject this odd experience, or you can accept it as a teaching. The Tantric tradition encourages us to explore the full array of our possibilities as human beings, and in this procession of faces, you will see that the range is infinite. Tantra, too, teaches that physical forms are ever-changing and are an expression of *maya,* the great illusion through which consciousness manifests itself as matter in continuous flux. Keeping this in mind, simply watch everything that you see with detachment, focusing on your breathing, and the procession of faces will soon return to the familiar face of your partner.

When you become familiar with the Soul-Gazing meditation, you can use it as a way of harmonizing with your partner before beginning new practices, or any time you feel the need to achieve a deeper connection.

⚜

In this chapter you learned intimate ways of connecting with your partner that will facilitate your intimacy and your experience of High Sex. You began by giving a gift to your beloved, opening up the doors of perception through the Sensory Awakening Ritual. Then you expressed the beauty of the god and goddess within, embodying your Inner Lover through the medium of dance. You learned the art of developing humor through the Inner Smile. You tuned in with each other through Soul Gazing, meeting your partner at a soul-to-soul level.

In the next chapter, you will learn to befriend your body and your partner's body. You will discover that when the body is honored as the temple of the spirit, it can show great intelligence.

❦

HONORING THE BODY ECSTATIC

Traditional Tantric masters tell us that for each of us the body is the location of an unfolding drama: "Matter ascending toward spirit, and spirit incarnating in matter." The Tantric attitude toward this delicate fusion of spirit and matter is to train the body gently to contain more and more "spirit"—that is to say, to refine raw sexual energy into more subtle and ecstatic states, thus gradually creating the Body Ecstatic. Tantra recognizes that the body has within itself the blueprint of its own perfection.

But such an attitude of respect for the body's innate wisdom is not prevalent in our culture. The vast majority of people think they must rule the body with the head. To them the head is the master and the body a kind of machine, like a car that can be driven in whatever direction the owner may desire. Rather than trusting and following the natural impulses, rhythms, and sensations of the body, most people compel the body to function in accordance with attitudes dictated by the intellect. For example, hair, facial configuration, and the shape and size of the body are altered—sometimes with extreme effort and at great expense—according to popular perceptions of what is stylish and acceptable.

In this way, the great majority of people rely heavily on social stereotypes instead of allowing themselves to feel their own intrinsic beauty. To be lovable they believe they have to possess the perfectly toned body of a model or movie star or the muscles and swagger of a professional athlete. They work hard at it, and most go around secretly disappointed that they don't measure up, no matter how much they diet or how hard they work out. Taught to view their bodies as machines that they have to tune up, fix, change, discipline, and train, they feel they'll

Energy is Eternal Delight.
—William Blake

never get the damn thing working right. The result is that they often end up distrusting their bodies—like lion tamers who, whip in hand, remain ever alert to the threat of sudden rebellion.

LEARNING TO LOVE OUR BODIES

A crucial element in the Eastern experience of oneself as an immortal being is the fact that this achievement occurs through working on the body, in contrast to Western occult so-called subtle body experiences which frequently happen independently of the body. The West attempts to create immortality and reach heaven mainly through good works, and more recently through psychological growth and self-knowledge. . . . But if the body is not integrated into self-knowledge, one becomes obsessed with its wellbeing. Psychological growth without body consciousness appears like a tree without roots.

—Arnold Mindell
Dreambody

Reared in a culture that for centuries has separated flesh and spirit and chastised the body as the abode of evil instincts, we are nevertheless bombarded by the media's tantalizing sex symbols that urge us toward unbridled hedonism. As a result, beneath our efforts to appear attractive and act sexy, there is an often unconscious layer of self-criticism that subtly sabotages our ability to love our own bodies.

Yet if we cannot love our bodies, how are we going to find somebody else to love them? How can we share with our lover something we ourselves do not value? If we secretly mistrust the body and order it around like a robot, how can we surrender to it during lovemaking?

Natural Grace

In High Sex, as lovers become more in tune with their bodies, more sensual, and more skillful in lovemaking, they naturally exude a feeling of style. But it is style of an entirely different kind than what is considered fashionable. They may not be dressed to kill or have flawless figures, but they are comfortable in their bodies and at ease with themselves. The grace with which they carry themselves conveys a sense of vital wellbeing and natural self-appreciation. This feeling comes from within and is not dependent on social trends. For a Tantric lover, the body is an intimate friend—accepted, cared for, and cherished—regardless of age, shape, or color.

I recall participating in a Tantra training in France many years ago, in which this issue of physical beauty was addressed by the instructor in a dramatic and provocative way. Cutting through fashionable façades, he invited any people in the group who felt they could to take off their clothes and show their bodies. To make it easier and also to add a little humor, each participant was challenged to find a unique way of undressing before the group. Some put on belly dance music and engaged in a striptease. Others wanted the group members to sing and clap their hands. One woman wanted us to be blindfolded until she had completely undressed. Most of us went through awkward moments, thinking, *My breasts are too small, my thighs are too big, my rear is pear-shaped. . . . How can I let them see me?* There was a tension behind most people's playfulness that arose out of the unspoken fear that their bodies were unacceptable.

At one point it was the turn of Michel, a man who had studied Tantra for many years. Although he had a very strong presence in the group, Michel until then had kept mostly in the background. He walked with a noticeable limp, and clearly had been severely injured at some point in his life. As he moved slowly toward the center of the group, my heart skipped a beat. Would he dare undress?

Unlike the others, Michel simply asked for silence. He sat down with the clumsiness of one whose thigh muscles have little strength. He did not seem in the least embarrassed by his body and apparently accepted its limitations as a matter of fact. He started untying his shoelaces, and in a moment a pair of crooked feet appeared, then two very bony legs, then a heavily scarred torso.

Michel proceeded as calmly as if he were in the privacy of his own bedroom. His hands were steady, his gestures flowing. The act appeared so simple, as if his body was not only undamaged but also free of the so-called imperfections that caused the rest of us so much doubt and worry. His blue eyes were ablaze with the fixed intensity of a warrior aiming at a distant target. There was a hint of defiance in his pride, yet such radiance in his composed features, such directness, even humility in his manner. The group remained absolutely silent for a long moment after he had finished undressing, then burst spontaneously into applause.

To me Michel's "performance" was a revelation. In a few minutes he had debunked everybody's myths about beauty being the reflection of perfected form. Yet if the beauty he exuded was not of the body, where did it come from? The answer that came to me was, *Beauty comes from the spirit. It is the spirit that "dresses" the body, not the clothes that are added to it.* This man knew that he was *not* the body. He was neither identifying with its shape nor judging it, yet his body was his friend.

Such an individual is an exception. Almost all of us—especially women—feel shy about taking off our clothes. In my groups many people look awkward in their clothes, as if they are trying to hide something. Yet I am always amazed to see how graceful these same people's bodies are in their natural state. This grace is a reflection of the spirit hidden within the form.

If life and the soul are sacred the human body is sacred;
And the glory and sweet of a man is the token of manhood untainted,
And in man or woman a clean strong firmfibred body is beautiful as the most beautiful face.

—Walt Whitman
Leaves of Grass

The Body as a Temple

In High Sex, the flesh is seen not as an obstacle to a pure and free spirit, but as the springboard from which the spirit takes flight. You need to be firmly rooted in the body in order to soar to the heights of ecstatic sex. The body is your temple, the abode of a unique divinity—yourself. As the one in charge of this temple, you honor it and keep its spirit high by keeping the temple clean and healthy so that it can support the divinity—the Inner Lover—that dwells within.

Throughout this book you will learn how to walk through the gates of this temple, into its secret gardens and waterfalls and the other delightful places that it offers for your pleasure. In so doing you are honoring and rediscovering your own body so that it can receive and assimilate subtler and more intense energies in lovemaking.

You can learn to revere the body as a marvelously intelligent and sensitive organism, for it represents the highest evolution of life forms. From the Tantric perspective, the body is the vehicle for transforming consciousness, the crucible in which the base metal of physical energy can be refined into the pure gold of ecstasy. And like the Tantric seers, as we love the body and discover its hidden wisdom, we come to understand that one who realizes the truth of the body can come to know the truth of the universe.

Good health is the touchstone of pleasure.

—George Leonard

In order to participate in this truth, you can happily put aside ideas about making your body fit some stereotypical ideal. Although in High Sex you do not need bulging muscles or shapely curves, it is important to achieve optimum physical well-being through a healthy diet, physical exercise, deep breathing, and relaxation. To help you relax, I recommend at least one full-body massage a week. High Sex also requires a fluid, supple body capable of changing positions easily and without discomfort during lovemaking.

Being weak and out of shape leaves us enslaved by many unconscious impulses. When we feel tense, anxious, and distracted, we do not have sufficient energy, concentration, and stamina to prolong and consciously guide the lovemaking experience to mutual enhancement and satisfaction.

In addition to physical fitness, you need to recognize, like Michel, that your body is your friend. This means accepting it as it is now—not as it could be or will be once it's "improved." In this way you and your body can become like two lovers who, after living together a long time, have formed a deep companionship. They do not need to be self-conscious, to prove anything, or to change each other. A reciprocity flows between them that is as natural as the ebb and flow of the tides.

From this perspective, working with the body is not tedious or serious. Rather, it is a joyful, playful celebration of life. In High Sex you do not subject your body to the commands of your will. You explore your body's potential, listening to its messages and trusting its self-regulating capacities. You heed and respond to its wild impulses, which are not siren calls to decadence and chaos but invitations to adventure—deep-seated yearnings to live life to the fullest.

Unlocking Forbidden Rooms

To prepare yourself for the following practices and to experience their value fully, it will help to imagine that you have recently inherited the marvelous castle in which you were raised—your body—and now you have returned to live in it. Slowly, day by day, you visit its many rooms. Some are cozy and full of light. You remember them from childhood and feel comfortable in them. They correspond to the parts of your body you accept and feel connected to—your chest, perhaps, or your face. Other rooms—perhaps your thighs and pelvis—are dark and foreboding, or locked and forbidden since childhood; others have never been fully furnished and require decorating.

Moving through the castle is not easy, especially when it comes to unlocking those dark, forbidden rooms. Sometimes you may feel as if some areas of your body are numb. They seem sealed and shuttered and won't let in any sensation—as when, during moments in bed, your lover's touch conveys little or no sense of aliveness. In such moments you do not know how to open up and allow the beloved's touch to reach your core. Indeed, you feel somehow "locked out" of yourself. What happened?

As children, we begin life as innocent, vibrant beings; our movements and energy are unrestricted, flowing. Research has shown that if, during those early years, we are held, cuddled, and stroked, we build up a healthy body image. This natural vitality gradually becomes constrained, however. Our natural tendency to say yes to our bodies and to life is thwarted by the well-intentioned but negative conditioning imposed by society: "No, don't touch this"; "No, don't do that"; and especially by direct physical references, such as, "Don't touch yourself down there!"

To know the truth of the body is to be aware of its movements, its impulses, and its restraints, that is, to feel what goes on in the body. If an individual doesn't feel the tensions, rigidities, or anxieties of his body, he is, in this sense, denying the truth of his body.

—Alexander Lowen
Love and Orgasm

In this way many of us come to believe that our natural way of being is wrong, even dangerous, and we suppress vital feelings of desire, attraction, arousal, and adventure. When we tighten and contract to avoid hurt, energy flow stops. We may not feel pain, but we don't feel pleasure either. This tightening can take place in any part of the body—not just the genital area—and still affect our sexuality.

For instance, the throat constricts and the face gets tight and frozen when, in childhood, we "swallow" noisy expressions such as sobbing, shouting, and screaming. The legs feel stiff and inflexible when the urge to kick, roll around, or dance is thwarted. And, most important, the pelvis becomes rigid and withdrawn when we tighten the anal muscles in order to repress anger, or when we contract the genital muscles in order not to give way to forbidden sexual feelings. These are typical reactions that, when repeated in childhood in response to condemnatory parental attitudes, gradually form into habits that deaden certain areas of the body. This deadening process was first recognized by Wilhelm Reich, the pioneer psychotherapist and sexologist, who called it "body armoring."

So we come to fear our ability to feel pleasure. To be sensitive means to be vulnerable—easily hurt. So we hold back. Our energies remain locked in certain parts of the body, which then feel stiff or dead. Being forbidden to touch, honor, love, and enjoy our genitals dulls the very source of our sensitivity. We build armor to protect ourselves from what we perceive as the potential threat of feeling deeply.

In this sense the body has been wounded and requires healing. In High Sex you learn to identify the wounded areas—exploring those parts that have been rejected, ignored, or denied—and to heal them, giving them recognition, care, tenderness, and a loving touch. By healing and integrating the parts of your body, you will naturally feel healthier and more whole and alive.

Releasing Pent-up Energy

Our feelings carry energy—the need to cry or laugh, to move and touch, to express anger or tender feelings of the heart. If this energy is held back, it is stored in the body, particularly in the muscles that form the layer between the body's core and its surface. Often, in relaxing our muscles, buried conflicts and memories and similar kinds of blocked emotional energy start to emerge from the subconscious. This happens when, for

The oft-heard complaint directed by women at the clumsiness, crassness, and incompetence of men in their sexual approaches and in sexual intercourse itself, men's lack of skill in foreplay and their failure to understand its meaning, almost certainly substantially reflects the lack of tactile experience that such males have suffered in childhood. It is difficult to conceive of anyone who had been tenderly loved and caressed in infancy not learning to approach a woman or a child with especial tenderness.

—Ashley Montagu
Touching

instance, people start an exercise program or receive a deep massage—tears may flow, memories may come flooding in, unnamed fears may surface.

In the following exercises we begin the process of releasing what has been constricted and suppressed for so long. In High Sex this release is of the utmost importance. The more you are able to flow emotionally and physically, the more your capacity to experience the pleasure of orgasm is expanded. Emotional and sensual fluidity is the language of lovemaking. You can't be orgasmic in love if you can't be orgasmic in anger or laughter. That means expressing and letting go of the emotional energy that builds up.

The body can build up a powerful energy charge. But it cannot contain this charge for an indefinite period without damage. The charge has to be released if the body is to function harmoniously. In the early stages of learning to practice High Sex, it is important for the body to be able to charge up and then discharge energy in a healthy and flowing way. By keeping fit, loving yourself, and using the exercises in this book, you are charging the body and storing energy. By expressing this energy through movement, sound, and dynamic lovemaking, you are releasing this stored energy. The charging, discharging, and recharging of energy represents the natural cycle of life. It is reflected in the cycle of lovemaking that begins with arousing and charging up sexual energy, peaks with orgasmic release, and is followed by relaxation and recharging.

When this has been accomplished, you will learn advanced practices in which you will build up a greater energy charge and then, instead of releasing it, you will contain and channel the energy toward higher levels of pleasure and ecstasy. The first step in this process, however, is to release the energy that has been locked away in the body by the logjams caused by our upbringing and past relationships. Initially this can be uncomfortable, but then it opens us up to a range of joyous feelings that are well worth the challenge.

Body armor prevents the full expression of our sexuality, and in order to become vibrant lovers, we need gradually to remove this obsolete layer of protection. When done in a safe way, loosening up our bodies and expressing our feelings can be fun and often feels like letting everything go in a great dance of liberation. This exhilarating, vibrant state is the way to ecstasy.

THREE KEYS TO BUILD UP AND DISCHARGE ENERGY

As I have indicated, the process of achieving an optimum flow of energy in the body involves more than just releasing energy. You also need to be able to charge up enough fresh energy to achieve the results you want.

Here are three major keys that are helpful in both discharging and charging the body with energy: deep breathing, movement, and expression. In any exercise that you do from now on, whether alone or with a partner, remember that these Three Keys can be used simultaneously. Their combined use increases the body's capacity to generate and maintain high levels of energy, which is experienced as intensified and expanded excitement in the body.

Deep Breathing

The most immediate way to build up energy in the body is to increase your intake of oxygen by breathing more deeply and fully, feeling as if the air is filling not only your lungs but also your belly, then exhaling fully. When your respiration becomes more active, your energy level rises, and the nerve endings beneath your skin become more sensitive, resulting in a sense of tingling and vibrancy, like champagne bubbles under the skin. During the following practices, and indeed throughout this book, remember to breathe deeply.

Deep, full breathing also expands sensory perceptions and lends sensitivity to whatever part of the body you focus on. In a matter of minutes, a few steady breaths affect the whole body, brightening and toning up its vitality while intensifying its metabolism and enhancing the flow of blood and energy to vital organs. When such breathing is combined with gentle touching and playful interaction, armored feelings are more readily released.

Breathing through the nose enhances control, slows down the body's metabolism, and holds in the energy charge. Breathing in through the mouth promotes the energy charge, and breathing out through the mouth speeds up the release of emotions. Crying, for example, happens only when you breathe through the mouth.

The conventional breath cycle is unconscious of Life. It receives very little, suffers chronic contraction of feeling and of the trunk and belly, and does not exhale fully. Such unnatural or contracted breathing expresses an emotionally reactive personality, self-possessed, self-protective, and separated from Life. The results of such breathing are a chronic buildup of tension in the lower body, particularly in the genitals.

—Da Love-Ananda
Love of the Two-Armed Form

Movement

Whenever possible, express your feelings through movement. Let your body act out fully what you are feeling inside or what you are saying. It is much harder to get energy streaming through the body when you are motionless than it is when your physical body moves, dances, undulates. Lack of movement encourages body tightness and stiffness that restrict your energies and block out feelings. When you visualize the part of your body that is moving, even small movements expand sensations in that area—a key practice in High Sex.

Sound

We tend to keep our feelings bottled up, but ecstasy comes only when we let them loose. So as you do the exercises, let yourself sigh, shout, and cry as the spirit moves you. Don't censor your vocal expression; don't hold things back. The ability to express your feelings vocally is a measure of good health. Sounds give color and tone to your energy, increase your sense of release, and help your partner to know what you're feeling.

For example, you can let out deep sighs as you exhale, or you can emit sounds from your belly as you dance. And when it comes to making love, you will experience a world of difference between silent sex—restraining the sounds—and expressing your feelings in sound, between the holding-back that is implicit in "I shouldn't say it," or "I'd better not show it," and the wild song of surrender to exploding energy.

Too many of us have learned to drive our bodies with the brakes on, but sexually our bodies are designed to be driven in high gear. Holding back or controlling the energy results in our feeling like victims who never get what we need. But that is only because we don't give it to ourselves. The Three Keys open the door to richer expression of sexual feelings and erotic sensations, as do the following practices.

THE RITUAL OF PURIFICATION

This ritual may seem simple, but it offers an effective way of enhancing awareness and appreciation of your body before beginning the practices that follow.

Purpose and Benefits

The ritual gives you the feeling of being firmly centered in your body, and this centering is vital to High Sex because it is within the body that the movement toward ecstasy happens. The Ritual of Purification can help you on a regular basis to make a distinct transition from your daily activities to the sacred atmosphere of your training in High Sex.

Preparations

You can regard the instructions for this practice and for the exercises that follow as stage directions that lay out the scenario in which you can honor and energize your body. You and your partner are challenged to act out the scenes in your own distinctive way. Let the playful child, the actor in you, have fun creating these rituals of body awareness.

These practices are most effective when done in a spirit of play, and there is no standard against which you must measure your performance. You can relax, knowing that as long as you give yourself wholeheartedly to each exercise, that's enough. If doubts arise about how well you are doing, don't fight them; just acknowledge that you have the feelings, and continue the exercise with calm commitment.

Each practice is designed to ease you gently into the next, so don't alter the sequence. You can do all of them in one evening, if you wish. The best way is for you and your partner to do the first three practices simultaneously but separately—using different rooms—then come together for the rest. This separation at the beginning allows you to focus on your own body, heightens the sense of mystery about the other person, and lets the drama build before you meet.

Before you start, agree with your partner about the time when you will meet. Give yourselves plenty of undistracted time. You will need about three hours to complete the whole sequence.

Allow about 45 minutes for this first practice.

Practice

Sit quietly and alone for 10 minutes. Breathe deeply and evenly. Watch your thoughts come and go. Tell yourself that you are putting your mind in a supporting role and that it is now the body's turn to come center stage and receive your attention. Support this focus on your body with assuring, relaxing, healing thoughts, such as: "I love and appreciate my body just as it is," or "My relationship with my body is happier every day." Imagine that you are preparing yourself for a great occasion, and let each step be done with a sense of ceremony.

When you feel calm and centered, stand up, slowly disrobe, and step into your shower. Begin the shower with very hot water. This relaxes the muscles and draws your vital energy to the inner core of your body. Exhale deeply as you allow the water to run longer on muscles that may feel tense. Imagine them gradually loosening under the water, melting away the contractions, as you continue to breathe deeply.

When you feel relaxed, change to cold water. Let yourself make sounds as your body responds to the shock. Successively expose each part of your body to the cold, starting with your legs, then your spine, arms, the front of your body, your neck, face, and the top of your head. The cold will act as an astringent to draw the energy of the body toward the surface of the skin and accelerate blood circulation. Breathe vigorously under the cold water, and jump, shout, and growl to energize yourself. You will emerge feeling revitalized, ready for adventure.

Towel yourself dry, slowly, sensually, paying full attention to the texture of the dry, clean towel on your skin.

Pay careful attention to your hands. Clean them thoroughly and trim your nails. It is important to have short, clean nails because you will soon begin to explore many forms of intimate contact, during which you can hurt each other or yourself with long nails. Put soothing cream on your hands so your skin is soft to the touch.

Brush your teeth and freshen your breath. Even though you are doing ordinary things, avoid falling back on routine behavior. Keeping the sense of ceremony makes them special. Put some drops of essential oil of mint on your tongue to freshen your breath, or use your favorite breath freshener.

Men would do well to shave just before a practice session. The rough skin of a day-old beard is unpleasant on a woman's skin. By contrast, the softness of a freshly shaved jaw, rubbed with a scented lotion, is irresistible.

My personal preference is to wear fragrances. Covering your body with perfumes and essential oils of plants creates an atmosphere of luxury and romance. The use of different fragrances on different parts of the body can surprise and delight your partner. For instance:

☐ Mint on the navel awakens the sense of power and centeredness.
☐ Lavender on the temples and behind the ears relaxes and soothes.
☐ Ylang-ylang or vanilla on the perineum acts as a sexual stimulant, warming skin tissue in the area. Make sure it is pure natural extract of the ylang-ylang flower—synthetics may hurt your skin.
☐ Lemon or lemon grass on the legs improves circulation.
☐ Eucalyptus on the chest and lungs opens up the breathing.
☐ Sandalwood between the eyebrows and on the crown of the head enhances calmness and meditation.

By now you should be feeling crisp, clean, and energized, ready to establish the strength of your body through the Basic Stance.

THE BASIC STANCE

This exercise is a simple yet important way of feeling rooted to the earth and being grounded and centered in your body.

Purpose and Benefit

This practice generates energy in the body and will be used in some of the later practices in the book. Returning to this posture is particularly beneficial when you find yourself drifting away from an exercise and when you feel afraid to confront a certain situation.

The basic stance.

Preparations

You need to be supported by a solid base. Mattresses and other unstable surfaces are unsuitable. If possible, choose either a thin carpet, tiles, or a wooden floor.

Give yourself three to five minutes.

Practice

Stand with your feet flat on the floor, parallel, as wide apart as your shoulders. Bend your knees in a slight crouch, as if you are skiing, while keeping your back straight, with your head straight forward and your torso leaning neither backward nor forward. Your vertebrae should be straight and your spine erect from your lower back to the top of your neck.

Let your arms hang loosely at your sides. Keep your jaw and belly relaxed, and breathe through your mouth.

Now settle comfortably into the stance. Feel how firmly you are planted on the ground, yet remain fully alert and ready to move. Explore how from this Basic Stance you can rotate from side to side, lean forward and back, and move into dancing and jumping while remaining centered and strong. Establish the feeling of strength and rootedness.

If you experience pain in your calves or thighs during this practice, rock back slightly, and shift the weight of your body to your heels. This should ease the tension. You also can try slowly shifting your weight from your right foot to your left and back.

Close the practice with a Heart Salutation to yourself.

THE CEREMONY OF RECOGNITION OF THE BODY

In this ceremony you greet your body as your temple, honoring each part in turn. You also prepare yourself in order to be able to honor your partner.

Purpose and Benefit

This ceremony helps you recognize that your body, whatever its particular form, is the essential vehicle through which you achieve the fullness of your sexual potential.

Preparations

The ceremony is done best in a quiet room with soft light from a few candles and with a mild incense burning. Place body lotion or oil mixed with your favorite perfume or essences in a bowl. You will apply it to each part of your body as you proceed.

If you feel stiff in the beginning, limber up, put on some music, and dance around for a while. When you feel warm and vibrant, stop the music and start the practice. Allow about 20 to 30 minutes for the ceremony.

Practice

Stand naked in front of a full-length mirror.

Do a Heart Salutation to your image in the mirror.

Taking a few deep breaths, observe your body image, and watch your reactions as you do so. If you have any judgments or self-criticism, simply observe them, and let them go without becoming identified with them. If you come across certain parts of your body that you cannot easily accept, remember that you are living in this temple, but *you* are not your body. You are the human spirit that inhabits the temple and is learning about it. Try to accept even your lack of acceptance.

Standing or sitting, apply perfume to each part of your body, touching each part with love and care, giving it conscious recognition. As you do so, repeat the following affirmations once.

"My feet are the vehicle of my spirit and I honor them."
"My legs are the vehicle of my spirit and I honor them."
"My hands are the vehicle of my spirit and I honor them"
"My arms are the vehicle of my spirit and I honor them."
"My pelvis is the vehicle of my spirit and I honor it."
"My sexual center is the vehicle of my spirit and I honor it."

*If I worship any particular thing
it shall be some of the spread
of my body;
Translucent mould of me it shall
be you.*

—Walt Whitman
Leaves of Grass

"My anus is the vehicle of my spirit and I honor it."
"My navel and belly are the vehicle of my spirit and I honor them."
"My heart is the vehicle of my spirit and I honor it."
"My chest is the vehicle of my spirit and I honor it."
"My mouth and throat are the vehicle of my spirit and I honor them."
"My nose is the vehicle of my spirit and I honor it."
"My eyes are the vehicle of my spirit and I honor them."
"My ears are the vehicle of my spirit and I honor them."

Finally, applying perfume on the top of your head, say, "The crown of my head is the vehicle of my spirit and I honor it."

Place the palm of your left hand flat on the middle of your chest. Then lay the palm of the your hand on top of the left one. Feel the warmth of your hands flow into your chest. Remain silent for a moment, feeling the heartbeats resonating in your hands.

Repeat aloud in a neutral, even voice, "I become conscious of my body as my temple and I honor it" until you have a really deep sense of the meaning of these words.

Close with a Heart Salutation.

Pointers

Initially, as I've indicated, this exercise is best done alone, but with experience it is a rich practice to do with your partner. When you do this ceremony with your partner, one receives while the other gives, and then you exchange roles. The giver touches and honors the receiver's body at the genitals, navel, heart, lips, nose, eyes, and crown, while applying perfume and saying, for example, "Your eyes are the vehicle of your spirit and I honor them."

After you both finish, spend a few moments in silence, taking slow, deep breaths, relaxing, and tuning into the effect of the ceremony. Then lightly caress your whole body. It may feel different than before, more sensitive, more charged.

The Ceremony of Recognition of the Body is also a beautiful practice to do before receiving a massage.

THE ART OF EROTIC TOUCHING

The next three practices introduce you to the art of erotic touching and restore the role of touching to its rightful place in your sensual and emotional life. Many people have been deprived in their childhood of the nourishment that comes through being touched, held, and cuddled. Research has shown that this deprivation can cause emotional disturbances such as depression, hyperactivity, and aggression. Because cuddling is often considered a prelude to lovemaking rather than a tender activity in itself, there is a tendency for some people—women especially—to engage in sex when their real desire is only to be held and caressed.

FEATHERING

Purpose and Benefit

Like the Melting Hug, the practice of each Erotic Touching exercise fulfills the desire for sensual contact independently of the goal of love-making and opens the way to an integrated sexuality.

Preparations

The truly sensuous takes time and a feeling for the deliberate, undulating rhythms of the body and of nature.

—George Leonard

Now that you have each prepared yourself with the previous rituals, you may feel excitement about meeting your partner. You'll need about 90 minutes for the Feathering, Fingertip Stroking, and Slipping and Sliding exercises, which flow naturally from one to the next. And you may wish to practice for a longer period.

You will need some long, delicate feathers—peacock feathers are best—that allow you to experience the quality of touching and being touched with the utmost delicacy. This provides an antidote to the tendency in busy daily life to touch brusquely and with little sensitivity.

You'll also need some good olive oil or, if you prefer, another thick massage oil.

Play soft, sensual music.

Decide ahead of time who will be the giver and who the receiver. Partner A is the giver and Partner B the receiver. The giver can be lightly dressed. The receiver should be naked. Make sure the room is warm enough.

Practice

If you are the man, enter the Sacred Space first. Focus on the Shiva within, your own inner grace. Play welcoming music and sit in quiet contemplation, awaiting your partner.

If you are the woman, focus on the Shakti within, your own inner grace, and enter the Sacred Space when you hear the music your partner has switched on.

Look at each other with fresh appreciation. It is time to forget any misgivings about each other, put aside past and future concerns, and declare an absolute truce in honor of your bodies.

Throughout the exercise remember to use the Three Keys—deep breathing, movement, and expression.

Begin with a Heart Salutation, followed by a Melting Hug.

Partner A, gently help Partner B lie down.

Partner B, close your eyes.

Partner A, slowly begin to stroke each part of Partner B's body gently with the feather, starting around the shoulders and throat, then moving gradually and sensuously down the body, then finishing with the head.

Partner A, be sure to breathe deeply as you stroke and brush with the feather, consciously letting the energy of your heart—your caring, your appreciation, and your love—flow down through your arms and into the touching. The strokes need barely contact the surface of Partner B's skin. The energy charge, the excitement, will be all the greater for the subtlety of the touch.

Partner B, express your appreciation through sighs and sounds that reflect the sensations rippling through your body. Move your body sensuously and slowly, welcoming the touching, turning so as to allow the feather to reach all parts of your body.

After you have finished, switch roles. Feathering can be a delightful game that tingles both the skin and spirit. Inevitably, tickling all over makes both of you smile and laugh. You can heighten the playful effect by tickling unexpected yet sensitive places—the ear lobes, inside the elbows, wrists, hands, ankles, inside the thighs—altering the touching sequence in surprising ways.

FINGERTIP STROKING

The whole body has the capacity to be erogenous, and this is especially true of the fingertips. In acupuncture, the meridians that carry energy through the body end in the fingertips, so they are able to relay energy from other parts of your body in a very precise way.

Purpose and Benefits

In this practice you will be using each fingertip as a magic wand or electrical conductor, conveying the energy of the giver to the receiver. This practice is not a massage. The connection is as much electrical as physical. Let your fingertips be the sensory antennae through which you can "read" your partner's body, discovering and stimulating the most sensual places.

Preparations

Continue to play soft, sensual music.

Practice

Partner A, vigorously rub the palms of your hands together to build up warmth and energy in them. Using your fingertip like the peacock feather, lightly touch Partner B's body all over. The touching should be extremely subtle, barely stroking the skin.

You may want to try making little circles and strokes on the skin's surface. This can generate a palpable electricity that for the recipient feels as if the skin is effervescent. If Partner B does not feel anything, try long, deep strokes at first, followed by lighter ones, and finally come back to fingertip touching.

Let your fingering dance in rhythm with your beloved's responses so that gradually Partner B's body becomes aglow with tingling excitement. Touch all the erotic parts of the body, both the usual and the

Fingertip stroking.

unusual: behind the ears; on the eyelids, above and below the eyes; on the lips; inside the elbows and the wrists; on the palms of the hands; around and on top of the nipples and the navel; around the pubic area; inside the thighs; behind the knees; inside the ankles; under the feet; and on other special places you will discover yourself.

Once you have covered the whole body with light caresses, stand above your partner, straddling the waist and facing his or her head, lean down, and with both hands energetically sweep from the navel up across the chest, down the shoulders and arms in unified flowing motions, inhaling and exhaling as you do so. Repeat the movement three or four times with the aim of interconnecting all the parts of the upper body. Then take a couple of steps back. Straddle his or her lower legs, and do the same light brushing movements, starting from the navel and sweeping down over the pelvis, thighs, legs, and feet.

Allow Partner B to rest for a few minutes, then end this part of the practice with a Melting Hug.

Sit facing each other. Partner B, tell Partner A which moments you most enjoyed in Fingertip Stroking.

When you have finished the verbal exchange, switch roles with your partner.

End the whole practice with a Heart Salutation.

Pointers

Often people do not express their full desires in lovemaking, especially about where they like to be touched, so use the verbal exchange in this practice as an opportunity to tell your partner exactly what you like.

In Fingertip Stroking and the next practice, the giver should take care not to get lost in the giving, forgetting his or her own bodily sensations, as this may make you tired. While giving, remember to breathe deeply and to remain in comfortable positions that do not deplete your energy.

SLIPPING AND SLIDING

As these practices progress, you will focus more on your sexuality, moving from subtle sensations to more erotic feelings. This practice offers a sensuous, full body contact.

Purpose and Benefits

This exercise first sensitizes your bodies, then offers a relaxing massage to reduce tension and to prepare you for the next stage.

Preparations

Because this practice will require you to cover each other with a lot of oil, you will want to protect your floor or bed by lying on thick towels. I like olive oil best for this practice. You may be able to feel that it comes from olives that have ripened in hot sunshine, and if you are sensitive, your body can absorb this feeling. Many people I know find this association with sunshine sexually stimulating. Also, olive oil is extremely beneficial for the skin.

Choose music with a more dynamic rhythm for this practice.

Practice

Take some olive oil, mix in a few drops of essential oil of mint and gardenia, and lightly massage your partner all over. Have your partner do the same to you.

Stand together, then slide your body around your partner's with the slow, undulating movements of a snake. Explore every possible way of slipping and sliding around each other.

Then one partner should lie down while the other slides over him or her, letting the various parts of your two bodies slip sensuously over each other, using your hands, feet, face, arms, legs, genitals, buttocks, and back. For example, bracing yourself with your arms, you can slide your breasts or genitals ever so slowly up your partner's entire body, starting at the feet and going right up the legs, pelvis, and chest and across the face. Or you can slither over your beloved's chest from side to side and then back across the genitals.

Keep your breathing deep, your body relaxed, the atmosphere playful. Let your weight connect you with your partner, but at the same time use your hands to prevent pressing down too much.

The partner who is lying down need not be only receptive. In fact, you can invent a kind of slow-motion ballet as your bodies writhe and intertwine in harmony.

Change roles so that the one lying underneath also can be on top.

When you feel finished with your snake game, one partner should lie on his or her back while the other, sitting at the head, gently massages the receptive partner's neck to relieve any tension. Take the head in your hands as if it were a delicate china bowl. Lift it a little and gently rotate it from side to side. Gently rake the top of the vertebrae and the neck with your fingers, being sure to breathe deeply, inhaling into the downstroke and exhaling on the upstroke with no jerky movements. After the neck you can massage the skull, gently working the scalp with your fingers. Then you can spread your massaging down to the upper back, shoulders, and arms.

Change roles.

End with a Heart Salutation. Then wash the oil from your bodies.

Slipping and sliding.

145

For some people, following the sequence up to this point may be enough of an adventure for one evening. If you feel tired, don't worry. Stop now, and save the following exercises for the next session.

I encourage you, however, to go on and finish the exercises if you can. You have sensitized the body, building up a charge that can be used to liberate untapped sources of sexual energy.

THE SQUARE STRETCH

You and your partner can have a good time together as you stretch the hip joints, the knee and ankle joints, and the muscles that connect the pelvic floor to the hip bone.

Purpose and Benefits

The purpose of this exercise is to make your pelvis more open and supple in preparation for the advanced practices in later chapters. This practice also helps you develop a dialogue between your two bodies, as you learn how to trust, take the lead and follow, let go, and find a common rhythm.

Preparations

If you like, you can play some gentle rhythmic music to accompany this exercise. I like *Totem* by Gabrielle Roth and *White Winds* by Andreas Vollenweider.

You will need a lot of free space in which to make wide rotations. Allow 20 minutes.

Practice

Sit on the floor, facing your partner.

Begin with a Heart Salutation.

Sit with your back straight and your legs stretched in front of you at a 45-degree angle. If you can't stretch them so that they lie flat on the floor, you can put a small pillow under each knee.

You and your partner should face each other in this position, with the soles of your feet flat against each other's. Lean forward from the waist, keeping your spine as straight as possible, and firmly hold each

The square stretch.

other's wrists. Look into each other's eyes, and take some deep breaths. Make sure you both feel well-balanced and comfortable and can maintain good eye contact.

Begin to sway gently backward and forward. Inhale through your mouth as you go backward, and exhale through your mouth as you come forward. Imagine that your breath is carrying the movement. Think of the Three Keys, and use your voice to make sighs and grunts as you exhale to express whatever you are experiencing. Test the range of your movements back and forth, and notice that the deeper you breathe, the wider your movements can go. Eventually, if your joints are relaxed enough, you'll be able to lie down with your back on the floor as you are inhaling and to bend forward with your forehead touching the ground between your partner's thighs as you're exhaling.

As you experiment with this seesawing motion, keep your spine straight, and bend from the waist only. Keep your arms outstretched at all times. It is not really a question of pushing and pulling, but more a matter of letting your weight shift forward and backward. Keep your neck loose by rolling your head around from time to time. Remember to make sounds as you breathe deeply in and out.

After a while, you can try stretching one arm forward and the other arm back while your partner does the opposite.

*A successful relationship with re-
ality must be learned as a dance
is learned—not by contemplation
but by participation, by an exer-
tion of will, by movement, action,
and response. In order to derive
strength from God and the an-
gels, it is necessary to enter into
active contact with them, to push
against them with our muscles
and feel them with our senses.
We are formed not by abstract
laws but by the intimacies of a
wrestling match.*

—Deane Juhan
Job's Body

Then shift to moving in circles from the waist, clockwise and then counterclockwise. This movement easily becomes a rhythmic body dance and is excellent preparation for the bodily interplay of High Sex.

This exercise calls for constant, fluid movement, so be sure to keep moving. Don't stop and start. Feel how you are loosening the hip joints, knee joints, and lower back. This will help relax the pelvis during lovemaking.

Notice how your interaction with your partner proceeds; observe when and how you take the lead and when you give in and follow. Use the practice as a way of exploring the patterns in your relationship, seeing where you resist and where you respond and surrender. Gradually try loosening up the joints more and more, while not going beyond the limits of what is comfortable for you physically and psychologically. Let your breathing carry your movement.

End with a Heart Salutation.

When you are finished, talk about what you felt for a few minutes. Then get up, shake out your hands, arms, and legs; wiggle your hips; and enjoy the tingling but relaxed feeling of standing on your own two feet again. You may notice that your pelvis feels wider, more open. This loosening and centering is integral to releasing your sexual potential.

Pointers

As in the Heart Salutation, your movements in this exercise should come from the waist and the hips, not from bending the back, which should be kept straight.

Do not push yourself or overstretch. If at any point you feel you're being extended too far, just say "No"; "Ease up"; "Slow down"; or whatever is appropriate.

If you have back problems, it's best to do this exercise on your own first so that you have better control in testing your limits. Avoid pulling each other too violently. Be gentle and respect each other's limits.

SQUATTING TOGETHER

This is an ancient exercise that has assumed many forms in different cultures through the centuries. In "getting down," you're instinctively connecting with the earth, your animal nature, your bodily roots.

Purpose and Benefits

Squatting strengthens the pelvic floor and abdominal muscles; massages the intestines; relaxes the anus; loosens the hip, knee, and ankle joints; and stretches out the spine.

Squatting exercises are especially beneficial for women who enjoy lovemaking on top of the man, because they strengthen the thigh muscles, allowing the woman to move up and down in an easy manner.

Preparations

This practice requires an uncluttered space in case you fall backward while working to maintain your balance.

Don't try to do this exercise in tight-fitting pants.

Keep your feet flat on the floor for the best stretching of the leg muscles. Avoid placing your weight on your toes or on the balls of your feet. If it proves difficult at first to keep your feet flat while squatting, you can elevate your heels with a pad.

Allow 15 minutes.

Play gentle, rhythmic music.

Squatting together.

Practice

Stand opposite your partner, and look into each other's eyes. Maintain eye contact whenever possible throughout the exercise.

Slowly sink into the squatting position. Breathe deeply through your mouth, and feel the breath massaging and expanding your rib cage, internal organs, and upper back.

Keep your feet flat on the floor, stretch out your hands by your sides—not touching the floor—and begin a gentle rocking motion forward and backward. The pressure will shift from one set of muscles to another as you move back and forth, stretching one set and relaxing the other. Test the range of your balance in both directions.

It is best if your knees rest under your armpits, thus keeping your shoulders and chest loose. Let your neck and head hang loose. Make no effort to keep them straight.

After you've done this rocking successfully for a while, imagine that the bottom of your spine has an anchor suspended from it that pulls it down toward the earth. Without moving your feet, slowly rotate around this axis. You'll notice a light twisting movement that stretches the pelvic

Squatting and rocking.

muscles sideways into the hip joints. Move side to side as well, exploring all the possible movements, big and small.

As you exhale, let out some healthy grunts or sighs, and see how they relax you even more.

While squatting alone, imagine that you are on top of your partner and making love in this posture. Then, keeping your head down and your knees bent, slowly raise your buttocks, feeling the strength in your thigh muscles. After a few moments lower your buttocks. Repeat this movement in rhythmic succession, slowly at first and then quickly, up and down. Make grunting or sighing sounds that go with these movements.

Continue this for three minutes or so on your own. Then stretch out and take your partner's hands or wrists in yours, and start the exercise over again, this time holding hands. Make sure your feet are close to each other's, while your arms are stretched out and taut the whole time to give you leverage. Pull each other so that you rock gently back and forth. Then you can try sideways circles and the other patterns.

Try going up and down together and holding the position for a while at the top. Feel the power and balance you have in this seemingly awkward position. Feel how the power center just below your navel gives

Squatting and stretching.

you a sense of the delicate point between pushing and pulling. You need only balance your weight against each other to maintain this position. This dynamic position can be an image that represents your whole relationship.

Pointers

In this practice you need to be sensitive and trust each other so that you can achieve the fine balance required. It can be great fun. Here, as elsewhere, a playful attitude will help you to avoid feeling stiff and awkward.

THE PELVIC CURL

These practices are based on the discovery by Wilhelm Reich and his successors in bioenergetic therapy that the release of orgasmic energy through the whole body is intimately related to the rocking movements of the pelvis, enhanced by certain breathing patterns. The following practices teach you how to simulate the orgasmic reflex and let go of muscular tensions that inhibit orgasmic release. It is possible that you will experience genital orgasm during these practices.

Purpose and Benefits

The Pelvic Curl is inspired by my friend Jack Painter, creator of the Postural Integration method of bodywork. It increases your pelvic flexibility and involves you in the rhythms of thrusting forward and drawing inward that are fundamental to energetic lovemaking.

The pelvis is your power house, the place where you generate, store, and distribute your sexual energy. In exercising the pelvis, you may come to a point where you need to release emotions connected with your upbringing and sexual history. This release will free your pelvis of fears and tensions and enhance your erotic sensitivity.

Most of the time you may feel only certain areas of your pelvic region, such as the hip joints or the bones you sit on. But the pelvic floor—the buttocks, anus, and perineum—remains relatively insensitive. This insensitivity is more learned than natural. For instance, rushed toilet training often teaches people to tighten up the whole pelvic musculature as a way of controlling their bowels.

The purpose of the Pelvic Curl is gradually to open up the pelvis, using rhythmic rocking, expressive sounds, and breathing to intensify the energy charge in this area. The pumping effect on the pelvic muscles increases blood flow, thereby enhancing sexual sensations in the genitals. This increased charge contributes to the experience of orgasm during lovemaking.

Preparations

In the previous exercises you have built up an energy charge through the whole body. Now you can focus on mobilizing this energy in the pelvis. You will know when this happens because you will feel a warm, tingling sensation in the pelvic floor and genitals, as well as perspiration, lubrication, and slight reflexlike vibrations priming you for sexual activity.

Once these feelings arise, you need to connect these sensations to fast, expressive breathing in order to spread the sexual excitement throughout the body. There is no established way of proceeding, because the Pelvic Curl is not an artificial aerobic exercise but a tuning into the body's natural, built-in patterns of erotic energy charging and release.

In my experience there is an energetic connection between the pelvis, throat, and eyes. In order to achieve maximum mobility of the pelvis in this practice, it is important to maintain eye contact, move the neck, open the throat, and let out sounds in sighing and shouting. When the pelvis opens and becomes energized, long-repressed emotions often come to the surface. You may feel like crying or shouting with rage. Simply let these emotions be expressed as you keep going. Don't be deterred or upset by them—the release will be healing and freeing.

In this practice you will be doing two kinds of Pelvic Curls, first downward then upward. The Downward Pelvic Curl is a gentle and feminine approach to charging the pelvis with energy. The Upward Pelvic Curl is more dynamic and corresponds to what the pelvis does automatically during orgasmic reflex, so it may feel like falling into a familiar groove. It is important to experience these different kinds of pelvic rocking. See which one feels most beneficial for you.

Maintain eye contact with your partner throughout. Or, if you are doing the practice by yourself, stand in front of a mirror so that you can gaze into your own eyes to stay centered.

Give yourself about 30 minutes for this exercise, and make sure you are not interrupted. Stopping abruptly may reinforce the kinds of muscular and breathing contractions that you are attempting to heal.

You can use dynamic music such as African drumming (see Appendix II) for this practice.

Practice

As a warmup, you and your partner can march around the room, shouting "Ha!" repeatedly and vigorously, pounding your feet on the floor and jumping up and down to the drum music for five to ten minutes. Then stand facing your partner, leaving about two feet between you. Adopt the Basic Stance and look into each other's eyes. If you practice alone, stand in front of a full-length mirror.

Let your arms hang loosely by your sides. Pay attention to the way your neck is connected to your whole spine so that sensations and movement in your spine can ripple up into your neck and head.

Close your eyes and focus on how you are feeling inside. Be aware of your sense of rooted balance. Breathe deeply through your mouth down into your belly, letting your belly hang loose. Allow your genital

Downward pelvic curl.

and anal muscles to relax. As you do so, imagine that you are breathing all the way down through your stomach into your sex center.

After a few minutes, open your eyes and look at each other. Sustaining excitement while keeping in contact with each other is a key ingredient in High Sex.

Begin the downward method of the Pelvic Curl.

THE DOWNWARD PELVIC CURL. Start a forward and backward rocking movement with your pelvis. Keep your chest and spine relaxed yet straight, with the rocking motion coming only from your pelvis. As you inhale, thrust forward without tensing the pelvic muscles. Let the squeezing of the buttock muscles be gentle and light. For these forward thrusts cultivate the feeling of "going for it," the driving, dynamic dimension of sexual experience.

As you exhale let your pelvis fall back, relaxing your inner thighs, buttocks, and pelvic muscles. It is less a question of doing something than

155

just letting the pelvis fall back into its natural position. In this backward movement cultivate the feeling of letting go.

Keep your torso still and relaxed, letting only your pelvis move back and forth. It may help to imagine your pelvis swinging back and forth on the horizontal base of your hips. Also, keep your knees slightly bent and still, not moving up and down.

Rock back and forth with strong movements, vigorously pulling and releasing these powerful muscles for at least five minutes. Add your voice to the movements, saying "Ha!" in a gentle, sensual manner each time your pelvis falls back.

After some practice you will feel the excitement build, especially as you coordinate thrusting your pelvis forward as you inhale and relaxing your pelvis as you exhale more precisely.

Gradually you can quicken the pace, going faster and louder, with stronger movements, making increasingly intense sounds, as if you are approaching orgasm. Your breathing can step up into panting, your shouts can get higher, moving up from your belly into your chest.

Keep up this faster pace for about three minutes. Then slow down, letting your voice come back down and allowing the "Ha" sound to fall down into your sexual center as you exhale, as if you are pushing it out through your genitals. Let your breathing move into your belly. Keep inhaling as your pelvis curls forward and exhaling as your pelvis falls backward. Let the "Ha" sound become lower and resonate in your belly. This cool-down also can take about three minutes.

Now you can start a new cycle, again building up gradually to a fast pace and a climax of excitement, then slowing down but continuing. This time include the rest of your body in the rocking. Let the pelvic movement run like a wave through your torso, neck, and head. Continue with the "Ha!" sound, abdominal breathing, and eye contact. You can do this for about three to five minutes.

Continue this cycle of charge and discharge for about 15 minutes, then slow down and stop. Close your eyes and focus inward on your pelvis and genitals, keeping your knees bent and your pelvis relaxed. Notice whether you feel any tingling sensations, warmth, vitality, pulsations. If so, you're well on your way toward the pelvic flexibility and charging necessary for High Sex.

THE UPWARD PELVIC CURL. Now we can proceed with the same practice, but invert the movement so that your pelvis arches back and up slightly as you inhale and drops down and forward as you exhale.

Upward pelvic curl.

Adopt the Basic Stance with your pelvic floor muscles relaxed, and let your arms hang loosely at your sides.

Start the pelvic rocking. Curl your pelvis backward as you inhale, and let it fall forward as you exhale, relaxing all the pelvic, genital, and buttock muscles.

Arch your back slightly as you inhale, and rotate your pelvis backward. As you exhale bear down and push out with the "Ha!" sound to release tensions and open the area. Again, your pelvis should swing back and forth while remaining horizontal, not going up and down. Imagine that your pelvis is a big ball rotating on itself.

Once you have the hang of this movement, you can intensify the rocking and the "Ha!" sounds. As you inhale, imagine that you are taking energy into your genitals and pelvis, as if you are sucking in your partner's love energy.

Experience the difference between this movement and the previous one. Many people find this one more masculine. There seems to be a natural tendency to want to push forward on the exhalation, and many enjoy the feeling of power in this movement.

You can accentuate this "macho" experience by tightening your anus and buttocks as you push your pelvis forward as you exhale. If you are a woman, you can imagine having an erect penis between your legs and penetrating your partner in front of you. In this way you can play out your aggressive sexuality as a wild game of release.

Feel the two-way rhythm of taking in energy as you inhale and giving it out as you exhale. Again you build the movement up to an intense pitch and then wind down. Let your whole body move with the rhythm.

Continue this practice for 15 minutes, then slow down and stop. Close your eyes, and again be aware of any new sensations in your pelvis.

Pointers

Do the Downward Pelvic Curl and Upward Pelvic Curl dynamically and long enough to allow a real energy charge to build up in your body. You will know this has happened when you feel sweat, body heat, aliveness, quickening of the breath, and a tingling in your genitals.

In the beginning it may be too much for you to concentrate on the exercise and keep looking at each other. In this case, keep your eyes closed until you feel you have mastered the exercise and are enjoying it. Then open your eyes. You can alternate between having your eyes open and closed, noticing the different feelings that arise. It can take several regular sessions of this exercise to get to the point of experiencing pelvic sensitivity and flexibility.

If you don't feel anything during this exercise, you may be holding tensions in your throat, mouth, or the back of your neck. Try to open and relax these areas by sucking your thumb or making sucking motions and noises with your mouth. These release energy in the throat, which has the effect of relaxing the pelvis.

If you still don't feel anything after several sessions, wait until you have gone through the practices in chapters 9 and 10, which will tremendously enhance your pelvic sensitivity.

You may find that you can enhance pelvic sensitivity during this practice by placing one hand lightly on your pubic area, loosely cupping your genitals and the pelvic floor, and the other at the base of your spine.

Imagine you are holding your pelvis like a cup. Feel how this position conveys a sense of being supported, contained, and rooted.

If you find that the Pelvic Curl exercises are too much of a challenge at this stage, you can work up to them by starting with the Pelvic Bounce, which is a helpful exercise in its own right. For the Pelvic Bounce you follow the basic instructions for the two versions of the Pelvic Curl, but you do it lying down. This is done by lifting your pelvis off the floor and then bouncing down. Proceed vigorously with this up-and-down bouncing, lifting your pelvis up as you inhale and letting it fall to the floor as you exhale while making the explosive "Ha!" sound.

See if you can move beyond the seriousness of following instructions into the playful excitement of simulating an orgasm.

THE OPENING LOTUS

After expanding your energy in an active and dynamic way with the Pelvic Curl, it will be beneficial to draw the energy back into yourself to a place of stillness and peace through a practice that I call the Opening Lotus. As I explained in the previous chapter, moving from high-energy exercises to stillness brings an alive quality to quiet, reflective moments.

Purpose and Benefits

The Opening Lotus posture is used in Tantra, yoga, Zen, and many other spiritual traditions. It promotes self-contemplation, calmness, and tranquillity and allows you to go inside your body easily and become aware of its subtlest sensations.

Later in the book you will be using the Opening Lotus posture in advanced practices of High Sex, in which the body is kept vertical. In the horizontal position of lovemaking, energy naturally gathers in the pelvis, but in the vertical position a connection can easily be established between the pelvis and the head, enabling sexual energy to be transformed into subtler and more ecstatic sensations.

My purpose in introducing it to you now is to help you familiarize yourself with the position. Although the Opening Lotus has no movements, it requires just as much practice as the Pelvic Curl. The more flexible and comfortable you can become in the Opening Lotus, the more easily you will be able to experience High Sex.

Preparations

You can do this posture alone or with a partner. Find a firm, comfortable, supportive cushion or pillow to sit on. The round meditation cushion used in Zen, known as a *zafu,* is probably the best. It is available in shops that sell Japanese meditation supplies.

Create the Sacred Space.

Minimize external distractions and sounds. You can use peaceful, relaxing music.

Allow 20 minutes for this practice.

Practice

Sit on the pillow so that your belly is relaxed and your knees can touch the ground. Fold your legs, Indian-style, and tuck them in toward your groin.

Let your belly hang loose. I call this the "Buddha belly." Do not constrict your waist with a belt or sash. Do not arch your back. Keep it straight yet relaxed. Keep your neck aligned with your spine, your chin slightly tucked in toward your chest, your shoulders relaxed.

Put your hands on your knees. Your palms can be turned up in a spirit of receptivity or down for a sense of strength and groundedness. For a taste of meditation, your hands can be joined, palms up, right palm resting in your left and thumbs touching. Experiment with each hand position, and note how it alters your mood.

Breathe slowly and evenly through your nose, feeling the air entering and leaving your nostrils. Feel the cool air moving in and the warm air going out. Let your jaw relax.

Sit for 20 minutes, observing your breath. Do not direct your mind or manipulate your thoughts. Simply observe whatever passes through it. Enjoy the relaxed, contemplative attitude of the witnessing state.

End with a Heart Salutation, either to yourself or to your partner.

Pointers

In this posture let your knees touch the ground. This relaxes the belly and opens up the front of the body. To help your knees drop down farther, you can use a higher pillow to raise up your pelvis.

The Opening Lotus.

Hands in meditation.

The Opening Lotus posture is difficult to maintain if your thigh and hip muscles are tense. To help relax them, practice the Square Stretch and Squatting Together. It is essential that you gradually familiarize yourself with this position until you can feel comfortable in it because it will prepare you for the advanced practices in chapter 12. Adopt this position every day for at least ten minutes.

☙❧

In this chapter you learned to center and ground yourself through the Basic Stance, to honor your body as the vehicle of your spirit through the Ritual of Purification and the Ceremony of Recognition of the Body, and to explore a progression of sensual sensations through the Art of Erotic Touching. You also learned to loosen and relax your body through Square Stretching and Squatting Together, to open and relax your pelvis and build up a strong energy charge through the Pelvic Curl, and to experience inner stillness and develop self-observation through the Opening Lotus.

Remember to repeat these practices regularly on a daily or weekly basis so that you can fully enjoy them and benefit from the advanced levels of this training, in which each of these practices plays an essential part.

In the next chapter you will develop the strength of your genital muscles, enhance sexual sensations, and open the Inner Flute—the secret channel that connects the body's energy centers, learning how to channel orgasmic energy through the Inner Flute to the entire body.

~ネ~

OPENING THE
INNER FLUTE

A t first the concept of an Inner Flute on a vertical line within your body may seem strange. To understand what I mean, imagine listening to a piece of music that has everything except the main instrument. It may be rock and roll without the lead guitar, or a Mozart woodwind concerto without the flute. You hear the rhythm, the piece is vaguely familiar, but somehow the essential element that would weave it together, set the mood, and give the music soul is missing.

Often ordinary sex is like playing music without the main instrument. The exchange begins beautifully, but the crescendo is interrupted, or the instruments are poorly tuned, and the experience is flat. Some element is missing that would allow the lovemaking to take off, to contain a "tune." In this chapter you identify the Inner Flute as the instrument that will make your sexual energies "sing." You will learn how to find it within yourself, and, step by step, how to begin playing it. As you open the Inner Flute channel, you learn how to amplify your arousal and redistribute your sexual energy, your orgasmic sensations, to your entire body. Without the Inner Flute the sexual music played on the single instrument of the genitals could not expand so readily into a symphony in which the whole body becomes involved. Through this practice you will discover the fallacy of the popular belief that sexual orgasm is exclusively a genital affair.

Traditionally, the Taoists have called this secret channel the Hollow Bamboo. I call it the Inner Flute because I experience it as an instrument on which I can teach myself and others to play the most ecstatic music. As the name suggests, it is an inner pathway that begins at the perineum— the point that lies between the anus and the genitals—and moves up

Love is the secret key; it opens the door of the divine. Laugh, love, be alive, dance, sing, become a hollow bamboo and let His song flow through you.

—Bhagwan Shree Rajneesh

through the middle of the body and the center of the head to the crown. Some women prefer to visualize the Inner Flute beginning inside the vagina, as it is easier for them to feel it there.

DISCOVERING THE INNER FLUTE

The discovery of your Inner Flute can be a deeply transforming experience. James, for example, was an internationally known photographer, a very attractive man, who participated in several of my training programs. His main complaint was that he was obsessed with seducing and conquering the young models with whom he worked. He was extremely successful in this, but gradually he came to understand that he had no control over the impulse. Instead of feeling like a lover, he began to feel enslaved by his own sex drive. When he felt turned on by a woman, he would immediately lose all sense of concentration until he had made love with her, and then he would resent the depletion of his vital energy.

"I follow my penis around like a dog chasing its own tail," he told the other participants. I explained to him the possibility of transforming his sexual energy by internalizing it instead of throwing it out in ejaculation, and channeling it upward through his body. I said that however strange this practice might sound, it would allow him to enter the more feminine and receptive aspect of his nature.

During the training I saw James struggle tremendously with this effort to switch the direction of his sex drive. He was a difficult case, with long-ingrained sexual habits, but he really worked hard at the practices. Then it happened. One morning he came to the session and told us about the lovemaking he had enjoyed with his girlfriend, Elsa, a gorgeous model, the night before.

"I was feeling very relaxed when Elsa approached me and offered to seduce me, saying, 'You don't have to do anything, I want to take the initiative,' " he said. "I readily agreed. I wasn't feeling particularly sexual, but an offer like that—well, I simply couldn't refuse. She caressed my body very softly and slowly, then massaged and kissed my genitals. It was a very pleasant sensation, but even though I quickly got an erection, there was nothing in me that wanted to take over in the conventional male way. I just lay there and received.

"I was aware of the exercises concerning the Inner Flute that we had been practicing, but at this point I was totally relaxed, open to anything,

The Inner Flute, a secret channel of sexual energy.

not expecting anything in particular. I felt myself coming close to a genital orgasm, but instead of pushing for it as I usually do, I remained completely passive. As the orgasm happened, there was a sudden, swift movement of energy that shot straight up through my body to the brain, where a much stronger orgasm happened—like fireworks silently bursting into pretty colors in the sky. It all happened very fast, but the movement of energy was unmistakable; it shot like a bullet or, perhaps more like a small tidal wave, right from my genitals to my brain. That's when I felt the Inner Flute for the first time. It was an exhilarating experience. I felt that all the practices I'd been doing had finally borne fruit."

James discovered that he could balance the pleasures of the explosive male orgasm with this new, more internal, quiet orgasm. From then on he was much more centered, and he experienced orgasm not only as a genital reflex but also as a gentle, ecstatic vibration that he could allow to spread through his whole body.

A Subtle Pathway

Imagination is the ability to create an idea or mental picture in your mind. In creative visualization you use your imagination to create a clear image of something you wish to manifest. Then you continue to focus on the idea or picture regularly, giving it positive energy until it becomes objective reality . . . in other words, until you actually achieve what you have been visualizing.

—Shakti Gawain
Creative Visualisation

Although the Inner Flute has not been recognized as an anatomical fact of life, it does follow actual physical and neurological pathways through the body that connect the endocrine glands. These seven glands—the sex glands, adrenals, pancreas, thymus, thyroid, pituitary, and pineal—regulate the body's vitality and energy flow. By opening the Inner Flute through the practices I suggest, you "irrigate" these subtle pathways, producing an impression of vitality, rejuvenation, and increased sexual energy.

To Tantric and Taoist masters, this approach to rejuvenation was well-known, and the concept of the Inner Flute is mentioned in several ancient texts. In the book *Tibetan Yoga and Secret Doctrines,* W. Y. Evans Wentz describes an exercise in which the advanced meditator, learning the art of self-rejuvenation, visualizes a nerve canal running from a point between his legs to the top of his head, possessing the following characteristics: "redness like that of a solution of lac, brightness like that of the flame of a sesamum oil lamp, straightness like that of an inner core of the plantain plant, and hollowness like that of a hollow tube of paper."

We, too, will be using visualization to create an experience of the Inner Flute, because imagery is a powerful way to influence physiology. Modern science is only just beginning to explore how this happens, but

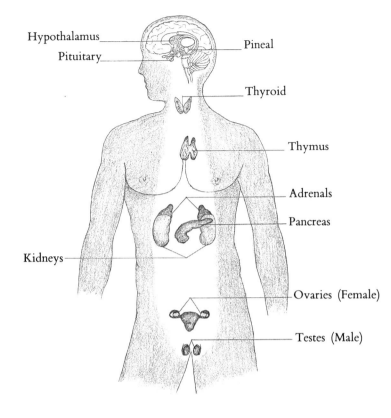

Hypothalamus

Pituitary

Pineal

Thyroid

Thymus

Adrenals

Pancreas

Kidneys

Ovaries (Female)

Testes (Male)

The endocrine glands and brain regulate your energy flow.

many people attest, for instance, to the power of visualization in healing common warts, and some doctors are teaching visualization to cancer patients to heal the sick cells in their bodies.

The experience of the Inner Flute will never come through intellectual persuasion, but only through repeated experimentation. It cannot be explained scientifically, but the results demonstrate that it works. You may be skeptical. Please don't let this prevent you from participating fully in these exercises. Here again, it is a question of practice making perfect. Many people never discover the bliss of High Sex simply because they cannot imagine that such a channel can be opened within them. Yet the potential for experiencing High Sex lies within everyone.

As you will see, the Inner Flute will not take anything away from the styles of lovemaking you have already developed and enjoy. On the contrary, it will enhance them, allowing you to modulate and expand your sensations and enabling you to choose from a variety of orgasmic experiences—implosive, explosive, localized in the genitals, expanded to the heart and the brain—that you will be able to develop through the practices in this book.

When you learn to feel and to play this Inner Flute, you will discover that you are the source of your own orgasm and that this orgasm can become an ecstatic energy event—stretched, expanded, subtle, colorful, like a beautiful balloon that gradually inflates and then soars into the evening sky.

Understanding the Chakras

The chakra is seen to be an intermediary for energy transfer and conversion between two neighboring dimensions of being, as well as a center facilitating the energy conversion between a body and its corresponding mind. As the chakras are activated and awakened, man not only becomes aware of the higher realms of existence, but also gains the power to enter those realms, and then, in turn, to support and give life to the lower dimensions.

—Hiroshi Motoyama
Theories of the Chakras

As a prelude to the Opening of the Inner Flute, I would like you to consider more deeply the implications of opening a channel between the genitals and the brain. You are going to learn to play this Inner Flute yourself, using seven finger holes that correspond to the seven chakras or energy centers in the body. These chakras are the symbolic representation of the energy fields created by the body's endocrine glands, mentioned earlier.

To get a better picture of what I am describing, think of the wind blowing through the blades of a windmill. This turns the mill, grinding the grain that produces flour for bread that people eat. In a similar way, energy that comes into the body through the throat chakra, for example, will stimulate the thyroid gland, affecting the growth of cells in the body and revitalizing the respiratory system.

Several physicians, including Dr. John Pierrakos, author of the book *Core Energetics* and cofounder, with Alexander Lowen, of the Institute for Bioenergetic Analysis in New York, are currently conducting research using the traditional Eastern system of chakras as a map of the body's subtle energies. Pierrakos calls the chakras energy wheels, and vortical centers shaped like funnels. B. K. S. Iyengar, a modern Indian teacher of hatha yoga, writes about the function of the chakras in this way: "As antennae pick up radio waves and transform them into sound through receiving sets, chakras pick up cosmic vibrations and distribute them throughout the body."

Pierrakos explains that the purpose of the centers is to draw energy from the surrounding atmosphere into the organism to charge it. "They [the chakras] are energy organs, as the kidneys and heart are physical organs, and they are as vital to human health. The energy they draw in

Energy funnels in the higher chakras.

is metabolized by the organism and distributed through the body, down to the cell level."

It may be easier for you to understand your own sensations during the practices if you understand the possible ways in which sexual energy may be transformed as it moves through the chakras while you open the Inner Flute. You don't have to believe in the existence of chakras, however, to benefit from the practices in this chapter. You can suspend both belief and disbelief, follow the indications I will give, and simply observe your own experience.

Rare are the people who, like Pierrakos, can actually see the chakras. But everyone can feel the sensations related to the chakras without necessarily realizing their origin. For example, chakra sensations include the sudden feeling of butterflies in the stomach when we are nervous or frightened; the tightness of a lump in the throat when we feel emotional and want to say something but cannot find the words; and the warm, erotic, melting sensation in the lower belly when we begin to be sexually aroused.

The middle of the chest is a particularly common place to experience sensations, for this is where the heart chakra is found. Recall, for example, a time when you had not seen your lover for a long time, and you went to the airport to meet him or her. The crowd of passengers was flowing out through the gate, and you were craning your neck to catch a glimpse. Finally, he or she walked out through the gate and smiled, and you felt as though your heart would surely burst because it had grown so big. This was not the physical heart you were experiencing, although it, too, was affected and was certainly beating a little faster. It was from the heart chakra that your love flowed, and it is the heart chakra, too, that produces the pain of heartbreak at the end of a love affair.

A Map of the Seven Centers

This secret of the higher level of Yoga is the stimulation and use of the latent nerve and brain centers, which are the seat of the spiritual centers, termed chakras *in the philosophy of Yoga, and the use of the only fuel absolutely indispensable for this purpose— sexual energy.*

—Elisabeth Haich
Sexual Energy and Yoga

In this section I provide you with a brief road map of the chakras and describe some of their qualities to give you an idea of the route we will be taking as this course unfolds.

When your sexual energy moves through the Inner Flute, it is modulated and transformed as it passes through each of these chakras, producing different sensations, feelings, and colors. Each color expresses and reflects the mood of a certain energy—for instance, the cheerfulness and brightness of yellow. Eventually you will get glimpses and tastes of the sensations related to all seven chakras.

THE SEX CHAKRA. The first chakra corresponds to the sexual center and is associated with giving birth, and the sensations of life and survival. When the energy is flowing freely through this chakra, you feel fired up with the sex drive, with a desire to go wild, and a need to be released or to be filled. Some people report having a mental image of this fiery energy as a dark red color that is diffused in the lower body, similar to the phenomenon of "seeing red" when a person becomes very angry. In the sex chakra you can have a sense of aliveness, a zest for life that for me is symbolized by someone like Zorba the Greek.

When this chakra is not fully relaxed and open, the energy is unable to flow freely, and the person experiences negative feelings such as a sense of scarcity, guilt about sex, fear of not having enough sex, or not being able to achieve a full orgasm. A person may also feel needy, both physically and emotionally, and unable to cope without a partner.

A map of the seven chakras—
the vital energy centers.

THE LOWER BELLY CHAKRA. The second chakra is located just below the navel. It is the body's natural center of balance and movement. In the traditions of China and Japan, where it is called *hara,* it is seen as the source of the body's vitality and the center of gravity for the martial arts. When your energy flows freely through this center, you feel strength, vitality, and an aliveness that exudes from a healthy, relaxed body. "Here," said one of my teachers, "the Tao of sex is fluidity and movement." Sexual energy is expressed through the movements of the pelvis, as in dance and physical playfulness.

When this chakra is closed, inhibiting the flow of sexual energy, a person can feel stiff, tense, critical of a partner, dissatisfied, jealous and competitive, and prone to sudden aggressive outbursts. In this closed state, one also experiences the "push-pull" syndrome commonly found in relationships: "I want you, but go away." Orgasm is reduced to a performance involving athletics, achievement, and release. One pushes so hard for the "big O" that it often becomes elusive.

This center is associated with the color orange, expressing the feeling of vitality.

THE SOLAR PLEXUS CHAKRA. This chakra is located in the central hollow just below the rib cage. Here sexual energy is felt as personal power, charisma, self-assurance—the ability to project yourself into the world and make things happen the way you want. When this chakra is relaxed and open, lovers feel as if they are masters of their emotions and capable of being equal partners. Their lovemaking expresses their power to transform and conquer, pouring their energy into each other. Orgasm here can be experienced as the ultimate expression of personal power—"you are mine."

When this center is tense or blocked, sex feels threatening; people fear that orgasm will take energy away or that they aren't up to it or good enough, or that premature ejaculation is an incurable condition.

This center is associated with the color yellow, expressing cheerfulness and radiance.

THE HEART CHAKRA. This chakra is located at the center of the chest, midway between the two nipples. Here sexual energy is experienced as a desire to merge and melt with another—a sense of two people being part of each other. There is a passion to share love, joy, and laughter; to be a playful child; to give just for the sake of giving. When this center is relaxed and open, you feel trust, empathy, and compassion. When it is closed, you experience doubt and cynicism and feel argumentative.

This chakra also marks a turning point in the voyage of the energy up the Inner Flute. Until now, the energy was oriented toward the physical body, pulled by gravity toward the earth, in need of being released through ejaculation. As love and sex meet, your experience becomes qualitatively different. Think of the difference between having sex and making love. When the heart is not involved, sex remains purely physical. You experience the momentary satisfaction of release, but it remains one dimensional. With love, sex is transformed into a higher, more healing, and ecstatic experience.

This chakra is associated with the color green, expressing hope and the springlike rebirth of freshness and creativity.

THE THROAT CHAKRA. When this chakra is open, you know who you are and what you want, and you can express it. You feel at ease with yourself and can remain authentic, even if it means being different from others, taking new initiatives, or even appearing rude or antisocial. For instance, you may enjoy shouting or saying wild things or communicating about your feelings truthfully during lovemaking. At this level you know exactly the style of lovemaking you like and the kind of lover you appreciate.

When this center is closed, you wonder what you are supposed to feel, and tend to cater to your partner's desires and needs rather than recognizing and following your own. As a result, you tend to imitate others and might fake orgasm to avoid appearing inadequate. Orgasmic sensations remain skin deep, as if someone else is experiencing them, not you.

This chakra is associated with the color violet, expressing the depth of wisdom.

THE FOREHEAD CHAKRA. The same energy, transformed and refined by its passage up the Inner Flute, arrives at a point in the center of the forehead, between and behind the eyebrows. When this happens, you feel like a person arriving at the top of the mountain after a long climb. The energy is crisp, fresh, and clear, with an expanded sense of space and freedom. You discover the powers of intuition and imagination, seeing inner visions—that's why this chakra is known in the East as the third eye. You follow hunches and understand things directly without having to use reason and logic. In this center, energy is often experienced as inner light.

When this center is closed, sexual experiences lose their sense of mystery and excitement, and life in general seems dull and devoid of higher qualities. There is no sense of a higher awareness or intelligence pervading the universe beyond the sense of "me" and "mine."

This chakra is associated with the color blue, expressing the coolness, panoramic vision, and detachment of a parachutist floating down through a clear blue sky.

THE CROWN CHAKRA. Finally, when the energy reaches the top of the head, you feel a joyful connection with everything and everyone around you. You feel you can expand beyond the boundaries of the body, as if you are pure space and larger than life. At this level sexual loving is an ecstatic, mystical experience, a merging with your partner on the physical, emotional, and spiritual levels. This is the part of you that knows, deep within, whether your actions are helping your life develop and fulfill itself. Through this center you reach to the realms of the soul—realms of peace, silence, and wonder. It is the center of higher creativity that creates a bridge between matter and spirit.

When this center is open, you are naturally spontaneous and playful, focused on what is happening here and now, in the present moment. You do not let the habits of the past control you. When this center is closed, you tend to live in a fantasy world or in some future utopia that you feel cannot be manifested in the real world. You do not have the capacity to transform sexual experience into a communion of the soul.

This center is associated with the color white, expressing clarity, neutrality, and illumination.

Generating Sexual Energy

None of the chakras is isolated from the others. They function as an interconnected system in which each one affects the energy of the rest. If one chakra is tense or out of balance, then the other chakras will be negatively affected and their vitality diminished. On the other hand, if one chakra gets healed and relaxed, this promotes the revitalization and expansion of the rest.

One of the benefits of the Inner Flute is that it can be used as an "irrigation system" to channel and distribute your energy evenly to each chakra, promoting health and vigor. The more you can learn to stimulate your chakras by using the Three Keys—breathing, movement, and sound—plus visualization, the more your energy will expand. Think of your chakras as beds of flowers and the Inner Flute as an irrigation channel through which they can be watered. You, as the gardener, must ensure that there is enough water to make the system work properly. That is why the following exercises are so important. They give you the energy you need in order to use the Inner Flute to maximum effect.

In this chapter we are primarily concerned with generating sexual energy and learning how to channel it into the Inner Flute. This is a step-by-step process, and you need not feel that you must open the whole Flute and all seven chakras immediately. At present, we are concerned only with the groundwork. You will need three to six weeks, practicing several times a week, to really acquire the art of generating sexual energy and channeling it into the Inner Flute. Then you will be able to expand orgasmic sensations through your entire body.

For women, these exercises can help you to heighten your sexual pleasure considerably and also teach you how to achieve vaginal orgasm *independently* of sexual penetration. For men, these exercises will help you to acquire greater staying power and a stronger erection, as well as the ability to spread pleasurable sensations beyond the genital area.

At first you should practice each of the following exercises independently. Then you can integrate the elements into a single, multidimensional experience.

THE PC PUMP

The pubococcygeus, or PC, muscle, spreads out like butterfly wings at the bottom of the pelvis to connect the anus and genitals to the sitting bones and legs. It is the basic muscle of the pelvic floor and controls the opening and closing of the urethra, seminal canal, vagina, and anus.

Your PC muscle is the one you have to rely on when you are stuck in a traffic jam, desperately wanting to urinate but unable to do so. You clamp down with your PC muscle to stop the flow of urine. It can feel like a valve, closing and opening around the genital area, and you may also feel a tightening around the anus. Men also feel the PC muscle when they bear down to squeeze out the last drops of urine. Women feel it most acutely when they push out during childbirth.

Purpose and Benefits

In an athletic workout it is helpful to pump and stretch your muscles, causing them to expand and fill with blood so the body is warmed up, less stiff, and more flowing. The same principles apply here. You will be pumping the PC muscle to give it more tone and vitality.

The PC muscles.

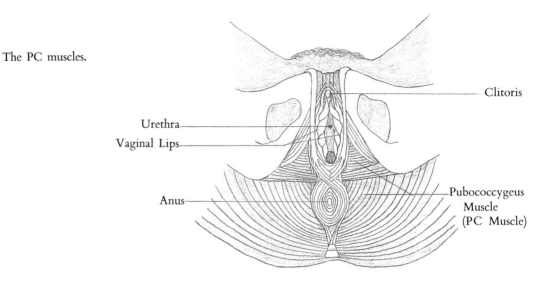

Clitoris

Urethra

Vaginal Lips

Anus

Pubococcygeus Muscle (PC Muscle)

For men this practice stimulates the flow of blood to the penis, enhancing both its ability to stay erect and its capacity to feel pleasure. Women can benefit by being able to hold the penis more tightly inside the vagina, thus improving erotic sensations for both partners. This pumping exercise not only conditions the PC muscle for sexual practice but also enables you to shoot sexual energy up the Inner Flute.

The rhythmic contraction and relaxation of the PC Pump happens naturally during sexual intercourse. It is also one of the main movements that occurs during orgasm at split-second intervals. So by making this movement slowly and consciously, you are strengthening your ability to expand orgasmic sensations during lovemaking.

Preparations

Prepare the Sacred Space.

Allow 20 minutes for your first practice.

Wear loose, comfortable clothing that does not restrict the hips and genitals.

Be ready to give yourself wholeheartedly to this exercise. Practicing the PC Pump is like doing push-ups in the pelvic area. It is very simple, but it takes a lot of practice to be able to do it smoothly and repeatedly.

In the beginning try it without music for better concentration.

Practice

For this exercise you can sit, stand, or lie on your back. The first phase of this exercise I call pulsing.

PULSING. Begin by tightening and relaxing the PC muscle in quick, short pulsations. At first you may involuntarily contract the abdominal muscles and the anus, too, because you are unable to differentiate between the muscles. Some people even contract the shoulders. But with practice you can detect and isolate the PC muscle while allowing other muscles to stay relaxed. It lies exactly between the genitals and anus, so focus your awareness in this area, making short, quick pulses with the PC muscle until you have a good feeling for it.

Now bring your breathing into the practice. Inhale, contracting the PC muscle as you do so, while keeping the rest of your body relaxed, especially your shoulders. As you exhale, relax the PC muscle. Repeat this for about three minutes, using your natural rhythm of breathing. Do not hold your breath, as you either inhale or exhale.

After a while see if you can feel a subtle tingling or tickling in the genital area. If not, continue pulsing with the PC muscle until you feel these sensations. Welcome any sensation of heat, coolness, tingling, sinking, or expanding. They are signs that your practice is yielding results.

PUMPING. When you are ready, move to the next step, which I call pumping. Tighten the PC muscle as you inhale. Then, when you have fully inhaled, hold it for a count of six seconds. Imagine that you want to urinate and are trying to hold in a full bladder. This will enhance your experience of the PC muscle.

Exhale, relaxing the PC muscle and gently bearing down as if you are forcing urine out of your body or having a bowel movement. Repeat this sequence for five minutes.

This pattern of inhaling while contracting the PC muscle, holding your breath, and then exhaling and relaxing the muscle, constitutes the PC Pump that we will be using throughout the book.

Women can increase their sensitivity in this practice by using visualization. Try imagining that your vagina is a mouth that, through the PC Pump, is slowly sucking in a medium-sized, ripe, juicy plum. It is sucking the plum from the vaginal opening to deep inside the vagina.

Allow your imagery to be colorful. Imagine this, your "lower mouth," sucking the juices of the plum, massaging its tender flesh, swallowing the fruit deeper and deeper inside you. When you have firmly established this image, imagine that instead of a plum your vagina is sucking, kissing, milking your partner's penis, massaging its sides until it feels so deeply drawn in that it cannot resist and grows bigger and bigger.

Men, as you do the PC Pump, imagine your penis is at the entrance of the moist, welcoming vagina of your partner. With each pump that you make, you are building up power for penetration, increasing your strength, showing your virility, coming to the entrance of the vagina, teasing the outer lips, gently pushing inside. As you penetrate, focus all your attention on the pumping movement. The more you pump, the more you establish the power of your penis's erected presence inside the vaginal canal, growing bigger, filling the space.

Feel the amplifying effect of your breathing on the rhythmic movement of the PC Pump. Through this practice you are beginning to open the Inner Flute, and as you move into the following practices, you will feel the sensations in your genital area grow and expand throughout your entire pelvis.

Pointers

If women practice the PC Pump while making love, they will discover after a while that they have the ability to bring a tired penis back to life, using the milking and sucking effect of their vaginal muscles. And later in this book, in advanced practices of lovemaking, they will enjoy the art of making love from within, without the need for external athletics. This is one of the secrets of High Sex.

Both men and women should contract and relax the PC muscle at least ten to fifteen times every day for a week. After a week, increase the pumping to at least 30 contractions a day. Keep it going daily. The development of this muscle requires regular attention. After ten days of daily practice, you will feel that your genitals have become more sensitive.

Gradually you can incorporate the PC Pump into other activities, such as sunbathing, reading, or watching TV. My experience is that if you can do 30 contractions a day, you will notice a difference in your lovemaking within a week.

If your PC muscle does not respond evenly—if, for example, you cannot maintain a tight PC muscle during the six seconds of holding your breath—this means the muscle is weak and unaccustomed to the demands you are now making on it. You simply need to practice to gain better control over its movement.

Some sexologists advocate training yourself to perform 100 to 200 contractions per day, but there is no need for such athleticism unless you happen to enjoy it so much that you naturally reach that level. Don't turn this practice into hard work. And don't overdo it, or you may get sore, especially in the beginning.

SEXUAL BREATHING

In this practice, using visualization, you will come to think of breathing as a function that spreads far beyond the lungs, all the way down to your genitals.

Purpose and Benefits

Sexual Breathing is essential to the art of learning how to play your Inner Flute. Combined with the PC Pump, it enables you to amplify sexual sensations and spread them through the body, bringing aliveness, awareness, and pleasure to areas that formerly lacked sensitivity.

Preparations

Make sure you have time to focus fully on this practice without distractions. Allow 30 minutes.

Create the Sacred Space.

You can be naked or dressed in loose-fitting clothes that are comfortable and do not restrict your breathing.

In this practice you are dealing with subtle energies. At first you may notice very little and wonder if you are doing it right. Don't worry—the feelings will grow as you tune into the rhythm of Sexual Breathing.

Avoid getting tense when practicing. Stay relaxed and use only the muscles required.

Sexual Breathing.

Practice

Lie on your back, and let your left hand rest gently on your genitals. Let your right hand cover your left hand. Feel that you are cradling and protecting your genitals. Close your eyes.

Pucker your lips, as if you are sucking on a large straw, and inhale gently and deeply through your mouth. Let the air make a sound like the wind as you inhale. Then relax your lips and your jaw, and let the air flow out. Inhale and exhale in this way until it seems natural. Imagine that you are a nursing baby, receiving warmth and nourishment from your mother's breast. Or, if you prefer, imagine that you are experiencing oral sex. Let the pleasure of these images comfort and relax you.

When you are ready, feeling at once relaxed and energized, combine Sexual Breathing with the PC Pump. As you inhale, contract the PC muscle. As you exhale, relax the PC muscle. Allow yourself a few minutes to become accustomed to this practice.

Now imagine, as you inhale, that you are sucking air into your body through your genitals. As you exhale, imagine the air flowing out again through your genitals. At first, as you inhale, imagine that the air is flowing only into your pelvic area. Then, as you become more familiar with the practice, visualize the air coming in through your genitals, entering the Inner Flute, and moving up through your body.

As the air moves into your Inner Flute, notice any feelings that come with it—a tingling sensation, perhaps, or warmth, or a feeling like trickling warm water. As you exhale, remember to allow the air to flow back down the Inner Flute and out through your genitals.

Continue in this way for at least five minutes, finding your own rhythm, concentrating on this image. Enhance any sensations in the genital area through your breathing and PC muscle contractions.

The spirit is the master, imagination the tool, and the body the plastic material. . . .

—Paracelsus

180

Then, as you inhale, keep your left hand on your genitals, and move your right hand up the path of the Inner Flute, starting at your genitals and, by the end of the inhalation, reaching your forehead or the crown of your head, whichever feels more natural. Pause, holding your breath for ten seconds. Then, as you exhale, move your hand back down your body. In effect, you are tracing the flow of air as it moves up and down the Inner Flute.

Let your visualizations become more detailed. As you inhale, imagine the air entering your body through your genitals and carrying your sexual energy with it up the Inner Flute through the seven chakras. Think of your breath as an elevator, your PC Pump as the motor, and the Inner Flute as the elevator shaft through which your breath is going to move. As you breathe in and contract the PC muscle, the elevator starts its journey up the shaft, moving through seven floors—the seven chakras in your body.

In your mind's eye, see the elevator arrive at the second floor, your lower belly, and as the doors open, make a quick check—no more than a second—of what you find there: a sensation of warmth and roundness, contented fullness, or perhaps a feeling that you don't want to be disturbed. Do not look for any particular response. Note what's there—a sense of color, an idea, a mood, or nothing at all—and move on to the third, fourth, and fifth floors with the same current of your inhalation. This practice of quick checking will help you to establish a firm impression of each chakra.

Go as far as your inhalation can take you—maybe the fifth floor—and exhale. Then start again, gradually inhaling deeply and slowly enough to take you all the way to the seventh floor. Soon you will get the knack of passing through all seven chakras in one breath. Let your right hand follow this detailed path of the Inner Flute as the energy flows up through your body. When it reaches the crown of your head, pause, holding the breath yet keeping the body relaxed.

Exhale, moving your hand downward, feeling or visualizing the energy as it descends from your crown through the Inner Flute and out through your genitals. As you exhale, let go and relax your whole body. At the end of the exhalation, again rest your right hand on your left hand, slightly above the pubis.

If you have trouble visualizing air leaving your body through your genitals, try this simple technique: Exhale in a very relaxed way, letting the breath flow easily out, making no effort to control it. Then exhale

Visualization is the way we think. Before words, images were. Visualization is the heart of the bio-computer. The human brain programs and self-programs through its images. Riding a bicycle, driving a car, learning to read, bake a cake, play golf—all skills are acquired through the image-making process. Visualization is the ultimate consciousness tool.

—Mike Samuels, M.D., and
Nancy Samuels
Seeing with the Mind's Eye

still further. You will find your belly drawing in as you push more air out. Then exhale as far as you possibly can. Your belly will draw in even further, and you will feel a contraction at the bottom of your pelvis— your pelvis may even rock forward a little—and you will feel as if you are pushing air out through that region.

It helps if you let your eyes fall into the same rhythm. Keep them closed, and just before you begin to inhale, look down—inside closed eyelids—toward your genitals. Start the inhalation, and slowly roll your eyes upward as your hand moves up your body, until by the end of the breath you are looking up into the top of your head. As you exhale, reverse the direction of your eyes.

Continue this for at least five minutes.

Eventually the energy from your breath will vibrate through the whole length of the Inner Flute, creating different tones, or feelings, throughout your body. At this stage, however, all that's needed is to feel the breath starting to flow into the Inner Flute.

Pointers

In this practice there is no specific goal for which to strive. In fact, too much effort will interfere. As you become familiar with the various movements of the breath, hands, and eyes, and as you learn to visualize the passage of air and energy through the Inner Flute, you will be able to relax more and notice new sensations happening in your body. While you're learning, do not force your breath through all seven chakras. Focus on how to open the Inner Flute by creating a sensation in your genitals, picking it up with your breath, and channeling it upward. Let this practice go as far as it can without getting tense.

In my workshops people imagine the movement of air in various ways. Some see it flowing through the pelvic region and into the Inner

Flute. Others feel it there—the way you feel air flowing into your nostrils. For some, it is more of an idea, a concept. Try all of these methods and notice which works best for you.

Different parts of your body will be sensitive to different degrees. In some areas you may get a strong impression of energy moving, while in others you may feel nothing. Do not get impatient or discouraged. In the following chapters we will be exploring ways to sensitize each area.

When visualizing the chakras, do not try to create overly elaborate impressions, such as the vortexes described by Pierrakos earlier in this chapter. Stay with the simple, immediate impressions that come to you spontaneously.

If it feels more comfortable, you can reverse the positions of your hands in this practice, tracing the movement of the breath with your left hand instead of your right.

Sylvia, a psychotherapist and mother of four, trained with me and reported enthusiastically about the improvements these practices made in her love life. "I used to make love and feel somewhat distracted," she said. "Different parts of me were not coordinated. My body, breath, and spirit seemed to be reacting in different ways and in different rhythms. Nothing seemed to be in sync. A distance existed between me and my sensations. Now, when I visualize the Inner Flute and practice the PC Pump and Sexual Breathing during lovemaking, I feel it's like the difference between watching a movie and being in it. An integration is happening. I am what I feel. I resonate to every sensation; I can expand it, stretch it. It is wonderful, particularly when I am on top of my partner. He thinks I have become a great lover because I can stimulate his penis through the PC Pump, bringing him to erection as many times as I want, and I also feel much more turned on through my whole body. These practices have allowed me to become totally involved."

Practice Sexual Breathing with the PC Pump consistently over several weeks, for at least ten to fifteen minutes every two days. Incorporate it into other activities, particularly lovemaking.

While practicing, you need not even say anything to your partner. Simply close your eyes and do the Sexual Breathing as you enjoy making love. Or you can apply Sexual Breathing together when you lie down and cuddle, before and during lovemaking. Gradually it will expand your pleasure.

PELVIC ROCKING

Pelvic Rocking follows naturally from the two previous practices. When doing the PC Pump and Sexual Breathing, sexual arousal automatically spreads through the pelvis, generating a rocking movement. It is also the basic movement that the orgasmic reflex triggers in the body.

In this practice you may feel as if you are riding a horse. This is a beautiful image to hold in mind: the horse symbolizes the power of the sexual energy carrying you toward High Sex. It is a mutual love affair: You are riding it; it is carrying you; together you can journey to ecstasy.

Purpose and Benefits

In this exercise you will practice Pelvic Rocking outside the sexual context, loosening the muscular attachments between the sacrum and the hip bones that normally tend to become stiff and fused through lack of exercise. A loose and alive sacrum is essential to the transformation of raw sexual energy into a subtler force capable of traveling up the Inner Flute through the whole body and vitalizing other centers.

Pelvic Rocking will greatly facilitate this process. In fact, it is the foundation for the rest of the training. Combined with the PC Pump, Sexual Breathing, and the Inner Flute, it provides you with a powerful way to spread sexual energy through your body.

Preparations

Pelvic Rocking is a simple physical exercise. All you need is a pillow to sit on—not a bed pillow, which is too soft, but something quite firm. If you have access to a shop that sells Japanese meditation supplies, get a *zafu.* This is a round cushion about 18 inches in diameter and about 6 inches thick, usually stuffed with kapok, a hard cotton fiber. If you can't find a *zafu,* you can also use several blankets rolled tightly and bound together for strong support.

If you carry tension in your upper back, ask your partner to massage your neck and shoulders as preparation for this practice. Or you can lie down on the floor, with a tennis ball under your upper back, and slowly roll your spine and neck up and down on the ball, staying relaxed, breathing deeply through your mouth, sighing as you exhale, letting your entire weight rest on the ball. Roll until the area relaxes.

Before you start Pelvic Rocking, try to accept the idea that whatever happens in this practice is okay. You have nowhere to go, no special goal to achieve, no extraordinary technique to master. You are doing this to turn yourself on, to try something new, and to have fun.

To encourage a relaxed mood, it is helpful to play soft, sensual music, like the melodies associated with oriental snake charmers, or the Mevlana whirling dervish music, or the sound of the sea.

To get maximum benefit, it is best to practice on an empty stomach. Any heaviness in this area will prevent energy from flowing freely in the pelvis and may make you feel nauseated.

To facilitate Pelvic Rocking you need to have already assimilated the practices for loosening the pelvis in chapter 5, such as the Square Stretch, Squatting, and the Pelvic Curl. If you need to, take ten minutes to review them before you start.

Allow 30 minutes for this practice.

Both partners should practice separately for ten days and then come together for the second part of the exercise.

Practice

Kneel on the floor Japanese-style, with your feet under your buttocks, legs parallel, toes pointing back. Place the *zafu* vertically between your thighs, and straddle it so that it supports your pelvis by pressing against the perineum—the area between the genitals and anus. In this position your back is well-supported, and you are free to rock your pelvis.

Make sure your perineum is resting against the surface of the pillow. For men, the pillow should be pressing right behind the testicles.

Let your belly hang loose. If you are wearing a belt, unfasten it.

Keep your spine and neck straight and your body relaxed, especially your shoulders and jaws. Shake your shoulders a little, and open your mouth wide for a moment to make sure the tension is gone.

Rest your hands in your lap in whatever way feels appropriate. Close your eyes. Recall a time when, as a child, you enjoyed some form of rocking or rhythmic, wavelike motion. Perhaps you were riding on a carousel; perhaps you were bobbing up and down on an adult's leg or on a seesaw; perhaps you were riding a bicycle or a pony. In any case, you were sitting on something that was pressing up between your legs, moving to a beat, and it felt good. As a child you may have responded to this pleasant sensation by rocking your pelvis—children often do.

Pelvic rocking: inhale.   Pelvic rocking: exhale.

Imagine yourself back in that situation, and reproduce the movement, the slight rocking back and forth of the pelvis. Feel this little
movement now as your genitals begin to rub lightly against the pillow.
Keep your eyes closed.

Find a rhythmic movement and then quicken the pace, breathing
faster as you rock faster. Keep going for a few minutes, intensifying the
rhythm until you feel a slight tingling sensation in your genitals.

Focus your awareness on your genital area, and enjoy the sensation.
Find ways to enhance it. Maybe you want to slow down for a while,
rocking and breathing slower, and then speed up again. Use your memories of riding or rhythmic movement to enhance the feelings you are
generating in your genitals. Enjoy these feelings, and relax into them as
you rock back and forth.

Now imagine that your pelvis is hinged on a horizontal bar that
passes straight through your hips. Rock your pelvis as if it is pinned in
this way, free to rotate back and forth but unable to move up and down.

Let the rest of your body be relaxed and still, especially your shoulders and neck.

Feel this rocking in your genitals, anus, and perineum, and rub them against the pillow. Familiarize yourself with this way of rocking. Turn yourself on. Be playful, like a kid discovering sexual sensations for the first time. Keep going for five to ten minutes.

Now bring your breathing into harmony with this movement. Still keeping the image of the horizontal bar through your pelvis, inhale as you rock your pelvis back, and exhale as you rock your pelvis forward. You can breathe either through your nose or your mouth, whichever feels easier. Continue the pelvic rocking and watch your breathing for some minutes.

When you feel that an easy coordination has taken place, you can connect the breathing and movement with the sensations in your genitals. As you rock slowly back, inhale deeply and hold your breath for ten seconds. The backward movement of your pelvis should be slight, so that your lower back and belly stay loose and relaxed. It will seem as if you have filled your belly with air that is almost touching the genital area. After ten seconds let go, slowly exhaling and rocking your pelvis forward. Repeat this deep "belly breathing" for two to three minutes, using it to open up a connection between your breathing and your sexual center.

Feel the breath going deeper and deeper into your pelvis. Make a sound or sigh like "Aaaah!" as you exhale. Feel as if you are relaxing and letting go as you make the sound.

When you feel you have mastered this form of pelvic rocking, bring in the PC Pump. As you inhale, rock your pelvis back and tighten the PC muscle. Hold the breath for three seconds. Exhale, rocking forward and relaxing the PC muscle. Continue for five minutes.

Keep your attention focused on the connection between your breathing and genitals. When your belly breathing connects with the pleasurable feeling in your genitals, the two sensations react with each other, and you will feel an expansion of pleasure in the genital area. Use the breathing and rocking to explore ways to stimulate pleasurable sensations, such as a tingling or tickling feeling in the perineum area, inside the vagina, on the clitoris, or in the scrotum.

PELVIC ROCKING, PC PUMP, AND SEXUAL BREATHING. As you continue this gentle, wavelike Pelvic Rocking combined with the PC Pump, expand the sensation by bringing in Sexual Breathing.

Inhale through puckered lips, as if you are sucking on a large straw, and imagine that you are breathing in through your sex center, drawing energy in as you rotate your pelvis backward and do the PC Pump.

Exhale, imagining that you are breathing out through your sex center, giving your energy out as you rotate your pelvis forward and relax the PC muscle. Continue this for a few minutes.

Then, when you begin to feel arousal, visualize that through your breathing, you are spreading this sensation to your entire pelvis.

Pointers

Many people confuse rocking the pelvis with a movement of the whole torso forward and back, especially when the pelvis is stiff. You can help to isolate the pelvic rocking by making sure your chest remains still. Only if the pelvis moves by itself will the sacrum and hip joints begin to loosen up.

If kneeling Japanese-style gets too hard on your knees, add another pillow to the one you are sitting on. The higher you sit, the less pressure there is on your knees. If this still feels uncomfortable, you can sit on a stool covered with a pillow.

Some people find it easier to fall in time with Pelvic Rocking if they reverse the breathing sequence—inhaling as they rock forward and exhaling as they rock backward. If this feels good to you, use it.

In the beginning you may not feel a connection between the breathing and the genitals. Again, be patient. The sensations may come a little later, when you are not expecting them. Often a new feeling or sensitivity will suddenly arise while making love or during some other activity, such as urinating or self-pleasuring.

DUAL PELVIC ROCKING

After practicing the Pelvic Rocking on your own for ten days, you can do it with your partner.

Preparations

For this practice it is essential to have fresh breath. So before you start, take time to brush your teeth and put a drop of essence of mint on your tongue.

Practice

Sit facing each other, kneeling Japanese-style. Relax your body, letting your belly hang loose.

You are going to make a breath connection with your partner, so breathe through your mouth throughout this sequence.

Look at each other for a few seconds, then make the Heart Salutation. Close your eyes.

Begin the Pelvic Rocking, and continue for three minutes.

When you feel you have established a good rhythm and feel centered in yourself, open your eyes and look at each other while continuing the rocking. There is no need to harmonize your pelvic movements immediately. Allow yourself to remain unaffected by any fears of judgment or comparison ("He's doing it better than I am," or "I don't look

Dual pelvic rocking.

good today") that pop into your mind. This is playful, nonserious practice. You are a couple of kids having fun on a rocking horse.

When you feel at ease, begin to connect with each other's rhythm and energy. Look for ways to harmonize your movements so you can breathe and rock together. Be aware of who has the shorter or longer breaths, and make allowances so that you can both find a single rhythm that feels comfortable. Take your time and stay relaxed. Don't hesitate to talk about any point that requires clarification during this practice, such as "Can you slow down a little?" or "Please match your breathing to mine."

Then move closer and hold hands. Feel a sense of trust in each other, in the process. In your heart, see if you can find a sense of oneness with your partner. Start the Soul-Gazing meditation that you learned in chapter 4. Gazing at each other, inhale together, rocking your pelvises back and feeling as if you are "drinking" your partner into yourself. Exhale together, rocking your pelvises forward and feeling as if you are giving yourself, your energy, to your partner. Keep going for five minutes.

INVERTED BREATH. When you have established a pleasant flow, try inverting the breathing pattern. Partner A inhales, rocking her pelvis back, tightening the PC muscle, and imagining that she is drinking in the energy of Partner B. At the same time, Partner B exhales, rocks forward, relaxes the PC muscle, and gives his energy to Partner A.

As you tune into this inverted breathing, feel as if you are making love through your breathing, gazing, and movement. Partner B, as you exhale, imagine you are blowing a kiss to Partner A, puckering your lips and blowing the air toward her lips, as if through a large straw. Feel that you are blowing your breath, your energy, your love, into her.

Partner A, as you begin to inhale, feel the soft breeze of Partner B's breath being blown toward you, and take it in—as if drinking him into you. Take your partner's breath, together with your own, down the Inner Flute through your throat, chest, diaphragm, navel, and abdomen and into your genitals. Hold it there for a second at the end of the inhalation, while keeping the PC muscle tight.

Exhaling, let your pelvis rock forward, and imagine that the energy stored in your genitals is released upward through the Inner Flute and out your mouth, then blown toward your partner's lips, who in turn inhales it. Keep going for five to ten minutes.

Feel that you are with an intimate friend, sharing the same energy, the same consciousness, the same heart. I like to call this "the kiss of the spirit" because it is so subtle and uplifting. Keep going for at least five minutes, gently, slowly.

Let the breathing be deep and the body relaxed. As you progress, you may wish to vary the rhythm and tempo. Follow your impulse. Just let it happen. Let yourself follow the energy.

Then slow down, stop the rocking motion, and come to a closure.

Close your eyes, and for one minute focus your attention inside your body, at a point below the navel, in your lower belly—your power center. In any practice with a partner, it is important to end by moving from togetherness back into your aloneness, so you can feel yourself, your individuality, your power, independently of the other. Feel how your energy has changed and expanded, because you shared it with your partner in this practice.

Finally, after exchanging a Heart Salutation, take 15 minutes for a conversation about what you experienced. Describe whether you felt that a subtle connection was established between you through the breath, whether the breath was strong or soft enough, whether your rhythms were matched. If you experienced any difficulties—for instance, differences in breathing rhythms that you could not harmonize—talk about that, describe what you learned from it, and how you could transform it during the next session. End the feedback on a positive note by telling each other what you liked most about this exchange.

Pointers

If you do not wish to exchange breath directly in this practice, breathe through your nose. Or you can sit close to your partner, with your lips near his or her right ear, and breathe into the ear, so you can feel and hear the movement of the breathing.

Tuning into a common rhythm doesn't always happen right away. Frequently you have to work at it. If you find yourself getting tense, impatient, or serious, it means that you are focusing too much on the technique and have been caught up in the performance syndrome of trying to do it right. In this tense atmosphere nothing is going to happen. Relax. Take a break, recover your sense of humor and playfulness, and start again.

꧁

The kundalini is a type of energy—a "power" or "force" (shakti)—that is held to rest in a dormant, or potential, state in the human body . . . at the base of the spine. When this energy is "awakened," it rushes upward along the . . . spinal column to the crown of the head. . . . Upon arriving there, the kundalini is said to give rise to the mystical state of consciousness, which is indescribably blissful and in which all awareness of duality ceases.

—Lee Sannella
The Kundalini Experience

In this chapter, you discovered that your sexual energy can be transformed as it travels through the chakras up the Inner Flute, and that you can stimulate and expand the power of your sexual sensations through the PC Pump. In addition, you found that through Sexual Breathing, you can generate and expand erotic sensations through the whole body, all the way to the head, thereby using erotic arousal as the fuel for ecstatic meditation. You also explored the first steps of working with a partner to find a common rhythm in moving energy through the Inner Flute together.

It may inspire you to know that in classical Tantra this practice of moving energy up through the body is seen as the ultimate union of Shakti and Shiva. Shakti, symbolizing the universal energy, is residing at the base of the spine in the form of Kundalini, while Shiva, the principle of divine consciousness, resides at the crown of the head. By leading the vital power of Kundalini-Shakti from the base of the spine through each chakra to the crown chakra, the female and male polarities unite and attain the state of divine rapture.

In the next chapter, Self-Pleasuring Rituals, you will have the opportunity to integrate the practices of the previous chapters into the sexual context of self-pleasuring. Everybody knows about masturbation. But who ever thought it could become a healing art? In chapter 7, you apply the practices that you learned here to enhance erotic pleasure, and you discover self-pleasuring as a way to further Awaken Your Inner Lover.

❧

SELF-PLEASURING RITUALS

Remember the first time you discovered how good it feels to have sexual feelings? As a girl, do you recall the electric tingling, the warm, alive sensation as you climbed a tree and felt the coarse rubbing of the branch between your legs? Or do you remember innocently holding the shower nozzle against your pubis and feeling the warm flow of water trickling over your clitoris? What a subtle tickle of unexpected pleasure! As a boy, perhaps you were sitting in class and suddenly discovered you had a big erection, right there, under your school desk, and you touched it for the very first time. Your blood was rushing, your energy was bursting through your skin, saying, "Hello! I am here, and I will make you feel good when you touch me!"

Many people in my seminars recall an atmosphere of joyful innocence in those early explorations, as they were being welcomed by these friendly messages to join life's dance. But it could not be. It should not be. It had to be outlawed by the adults. It was dangerous. The unspoken fear was that the sexual organs wielded such formidable power, unbridled instincts, and passions that they had to be kept under strict control.

So our educators—our parents, clergy, and schoolteachers—gave the sex organs a bad reputation. These parts of the body were vigorously condemned, and as a consequence they were given coarse, ugly names: prick, bone, one-eyed trouser-snake for the male organ; slit, cunt, squeeze-box, pussy for the female. Their dignity was denied. Their power was crushed, and at the same time, your body's natural ability to experience ecstasy and joy through feelings originating in your genitals was greatly decreased.

Sex is play. You begin to win in your sex life when you come from this position.

—Margo Woods
Masturbation, Tantra and Selflove

Later, as you grew up and began to encounter sexual partners, this self-condemnatory attitude may have compelled you to hide your sex organs and prevent you from honestly sharing your feelings about them. Such things were not to be talked about, even with lovers. As a result, you probably had difficulty telling your partners what to do, how to do it, or how it felt.

Often, for example, women pretend to have a great time, but when they come to my seminars they say, "He doesn't know how to touch me," or "I can come better when I do it myself, but I don't dare to do it to myself when I am with him. He might think he isn't good enough." And men say, "She doesn't like to touch my penis," or "She doesn't touch me strongly enough."

For many people, the only safe way to experience genuine sexual satisfaction is to do it by themselves, in secret, masturbating. But masturbation is also filled with feelings of guilt and considered by many to be wrong. If children are caught doing it, they are punished or threatened with dire consequences. I recently heard a wonderful anecdote about this. One little girl, who was warned she would go blind if she masturbated too much, replied, "Couldn't I just do it until I need to wear glasses?"

Whether as a child you rebelled and did it more or accepted the prohibitions and did it less, the chances are that the guilt associated with masturbation has carried over into your adult life. As a result, you may regard it distastefully as "jerking off," throwing energy away, or an uncontrollable tickle that you want to get rid of. It is done hurriedly in unaesthetic places like bathrooms, garden sheds, and dark corners, never joyously and proudly and never with your partner.

LEARNING TO LOVE YOURSELF

This chapter offers an alternative perspective. The goal here is to bring the art of self-loving down home to its roots by changing the way we think about our sexual organs and learning to love them and to pleasure ourselves without guilt.

Overcoming Guilt

Negative attitudes about masturbation can linger on, long after people believe they have become sexually liberated. I recall an incident in my own life that showed me how deeply I was still being influenced by such taboos. It happened in the late seventies. I had been leading one of my first Tantra seminars. For hours I had been teaching people some of the practices that you are exploring in this book and consequently was feeling extremely aroused. I went home and waited eagerly for the arrival of Alan, my beloved partner, hoping to seduce him into a great evening of lovemaking. He smiled at me as he came in and gave me a gentle hug that I artfully turned into a long, tender embrace. Soon we had undressed, taken a shower, and slipped into bed.

I awaited his approach with trembling, vibrant expectation. It was up to him to make the first move, I thought, but nothing was happening. My sexual desire was so intense that I found myself too embarrassed to initiate a move. It was a familiar pattern: the stronger my desire for him, the more incapable I felt of expressing it. I tossed, turned, stretched, and with a timid hand started stroking his chest. I nestled my head against his shoulder and kissed his ear. But he lay there, limp, unresponsive. After a while I confessed, "You know, I have to admit that I am very turned on. I am dying to make love."

From his side came a sleepy response, "Yes, I understand, but I can't muster the energy, and I'm tired, so let's sleep. We'll do it some other time."

I could not believe what I had just heard. Could he possibly let me down at a moment like this? I lay there, abandoned, turned on, and distraught. What was I going to do with all this energy? Where was I going to go? How was I going to manage this situation? I did not dare to pleasure myself, which should have been the natural conclusion to this situation. I felt intimidated by his presence. Lying there, however, I began to reflect on all the times in my life when I had not taken action to fulfill my sexual needs. I felt a mounting frustration until I could stand it no longer. This time I had do something.

So very discreetly, I crawled out of bed and tiptoed into the living room with the firm intention of taking responsibility for my own pleasure. Of course, I had masturbated many times before in my life, but this was different. I wanted to find a way I could use self-pleasuring to heal my sexual wounds. As I started stroking my body and approaching my genitals, I heard myself think, "What if Alan walks in? You can't really let yourself go like this. You'll wake him up. . . ." and so on. But instead of allowing this to stop me, I breathed deeply and used the waves of pleasure as a force to carry me beyond these guilty feelings. It seemed

It can be as important and necessary for a woman to enjoy sex as it is for her to enjoy her work, children, environment, food, or recreational activities. It's just another potentially satisfying aspect of life.

—Lonnie G. Barbach
For Yourself

that all the negative attitudes about masturbation that I had ever heard were welling up inside me, but I consciously maintained a mounting tension of sexual excitement and did not give in. I stayed with my sensations. I did not let myself down. I put aside thoughts of giving myself a hasty, furtive orgasm and took my time, making a feast out of pleasuring my whole body until I was fully ready to have a most wonderful climax.

In this moment I discovered the importance of self-pleasuring as a healing force and decided to make it part of my work. I also found myself making a sudden decision that shocked and thrilled me. Next time, I would pleasure myself in front of Alan and encourage him to do the same in front of me. Intuitively, I felt certain this would bring a new eroticism and vitality to our sex life. My insight proved correct.

The Healing Power of Pleasure

In High Sex the negative ideas associated with masturbation need to be healed. This is why I have replaced *masturbation* with the term *self-pleasuring*. *Masturbation* has something cold and clinical about it, something furtive and shameful that separates people from their hearts and prevents self-acceptance. *Self-pleasuring,* on the other hand, implies that it is good and healthy for the self to be pleasured, celebrated, and enjoyed. It also suggests that the whole body is involved, not just one part of it.

I know that some of you will find it hard to believe that it is possible to discard lifelong feelings of guilt about giving yourself sexual pleasure. I want to assure you that, in my seminars, however, I have seen many people transformed and healed through the Self-Pleasuring Ritual. For me the example that stands out most prominently is that of a 62-year-old grandmother who, having spent her life taking care of two husbands and two families and continuously postponing her own pleasure because of her duties, was absolutely convinced that she would not be able to do this particular practice. "It is out of my reach," she told me. I spoke to her about her beauty and the importance of finding out how much pleasure was still available to her. I did everything I could to encourage her, playing evocative music, arranging soft lighting, burning incense, and eventually she fully participated in the ritual, even allowing herself to reach orgasm. She emerged from the Self-Pleasuring Ritual like a joyful little girl, a girl who, until then, had been locked away behind a life of responsibilities and never given a chance to express herself. Her

In the erotic art, truth is drawn from pleasure itself, understood as a practice and accumulated as experience; pleasure is not considered in relation to an absolute law of the permitted and the forbidden, nor by reference to a criterion of utility, but first and foremost in relation to itself; it is experienced as pleasure, evaluated in terms of its intensity, its specific quality, its duration, its reverberations in the body and the soul.

—Michel Foucault
The History of Sexuality,
Volume I

discovery of a hidden wellspring of pleasure within herself gave her a new radiance and allowed her to open herself up to a whole range of sensual possibilities she had never imagined could be hers. Her self-esteem as a woman rose dramatically, and as a result, she attracted the attention of a younger man who subsequently became her boyfriend.

So I know that if you are courageous, you can begin to put your superstitions about this activity behind you. And remember, you are not alone. Alfred Kinsey, who in 1948 wrote the ground-breaking book *Sexual Behavior in the Human Male,* has stated that, even then, 64 percent of all women and 94 percent of all men self-pleasured themselves, well before the so-called sexual revolution of the 1960s. More recently, in her 1981 nationwide study of female sexuality, Shere Hite reported that of the 3000 women who replied to her questionnaire, 82 percent said they enjoy self-pleasuring.

Self-pleasuring is a natural activity. Alexander Lowen, founder of bioenergetic therapy, recalls a conversation with his teacher, psychotherapist and sexologist Wilhelm Reich, in which Reich observed, "The patient who cannot masturbate with satisfaction has not completed his analytic therapy." In other words, Reich was saying that the ability to give oneself pleasure is a key indicator of self-acceptance.

As I explained earlier, this practice can help you to heal sexual guilt and fear. Usually such fears arise at the moment when you are starting to pleasure yourself. That is when the admonishing voices say, "Watch out!" At that point you have a choice: either to go with your past conditioning and feel guilty or to take a deep breath and find the courage to explore the new dimension of self-pleasuring, healing the fear and guilt through a positive experience of consciously directed pleasure.

Discovering the art of self-pleasuring is essential in High Sex. In a way, it is the fountainhead from which everything else flows. In this chapter you have, for the first time in this book, the opportunity to integrate the previous steps of the training in a sexual context that feels secure and safe because you are in complete control. You learn how to give yourself all the erotic stimulation that you ever wished to receive from another. Then you are ready to teach your partner exactly what turns you on and how best to give it to you. In the coming pages, you'll discover that you are the source of your own orgasm. Many people still place the responsibility for inducing orgasm outside themselves, believing that it depends on the skills of a partner. Yet, as we shall see, it is possible to discover an inner-directed type of climax that you can induce com-

The effects of pleasure are wholly positive. Physically, pleasure improves circulation and increases energy. The emotional effects include greater self-esteem, increased self-confidence, and a generally sharper mind. Spiritually, enjoyment enhances your appreciation of your blessings and contributes to a brighter outlook.

—Harold H. Bloomfield
and Robert B. Kory
Inner Joy

Once you know the centers of your pleasure, you will be better able to share pleasure with another. This is the whole of the Tantra: that you must perceive what you are through knowing yourself and your pleasures; for only then can you give the pleasure you seek and accept the pleasure given to you.

—Ashley Thirlby
Tantra

pletely by yourself, whether alone or with a partner, through the exploration of self-pleasuring in conjunction with the PC Pump, Sexual Breathing, and Opening the Inner Flute. The more you are capable of developing this skill, the more accomplished and autonomous a lover you become.

Self-pleasuring is also likely to improve your relationship with your lover, because you don't feel dependent on him or her for your satisfaction. Your partner, in turn, doesn't have to feel responsible for your ecstasy. The whole performance pressure of satisfying the other person is removed, allowing more freedom and more sense of equality.

Through this practice it becomes clear that only you can improve the quality of your orgasm. Your partner can help you to have an orgasm, but not to be orgasmic. This is your responsibility. And because the actual quality of the orgasm depends on you, it is important to develop an awareness of how your body moves, how your muscles react, how the depth and rhythm of your breathing can help in the experience of pleasure, and how pleasure can be intensified and made to last longer. You become at once the giver and the receiver, a unique position in which to learn how to use your breathing, movement, imagination, and voice to expand your sexual arousal through your whole body.

As you learn the techniques, you'll strengthen your trust and confidence in yourself as a sexually attractive individual, and you'll discover that pleasuring yourself physically is an essential part of loving yourself emotionally, bringing together your sexual energy and your heart. Self-pleasuring makes your heart happy.

Betty Dodson, author of *Liberating Masturbation*, recently said at a conference, "For me, masturbation is a form of sexual meditation. I was measured by scientists during a masturbation session. They wired my brain, and the scientists in the control room thought I was about to have heart failure as I was on my way to orgasm because my metabolism was so aroused—I was going wild to the music of the Allman Brothers' 'Eat A Peach.' But my brain waves were in Theta—deep relaxation. So while the body is pumping pleasure and moving, the brain is in a meditative state."

Betty continued, "I have the first big 'O,' then the second, then the third. I'm already in it for one hour, but it's in the second hour that it starts getting interesting. You are no longer going for anything; you are there already; you are in ongoing ecstasy. So the idea is to go on pumping pleasure, to break into a sweat, to work past the orgasmic response into ecstasy. Then you feel the chills and thrills up and down the body, and there is nowhere to go. You are there. So you have to keep it going, keep it going, go to excess, keep riding the waves of pleasure until you break into ecstasy."

Betty was describing the benefits of going beyond one's ordinary limits and moving from the first degree of pleasure, which is having an orgasm—usually a momentary release—to the second degree of being orgasmic—the ability to prolong this experience until it becomes an ongoing state of being. Instead of orgasm being something that you *do,* it becomes something that you *are,* and out of this state is developed the High Sex perspective that life is basically to be enjoyed, ultimately enjoyed, not endured.

These experiences may sound remarkable—beyond your reach—but they are not. After the first hour of self-pleasuring and even after orgasm, you can find ways of going into a second hour. It is the equivalent of an athlete who is training himself to run longer and longer distances with more and more ease. It is a training in pleasure.

You are not training yourself to set endurance records, however, but to heighten sensitivity. The more sensitive you become, the more pleasure you are capable of giving yourself. In practical terms, this means constantly moving beyond the limitations and boundaries you set for yourself. The more you learn to understand and modulate your sexual responses, the better lover you can become.

THE SELF-PLEASURING RITUAL

Through the Self-Pleasuring Ritual, you will learn the kinds of touches, positions, breathing, fantasies, and music that can intensify your pleasure, help you contain it, and feel it more deeply; then you will consciously direct it to other parts of the body.

Purpose and Benefits

From the perspective of High Sex, the purpose of learning to give yourself pleasure is not to achieve a bigger and better orgasm of release and ejaculation. This is only an enjoyable side effect. The true purpose is the transformation of genital orgasm into whole-body ecstasy.

This process will require discipline, because at first you will be asked to arouse yourself sexually and then stop just before "the point of no return." Ordinarily, we are accustomed to associating masturbation with release, so stopping before the climax may not seem a very attractive proposition. It is well worth it, however, as you will find that the pleasure you are delaying is much less than the pleasure you are building up to.

This form of self-pleasuring is particularly beneficial for men who experience premature ejaculation or who have difficulty maintaining an erection because it teaches them greater control of the orgasmic response. It also enhances staying power, allowing the charge of arousal to build up so that ultimately, when the decision is made to let go, the experience of ejaculating is much more intense. For men with these kinds of concerns, self-pleasuring is easiest when it is done alone, and it should be continued alone at least three times a week for a month. Only after you feel an improvement in your staying power should you proceed to the next steps of the ritual indicated below.

Women report that the Self-Pleasuring Ritual accelerates the speed with which they can feel sexually aroused and that this arousal spreads more easily beyond the genital area, enhancing their sensuality. This acceleration of the female response helps to reduce the "arousal gap" that

The masturbation that belongs to the androgyne's experience is performed consciously; *the reason for it is understood and accepted; and it is entered into with the fantasy which allows the soul to participate in the experience of the body without guilt or shame.*

—June Singer
Androgyny

is such a common source of friction between men and women. So often the timing is off. Because men are usually more genitally oriented, they are ready for lovemaking within a few minutes, whereas women, being more heart-oriented, usually require a lot more time and preparation. The feedback I get from couples in my seminars is that self-pleasuring balances out the gap: Men learn how to diffuse their genital sensations, paying more attention to whole-body arousal, while women tend to be more readily aroused genitally.

Preparations

The following practices should be done in the given order but are not intended to be done all at once. Practice each sequence as often as you can for one month, at least two or three times a week. When you feel ready—that is, when your practice has become very enjoyable, you can move on to the next phase.

In contrast to the often hurried nature of masturbation, the Self-Pleasuring Ritual can take up to an hour at first. It is important that you take as much time as you want. After three or four sessions, you will probably be able to complete it in half an hour.

Make sure you will not be disturbed by telephone, children, or other disruptions, and that you have plenty of time. There should be no sense of hurry, no anxiety.

Create your Sacred Space. Use your imagination to create an erotic environment with red satin sheets, provocative pictures or movies, dildos, romantic or wild rhythmic music. Use the things that turn you on.

It is especially important to have pleasing lubricants available, such as KY jelly or Astroglide, because these greatly increase your ability to touch erotically. The fingers need to be moist in order to slide smoothly over your skin without irritating it and to be able to maintain a steady, rhythmic speed without interruption.

I'd like to add a word here on the use of vibrators to enhance genital stimulation. Even though they work wonders for some people, my suggestion is to use them infrequently, if at all, because they tend to dull the nerve endings in and around the male and female sex organs, thereby reducing sensitivity. In High Sex, instead of intensifying stimulation, we are developing an expanded awareness of increasingly subtle sensations in the whole body. In other words, instead of banging a single drum louder and louder, we are learning to hear an entire orchestra.

Female genitals in a mirror.

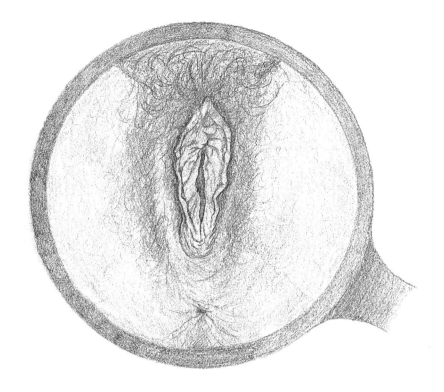

Before you start, unwind in a warm bath in which you have mixed three drops of essential oil of lavender to help you relax, three drops of ylang-ylang—a sexual tonic—and three drops of peppermint to keep you alert. Or you can use any other favorite bath oil.

Make sure your nails are trimmed.

Practice

Turn on your favorite rhythmic music.

Take off your clothes, spread your legs, and look at your genitals in a mirror. For some women, this can be a revealing experience because unless we set up the means to see ourselves, we may never know what our full, open genitals look like.

Stroke your genitals, and imprint their image in your memory. Practice this by closing your eyes and seeing if you can hold a visual image of them in your mind. To strengthen the image, open your eyes, look in the mirror, then close them again. Keep alternating until you can

Male genitals in a mirror.

see your genitals clearly in your mind's eye. Call forth this image as often as possible during self-pleasuring. Subconsciously this will help you make friends with this precious part of your body until it becomes as legitimate as your nose, hand, or foot.

Sensually cover your body with oil. This is the foreplay of self-pleasuring. Take your time and include the whole body. Some men may feel uneasy and impatient doing this because they are accustomed to focusing exclusively on genital stimulation. But do it anyway. Learn what feels good, and seek out pleasure in unexpected places: your nipples, neck, inner thighs. Your whole body has the potential to be orgasmic, and this is one step on the path to High Sex.

After completing the massage, lie on your bed, your body relaxed, your hands at your sides, breathing deeply all the way down to your genitals. Close your eyes, and take a moment to allow your body to resonate with the vibrations of the music.

Recall a pleasant moment in your love life. Visualize a time when you felt secure, loved, confident, open. As in the exercise for Awakening the Inner Lover, allow yourself to enter into the scene fully. Feel the flow of blood through your veins, the beating of your heart, the throbbing of vital energy in your navel and stomach. Feel a sense of expectation, of excitement, as if you are preparing for a date with your most beloved partner. This time, however, the partner is yourself.

Without moving your upper arms, raise your forearms to the vertical position, and bring your awareness into your hands, breathing energy into them. They are going to open the sacred doors of your temple so that you may, through this offering of pleasure, go inside and meet the Inner Lover. As you breathe deeply and shake your hands for a minute, feel the tips of your raised fingers turning electric. Now let them gently and delicately touch your naked body, like feathers.

Stroke your body, breathing into each sensation, feeling the grain of your skin, the texture, the places where it is warm and mellow, and the places where it is cold and unwelcoming. Massage these cold areas, warming them, giving them love, support, and tenderness.

Yes, touch yourself all over. This is all you, and you are beautiful. You deserve every moment of pleasure. This moment of delight is your only purpose now.

As your hands move over your body, stay tuned to the imagined love scene with which you began. Recall the way you were touched by your lover and the way you responded. That lover is now you. You are the lover, and your body is the beloved. Go into the scene, and breathe into those feelings, as if you were there again. Your hands, the hands of your lover, are touching you, and your body is moving in response—undulating and arching upward, seeking the lover's touch, honoring it, welcoming it.

Let your body direct you. What position does it want to take, standing up, lying on your back, on your stomach, kneeling? Find out what arouses you the most.

In the following section I give separate guidance to women and men. Then I return to guidance for both partners.

WOMEN: EXPLORING THE FORBIDDEN FRUIT. Let your hands slide over your belly; let your fingers move through your pubic hair; and gently touch the lips of your vagina. Tease yourself—don't be in a hurry—and caress your pelvic area, perineal area, and anus.

Then lubricate your major and minor labia, your clitoris, the opening and the inside of the vagina. Enjoy the softness of the vaginal lips

Lubricating your vagina.

opening under your fingers like the petals of a flower. Feel the moist cave within, as its elastic walls tighten their grip around your fingers. Feel how your inner temple is becoming moist and soft, opening up to love, life, and joy. When you are ready, lubricate the perineal area between your vagina and anus, and finally, your anus itself.

Explore different strokes, touches, pressures. Lightly pull the pubic hair. Tease yourself by stimulating the area around your clitoris, gradually making circles and brushing lightly onto the clitoris. As you stimulate it directly, find out which part is more sensitive, the shaft or the tip? The left side or the right side? Experiment. Try holding the clitoris between your thumb and index finger. Try moving the index fingers of both hands up and down the shaft. When you find a stroke you like, maintain it in a rhythmic progression, increasing arousal.

Caress the area around your anus, tightening and relaxing the anal muscles, accepting this region as an instrument of pleasure. As you will discover later in this book, the anus has great orgasmic potential for men and women.

You may want to explore what I call "blended stimulation"—stroking your clitoris and your nipples simultaneously. For many women this intensifies pleasure. Or you may want to insert an object inside the vagina and simulate the rhythmic movement of the penis during lovemaking. Some women use their fingers; others use a dildo or some other phallic object. Simultaneous, blended clitoral and vaginal stimulation can be extremely effective in bringing you to the edge of orgasm. Remain on this edge without going into the orgasmic reflex.

MEN: DISCOVERING THE MAGIC WAND. First, lubricate your belly and caress it. Then lubricate your genital area—your scrotum and perineal and anal areas. Finally, lubricate your penis. Enjoy your shaft, your scepter. Touch it delicately at first, then begin moving your hands from the base to the tip, holding your penis with your whole hand, turning your hands around it, pulling it, caressing the skin under it, feeling the sensitive ridge around the glans. Quicken the movement, milking your penis. Then feel the

Lubricating your penis.

sensitive skin of the scrotum, then the perineal area, caressing it with both hands, curling your thighs up to feel it better, moving your fingers around your anus, accepting it, too, as an area capable of erotic sensitivity. Play with it; tickle it.

Some men require deeper and longer massage before their penises respond to pleasuring. If you find this is the case, sit with your back against a wall so that you can touch your perineum, scrotum, and testicles more easily. Press hard with both hands on the perineum. Beneath this area is the prostate gland, located inside the body. Massaging the perineum stimulates the prostate, which in turn increases sexual arousal. The best way is to apply steady pressure with two fingers—be sure your nails are well trimmed—then rhythmically and regularly press into the area while stroking the penis in the same rhythm. The deeper the pressure on the perineum and the faster the stroking, the faster you will arouse yourself.

MEN AND WOMEN: SPREADING THE SEXUAL FIRE. As you pleasure yourself with one hand, with the other caress the whole area around your genitals, including your anus and the abdominal area above the pubis. Amplify your breathing and body movement, helping the arousal to spread warmth and aliveness to these areas.

Inhale, visualizing that you are drawing your pleasure energy, your sexual fire, from your genitals into your pelvis. Help this visualization process with the sucking motions of the PC Pump, and as in Sexual Breathing, imagine a warm tickle of pleasure being sucked into the lower part of the Inner Flute as you breathe in through your genitals.

Exhale, imagining the sexual fire spreading, expanding, filling your entire pelvis with ripples of pleasure. You can help to spread this energy by stroking your belly in a slow, circular fashion.

Continue self-pleasuring until you reach a near-peak, on the edge of orgasm, just before the point of no return. Then completely stop stimulation and inhale, holding the pleasure energy in, allowing it to fill your pelvis. Hold it for a long moment and then relax, exhaling, allowing the energy to spread. You have resisted the temptation to go for a quick release. This is an important moment on your path to sexual ecstasy.

MOVING PLEASURE ENERGY TO THE HEART. Stimulate yourself again. Take your time, as if you are strolling through the woods rather than sprinting for the finishing line. Observe any feelings of doubt or frustration, or an

Sending energy to the heart center.

urgent need to climax. Let them be there, but focus on your breathing, and keep stimulating yourself.

This time you are going to start to move the same pleasure energy toward your heart center, the point in the middle of your chest, halfway between your nipples. At the peak of arousal, inhale once, deeply and quickly, much like a diver about to go down to the ocean floor, and tighten or clench the PC muscle and imagine that you are drawing sexual energy up to your heart center through the Inner Flute. Use your imagination. You are guiding, pulling, sucking the fire of arousal upward toward the center of your chest. Let your hand help this imaging and movement by stroking your body gently in an upward motion, from the genitals to the heart.

Hold your breath for a few seconds. Become aware of the rest of your body, and allow everything except the PC muscle to relax. This may be difficult at first, but it becomes easier with practice.

As you exhale, relax all the muscles of the pelvic floor, and imagine the energy rushing back down to your genitals and out your body through your genitals. As you do so, let your hand slide down from your chest to your genitals. As in Sexual Breathing, the movement of the hand emphasizes and supports the upward and downward energy currents.

Resume genital stimulation. As before, build your arousal, and when you approach the peak, stop stimulation, close the "lower gate"— tighten the PC muscle—and inhale once deeply, sucking the energy of arousal all the way up to your breasts, filling and expanding your chest. Let your chest be as relaxed as possible, and let the pressure of the inhaled air push out against it. Feel that your chest is expanding, vibrating. Look for a tingling, warm, expansive sensation. This is the first glimpse of what I call "an orgasm of the heart." After holding it for a few seconds, exhale, let go, and let your mental focus drop down from your heart to your sex center.

Move to this peak of arousal three times, stopping just before orgasm and, in your own way, moving the energy up to the heart center each time, holding your breath before allowing the energy to rush back down the Inner Flute and out through your genitals. Each cycle should last five to ten minutes.

Finally, go for it! After the third cycle reward yourself with a full orgasmic release.

Practice this technique three times a week for at least a month. Then you will begin to reap the benefits. You are now in the process of mastering a previously uncontrollable reflex. This gives you a feeling of greater strength and greater freedom. You are in charge.

SENDING ENERGY TO THE THIRD EYE. After you have experienced some of these intensified responses, you are ready to move to a more advanced level of this practice, stimulating yourself almost to the point of no return and then pulling the energy up to the third eye.

This practice may seem a little strange, but it is an ancient and widely used technique found in Tantric scriptures. Many books have been written about the ecstatic quality of the third eye experience, and you will develop it further in a later chapter. For now it is enough to know

Sending energy to the third
eye.

that directing pleasure energy to the third eye brings an expansion of
consciousness.

Do not try this technique until you have practiced pulling the
energy to the heart center.

As with the prior exercise of stimulating the heart center, begin by
inhaling, pulling your pleasure energy up through the Inner Flute, mo-
tioning with your hand. At the beginning of the inhalation, look down
toward your genitals behind closed eyelids. Roll your eyes upward as you
breathe in, so that by the time you have inhaled fully, your eyes are
looking up into the region of the third eye, with your eyelids still closed
or half closed. This will help lock the energy at that point.

As before, hold your breath for a few seconds while relaxing your
body as much as possible. It is very important to keep the body relaxed.
Even though you are holding in your breath and the lower gate is closed,
the rest of the body should not be tense.

At this stage students sometimes report a sense of feeling light, or floating, as if their energy has expanded beyond the boundaries of the body. The long moment of holding the inhaled breath and focusing on the third eye is very important because it is at this moment that the feeling of lightness occurs.

Then exhale, sending the energy back down the Inner Flute and out through the genitals.

Pointers

In self-pleasuring, one of the biggest challenges for men is avoiding ejaculation. This is important in lovemaking, too, so I will give a few tips to men on how they can last longer, controlling the emission of sperm so that it becomes a conscious act rather than an involuntary reflex.

For some men ejaculation can be triggered by muscle tension in the buttocks or pelvis. When you feel that you are approaching the point of no return, remain completely still, and relax the anal and genital muscles while pressing your tongue against the top of your palate. Pressing there creates a sense of feeling anchored and can help delay ejaculation.

Pressing your tongue to your palate.

Just before the point of no return, the man or his partner can squeeze his penis, clasping the frenulum—the area just behind the glans—between thumb and forefingers. Try it with one hand, then two, and see which feels best for you. You may want to squeeze gently for ten seconds, or more firmly and deeply for five. Keep squeezing until the urge to ejaculate subsides. Repeat this process several times during each self-pleasuring session. This technique will also help women postpone orgasm.

Immediately before you start a self-pleasuring session, do 30 PC Pump contractions. The tightening action of the anal muscles has a pumping and massaging effect on the prostate gland. This preventive massage will strengthen the gland and delay the onset of a preejaculatory spasm during self-stimulation.

Before the point of no return, press deeply and firmly on the perineum point, located halfway between the scrotum and the anus. When you find the right point, you will feel little or no resistance, because there is a small indentation. If you press exactly on the perineum point before you are about to ejaculate, you will prevent the emission of semen into the urethra. Do not press too close to the scrotum or too close to the anus, or the benefit of the exercise will be lost. You can press on the perineum from the front or reach around behind your buttocks. Press hard.

One of the advantages of this approach is that you can experience the pleasurable sensations associated with the pumping of the prostate that occur at the onset of orgasm, yet you avoid the emission of semen that usually accompanies it. This is how men experience multiple orgasms. There is no refractory (or recovery) period following each orgasm so that

Pressing behind the glans to avoid ejaculation.

Pressing the perineum to avoid ejaculation.

erection can be maintained. This is very pleasing for a woman as love-making lasts long enough to allow her several orgasms. If ejaculatory orgasm happens accidentally, however, enjoy it, let it be, and resume stimulation after a few minutes.

For a complete discussion of this matter, I recommend two excellent books: *Sexual Solutions* by Michael Castleman, and *The Tao of Sexology* by Dr. Stephen Chang.

A warning: when channeling energy up the Inner Flute, don't expect an immediate "cosmic" orgasm. This is just putting yourself under unnecessary pressure and guarantees disappointment. Self-pleasuring is not about "getting" an orgasm. It's about expanding your range of pleasurable sensations, about loving and accepting yourself as you are and starting from that point. So don't get disheartened if sparks don't fly at first. In the beginning you may not feel any connecting sensation between your genitals and your heart. Be patient, keep up the practice, trust yourself, and eventually it will happen, especially when you are willing to intensify stimulation for a longer time while using the Three Keys—breathing, movement, and sound.

Some people report feeling bored during self-pleasuring. This resistance to giving yourself great enjoyment probably has to do with early negative self-pleasuring experiences, or a generally low self-esteem that prevents you from experiencing a successful conclusion. Work with these practices for a while. Then, if you still feel your problem is specifically sexual, such as anorgasmia or premature ejaculation, seek sexual counseling. None of these problems is insurmountable.

Also, when touching your genitals, avoid falling into patterns of familiar behavior. Even when you have become skilled at self-pleasuring, never reduce it to a habit. Take your time, remain alert, experiment with new strokes.

In self-pleasuring, feelings of discomfort may arise either because you are experiencing more pleasure than you know how to contain or because your body seems numb and unresponsive. If you feel numb in a certain area, focus your awareness there, using the Three Keys to help the energy move through it. You will know energy has started moving when you feel a tingling sensation, a vibration, spasm, contraction or relaxation of a muscle, or a pleasant feeling of bubbling, like uncorked champagne, under the skin.

If you are feeling too much, reduce the stimulation, slow down, and deepen your breathing so that the intensity can spread through your body. In all cases go easily and be patient with yourself. Your limits exist as protection. They allow you to absorb only as much energy as your system is ready to assimilate at this stage. So respect them and proceed step by step, gradually stretching your boundaries.

Don't judge or criticize yourself. The more you replace self-criticism with self-acceptance, the more easily your energy will begin to flow, and the more life will be able to dance within you.

THE SEXUAL DIALOGUE

So far, we have explored "safe" self-pleasuring—that is to say, doing it alone. When you feel more confident about accepting and modulating pleasure, you can emerge from privacy to develop self-pleasuring in your partner's presence.

For me, the practice of self-pleasuring with, or in front of, my partner was the most delicate and difficult challenge. From feedback from others in my seminars, I know that this is true for many people. So I have developed a delightful method through which you can "dedramatize" this potentially serious and uncomfortable situation. I call this method the Sexual Dialogue. By introducing a sense of humor and playfulness, this dialogue can help you to heal old sexual wounds, replacing negative attitudes about the male and female genitals with positive ones, and also take a major step toward deeper intimacy with your partner. Once you have participated in the Sexual Dialogue, you will find self-pleasuring with another person much easier.

Purpose and Benefits

This practice provides you with an easy and effective way of transforming old patterns of shyness, shame, and guilt about "those hidden parts," giving them a voice and listening to what they have to say. By experimenting with a dialogue between your genitals, you can let your lover know what you want and what works for you in a humorous and charming manner. Moreover, using poetic expressions for your genitals enhances erotic feelings and brings gentleness into your lovemaking.

Preparations

To do this exercise and others in the book, you need to prepare not only a place, a time, and your body, but a personal language as well. As I noted at the beginning of this chapter, our culture has given our sex organs both a bad reputation and many crude and derogatory names that diminish the possibility that anyone could find spiritual expansion and ecstasy through them. To remove them from this common level and help restore their dignity, I suggest you create special names for your sex organs, christening them, as it were, for their new life in the world of High Sex. When I engage in lovemaking, I call the penis *Vajra,* a Tibetan term that means "thunderbolt" or "scepter of power," as well as penis. Other names given to the penis in the East include the Peak, the Warrior, the Hero, the Emperor, the Jade Stalk, and the Magic Wand. And I call the vagina *Yoni,* which in India means the vulva, in the sense of the great womb of Creation. Other names given to the vagina in the East include Valley of Joy, Great Jewel, Pearl, Lotus Blossom, Moist Cave, Ripe Peach, Enchanted Garden, and Full Moon.

You can use these names, or better, invent your own pet names that carry a happy, positive meaning for you. I will use the names Vajra and

Behold the Shiva Lingam, beautiful as molten gold, firm as the Himalaya Mountain, tender as a folded leaf, life-giving like the solar orb; behold the charm of his sparkling jewels!

—Linga Purana

215

Yoni in some exercises, and you are free to replace them with the names you have chosen. In fact, you could introduce a whole variety of poetic expressions into your lovemaking. Rather than dismissing these sacred encounters with terms like *screwing* or *getting it on,* I suggest you use supportive metaphors. In my seminars I suggest that participants use theatrical phrases, such as:

"Beloved, may I visit your Enchanted Garden tonight?"

"May I dwell in the Valley of Delights?"

"The Great Warrior wishes to rest in the Moist Cave."

These evoke much mirth and laughter, and that is exactly the response I wish to elicit. Exaggeration here is a device to bring forth playfulness in an area formerly loaded with negativity and tension.

A man will be greatly appreciated by his lover if he shows his tenderness and respect by asking her whether he can "penetrate her garden," and then, later, whether Vajra can leave the "valley."

This kind of language may be awkward at first, but over time such expressions, particularly your own, will add greatly to the specialness of High Sex. I encourage you to experiment with these poetic expressions, both in the following practice and in your lovemaking.

Prepare the Sacred Space.

Both partners should be naked for this exercise.

Allow 30 minutes for the dialogue.

Decide who will be Partner A and who will be Partner B.

Practice

Sit opposite your lover. Hold your own genitals, feeling their warmth and breathing down into this area.

Partner A, close your eyes for a moment, and feel that you are listening to this part of your body as if you are waiting to receive an important message. Partner B, sit silently and wait for Partner A to begin.

Partner A, allow your mind to bring up different images, memories of times past, sexual sensations felt by Vajra or Yoni, letting these images fuse into a kind of life history. Prepare yourself to give a voice to Vajra, your penis, or to Yoni, your vagina, as if they can speak through you. They are going to tell you what it is like to live with you, in your body.

Open your eyes, and maintain eye contact with your partner for the rest of the practice. Partner A, while continuing to hold your genitals gently, begin to speak as if you are giving them a voice. Speak as if you *are* your genitals, and describe what it is like to live with you. For example, suppose Partner A is a woman called Sarah and Partner B is a man called Steven. Sarah's Yoni may say something like this:

"Sometimes Sarah pretends that I don't exist. She becomes serious and heady. She doesn't listen to me. She takes a long time to come out of her shell, and she usually thinks she'll never get what she really wants. So I often don't get what I need.

"I want Steven's Vajra to visit more often and for longer. If Sarah listened to me and let me lead the show more, she would be happier. But she always expects to be disappointed, and Vajra can feel that, so he gets scared and pulls away too soon. I feel that Sarah is like a little girl who needs to be taken carefully through a sexual experience by someone who is very caring and sensitive. This will help Sarah not to give up before she has even given herself a chance.

"Sarah and I, we both like caring lovers. I don't like it when Vajra pushes his way rudely inside me. I like to unfold slowly, like a flower; otherwise so much is lost.

"Yes, I like passion too. I like the hard thrust of a hot Vajra, fierce and demanding, but that comes later, when I am wet and moist, open and receptive. I need a beautiful and patient Vajra to help Sarah open herself to what I have to offer when I dance inside her. . . ."

Partner B listens as Partner A speaks, giving his full attention and support.

Partner A, give yourself about ten minutes. Don't feel hurried. At first you may need a little more time to say what you feel. If you need to, close your eyes once in a while and focus on your genitals, listening to what they want to tell you.

After speaking, spread your legs and, gently caressing your genitals, show them to Partner B. Feelings of shyness, shame, or doubt may be coming up. It's important that you accept them, allow them to be there, and acknowledge them, but don't stop the exercise. Maintain eye contact. When uncomfortable feelings start to surface, you may feel yourself starting to contract. This is how people react to fear, instinctively holding energy in. When you feel this contraction, that is the right moment to expand your breathing, releasing the energy and dissolving the fear. This is what I call "breathing through difficult moments." You can use this approach each time you feel yourself shying away from an uncomfortable situation.

Take three minutes to show your "precious jewels."

Then Partner B should tell Partner A, "Thank you for this beautiful gift," and hold your beloved close to you for some minutes.

End with a Heart Salutation and a Melting Hug.

Exchange roles. Partner B, who in this case is a man, will speak on behalf of his Vajra:

"Well, I am a bit impatient, and Steven tends to get locked into the goal of orgasm as soon as I start to grow! But Steven and I, we really want to give Sarah pleasure, so Steven is learning to relax more, even when I perk up. I like sex, and I think I am very good-looking and very reliable. I've never let Steven down—even when the poor guy is drunk! But you are such a beautiful Yoni. So sometimes we get carried away. Please forgive us. I want to learn your secrets, and I know you are shy. I will be gentle and tender with you. Later I will go wild, but I will go slowly at first and knock at the door patiently until it feels okay for you to let me in."

Partner A listens attentively while Partner B speaks.

Partner B, when you have finished, gently caress your genitals and show them to Partner A. Do this for about three minutes.

Then Partner A should tell Partner B, "Thank you for this beautiful gift," and hold your beloved close to you for some minutes.

End with a Heart Salutation and a Melting Hug.

Pointers

What Steven and Sarah convey through this seemingly light and innocent dialogue are essential points about caring lovemaking: asking your partner's permission to "enter" and to "leave," revealing past hurts, expressing needs, and so on.

As I have indicated, the Sexual Dialogue aims to endow our sex organs with personalities of their own. You discover them as you would enjoy looking at your face in the mirror or chatting to a friend. It allows lovers to develop a rapport, not only with their own genitals but with those of their partner, clearing away misunderstandings and encouraging playfulness and innocence, both of which are essential to the art of self-pleasuring with a partner.

In this exercise both the speaker and the listener are likely to have difficult moments, but if you stay with it, breathing through the uncomfortable feelings, shame and guilt will drop away and intimacy will deepen. It is important not to judge yourself or your partner during this delicate time, when you are both vulnerable. Do not interrupt the exercise until it is finished.

Although the Sexual Dialogue can be a wonderful introduction to lovemaking, I suggest, at this stage, that you use it as preparation for the following practice.

SELF-PLEASURING UNDER THE EYES OF YOUR BELOVED

Now that Yoni and Vajra have expressed their insecurities and desires, they are ready to move into new and exciting territory. In this exercise Partner A is going to give herself pleasure while Partner B watches. Then Partner B will give himself pleasure while Partner A watches.

Purpose and Benefits

The biggest victory here and the most important teaching of this phase is allowing yourself to display your most intimate erotic behavior to someone else. At first this may seem difficult—almost impossible for some people. This is why I advise you to wear a blindfold; it helps you to stay focused on your own sensations and diminishes the risk of being distracted by the presence of your partner. In addition, the one who is watching will feel freer to look and learn the movements and gestures that please you, without being an intruder.

This practice has tremendous benefits: You are learning how to stay tuned with your own orgasmic source, independent of any feelings of shyness or guilt, and this gives you strength, trust in yourself, and a sense that it is okay to have pleasure and to show it. You will enjoy a kind of joyful pride when you break through the secrecy-shame taboo.

Preparations

Create the Sacred Space.
 Allow 45 minutes for each partner.
 You will need a comfortable blindfold.
 Choose who is going to be Partner A and Partner B.
 Play sensual, rhythmic music.

Practice

Begin with a Melting Hug, and give a Heart Salutation to each other.

Partner B, make a Heart Salutation to the Vajra or Yoni of Partner A, expressing the feeling, "I honor the gate to your temple." This will give reassurance and support to Partner A, who is about to start.

Partner A, put on the blindfold.

Partner B, watch silently and attentively. This is an opportunity to see exactly what it is that gives Partner A pleasure—what touches and pressures are used. Remember the strokes so that you can repeat them later.

Partner A, find a position that feels good—standing up or reclining on a pillow, perhaps—and begin self-pleasuring. Don't be in a hurry. You don't have to go straight for the genitals. You can caress yourself sensually, gradually building your arousal in whatever ways you enjoy most.

Partner A, stay focused on your own sensations, and constantly bring your mind back to what you are feeling. Even when part of your mind is telling you, "I can't do this; this is wrong"; "What is he going to think of me?"; "What if I don't come?"; and "What if I don't get an erection? . . ." you can pass through these negative thoughts by staying with your breathing and sensations. They anchor you in the present moment.

If you feel uncomfortable, it also can be helpful to remind yourself of an appropriate affirmation, such as, "I am learning to break new ground. I am courageous. I appreciate myself. It feels good to turn myself on while my beloved is watching."

As with the solo exercise of self-pleasuring, Partner A approaches the peak three times, moving the energy up the Inner Flute to the heart center each time before finally experiencing orgasm. Follow exactly the same steps as in the solo practice of self-pleasuring.

Partner B, you are learning how to give nonjudgmental support and love. Be generous! When Partner A is finished, let him or her rest for a few minutes in silence, then lie close, taking your lover in your arms, and offer words of appreciation and gratitude for his or her openness, such as, "Dear one, I appreciate the gift I have just received, for your willingness to show yourself in front of me, revealing your most intimate actions. I have learned better how to pleasure you."

When you are both ready, sit up and do the Heart Salutation.

See if you feel like talking about what took place, or whether you

Self-pleasuring while your beloved watches.

prefer to hold the discussion until you have exchanged roles and completed the whole exercise. Choose whichever way feels most appropriate.

When you do begin to give feedback, focus on the following points.
Partner A, what was the most difficult moment? The most pleasurable
one? Which part of your genitals felt the best? Did you have any
fantasies? Any images? Partner B, how did you feel watching your
partner?

Exchange roles. Partner B puts on the blindfold and begins self-
pleasuring while Partner A watches.

The session is complete when each partner has watched once and
self-pleasured once.

221

You may wish to repeat this practice at a later date or perhaps on several occasions, until you can move beyond any resistance and thoroughly enjoy it.

End with a Melting Hug and Heart Salutation.

Pointers

Some people may feel safer and better able to concentrate on their own sensations if their partner watches in silence, without touching them, while others may enjoy the support of their partner's caress or of whispered words of tender encouragement. Decide in advance which course you prefer.

When fears come up, you may feel that the pleasurable sensations are beginning to disappear. This is usually due to pressure—you may think you have to perform. When this happens, it is important to change the focus from the sex organs to the whole body, diffusing the sensations by caressing yourself all over. Remember to use the Three Keys during this process and to use as much of your favorite lubricant as you wish.

The observer should pay particular attention to the ways the active partner directs the energy upward, because later in this book you may wish to help each other master this important practice. Does she try to move it up too soon, long before the point of no return? It could mean she is tired or doesn't trust herself or feels scared of pleasure and later will need encouragement from you to build up more arousal.

Is your partner very expressive, making sounds, or silent and totally internalizing the experience? Is he or she taking this too seriously? If so, wait for an appropriate opportunity to tickle her, blow in his ears, anything to get her to smile. It's important to remember that this is play, a celebration.

Both partners should remember to be gentle with themselves and with each other. Whatever happens is okay. You don't have to show your partner you are capable of having a cosmic orgasm. It's enough to get used to the practice of self-pleasuring with someone else present.

At this point in the book, one of you may feel resistant and unwilling to continue. Take this resistance as a challenge to learn how to improve your communication skills together. Put the practices of this chapter on hold. Go back and review the practices of chapters 2 and 3, particularly the exercise Moving beyond Resistance. Use these practices for resolving tensions concerning self-pleasuring.

For example, by expressing fears, hopes, fantasies, and peak moments in the realm of self-pleasuring, you may find yourself opening up to the possibility of experimenting further. It is my experience that if both partners are committed to the goal of High Sex, they can find a way to proceed harmoniously, using the tools provided in this book.

SELF-PLEASURING IN FRONT OF EACH OTHER

Next you are ready to watch your partner self-pleasuring while you give yourself pleasure at the same time.

Purpose and Benefits

This practice will help you break through inhibitions and taboos in a playful and exciting way, freeing your sexual energy. When you can easily do self-pleasuring in front of each other, you also relieve the pressure one of you may feel to have intercourse at any given time.

Preparations

Prepare the Sacred Space.
    This exercise is both outrageous and fun. Approach it in the spirit of high adventure.
    It is important to be very comfortable and relaxed. A luxurious setting of big pillows will be very helpful.
    Allow 45 minutes for this practice.
    Mellow, sensual music will help.

Practice

Begin with a Heart Salutation and a Melting Hug.
    Lie back on the pillows slowly and luxuriously in a half-sitting, half-lying position, so you can easily see your partner. Make sure your neck is well-supported and relaxed. There should be no tensions in your body.
    Gently caress your body, maintaining eye contact with your partner. Be sensual, erotic; show your partner your movements, the way you give yourself pleasure. Be creative! Moisten a finger and slowly move it across

223

Self-pleasuring together.

your lips, make undulating movements with your pelvis, turning yourself on.

Take your time before moving to your genitals. There is no hurry. When you reach this pleasure point, begin slowly. Use your imagination, watching, for instance, the erect Vajra of your partner and imagining it coming inside your Yoni. Or watch your partner's Yoni contract and imagine how it would feel if you were inside her.

Show your wild self. Make sounds. Feel sexy. Feel the pleasure that comes with allowing yourself to go into the forbidden, breaking the rules. See how much of yourself can flower when you give each other unconditional approval and support. Bring in some sexy talk, a tickle, or a smile.

It's important not to interrupt the practice until you've completed the full cycle, going to the brink and pulling up the energy to the heart center three times before bringing yourself to a climax. If you can't complete the whole cycle the first time before achieving orgasm, don't worry. Go as far as you can. Pick it up one step further next time.

COMING TOGETHER: PLEASURING EACH OTHER

In the last exercise in this series, one partner pleasures the other, each taking a turn to be the active partner and the receiving partner. This practice offers you new ways of bringing your partner to orgasm.

Preparations

Create a luxurious, erotic Sacred Space.
    Allow 45 to 60 minutes for this practice.
    Choose who is Partner A and Partner B.

Practice

Proceed with a Heart Salutation and Melting Hug.
    Partner B begins by giving pleasure to Partner A. Partner B follows
the format of the Self-Pleasuring Ritual, sexually arousing and bringing
Partner A to the brink three times.
    Partner A should be receptive. Let Partner B do the movements that
you have been doing yourself. Focus on your breathing and the movements of your pelvis. Don't hesitate to communicate if you want Partner
B to change the stroke or intensity. When you come to the brink, tighten
the PC muscle, inhale deeply, move the energy up the Inner Flute to the
heart center, hold your breath for a few seconds, then relax and send the
energy back down to your genitals as you exhale.
    Partner B, the moment you feel Partner A on the threshold of
orgasm, cease all stimulation and stroke him or her from the genitals to
the heart or, if it feels appropriate, all the way up to the head. Help your
partner to pull the energy upward. Both partners need to be very alert
and sensitive, because in this practice it is easy to move quickly across the
threshold from arousal to orgasm and release.
    If you need a signal, Partner A can say, "Now," and that will be
the moment to stop all stimulation and, if necessary, to press on Partner
A's perineum point with the fingers of one hand to prevent orgasm or
ejaculation. Continue to stroke the energy up to the heart—and all the
way up to the head if it feels right—with the other hand. Then, on the
exhalation, bring your hand back down to the genitals.
    Partner B, as you pleasure Partner A, be open to whatever guidance
Partner A wants to give. You may feel that technical information such
as, "Put your fingers more to the right," or "Press harder," can cut off
your enthusiasm, but once again, you have to be patient. Most people
need two or three sessions of this kind before they feel easy and familiar
with each other's bodies. Then there can be more of a pleasurable flow
without interruptions.

Partner A, as the receiver, you are facing a new challenge, which is to guide Partner B as specifically as possible to what works for you. Dare to tell your partner exactly what you like, how you like it, and especially to encourage your partner, once the stroking feels right, to continue the same rhythm at a regular, uninterrupted pace for at least two to five minutes so that you have time to climb to a peak of arousal.

GUIDANCE FOR MEN ON AROUSING WOMEN. One comfortable position is for the woman to lie with her head and back supported on pillows, legs apart, the man sitting between her legs. The man's legs can be either extended or crossed. The woman's legs can be flexed, her knees up and her thighs resting over those of the man. Feel free to shift positions as needed so you remain relaxed and comfortable and can focus your attention on building up arousal.

Be aware that most women need a very light, feathery touch to start with and desire gentle stimulation of the whole body and pelvic area before you zero in on the genitals. Use ample massage oil and lubricant for the entire genital area, including the perineum and anus.

In the beginning, such sessions are scary for most women. When you are self-pleasuring, you are in charge. But putting yourself in the hands of another requires trust. This has to be built up through a caring touch, humor, patience, and loving words of appreciation on the part of the man. During this exercise, whisper in her ears, asking to be guided to her inner secrets, to be taught how to bring her to ecstasy.

Gently tease and tickle the area around her vagina, pulling on the pubic hair, stroking the major and minor labia, circling closer and closer to the clitoris. Touch the clitoris only very lightly. It is very sensitive. Take time to spread the labia apart and look closely at this bud of pleasure. Feel the wonder and peaks of delight that such a discreet organ may generate when properly treated. You are about to learn a subtle new language—the language of female orgasm. Go step by step, with patience and devotion.

Remember those strokes with which your partner pleased herself, and apply them now. Listen to her guidance. Experiment and accept the idea that at first you must proceed by trial and error; even though you watched, you don't know for sure what works. When something feels right, repeat it long enough so that she can assimilate it, relax into it, and integrate it. Don't change strokes too fast.

Find a basic stroke that pleases her the most. It could be teasing the clitoris as you hold it between your finger and thumb, moving up and down, circling around it, or on the side or top of it. The most important point is to be consistent with your stimulation. Apply ten to twenty strokes in a stimulating, yet regular, dependable rhythmic pattern that helps her to climb higher in her arousal. Then, for a few seconds, slow down, change to another stroke and start again.

When your partner's arousal is rising, her vaginal lips and clitoris will swell and become engorged from the increased blood flow, darkening in color. Her pelvic muscles will tense; her toes and fingers may spread

Concentrate fully on the sensations of arousal.

and curl; her torso or pelvis may arch toward your fingers, signaling the need for more and stronger stimulation.

At this stage you can insert the index and middle finger of one hand into her Yoni while the other hand is stimulating her clitoris, simulating the thrusting of the penis in lovemaking. Or you can stroke the G spot—an area the size of the tip of your middle finger, located behind the pubic bone, in the front and center of the vagina—consistently and rhythmically. The G spot is an important trigger point for the vaginal orgasm. When stimulated, it becomes engorged and firmer than the softer tissues around the vaginal walls. Continue with ten to fifteen stimulating strokes for the clitoris and the G spot, followed by a time of rest. If you are unfamiliar with the G spot, stay with the areas you can feel and recognize now. We will explore the G spot in more detail in chapter 10.

For receptive women: At this stage, you should practice the PC Pump consistently and vigorously, increasing your buildup to higher and higher stages of arousal. Forget everything else, and concentrate fully on the genital-pelvic sensations of arousal. Inhaling, draw your partner's

Stimulating the G spot.

fingers into your vagina as you tighten the vaginal muscles. Exhaling, relax the vaginal muscles and bear down, opening the vagina. Keep going with a regular rhythm.

At this point many women tend to lose control, scream, thrash about on the bed, and become extremely desirous of the final orgasm of release. This is understandable, but hold on nevertheless. Don't step across that point of no return. Remember that you are going to build up the delicious energy of arousal and say to your partner, "Now!" Then, with a strong, quick, deep inhalation, you will pull the energy up to the heart or the third eye while closing the lower gate.

The man can help his partner redirect her energy by pressing on the perineum point with two fingers of one hand or pressing the palm of his hand flat against her vagina while firmly but gently stroking upward with the other hand. He should follow the movement of her inhalation up the front of her body, from the pubic bone to the navel, chest, and all the way to the crown of the head, as explained in chapter 6.

At the end of the inhalation, gently pull on your partner's hair on top of her head, pulling from the roots to the tips. This emphasizes the upward movement of her energy. Freeze for a few seconds while she holds the energy in. After you get a feel for this, you will both feel like a plane taking off into the sky: peaceful, silent, expanded, and light.

Then, when she begins to exhale, let your hand accompany her breath with a downward stroke from the crown back to the genitals. Make sure your stroke follows exactly the upward and downward movement of her breathing pattern. As the giver, you may want to follow the same breathing pattern, inhaling deeply, holding the breath, and exhaling in synchronicity with your partner. This will add strength and scope to the experience.

If you sense that your partner is becoming discouraged, help her through her difficulty. Stop the stimulation; take a break; bring her a glass of water, fruit juice, or champagne; and lovingly encourage her. She may want to stop altogether, but feeling discouraged is not a good note on which to end the practice, and you should gently insist on continuing after this pause.

Another way to help is to encourage her to increase her breathing rate and redirect her attention to bodily sensations while you increase and intensify stimulation. Remember, everyone reacts differently, so don't impose your rules or vision of how this should be onto her. Be receptive yet supportive. That is your challenge.

Pressing the perineum to direct
her energy up.

GUIDANCE FOR WOMEN ON AROUSING MEN. Women need to be aware that most men require direct, strong, intense stimulation of the penis in order to reach erection. Do not expect your partner to get an erection automatically, and do not get discouraged if he loses it. Rather, ask him to specify what he needs and how he wants it.

Give him support and encouragement as he expresses such fears as putting himself in your hands and not being in charge of the situation, and as he ponders such anxious thoughts as, *Is she getting bored?* and *Am I doing this right?* Men are great thinkers, especially about "serious" matters such as sexual performance. So do what you can to defuse the situation—make faces, crack a joke, or make him laugh while you continue to stimulate him.

Most men need stimulation to reach erection.

Many women think they have to slow down, lowering the intensity of the stimulation, when they feel their partner doesn't seem to be with it. The opposite is true in most cases. You need to take your partner by surprise, diverting his mind through humor while stimulating his Vajra rapidly with strong pressure and hard strokes. Give him the sense that you are in charge, that you trust yourself and you know what to do. This will help him in the delicate situation of surrendering control to you.

Use plenty of lubricant on both your hands, and stimulate the whole genital and anal area. In the beginning apply strong pressure and slow, heavy strokes up and down the shaft of the penis. Stay with it until erection is achieved, gradually incorporating the strokes he prefers, which

231

you observed during the previous phases. Be experimental. If you are not sure, ask your partner, "Is this right for you?" Keep communicating with each other about what feels good.

When your partner has reached a full, hard erection, work to maintain it for at least ten minutes.

When your partner has relaxed into his state of sexual arousal, you can begin to alternate between giving his Vajra localized attention and stimulating the whole area—spreading out your caresses to include the scrotum, anus, pubis, belly, and the rest of the body.

When your partner approaches ejaculation, his testicles will draw up against his body, his buttocks and legs may tense up, and his pelvic muscles may contract. Be watchful for these signs of intense arousal and for his signal, "Stop!"

Help him control the urge to ejaculate and to hold the energy in, directing it upward. When he applies the control method described in the previous sequences—inhaling deeply and squeezing the PC muscles— help him by applying deep pressure on the perineum in one single, steady act.

With your free hand, lightly stroke the front of his body from the genitals all the way to the crown of his head. End the stroke by pulling lightly at the roots of his hair around the crown. Hold this position for the duration of the time your partner holds his breath, then relax your pressure on the perineum and sweep your hand downward as he exhales.

BOTH PARTNERS. When the receiving partner has been pleasured and brought to the brink three times, you can complete this part of the practice by giving him or her a full orgasmic release. The delay in reaching this moment of release will have greatly increased your partner's capacity for pleasure. Ask your partner, "Are you ready for the final celebration?" Then, as you stimulate your partner, give words of encouragement, such as, "Now you can open the floodgates. Allow yourself to go fully into your pleasure. Take it. I am with you, and I love you."

Afterward, allow 15 minutes to rest, integrate the experience, and give each other feedback. Recount the difficult moments, highlight the most pleasurable ones, and communicate in a supportive and loving way.

End this first half of the practice with a Heart Salutation and Melting Hug.

Exchange roles. Now it is the turn of the receiver to be the giver. Go through the whole sequence again.

Pressing his perineum to direct his energy up.

Pointers

When receiving pleasure in this practice, most people tend to breathe too hard. At the end of the inhalation, after holding the air in, they push the air vigorously out as they exhale. But it is better to exhale slowly so that you can mentally follow the flow of energy step by step down through the Inner Flute.

Many people also have a tendency to stop breathing as they approach orgasm. This increases tension, as well as the probability of orgasm or ejaculation. You can offset this by reminding your partner to breathe deeply, playfully breathing in his or her ear. Try not to speak at this stage.

Often, at the height of pleasure, we feel, *Aha! This is it—the right touch, the right sensation, the right speed!* But before we have a chance to settle comfortably into this peak of arousal, our partner has already changed the stroke because we haven't told him or her how good it feels. Be sure to communicate your pleasure in these moments. If you can

233

exlaim, "Yes! Yes!" that will be a clear indication to your lover to keep doing whatever is pleasing you so much.

However tempting it may be, your partner's orgasm is not the goal during this practice, nor should he or she attempt to persuade you otherwise until the energy has been moved up the Inner Flute three times. If you sense that your partner has become lost in the peaking sensation and is not going to stop, use your own intuition to decide when to cease stimulation and direct the energy upward.

Remember to use the Three Keys—breathing, movement, and sound. It is especially helpful for the person who is receiving to express what he or she is feeling through sounds. This is an excellent way of telling the active partner that his or her actions are effective. Make cooing, growling, or purring sounds that bring the energy down into the belly.

Another very important point, especially for women, is not to fake it. Be truthful and honest. If something doesn't feel right, say so. Be patient and consistent in your guidance, and assume that your partner wants to learn. Avoid starting the exercise with expectations that you have to do it right. Stay in the moment.

If negative feelings of impatience, frustration, self-doubt, boredom, or fatigue come up for you, let them move through your mind like the clouds in the sky. Don't attach too much importance to them. Relax, take it easy, take a break, drink a glass of wine. And take good care not to criticize each other, always addressing each other with a sense of positive support.

❧

Congratulations! You have just completed the most intensive marathon training in the art of loving yourself. I know this chapter required discipline, courage, and perseverance. By holding the vision of the most positive outcome that you wanted to achieve, you have overcome and healed many fears.

Going through the self-pleasuring rituals, you have learned how to develop autonomy and precision in the way you stimulate yourself, and you've come to a greater understanding of your body. You know that it is healthy to pleasure yourself and that you deserve the enjoyment it brings. You've discovered how to hold and contain the tension of arousal to a peak, and then redirect this energy to your heart, thus connecting your sensuality to feelings of love and acceptance.

Through the Sexual Dialogue, you've learned how to communicate with honesty and humor about your needs and desires, and in the ritual of Self-Pleasuring Under the Eyes of Your Beloved, you've shown your most erotic self to your partner—and have become empowered by it. Finally, through Pleasuring Each Other, you've learned how to bring your partner to a peak of arousal while enjoying your own strength and confidence.

Having accomplished so much, you will have established a deep bond of caring and intimacy with each other through the agony and ecstasy of it all. Repeat each of these practices until you know and enjoy each step.

As you are becoming a skillful and erotic lover, the time has come to focus on the art of building a balanced partnership: a playful relationship full of adventure and creativity.

The next chapter answers these questions: Who are you as a man? Who are you as a woman? How do these ideas about yourself limit both your sexual potential and your relationship? You will discover that when you harmonize your Inner Man and your Inner Woman with your partner, the love between you can sing like the songs of mating birds in spring.

❧

CHAPTER 8

HARMONIZING YOUR INNER MAN AND INNER WOMAN

According to tradition, the wise fool Mulla Nasruddin, a legendary Sufi, once wrote the following letter to his wife, complaining about the dire state of their sex life:

Only the united best of heart and sex together can create ecstasy.

—Anais Nin

To my dear, ever-loving wife,

During the past year I have tried to make love to you 365 times, an average of once per day, and the following is a list of the reasons you gave for rejecting me:

It will wake the children: 7; It is too hot: 15; It is too cold: 3; Too tired: 19; Too late: 16; Too early: 9; Pretending to sleep: 33; The window is open, neighbors might hear: 3; Backache: 16; Toothache: 2; Headache: 6; Not in the mood: 31; Baby restless, might cry: 18; Too drunk: 7; Visitors sleeping in the next room: 7; "Is that all you think about?": 62.

Dearest, do you think we can improve on our record during the forthcoming year?

Your ever-loving husband,

Mulla Nasruddin

Even if the poor Mulla didn't want to face the fact directly, it is clear that, to his wife, sex had become an unappealing and boring proposition. We may laugh at the poor Mulla's plight, but it reflects a contemporary concern. Why are so many people, in a culture so fascinated by sex, losing interest? Why do relationships that started out with intense sexual excitement frequently degenerate into the occasional fulfillment of a dreary obligation?

Only out of deep experience of love, sweet and bitter, pleasant and painful, high and low, heaven and hell, only out of deep experience of pain and pleasure through love does one become aware. They are needed to make you aware.

—Bhagwan Shree Rajneesh

The clinical answer is that lack of sexual desire can result from depression, stress, marital discord, or physical causes such as hormone deficiencies. But psychologists and counselors know that the origins are often more elusive. There is a great fear of intimacy today, and hence a fear of sex as the ultimate act of intimacy. People are afraid to be vulnerable, to let down their defenses and open up themselves to one another. Busy two-career couples cite fatigue and the inability to find time for more than quick, routine, weekly encounters as their reasons for avoiding slow, easy sexual intimacy. But the difficulty is deeper than reserving bigger chunks of time in your datebook for sex with your partner. The problem has reached such proportions that psychologists have come up with a clinical name for this widespread syndrome— Inhibited Sexual Desire. Complaints about disinterest in sex come as much from men as from women and focus as much on one's own lack of sexual desire as on a partner's lack of interest.

CONFRONTING SEXUAL BOREDOM

From the perspective of High Sex, the underlying problem may be deeper. I believe that people have become locked into fixed, restrictive gender roles and, as a result, have grown one-dimensional in their love-making, following a set of culturally determined responses. So we become bored and uninterested in the repetitious nature of sex and unable to draw upon other parts of ourselves for intimacy.

Transcending the Gender Trap

Cultural standards heavily influence the individual's perception of what it means to be a man and a woman. Because the existing culture clearly segregates the genders, as you grew up, you may have felt caught in the "gender trap" that this division has created. You may believe that, as a person born into a woman's body, you are exclusively female and therefore compelled to act like a woman, meaning to follow a set of socially predetermined roles. For example, in relating to a man, you may feel obliged to be soft, dependent, and supportive, to do what is pleasing to him, and feel that you always have to look sexy in order to be lovable. As someone born into a male body, you may believe that you are exclusively male and therefore expected to act like a man. For example, you may feel you must always be in charge, project a tough and capable image, and believe that your manhood is determined by the size of your bank account.

Because much of what we call femininity and masculinity is a set of roles pervasively taught and rewarded by society, overstepping the boundaries defined by these roles can feel risky. Many men, for instance, feel compelled to avoid their more feminine side. Some fear that any expression of gentleness or vulnerability might be interpreted as a sign of latent homosexuality. Others fear that if they are too tender with their mates, they will be manipulated or overpowered. Similarly, many women do not allow their independent, masculine side to be expressed. They fear that by taking initiative or being straightforward about their sexual needs, they will lose their attractiveness and no longer be considered desirable by men.

These one-dimensional attitudes are reflected in the ways we make love. Like most people, you probably learned that the man initiates and the woman responds. These roles are loosening and changing, especially as women claim a more active role in a hitherto male-dominated society. The basic stereotypes still exert a powerful hold on our subconscious minds, yet I believe they are purely arbitrary, rigid ideas imposed by fashion and tradition. In most cases they have little to do with our authentic individuality.

The multiplicity of the gods correspondeth to the multiplicity of man.

—C. G. Jung

Expanding Your Sexual Identity

The goal of this chapter is to free you from these stereotypical roles. You will learn to expand your gender identity, recognizing both the male and female aspects of your personality, welcoming them, exploring them with your partner, and expressing them in your lovemaking.

From the perspective of High Sex, no man is just a man, and no woman is just a woman. Each man is both male and female. Each woman is both female and male.

High Sex acknowledges that each of us has a dominant polarity and a recessive one. In a man the dominant side is masculine, and the subordinate is feminine. In a woman the dominant is feminine, and the recessive is masculine. From this perspective stable, happy relationships between men and women require an understanding that a balance, an inner partnership, must be achieved within each of us between the male and the female aspects of our nature. Each of us has an Inner Man that is associated with dynamic, active energy; with setting and achieving goals; and with getting things done. This is what the Taoists call the Yang aspect of our nature—the engaged, noncontemplative self. And each of us also has an Inner Woman, a natural capacity for letting things happen, for going with the flow of life without setting goals, for relaxing and being playful. This is what the Taoists call the Yin aspect of our nature—the contemplative, intuitive, communing self.

We are all familiar with legends about an earlier, more harmonious and peaceful age. The Bible tells of a garden where woman and man lived in harmony with each other and nature—before a male god decreed that woman henceforth be subservient to man. The Chinese Tao Te Ching *describes a time when the yin, or feminine principle, was not yet ruled by the male principle, or yang, a time when the wisdom of the mother was still honored and followed above all.*

—Riane Eisler
The Chalice and the Blade

This concept of combined male and female energy within the individual has a biological basis. Scientists have acknowledged what they call the essential bipolarity of our nature through the coexistence of male and female hormones in each man and woman. Hormones regulate growth, gender, and the development of our sexual energy. From the Tantric perspective the man is given the possibility, through the existence of female hormones in his body, of tasting and experiencing the feminine within himself. Likewise, through the existence of the male hormones, the woman is given the possibility of experiencing the masculine side of herself.

This biological reality has its psychic counterpart. C. G. Jung studied the interplay between the masculine and feminine components of the individual psyche. He recognized a feminine element in the male, calling it the anima—the Latin word for "soul"—and noted that it remains largely unconscious. He also conjectured, however, that man's most creative work emerges from his anima—his dreams, visions, insights, inspiration, and intuition. Similarly, Jung postulated a masculine soul, or animus, for the female, and he argued that both men and women would benefit from the development of the opposite polarity.

Integration of the Inner Man and Inner Woman

What Jung envisioned is now becoming a reality. Both men and women are striving toward a greater awareness and integration of these inner polarities. In order to do this, the woman has to recognize the functioning of the animus, or male aspect, when it manifests itself in assertiveness, ambition, intellectual striving, and questioning. To integrate the Inner Man, she has to exercise masculine qualities that used to be repressed in

Krishna and his beloved Radha, in a drawing taken from an eighteenth-century Indian painting, symbolize the embrace of Yin and Yang.

women by a patriarchal, male-dominant society. In the same way, the man has to develop feminine qualities of caring, nurturing, sensual abandon, and receptivity that in the past have also been repressed because they were considered unmanly.

In a loving relationship, when these feminine and masculine qualities are developed and understood, the union of the two polarities can happen within each person. This is what is meant in Tantra by "ecstatic awareness." It is a state of consciousness that embraces both sexes in one body and then rises above the inner duality to a state of oneness.

At this point you may react by saying, "This sounds wonderful, but how do I get there?"

Happily, I have mapped out a path, and the first step is for you to recognize what your own attitudes are toward your Inner Man and Inner Woman.

Contrasting the Two Attitudes

Here are some illustrations of the kinds of attitudes a woman may have when her Inner Man is not awakened, as opposed to her attitudes when she has embraced both polarities:

Unawakened: She never or rarely says no. She feels compelled to say yes because she fears that if she shows her real feelings, she will be rejected.

Awakened: She risks saying no when she feels like it, because she respects herself, knows her limits, and does not feel afraid to express them.

Unawakened: When making love, she sometimes fakes her orgasm to protect her partner's self-confidence.

Awakened: She tells her partner that she did not reach orgasm, explains why, and suggests ways in which they can mutually increase their pleasure.

Unawakened: She dreams about a charming prince or eloquent poet who will take her life in his hands, think for both of them, and make the important decisions.

Awakened: She sees herself as a charming princess, riding alongside the charming prince, holding her life in her own hands. To her, life is a cocreation between equal partners.

Here are some similar examples contrasting male attitudes about the Inner Woman:

Unawakened: During lovemaking he never says a word. If the woman wants to express herself, he replies, "Be quiet. You're spoiling things."

Awakened: He enters into lovemaking with no preconceived ideas, open to change at any time and willing to listen to his partner.

Unawakened: Housework is a woman's job.

Awakened: Let's share the responsibility.

Unawakened: Even in emotional moments he dares not cry because he thinks he will look like a sissy.

Awakened: When he feels vulnerable, he asks for support and allows the tears to flow.

We all have such one-sided attitudes, but we can recognize and change them with a little patience and practice.

Celebrating the Whole Spectrum

You, too, are a rich blend of masculine and feminine qualities, all of which can be celebrated and enjoyed. From the perspective of High Sex, a balanced relationship between a man and woman, based on love and intimacy, begins with the harmonization of these two polarities within oneself. In Tantra this was exemplified by the relationship between the male deity Shiva and his consort Shakti. One of the most beautiful

Most of us in committed, stable relationships settle for predictability, comfort, and companionship because we fear exploring the mysteries that we embody together as man and woman, the exposure of our deepest selves. Yet in our fear of the unknown within us and between us we ignore and avoid the very gift that our commitment sets within our reach—true intimacy.

—Robin Norwood
Women Who Love Too Much

According to the Second Epistle of Clement, *when Jesus was asked at what moment the Kingdom would come, He replied: "When the two shall be one, outside like the inside, the male with the female, neither male nor female."*

Tantric scriptures consists of a loving dialogue in which Shiva teaches Shakti the methods by which she might attain spiritual enlightenment. Then they switch roles, and it is Shakti's turn to become Shiva's guru, his spiritual teacher, and to teach him the ways to an enlightened sexuality. Thus they symbolize the change and flow between the feminine and masculine principles of Yin and Yang, receiver and giver, student and teacher. This is a beautiful example of loving respect between equals in the attainment of sexual ecstasy.

In High Sex when the lovers are joined in a deep meditative embrace, the woman becomes the door through which the man recognizes and feels his Inner Woman within himself. Simultaneously, the man

243

awakens his partner to the presence of the Inner Man within her. It is through this awakening of both aspects of their nature within themselves that love is born. This recognition is beautifully expressed in the Tantric scriptures, when Shiva says to his partner, "You, O Shakti, you are my true self, there is no difference between you and me." This is why, in Hindu mythology, the union of Shiva and Shakti symbolizes the ecstatic union of male and female energies within one body, not in two bodies as superficial appearances suggest.

When I introduce this idea in seminars, I often begin by ringing a powerful gong. After the rippling echoes of sound have subsided, I ask, "When you heard that sound, who did the hearing?" In the discussion that follows, it becomes clear that no one hears the sound as self-consciously male or female, but from a state of consciousness that transcends both polarities. This is a simple and direct experience of the true nature of consciousness, which is androgynous, including the male and female polarities yet transcending both. It is to this blissful state that the union of man and woman leads in High Sex, a state that is already present in each of us, ready to be tapped as a source of energy and joy. It is a key that can unlock the prison of gender.

As I have already mentioned, men are often afraid to express their feminine qualities, fearing that they will lose their sense of manhood. But in working with men in my seminars, I have observed a strange paradox: The awakening of the feminine qualities in the man happens most strongly when he has the opportunity to contact the wild, passionate side of his maleness through dance, drumming, and ritual celebrations that allow him to feel strong in himself. In such moments he is truly a man. He knows it. He does not have to prove it. Consequently, it no longer feels threatening for him to become soft, feminine, and vulnerable. It does not take anything away from him but rather complements what he already has. Moreover, he finds that in allowing the emergence of his femininity, he is developing qualities that women yearn for in their male partners— attention, gentleness, patience, empathy, receptivity, and a capacity to harmonize his rhythms in lovemaking to those of his partner. Far from losing his attraction as a man, he is greatly increasing his personal magnetism.

For women the process is very much the same. When a woman has the opportunity to celebrate and enjoy the earthy, seductive, sexy, passionate aspect of her femininity, she comes to know who she really is.

Integration, or spiritual wholeness, is the incarnation and expression of the self, which includes and transcends the male-female alternative.

—Ann Belford Ulanov
The Feminine in Jungian Psychology and in Christian Theology

A woman's roles.

She can declare, "I am woman. I feel, I express, I show, I play, I dance the woman in me." She has contacted her root energy, and her femaleness cannot be shaken by external circumstances. Then it becomes easier for her to move to the other polarity, the male dimension, owning her power, asserting her needs, exploring her creativity. She no longer fears that by being self-assertive, she is sabotaging her femininity. Nor does she feel the need to use her newly found masculine qualities to compete with the man—a trap that many women tend to fall into as part of today's reaction to male dominance. She can draw upon the dynamism, creativity, and initiative of her male polarity to help project the beauty and radiance of her female nature. In my experience men are fascinated by women who have achieved this inner balance. Feeling the woman's confidence, a man can relax in the knowledge that he does not have to be continuously in charge. Because she is willing and able to teach him what she needs, he can relate to her as an equal.

A man's roles.

Women are peonies, spring
* flowers, lotuses and bowers.*
Women are pomegranates,
* peaches, melons and pearls.*
Women are receptacles, crucibles,
* vessels and worlds.*
Women are the fruit of life, the
* nourishing force of Nature.*

—Yuan-Shih Yeh-Ting
Chi, Tao Tsung-I

In this chapter you will explore many roles in order to give full expression to your Inner Man and Inner Woman. Women will have the opportunity to experience their male partners as brothers, husbands, lovers, sons, fathers, teachers, and healers. Men will have the opportunity to experience their female partners as sisters, wives, lovers, daughters, mothers, teachers, and healers. Moving through these roles, you will both discover new depths and dimensions to your erotic life. You will see that the rewards of High Sex come to partners who are dedicated to creating the deepest and most varied experiences in lovemaking, exploring beyond the gender trap into multidimensional sensations and feelings, sharing the delight of moving together, playing out different scenes and fantasies, initiating and adapting constantly.

Think of great ballroom dance partners you have seen, or ice skaters in the Olympics—the costuming, music, intimate coordination, physical grace, experimentation, risky moves, and dedication of each partner to a harmonized performance. The result is the thrill of dancing in harmony. That's what High Sex can be like.

VISUALIZING YOUR INNER MAN AND INNER WOMAN

This practice will take you on a journey in which you allow your own image of your Inner Man and Inner Woman to emerge from your subconscious mind.

Purpose and Benefits

By forming a picture of your Inner Man and Inner Woman, you will see his or her characteristics more clearly. Rather than wondering which aspect is dominant in you, you will focus your attention on how these aspects relate to each other, observe your attitudes toward both of them, and discover what they can teach you.

Preparations

Do this practice by yourself. Allow 30 to 40 minutes.

Create the Sacred Space, and make the atmosphere as mystical as possible. Use candlelight, incense, and power objects to create a mood in which other realms can be entered.

Play soft music as a gentle background, or listen to recorded sounds of the ocean. Wear clothing that is loose and comfortable.

In this practice both men and women first will visualize the Inner Woman and then the Inner Man.

Practice

Make a Heart Salutation to yourself. Lie down, close your eyes, and begin to breathe slowly and deeply into your belly.

As you exhale, imagine that you are sinking deeper into the mattress or floor, letting go of any worries or tension. Focus on your breathing, and let the traffic of thoughts in your mind flow past without paying attention to it. Feel yourself getting lighter, free of concerns.

Behind closed eyelids imagine that you are looking at a blank screen, waiting with enthusiastic expectation for a movie to start. Place your hands on your heart, and ask your inner self to reveal your Inner Woman. Don't be in a hurry to create an image of her on the screen all at once; you can build her slowly, line by line.

When opposites no longer damage each other,
Both are benefited through the attainment of Tao . . .
Therefore, the wise identifies opposites as one,
And sets an example for the world.

—Tao Te Ching

247

Place your hand on your heart and ask your Inner Self to reveal your Inner Woman.

As she appears in your mind's eye, observe what qualities this woman may possess. Is she contemporary, or is she from another time—from ancient Greece, perhaps, or a Native American tribe? Look at her clothes. How is she dressed? In what landscape or context is she situated?

What mood is she in? Is she serious, sad, happy, lighthearted? What general feeling does she convey—an air of mystery, dignity, ceremony, gaiety, tragedy, or smoldering passion? What color is her hair? What color are her eyes, and what is the texture of her face and skin? Look at her nose, her mouth, and see what form they take. Is her body round and full-breasted, or slim and sleek?

Slowly, through answers to these questions, build her image on your inner movie screen until you have firmly established the shape, mood, and qualities of your Inner Woman. Let her engage in a daily task, leisurely activity, or ritual so that you can see the way she moves and behaves.

When you have given as much solidity and reality to this Inner Woman as you can, let her turn toward you and approach you, so that she fills your movie screen. Prepare to listen to the important message that she is about to give to you. She will tell you how it feels for her to live with you, in your body. She will also tell you what she requires from you in order to feel more in harmony with you.

Listen as she begins to answer. Does she feel that you allow her to express herself in your life, or does she feel imprisoned and hidden away? Does she feel that you listen to her, or does she feel ignored? Does she feel nourished by you?

Let her feelings come forth. Let her weep or laugh if she wants to, and allow yourself to be receptive to everything she says. Listen particularly for some central suggestion from her that can create more harmony between the two of you. For example, she may say, "Yesterday you felt angry. I wanted to tell you that behind your anger, you were feeling hurt. But you didn't listen to me because you are afraid of being vulnerable. Yet if you remain unguarded, I can come close to you and heal you. I long for you to be soft and open sometimes, for that is when I can live in your heart and look out through your eyes."

Let your Inner Woman speak for as long as she wishes in this internal dialogue. You may ask more questions if you wish, until you are satisfied that she has expressed herself fully, and you have the answers you want.

When you have both finished, thank your Inner Woman and let her slowly fade from the screen.

The union of the sexes is four-membered rather than two-membered: it always means the complex union of the male element of the one with the female element of the other, and of the female element of the first with the male element of the second. The mystical life of the androgyne is realized not in one bisexual being but rather in the quadripartite union of two beings.

—Nicholas Berdyaev

Then take a distinct break. Get up, sip some tea, stretch, move around the room. Give yourself a chance to clear your mind of the image.

Then, when you are ready, lie down again, close your eyes, and resume deep, slow breathing. Again visualize the blank movie screen behind your eyelids. Rest your hands on your heart, and ask your inner self to reveal your Inner Man. Build the image slowly. Ask yourself the same questions as you did for the Inner Woman: In what culture is he placed? In what landscape? How is he dressed? How do his physical features look? What is his mood and general bearing?

When you have given him as much substance as possible, allow him to look at you and approach you, filling the screen. Prepare to listen to the message he is about to give you. He will now tell you how it feels for him to live with you in your body. He will tell you what he requires to feel accepted and understood by you.

Listen to his responses. Does he feel that you allow him to express himself in your life? Does he feel that you listen to him, or does he feel ignored? Pay attention to his heartfelt suggestions, which can make your internal relationship more harmonious. What would he most like to receive from you?

For example, your Inner Man may say, "You know, I really wish you wouldn't sell yourself so cheap. When you do things that you don't really want to do, just to please others—just for peace of mind—it makes me so mad! If you would only call on me in those moments, I could give you more support, self-respect, and courage."

Listen to everything your Inner Man wants to tell you, and ask more questions if you wish. End by thanking your Inner Man, and give him a Heart Salutation. Let the image slowly fade from the screen. End the practice by giving yourself a Heart Salutation.

Pointers

Be flexible in your approach to this exercise. You may not be the kind of person who visualizes very well. If so, try sitting in front of a mirror, looking at your reflection, and seeing in it the Inner Woman and then the Inner Man. Ask the questions of your reflection, and answer as if you are the Inner Man or Inner Woman.

Perhaps you do not see a movie screen inside your head but instead find yourself projecting the images into a sort of abstract blankness. You may not see human figures but symbolic male and female animals, or you

The bodily experience of androgyny can find its ultimate expression through sexual intercourse, when this is experienced in the spirit of evolutionary consciousness. In this act are combined the potencies inherent in the union of the cosmic Masculine and Feminine, with those generated in the union between two human beings, in each of whom the "mystical marriage" has come to pass.

—June Singer
Androgyny

What is the message of your
Inner Man?

may experience male and female feelings that are not clothed in a specific body. All these responses are adequate, as long as you get in touch with the male and female aspects of yourself and are receptive to their messages.

After doing this practice in my seminars, people often have such questions or comments as, "My Inner Woman was very sad," or "My Inner Man had a body but no face," or "I saw a shape or color but no person," or "I saw several people, not one," or "I didn't see anything at all." In these instances I encourage people to reflect on the significance of what they experienced. For example, in the case of the person who received an image of a man with a body but no face, this could mean that to him or her the body is more important than the mind, or that a conflict exists between the mind and body. In the case of the person whose Inner Woman was sad, I suggested, "Ask yourself why. What does this mean for you? It could be that you never listen to her, and she doesn't feel acknowledged."

If you get a clear message from your Inner Man or Inner Woman, you are on your way to a deeper relationship with your inner polarities. If you do not get a clear response, there is no need to spend a lot of time analyzing the situation. My basic rule is to repeat the visualization practice until you can establish a clear image of your Inner Man and Inner Woman and can hear the messages they bring to you. Each time you do this exercise, the visions and answers will be clearer.

The sign of your success will be that you begin to integrate an awareness of both polarities into your daily life. At various times of the day, in different situations, you will notice whether your Inner Man or Inner Woman is present or whether you are suppressing one of them in a situation in which he or she could naturally take charge.

A woman client gave this example: "We were lying in bed, and my partner was falling asleep, when I heard my Inner Man saying, 'Take the initiative and create what you want.' So I discovered a way of seducing him out of his sleep, but I did it in a very feminine and gentle way, using the talents of the Inner Woman while listening to the initiatives of the Inner Man. It turned out beautifully. In previous times I would have resigned myself to an uneventful night and gone to sleep."

A male client told me, "My wife had been away for two weeks on a business trip, and I was happy and excited to meet her when she got back. We found ourselves lying on the bed. I was extremely hot sexually and wanted to make love. However, I heard the voice of my Inner Woman saying, 'Wait—she needs more time.' Intuitively I felt that my wife was still preoccupied with problems that had arisen during her trip. I held her close, allowing her time to relax and open up. She greatly appreciated my tenderness. I felt her body unwind. Slowly she became warm and vibrant, and my Inner Man was rewarded with a green light to proceed."

ROLE-PLAYING EACH OTHER

Now that you have become aware of your inner polarities, the next practice will help you to discover the attitudes and patterns through which you express being male and female *with each other.* This is one of the most delightful games I have ever played. It involves role-playing your partner and then having your partner role-play you. You exchange names, clothes, makeup, personality, gait, everything. For a while you become the other person, adopting as best you can every aspect of his or her behavior, from speech patterns to stance to quirky gestures.

Purpose and Benefits

Ordinarily you do not see yourself through the eyes of someone else. This game gives you the chance to experience how you come across to your partner. You hear how you talk—both your distinctive speaking style, and what you tend to talk about. You see how you walk, gesture, listen, kiss, and hug, and in return you show how your partner comes across to you. The game can be incredibly funny, and it's surprising how many deep revelations can emerge in this atmosphere of merriment and parody.

Both men and women can get in touch with their own masculine and feminine sides by role-playing their partners. This will create more flexibility and freedom from gender stereotypes. You can reveal to your partner—and vice versa—in a playful, nonthreatening way, those things that make it difficult for you to relate and that stand in the way of harmony. You can disclose those character traits that your partner is not aware of because they are so ingrained and habitual. In this mutual exchange of roles, you also reveal to each other the fixed attitudes you both have about what it means to be a man or a woman, and how these assumptions affect and determine your relationship.

In Role-Playing Each Other, you can illustrate patterns of jealousy, clinging, inattention, controlling, and interrupting. It takes courage to

There is something so inspirational about any relationship entered into with the acknowledgment of a higher dimension, that with just a little preparation most people can be taught to touch this new level of experience.

—Richard Moss
The Black Butterfly

253

expose your partner's foibles, and it can be unnerving to have your own
blind spots revealed. But the atmosphere of the game should render this
healing communication innocent and even erotic.

Preparations

Create the Sacred Space.

Allow at least an hour or two for this practice. Be clear about the
time frame, and stick to it. It is important for this practice to have a
definite beginning and ending so that you can establish boundaries to the
dramatic comedy you will be enacting.

It's more effective if you start in separate rooms, dressing up in each
other's clothes. Try to find clothes that more or less fit you—a few
temporary alterations should do the trick.

See if you can arrange your hair like that of your partner—a wig
may help, if you can find one. If not, a hat is a useful way of hiding your
own hair, or perhaps you can find a substitute for a wig—colored paper,
perhaps, or a piece of cloth.

Remember your partner's face, and try to reproduce it on your
own—putting on makeup, penciling in or pasting on a mustache or a
beard. Fill in the accessories that distinguish your partner: jewelry, shoes,
scarves, vests, ties.

Before coming together, adopt the Basic Stance for a few minutes,
with your eyes closed, breathing deeply. Focus on becoming like your
partner in every way.

SUGGESTIONS FOR WOMEN. Your challenge is to submerge yourself in your
male partner's personality. Become him. Feel how he carries himself. Are
his shoulders sloped, hunched, or level? Is his torso drooping forward,
leaning back, erect? Does his manner of walking flow sensually from the
hips, or is the movement confined to his knees and lower legs? Try
walking as he does. Is it fast or slow? How do his feet meet the floor?
Does stand on the balls of his feet or on his heels? Do his toes point
in or out? How does he hold his neck, rigidly or loosely? How about
his head—does it remain fixed, bent forward, jerk around, have a habitual
twitch? How do his eyes and mouth move? Keep adding the characteristic
features, gradually becoming more and more like him, externally and
internally.

Remember how your male partner speaks, and try talking that way. Is it more from the belly or from the throat? Is his voice high-pitched or deep? How does he gesture when he speaks? What does he talk about? Rehearse some lines, capturing his speech patterns. And be sure to exaggerate so that you can let him know what it's like to hear some of his common refrains.

Depending on how you plan to spend the next hours, you can also recall how he eats, how he drives, and so on. Get ready to be him in every possible way.

SUGGESTIONS FOR MEN. You are becoming like your female partner. You are imagining and feeling how she moves her body, how it feels to have her hips, how it feels to have her breasts, her skin. Imitate how she carries herself, how she stands, walks, carries her head, and moves her arms. Feel the pleasures, the sensations, the surprises of being in a woman's body. Is she fluid, sensual, and overtly sexy, or stiff, withdrawn, and uptight? Imagine that you're a great actor, and immerse yourself in the role of your female partner.

Then, when you feel that you have successfully impersonated your partner, let him or her know that you are ready, and meet in your Sacred Space. Stay in your new role.

Practice

When you meet, the first thing you are both likely to do is burst out laughing. It takes a little discipline to maintain your new roles, but remember this is the vital ingredient that makes the game work. So be dedicated actors, even if you're playing comedy.

These first moments offer a precious opportunity to meet again, as if for the very first time. So before throwing yourself into the more familiar task of playing each other in the context of your current relationship, imagine that you have never seen each other before this moment.

Introduce yourselves. If it feels right, the man can be shy in playing the woman, and the woman can feel what it is like to be the man in this situation—the initiator, the one is who supposed to make all the right moves. Think for a moment—how did you feel when you met? What was the attraction? You may wish to enact a whole evening in which you come to know each other for the first time—not necessarily repeating the exact situation in which you met, but staying firmly in character. This could include flirting and seduction, but don't be in a hurry to jump into bed. Take your time, and feel the person you are playing as deeply as possible.

Once you have played these opening scenes, you can proceed to the current situation, reenacting some daily activities, such as cooking a meal, talking about your plans and your concerns, dancing together, seducing each other. As you make the transition from newly introduced strangers to familiar partners, notice whether anything has been lost through this increasing familiarity. Are you taking each other for granted? Are you less open, more demanding? Do not hesitate to enact those behavior patterns in your partner that you feel have made it difficult for you to be heard, seen, and understood.

When watching your partner impersonating you, try not to get upset by what you are seeing. Rather, learn about yourself through this opportunity. This can be a moment of great insight in which you clearly see the patterns that have prevented a deeper intimacy in your relationship. Most people find they can laugh at themselves, because the whole exercise is well-intentioned. If feelings of anger or embarrassment arise, do not try to hide them, but open yourself to the truth of the portrait you are seeing.

Make sure you end the game at the appointed time.

Sit facing each other. Close your eyes and be silent, taking a few deep breaths and integrating all that has happened.

End with a Heart Salutation and Melting Hug.

For the next half-hour do not speak about the game you have just played. Then give each other feedback, recollecting the most difficult, revealing, and humorous moments. Tell your partner what you learned that can improve your relationship.

Pointers

At first you may wish to role-play for an hour or so. Then, as you get better at the game, see if you want to play for a whole evening, acting each other around the house and possibly even in bed.

Even if you feel that your acting is amateurish, that you can't mimic the details of your partner's looks and habits, do your best to stay with the basic feeling of being him or her. After a while you may discover a natural ability to play this character. You'll soon see that your observations of your partner are keener than you realized.

In my seminars people often play this game over an extended lunch, with the whole group participating. It's also a hilarious and healing game to play at parties, once you get a little experience of doing it and reaping its benefits.

A word of caution: The aim here is to use role-playing to create more understanding and harmony with a loving and humorous attitude, not to humiliate. So if the temptation to be hurtful comes up, resist it and carefully toe the delicate line that divides revelation from revenge.

You may stumble into awkward moments when the easiest thing would be to say, "Let's stop being silly. I'm me, you're you. Let's drop this charade." But be courageous and stay in the roles. Your play-acting will deepen in these moments if, instead of quitting, you sincerely share your feelings while staying in character.

Vera, a young singer from San Francisco, had this to say after playing the game with Don, her husband: "Don acted 'me' to perfection. I saw myself as never before. It's true I am spoiled, always demanding, impossible. I see it now. And I am much more aware of what I say, how I say it, what I do, and the consequences of my acts. As a result, I feel more at ease with myself and with Don. I am able to see that he and I are two different, autonomous beings. Now I can listen to him and really *hear* him. Before I couldn't. I was always reacting to him without thinking. Now I observe myself while I act. It feels so good to be able to take some distance."

THE YIN-YANG GAME

Having found ways to harmonize the male and female aspects of your nature with each other, you are now ready to proceed to the Yin-Yang Game, the most popular game in my seminars. The idea for this game came to me after spending ten delightful days roaming around New Mexico with Alan Watts, one of the first Westerners to popularize Eastern philosophy. We had intense conversations, played crazy games, shared sacred rituals. One day he talked about a special ingredient in human relationships that made them exciting for him: the magical combination of being constantly surprised, while at the same time having your fondest fantasies fulfilled.

From this idea emerged the following game. It is one of the most revealing practices for couples to gain an understanding of how to balance their male and female polarities, to be equally active and receptive with each other.

The game is simple. One partner has wishes, and the other acts as the facilitator who makes the wishes come true. Then these roles are exchanged.

The game can be seen in terms of the ancient oriental concept of Yin and Yang—symbols of the complementary principles of negative and positive, receptive and active, female and male. The Yang partner makes wishes, the Yin partner fulfills them, and then they exchange roles. Both people have to flow in dynamic harmony between these two polarities, moving from Yin to Yang and back again, switching back and forth.

In this game you learn to take responsibility for what you want. You express it clearly, and you make it happen, including your wildest fantasies.

Both people have to be inventive, creative, challenging, generous, risk-taking, daredevilish, and at the same time open, receptive, and responsive.

Purpose and Benefits

This practice is one of the best ways I've discovered to build trust and intimacy between partners, which in turn creates the context for experiencing High Sex together. The Yin-Yang Game heals and improves the way partners relate to each other. This is essential in High Sex because in my experience methods for transforming sexual energy work better when there is an atmosphere of intimacy and trust, spontaneity and sincerity, love and playfulness between the two people who are practicing them.

I sometimes call the Yin-Yang Game "How Good Can You Stand It?" because it challenges your inhibitions about deserving pleasure, asking for what you have always wanted, especially in sex, and feeling that you deserve the best. Let's face it—the times when we allow ourselves to receive gifts of pleasure without feeling that we have to reciprocate are rare. And the times when we dare to ask for what we want in love are equally infrequent. The Yin-Yang Game is set up to create one of

Relationships have a chance of being successful if each person in the relationship is self-centered, that is, focused on her/his own needs, and on becoming acquainted with the internal masculine or feminine self. One must also have one's own creative work and a sex life with oneself in addition to the sex in the relationship.

—Margo Woods
Masturbation, Tantra and Selflove

these rare moments. Through it you can discover that giving yourself permission to ask for what you want is a giant step in your growth as a happy, fulfilled, mature human being. In addition, the changes and reversals in roles will enrich your experience of the masculine and feminine qualities present in your own nature.

You will also experience the fact that creative freedom in love emerges when a balance is reached between the feminine and the masculine—the yielding and initiating roles—within each player. The game is also a training in the art of switching from one role to the other quickly and freely.

It's not just giving that brings pleasure; it's also receiving. In concert, these two essential human acts join in a circle of interaction that expands with use. When the circle is complete, the more you give, the more you get, and vice versa.

—George Leonard

Preparations

The game is usually played between two partners—friends, lovers, husband and wife. But if you feel adventurous, you can play it with three partners. Experience has shown that it doesn't work with more than three people. You are free to play the game in your house or outdoors, or you can travel to another place if you wish, such as a romantic hotel or a great restaurant—whatever catches your fancy.

Decide on a time period during which you will play the Yin-Yang Game, and stick to it. Ideally, you should play it over a period of 48 hours, although 24 hours is also good. Six hours is about the minimum.

Then decide on the time periods you will reserve for each role. In my experience the deepest results come from dividing the whole time into two equal periods. But if you wish, you can start by reserving two or three hours for one partner to play Yang and the other Yin, then exchange roles for an equal period of time and keep changing off until the end of the game.

Practice

To start the game each of you should go alone to a quiet place with a pencil and paper to create a scenario called "My ideal day in heaven," or "What I always wanted to receive and never dared to ask for." Make a complete list of your wishes, even the most outrageous ones. Keep going until nothing more comes to mind. Be aware as you do so that you may not be able to play out some of them because they are too impractical. Listing everything that comes to mind, however, will inspire both partners to create new strategies for pleasure.

Then review the list and arrange the items in order of priority. Give priority to the ones that are feasible.

When you have compiled your list, meet with your partner in the Sacred Space. Exchange a Heart Salutation. Decide who is to start the game as the Yang partner and who is to be the Yin partner. Then read and discuss your lists with each other. It will be the Yin partner's task to carry out the desires of the Yang partner; afterward you will change roles.

"When I wake up, I want you to serve me breakfast in bed."

The practice of this exercise depends mostly on what the lists contain. For example, let's say that as the Yang partner, you wish to create a scenario that pampers your self-confidence and gives you a sense of culture and class. You make the following requests to the Yin partner:

"When you talk to me, end every one of your sentences with a compliment, such as, 'Pass me the salt, O beautiful and wise one.'"

"I am going to bed now, and I want you to read me my favorite poems or stories. Read them with gusto and style. Act them out. Look at me between the lines."

"When I wake up, I want you to serve me breakfast in bed—breakfast for two, with chocolate mousse, croissants, Viennese coffee, and a flower and poem on the tray."

Or let's say that you crave a sense of abundance, a great romance, a honeymoon, or a feeling that you are entering exciting and forbidden territory. You may ask:

"I want to lie down naked by the fireplace while you cover my body with flowers and dollar bills. Stand over me, and let flowers and bills rain over me until every inch is covered."

"I want to lie here and be cuddled for at least an hour. I want to be five years old—innocent, silly, spoiled, loud, unpredictable, and completely accepted. Touch my heart, and tell me you love me. Hold me tight. Breathe with me. Let me relax in your arms."

The game offers endless opportunities for sensual delight:

"Kiss my left nipple for 20 minutes."

"Seduce me under the kitchen table."

"Be my sacred harlot and do a striptease for me."

As I have already mentioned, this game helps you to build intimacy in a multidimensional way, but this does not necessarily imply sexuality. You are not obligated to make love or to do anything you feel is inappropriate for you, even when it is your turn to be Yin and to surrender.

SUGGESTIONS TO THE YANG PARTNER. Begin by taking full responsibility for making your desires and fantasies come true. You are king for a day, and you have the right to ask for anything that you wish, the fulfillment of any fantasy. Be daring, inventive, and creative, beyond the ordinary limitations of everyday life. You are learning what you like, how you like it, and how much of it you want. You are learning how to receive more pleasure.

I learned this, at least, by my experiment: that as one advances confidently in the direction of his dreams, and endeavors to live the life which he has imagined, he will meet with a success unexpected in common hours. He will put some things behind, will pass an invisible boundary; new, universal, and more liberal laws will begin to establish themselves around and within him; or the old laws be expanded, and interpreted in his favor in a more liberal sense, and he will live with the license of a higher order of beings.

—Henry David Thoreau

261

"I want to be five years old
and cuddled for an hour. Hold
me tight . . . and tell me you
love me."

As Yin, you are training in the art of surrender to Yang.

As the Yang player, avoid giving tasks to your Yin facilitator that could be unpleasant or perceived as a punishment, such as house chores, for instance. This would be a misuse of your power, and you are to be a benign monarch. A wise king is also a servant. Devise a scenario that will benefit both of you.

Your Yin partner will no doubt be facing the insecurities inherent in the role, wondering whether he or she is doing it right. In such moments it is easy for Yin to feel a loss of energy and enthusiasm, to feel empty and tired. As a wise Yang, do not simply receive mutely. When you feel good, give positive acknowledgment to your partner so that the pleasure you receive may in turn energize your partner.

As the Yang partner, be compassionate and generous. Thinking that the Yin partner likes the role you have devised, you may become greedy, ask for more, give too many new tasks, or even become pushy, contending, "You owe it to me!" As a result, Yin may feel used and cease to enjoy the event.

Being a good Yang partner is a subtle art that requires a receptive awareness of Yin. Ask for only as much as your supporter can assimilate at any given moment. Invent tasks that will be pleasing to Yin because they correspond to his or her nature. If Yin never liked cooking, go to a great restaurant rather than ordering a specially cooked meal. And don't limit yourself to directing. For example, if Yin is a creative person, you may wish to say, "I don't feel like being active. Why don't you devise a surprise journey for me and lead the show?" That, too, is your privilege as Yang.

SUGGESTIONS TO THE YIN PARTNER. As Yin, you are the nurturing one who helps Yang to realize his or her wishes. You have the opportunity to cultivate a state of mind that is fundamental to a creative relationship—moving beyond self-importance or the sense that "I know better" or "We must do it my way." It means you are willing to put "me" aside for the sake of your partner. For this chosen period, the other becomes more important than you. Think of the unconditional acceptance of a mother toward her young child, or the devotion of a student or disciple to a spiritual teacher. In both cases there is a heightened quality of listening, availability, and openness to receive the other.

As the Yin partner, you are training in the art of moving from no to yes. Many people have learned that it is safer and more comfortable to say no. It gives a feeling of being in control, of power and freedom. It is a needed step in the evolution of the maturing ego toward adulthood—the capacity to be strong, different, independent, and to develop free will. But nay-saying can degenerate into fear of exploring new, unknown, risky situations that confront our fixed attitudes toward life. Habitual negativity prevents you from exploring the mysteries and delights that lie beyond your present boundaries.

Saying yes opens you up to new challenges. You become willing to act without imposing your own likes and dislikes on your partner, and in this way you discover precious moments of feeling "egoless" or transparent.

Being Yin does not mean, however, that you are supposed to do whatever the other person asks, even if you dislike it. This is not a master-slave situation. The symbols of Yin and Yang represent polar opposites that are in fact complementary, so there should be no question of subservience or loss of face.

As Yin, you are training in the art of truthful surrender to Yang. This means saying yes in many different situations so that you can touch the feminine principle inside you at its deepest level. But if you feel that Yang's request makes you uncomfortable, that it is too much or doesn't feel right, then politely demur with humor, love, and respect. Say something like, "Beloved, I feel unable to follow this scenario. Could you possibly change your wish so that I may support you within the limits of my capabilities?" Then keep playing the game while maintaining a sense of self-observation and openness to each other.

After both partners have played both roles, end the practice with a Heart Salutation.

Part company for about an hour and review in your mind what happened. Then meet once more in the Sacred Space, and take turns asking and answering the following questions:

- ☐ What were your expectations before you started? Describe how the game matched your fantasies and where it failed.
- ☐ What was the most difficult moment for you? Can you describe what energy sensations you felt in your body during this moment? (It will help if you conclude this section by telling yourself, "I am willing to take responsibility for what happened and to look at the difficulties I encountered as opportunities to teach me something about myself.")
- ☐ What was the most fulfilling moment for you? Have you felt this way in other situations? Describe what thoughts, images, and body sensations came up. Ask yourself, "Did I take my opportunity fully, or did I play it safe?"
- ☐ What did you learn, and how can you apply it to your daily life and integrate it into your relationship?

When you are the partner who is answering, spend three to five minutes on each reply, and be as specific as possible, giving examples from the game. When you are the one who is listening, do so without interruption. Be attentive and supportive. Speak only if you need to ask your partner to clarify his or her answer.

The purpose of these questions is to see how at ease you were in the two polarities of Yin and Yang and how well you flowed between them. Through this feedback you can gain insights into how you can improve your inner balance between the two. This new awareness can help you to harmonize the polarities, which will, in turn, make it possible for you to expand the range of your roles in lovemaking, adding variety, creativity, and freedom to your erotic possibilities.

Thank each other for what you learned. Look into your hearts and see if you can forgive each other for any shortcomings you experienced during the game. End with a Heart Salutation and Melting Hug.

Pointers

When you feel that you are in the right mood to play the game, don't wait too long before you start; the more freshness and spontaneity, the better. Be sure to discuss your overall scenario for the game; otherwise the logistics of time, place, and availability may not work out as you wish.

Some people find it helpful to play outside their home environment. At home it is easier to fall into the trap of daily routines, and you tend to behave according to set roles—the nurturing mother, the dutiful husband, and so on. Playing in a new environment challenges you to be bold. Without the usual setting, you have to create everything from scratch, like actors improvising without script or props.

You may wish to use the game as an opportunity to go through some of the practices in this book. Create an inventory of practices for the evening, but be willing to drop the plan if something else unfolds spontaneously.

Make a real commitment to follow the ground rules of the game. Make sure you understand what they are. If not, discuss them with your partner beforehand. The rules are there to help you find out more about yourself.

Some participants report being confused because they didn't know what they were supposed to feel. Usually, this is a sign that they harbor resistance to what is happening. If you encounter such feelings, ask yourself, "Do I want things to happen differently? Am I willing to initiate change? To express my need?" Nobody can tell you what you are "supposed" to feel. It is up to you. There is no right or wrong.

Be sure to switch roles at the agreed time, and resist the temptation to stay in a role that feels comfortable. For example, many women find it easy to be Yin and giving, but they can become intimidated when it is their turn to be Yang. They have not yet learned how to awaken their Inner Man—their outspoken, dynamic, commanding side.

Take Christina, for instance. "I was very comfortable being Yin," she said, after doing this exercise in one of my seminars. "I just went into it with the usual attitude I'd always had in my interactions with men:

'I'll do anything you want, as long as it's not painful.' Later, though, I couldn't go to sleep because I was terrified of having to wake up the next morning and play Yang. I realized that until that moment I had never allowed myself to have a fantasy involving complete self-gratification. In the end I asked for a short massage and breakfast in bed, and that was the end of it. I just couldn't ask for more."

For Christina, this was a great teaching. She reflected, "I became aware of something I hadn't really noticed before. During my whole life I had never allowed myself to ask for what I wanted, only to give. So from then on I realized I had every right and privilege to ask for things in my life, to ask a man for what I wanted. For the first time, too, I became clearly aware of *what* I wanted—a Tantric partner with whom I could practice High Sex. I wanted to create a two-way exchange, rather than just surrender."

Here is how Paula, a teacher in her thirties, successfully transformed a situation in which, as Yin, she felt unable to fulfill the demands of her Yang partner, Adam, a retired stockbroker.

"We began with Adam playing the Yang role and me the Yin. He wanted to drive to the beach. As soon as we parked the car, Adam started necking like a teenager, mauling me all over. It felt cheap and crude. I didn't like it. I started thinking, *Oh, God, do I have to go through this? As Yin, do I have to let Yang do whatever he wants?*

"I waited, trying to play my role a little longer, but my whole body was reacting negatively. I decided to be honest about my feelings. I said, 'Look, Adam, this doesn't feel very good to me. It's turning me off. Is that what you really want?' He looked at me and said, 'No, no, I don't want that. Why don't you take over the Yang role for now?'

"So we drove back to the house. I lit a candle and placed it between us. We relaxed and looked at each other. Then I said, 'I want to connect with you at the highest level of which we are capable.' Adam did a total turnabout and became really aware of my feelings. We talked for hours, sharing our hopes and fears about the way we wanted to grow together, the future, the goals we wanted to set for ourselves. It was amazing. I found a depth and beauty in him that I'd never seen before, and later on we moved into a night of sheer lust and great lovemaking. It was fine then to move into what he had wanted earlier, because of the depth of trust and agreement we had reached. In fact, it was a fabulous experience."

The partners understood the game correctly. They were able to shift easily from one polarity to the other. As Yang, Adam was open to switching unexpectedly to Yin in order to keep the lines of communication open with Paula.

A further example is the erotic scenario that my partner once asked of me. It took place on a Greek island in the Mediterranean that inspired him. He said, "I hold power and prestige in the Greek Imperium. My attendant recently acquired you as a slave in the marketplace and brought you to my household. A subtle attraction develops between us. We are going on an excursion in nature. Wear a beautiful dress. No underwear. You will carry the basket with the picnic. You are never to look up into my face or eyes, or to talk to me. Only I can talk to you and look at you. You will walk ahead of me, feeling the sexual tension between us. Stop when I say so. If I caress your shoulders, your hair, your face, you may receive, but don't respond with any movements of your own."

The nerve of the man! Yet I agreed to play the fantasy. By the time we arrived at the picnic spot, I was literally burning with desire, and it turned out to be one of the most erotic days of my life.

What I learned from this moment was the incredibly erotic potential of the Yin role of surrender. Usually I am a person who likes to be in charge. Had it not been for the sense of security provided by the structure of the Yin-Yang Game, I might never have trusted my partner enough to yield so deeply and experience the beauty of the opposite extreme. I am not encouraging you to enter into such adventures unless you feel an enthusiasm for them that is rooted in love and trust for your partner, as mine was. Otherwise, instead of benefiting from the experience, you may feel humiliated. So be very aware, in such cases, whether you are entering them in a spirit of freedom and full assent.

Another participant, David, was able simultaneously to expand his idea of what it means to be Yang and to discover the delights of being Yin. "My lover created a ritual to adorn my penis and honor it as my Vajra, my power wand," he recalls. "I became very excited and longed for quick penetration and release. I thought, 'If I don't go for it now and pour my energy out, I won't be a man.' She sensed the narrowness of my focus and started caressing me around the perineum and the anus, up the sacrum, and up my spine to the crown of my head. The sex drive mellowed out. There was no longer such a gravity pull around my genitals. I lay down and relaxed, while my lover danced naked over me. Breathing deeply and looking at her, I suddenly felt as if I could open deeply and had a vagina too. At this moment all the energy in me expanded through my whole body and vibrated. It was extremely pleasurable to feel that, as Yang, I could be completely Yin, at once male and female. It is wonderful to feel that I can now live my Yin side, my Inner Woman, with my lover and it is not threatening. It brings us closer together."

Amanda, a real estate agent, realized that until playing the Yin-Yang Game, her Yin quality had not been authentic. Through experiencing the Yin role unconditionally, she discovered an ecstatic state of consciousness beyond both Yin and Yang. "There was a real joy in serving totally when I was in the Yin role," she said. "I realized that normally there is a subtle power struggle between Brad, my partner, and me. Usually, even when I give in and say yes, I hold something back. We were in a restaurant, and music was playing. As Yang, Brad asked me for a dance. Inside my heart I prayed, 'Let this be the most beautiful dance I have ever given or shared with anyone.' Well, all the musicians gathered around us and played for us. And other people joined in. It was as if Brad, the leader of the dance, was serving the dancers, and the dancers were serving the leader, and I was simply allowing and supporting this exchange. The sense of 'I' completely disappeared. I became transparent, just a presence, a flow. The act of serving became a state of grace, sufficient unto itself, independent of any doing or any goal. I felt as if the server was becoming the served, as if Yin and Yang had merged beyond distinctions."

I hope these examples have inspired you to plunge wholeheartedly into the Yin-Yang Game.

When the heart is flooded with love there is no room in it for fear, for doubt, for hesitation. And it is this lack of fear that makes for the dance. When each partner loves so completely that he has forgotten to ask himself whether he is loved in return; when he only knows that he loves and is moving to music— then, and then only are two people able to dance perfectly in tune to the same rhythm.

—Ann Morrow Lindbergh
Gifts from the Sea

❀

Through the Yin-Yang Game, you now have a structure through which you can bring harmony and balance to the way you interact with each other. You have paved the way for a new beginning in your love life.

Learning who you are as a man or woman has been one of the important lessons of this chapter. Through the practice of Visualizing Your Inner Man and Inner Woman, you discovered how to acknowledge these two polarities within yourself. You have become aware of how you express these roles in your daily life, thus expanding your gender role to include both male and female qualities.

You have come to realize that the relationship with your outer partner is but a reflection of the inner relationship between your Inner Man and Inner Woman, and that when these two aspects of yourself are fully expressed and balanced you become more attractive to others and can bring more joy into your love life.

You also explored and expanded the way that you express yourself to your partner through the practice of Role-Playing Each Other, thus improving communication between you. And through the Yin-Yang Game, you became aware of what you want in love. You developed the art and tactfulness to make it happen and learned the benefits of giving and accepting pleasure wholeheartedly.

Now that you have developed trust and intimacy with each other, you are ready to move to the next step in this training. In the next chapter you will discover orgasm as an energy event that can trigger an Ecstatic Response within your body. You will learn how to focus this energy at the genital level and share it with your partner, discovering the delicious art of melting within each other.

꧁

AWAKENING THE ECSTATIC RESPONSE

Many people think of orgasm as starting and ending with the genitals. In High Sex, however, orgasm is experienced as an expression of energy involving the whole body. Instead of focusing on the intense, localized sensations created through friction between the male and female sexual organs, High Sex uses breathing and movement to expand orgasmic energy beyond the genitals. In this chapter I will teach you to build up orgasmic energy progressively throughout the body while remaining relaxed so that this energy can be contained for longer and longer periods of time.

The idea of containing orgasmic energy may seem strange to you. You may have felt whenever you were very aroused sexually that you immediately wanted to do something about it. This tendency follows the cultural norm of sexual arousal followed by orgasmic release. But sexual arousal is a form of energy, and energy can take many forms. By transforming sexual energy and experiencing it independent of the genital context, you can create a regenerative orgasm of the whole body.

Although you may never have thought about it, you may have already experienced forms of nongenital orgasm in lovemaking. A good example of this was given by Dale, a teacher from San Diego, who in one of my seminars explained how this ecstatic condition happened to him. "Recently I fell in love with a beautiful woman who happened to be a student in a program that I teach," he said. "Now, the ethics of the program are quite strict—you don't make love with your students. Yet I was completely in love. I had the feeling, *This is the real thing!* Finally we got together, went to my apartment, and acknowledged that we both felt very attracted to each other. So we lay on my bed. I was utterly

We are highly—perhaps instinctively—conditioned to express the energy genitally once it becomes "sexual." But from another perspective what we call sexual energy is actually a mode of attention. If we free our attention out of the genital dynamic and remain present for the energy, something else begins to happen.

—Richard Moss
The Black Butterfly

271

excited, but we agreed we would not have sexual intercourse. So we lay in each other's arms, relaxed, and enjoyed the warmth, the intimacy of each other's presence. After some time it seemed that our hearts, breathing, pulse, movements, and rhythms became effortlessly synchronized. Sometimes the boundaries of our bodies simply melted away, and we felt merged into one timeless being. Then we looked in each other's eyes, felt the stirring of passion, and our bodies would begin to shake and quiver all over. We felt this delicious electric energy moving within us, filling us to overflowing. We lay the whole night this way, caressing each other, kissing, smiling, then falling back in a silent state of luminous oneness. We did not have intercourse, yet this was one of the deepest experiences of ecstatic lovemaking I have ever had."

Later, as he wondered about what had happened, he said, "It's really simple. When your energy is very high, you relax the body, and the energy charge is allowed to diffuse and spread from the core to the limits of the body and even beyond it in a wavelike movement. This gives one the feeling of becoming one with everything—the sound of a lover's breathing, her fragrance, the whole environment."

The purpose of this chapter is to help you experience orgasmic sensations that are not confined to the genitals. This will involve a major shift in values. In High Sex the usual hunger for the sharp, intense pleasure of genital orgasm is replaced by the discovery of the joys of a diffused orgasm. The physical tension and stress of dynamic genital sex is replaced by a deep feeling of relaxation that allows orgasmic sensations to ripple through the whole body. This is one of the basic secrets of High Sex: the art of staying relaxed in high states of arousal so that nongenital forms of orgasm can be experienced.

Usually when I ask lovers what the most important quality in sex is, they say it's the ability to reach high states of arousal. Tantric lovers, on the other hand, give a different answer—one that sounds almost paradoxical. They say the highest quality in sex is not merely to reach high states of arousal but to stay relaxed in them. We usually associate relaxation with doing nothing. It's a cooling-out state—a nap after hard work, an hour in the hammock or, for some, a slump in front of the TV. What can relaxation possibly have to do with sex, when sex is about getting excited and going wild with body temperatures soaring? Contrary to these popular ideas, lovers who practice High Sex report peak experiences connected with an ability to stay relaxed in the midst of sexual heat instead of allowing the fire to reach its climax and burn out quickly. This ability, or art, is the key to Awakening the Ecstatic Response. It is what the ancient Tantric lovers meant when they declared, "Stay with the fire in the beginning, and avoid the embers at the end." They knew that ecstasy is achieved by relaxing into the "fire" of excitement so that their energy is not "burned" by being thrown out of the body, leaving only "embers" of passion behind.

The word *ecstatic* literally means "being called out of stasis," feeling lifted out of the status quo, the daily routine. *Ecstasy* comes from the Latin *ex-stasis,* meaning to stand outside oneself, as illustrated in the expression, "I'm simply beside myself with joy." This implies that we are being filled with an emotion or energy too powerful for the body to contain or for the rational mind to understand. Some vital life energy is overflowing, and we are transported to another realm in which the spirit, released by some extraordinary event of great intensity—giving birth, making passionate love, confronting death—soars beyond the ordinary boundaries of perception and consciousness.

Ordinarily people think of ecstasy as an unpredictable event that happens rarely and accidentally—the product of an arbitrary set of circumstances that cannot be consciously duplicated. Or they see it as a mystical state that is extremely hard to achieve—something reserved for ascetics who renounce earthly pleasures and rigorously train their minds and bodies for years in order to catch a glimpse of "the beyond." It is neither of these.

Abraham Maslow, the founder of humanistic psychology, discovered in the 1960s that almost all people at some time in their lives have peak experiences involving joyful and ecstatic states. In High Sex the same is true. We all have the potential to experience joy and ecstasy through expanded orgasm. My personal experience and the experiences of the hundreds of people who have taken my seminars all point in the direction Maslow has indicated. Each of us has a built-in ability to experience ecstatic states of consciousness, and the goal of this chapter is to establish conditions that will give you this experience, primarily through the development of the Ecstatic Response. This requires training, but unlike the traditional ascetic approach, it does not require the renunciation of earthly pleasures or years of rigorous discipline.

The healthy person, according to Wilhelm Reich, is one who regularly engages in lovingly uninhibited sexual exchange leading to a thoroughly satisfying orgasm.

—Ken Dychtwald
Bodymind

THE ECSTATIC RESPONSE AND ORGASM

The best way to understand the Ecstatic Response is to compare it with genital orgasm—the body's response when it reaches the peak of sexual arousal. There are two basic phases in genital orgasm. First you become sexually aroused or turned on. This is a deliberate process, often called foreplay, in which you become excited through a form of doing. Then, at a critical point, the body starts to respond of its own accord, and shortly before the moment of climax, there is a sudden switch as the arousal abruptly moves beyond your control. Some inner dam bursts, releasing a flood of sensations that stream through the body for a period that lasts from twelve seconds to four minutes.

It is this orgasmic model that you will duplicate in this chapter, independent of the sexual context. You will learn how to generate arousal through intense breathing connected with specific movements of the body that seek to duplicate the vibrations felt during the orgasmic reflex in sex. Then, when you reach a state of high energy arousal, your body will start to respond of its own accord, and you will experience the same "streaming" sensations associated with orgasm. The Ecstatic Response begins when the sensations you are deliberately creating become involuntary, when planned arousal switches over to spontaneous streaming.

The body acts as a natural conductor for these streaming sensations. It is composed of 90 percent water and other fluids, which means that in more than a poetic sense, sensations, feelings, emotions, and energy can flow as tidal currents and waves, rippling and pulsing through the body's streams and rivers. These vibrations are the key to your aliveness. Dr. Alexander Lowen, the founder of bioenergetics, said that a healthy body is in a constant state of vibration, whether awake or asleep. Such vibrations happen at different intensities and amplitudes. They are found at the cellular level, where each cell rhythmically contracts and expands as it receives nutrients from the blood and transforms and distributes them. They are also present in our organs, such as the lungs, heart, and intestines, which are in a constant state of pulsation. When bodily vibrations happen at a high amplitude—that is, when they are intensified through strong arousal or excitement—they produce joy, vitality, and ecstasy in your being.

In High Sex you will seek to generate these vibrations. The following exercises aim to help you move vibrations through your body, first in a strong, voluntary fashion and then in an increasingly subtle way until the body starts streaming by itself. When all the various body parts— knees, pelvis, neck, and head—are properly aligned and resonating with one another, streaming takes place in a continuous flow. If, however, there are muscular tensions, the flow of energy will be interrupted at the tension point. Wilhelm Reich was the first Western scientist to demonstrate the fact that if bodily tensions are released, there will be an improvement in the flow of sensations that he called "streamings." Everyone has tensions that inhibit streaming, but there are effective methods for dissolving them, some of which were developed by Reich and his followers and some of which have been known for a long time by mystics in the East.

In the Eastern philosophy of Kundalini yoga, vital energy lies dormant at the base of the spine and is channeled upward through the body to the brain. Lee Sanella, an American doctor and author who has researched extensively the awakening of this energy, or Kundalini, asserts that its rise through the body has an interesting and very positive side effect: It causes the central nervous system to throw off stress. As the energy rises through the body, it encounters blocks in the form of armored or tense muscles and tissues. Rather like an electrical current, the friction created by the resistance of the armoring to the rising energy produces heat, and this burns away the tension, cleaning and purifying the channels to allow a freer flow—or streaming—of energy. As blocks dissolve, a subtle shift occurs, and you sense that the streaming sensation becomes more deeply internalized, running through the body first from the feet to the head and then back down to the feet. If you can observe this streaming—through the heart, navel, and genitals—without interfering, it develops into a sense of expansion, like an undercurrent that is taking you beyond the boundaries of the physical body. This is what I call the Ecstatic Response. It is an intense sensation of joy, a feeling of being cleansed and relaxed.

In the following exercises you are going to experience this cleansing process by building up an energy charge and allowing it to dissolve blocks in the body. The more blocks you dissolve, the more possibility you have of experiencing ecstasy as a whole-body phenomenon. These exercises may seem simple, and in a way they are. But appearances are deceptive. You are being given powerful tools for dissolving blocks and enhancing energy flow. It would require several sessions of deep tissue massage to achieve the same effect. I suggest that you not yield to the temptation of breezing past this chapter in search of more complex and challenging techniques. These four exercises are tremendously important because through them you will learn how to discover, stimulate, and direct the inner sensations of your body that will lead you to an experience of ecstasy.

The awakening of Kundalini is, somehow, the awakening of the latent cosmic energy lying in every human being, for such an energy is the origin of all his powers, all his strength, all the forms of life he may assume.

—Lilian Silburn
Kundalini

275

Even if you have encountered practices of a similar nature in bioenergetics or yoga, you are now exploring the dimension of High Sex. These practices are unique in their organization, sequence, and aim. So enjoy them in a spirit of innocent inquiry, putting aside the past.

To enhance your chances of developing the Ecstatic Response, do each practice in sequence. Each practice will take approximately 20 minutes. The whole session will take about one-and-a-half to two hours. In the beginning, however, you may wish to explore the practices in isolation from one another, going fully into each one until you get the hang of it. In this case, please take your time—up to 30 minutes per practice—and enjoy the ride.

SHAKING LOOSE

In the first practice, you experiment with voluntarily creating shaking and trembling sensations, cleaning the body of tensions and preparing it for the next practice, the Streaming Process.

Purpose and Benefits

In this practice you will be shaking each part of your body with gentle movements at first, then more intensely. The purpose is to prepare the body for streaming, bringing awareness and energy to each part. It will also help you to bring warmth, aliveness, and tingling sensations to areas of your body that until now have been insensitive.

Preparations

Create the Sacred Space.

Make sure the room is warm so you can wear little or no clothing. It is important that you have enough space to move, dance, and roll around freely.

You will need a glass of water nearby—this can be thirsty work—and a few soft pillows on which to relax when you are finished.

Doing this exercise with your eyes closed will help you to focus better on your internal sensations. To be fully concentrated, it is helpful to wear a blindfold.

Gently shake your hand while the rest of your body remains still and relaxed.

Use music that offers a steady, repetitive rhythm such as African dance music (see Appendix II).

Allow 20 minutes for this practice. You may need a little longer when you try it for the first time. Don't cramp yourself into a tight time frame.

Practice

Adopt the Basic Stance, with your arms relaxed at your sides. Breathe evenly through your mouth. Feel your connection to the ground, establishing a sense of balance in your body.

Gently shake your left hand for about a minute while the rest of your body remains still and relaxed. Breathe deeply through your mouth as you do so. To keep your mind on this activity, tell yourself, "I shake the left hand, I clean the left hand." Or, if you prefer, you can make sounds that express how this part of the body feels. In either case, don't let your mind stop paying attention to what you are doing.

Stop and compare the difference in feeling between your left and right hands. The left is probably warmer, more tingly, looser—the first indication of what is going to happen to your whole body in this and the next practice.

Next, shake your left hand, arm, and shoulder together for one minute. Breathe deeply. Make sounds that reflect how this part of your body feels—a sound of protest, a cooing of delight, gurgles of happiness, a hoot of disgust, a creak of rustiness. Stop and compare your left hand, arm, and shoulder with your right. Again note the differences. Does the right side feel denser and duller?

Now shake your right hand for one minute. Stop and compare. See if there is more evenness now between the sensations of the two hands.

Shake your right hand, arm, and shoulder for one minute. Remember to breathe deeply through your mouth and to make sounds. Again stop and compare.

Shake both hands, arms, and shoulders, allowing the vibrations to move into your neck and head so that they, too, become part of the shaking. As you do this, imagine someone shaking a plum tree to get the plums to fall, or think of the wind blowing through a tree, shaking the leaves. Check to see if your jaw and facial muscles are relaxed. If not, relax them.

After two minutes add your chest and back, shaking the upper part of your body to the waist. Breathe vigorously through your mouth. Continue for three minutes.

Stop and check your sensations. Do you feel a difference between your upper body and the lower part? This is an opportunity to become progressively aware of the sensations of aliveness—what it means to be warm and tingly instead of dull and insensitive.

Shake your left foot for one minute, keeping the rest of your body still. Stop and compare it with your right foot. Can you feel your connection to the ground and balance better on the left side?

Shake your left foot, calf, and thigh for one minute. Keep your right knee a little bent and the muscles of the pelvic floor relaxed so the shaking can come into your hip and pelvis through your left side. Keep breathing deeply through your mouth. Sigh as you exhale, or make any sound that feels right.

Stop and compare your lower left side with your right side. Does your left leg feel more flexible, more ready to jump? The joints should feel looser, and you should be able to feel them better.

Proceed in the same way for the right side: first the foot, then the calf and thigh.

Start again from the beginning, shaking each part, maintaining the sequence—left hand, arm, shoulder; right hand, arm, shoulder; neck, head, and torso; left foot, calf, thigh; right foot, calf, thigh. If you notice any areas of the body that are particularly tense, slow down and focus the shaking there. Focus your breathing there, too, imagining as you inhale that you are sending air to the tense area, literally breathing life into it.

If you feel very tense, imagine that you are shaking yourself loose from whatever is cramping your style. Did you have a bad day at the office? Imagine you are shaking yourself free of the boss. Do you feel silly? Imagine you are shaking yourself free from those who are judging you, including your own mind!

Make appropriate sounds, such as, "Let go of me!" or "Let me loose!" This attitude should help you feel lighter, springier. Then put on your favorite dance music, and allow yourself to dance and shake freely, breathing deeply, jumping, and loosening your whole body, including your head. Let yourself go wild, make sounds, and enjoy yourself. Do this for five minutes.

Pointers

In the beginning do not shake hard and violently; otherwise you will not be able to focus on your inner sensations. Start this practice slowly. Let yourself tune into the rhythm of the music and intensify the shaking until you feel capable of shaking as strongly as you can. If, after the first part of the practice, in which you shake each limb independently, you do not feel there is more aliveness in your body, continue to shake your body parts in isolation until you notice improved sensations.

Now that you have cleansed your body of tension, you are ready to proceed toward generating finer vibrations.

THE STREAMING PROCESS

In this exercise you discover how to trigger the Ecstatic Response in yourself.

Purpose and Benefits

This practice will help you experience energy streaming through your body. As in meditation, this process requires you to turn your awareness inside yourself and become very sensitive and alert to your inner sensations. You focus on following each little sensation—a shivering, trembling, or streaming in any part of the body—developing the same skills of self-observation that meditators acquire. You will learn to amplify these inner sensations, allowing them to expand and producing an involuntary, pleasurable vibration through your whole body.

Preparations

Keep this process going for at least 15 minutes.

Do it wholeheartedly so you can give yourself a chance to build up the energy charge, generating heat to the boiling point, as in a pressure cooker. The more charge you have, the more easily your energy can penetrate any blocks in your muscles and tissues.

Do this practice with your eyes closed. Use a blindfold if you wish. Sometimes people have difficulty maintaining their sense of balance in this practice when blindfolded, so you need to experiment. Even though your eyes are closed, it is helpful to practice together with your partner so that you can feel encouraged and supported by each other's presence.

Have a glass of water nearby; this too can be thirsty work. Choose your music from *Rajneesh Kundalini Meditation* or *Einstein on the Beach* by Phil Glass (see Appendix II).

Practice

Start the music.

Close your eyes or put on your blindfold. This will help you focus on internal sensations and build up energy. Every time you open your eyes, you lose concentration, and a little bit of energy leaks out.

Adopt the Basic Stance.

Bend your knees, as if skiing or skipping rope. This simple strategy creates a stress position around the knees, legs, and thigh muscles from which the first tremblings will arise.

Let your arms hang naturally at your sides.

Keep your spine and neck straight, yet relaxed. Let your belly relax.

It is very important for you to keep your anal and genital muscles relaxed throughout the exercise so that the streaming energy can move through your pelvis.

Open your mouth slightly, relax your jaw, and breathe in and out through your mouth.

When you feel comfortable in this position, rock slowly forward onto the balls of your feet, shifting the weight of your body to the front of your feet. Then rock back, shifting your weight to your heels, as if you are allowing yourself to fall backward, but stop yourself at the last moment, using your leg muscles. Hold yourself there, on the brink between standing and falling, as long as you can. Keep breathing deeply.

Do this five or six times, gently, and then come back to your original position. "Listen" for a slight tremor that may be developing around the knee and ankle joints as a result of the stress from maintaining this position.

Begin the rocking motion again. Notice which part of the movement produces the most trembling sensations, and accentuate it.

Some of my clients have difficulty detecting these sensations, and I encourage them to "fake it until you make it." Call forth an image that will help, and voluntarily begin to tremble in the knees. Imagine you are standing naked in a field of snow, or you're coming out of the sea and shaking water off your body. In nearly every case, after two to five minutes, your knees will take the hint and begin trembling by themselves.

As soon as you detect the slightest shaking, relax and breathe into it, bringing your attention to this area. Feel the trembling spreading to surrounding areas, creeping from your knees up into your thighs. Keep your body as relaxed as possible. Let the vibrations expand gently upward into your pelvis, *through* your genitals and waist. Breathe into these areas.

To expand the sensation, focus your whole attention on your knees, thighs, genitals, pelvis. Visualize them trembling. Let the shaking continue at a mild level for a while, then give yourself permission to amplify it. Breathe deeper and make sounds as you exhale that express how you feel. Don't censor yourself.

If you find that your pelvic area is not responding, experiment with deliberately making it move. Dance with your hips, and use the PC Pump to contract and relax the muscles in quick pulses. This will help to sensitize the pelvic area and also give you a better idea of the feeling when it is relaxed.

As you become more aware of what is happening in your pelvis, intensify the rhythm and tempo of your vibrations. Allow the excitement to build.

Hand over control from your mind to your body, welcoming the experience of involuntary streaming. Visualize the vibrations moving through your Inner Flute.

AWAKENING THE ECSTATIC RESPONSE. Keep going. Feel that you are developing the ability to sustain this new level of intense excitement.

Prepare to hand over control from your mind to your body, welcoming the experience of involuntary streaming. Look for a delicious shiver of energy moving into and through your pelvic and genital areas, like the first hint of sexual arousal. Like ripples in a pond, these tiny sensations are going to spread through your body, and you must follow them on their journey. Don't get frustrated if you lose track of them. Repeat the rocking motion until you rediscover them.

Again focus on relaxing the muscles around the anus and genitals, so that the vibrations can flow through the pelvis and genital area. When the involuntary vibrations take over, you may experience orgasmic sensations in the genitals without ejaculation. Let this happen (but don't worry if it doesn't), and relax into the sensations. Visualize the vibrations moving from your pelvis up into your belly, diaphragm, and chest. You can make light stroking movements with your hands to help. Let the shaking ripple up your spine and through your shoulders and neck.

Keep your spine and neck aligned and vertical. It is a common error for people to throw the neck back, tilting the head, which prevents streaming from flowing through the neck into the head.

Let your arms participate in the vibrating. Finally, let these vibrations move all the way to the top of your head. Coordinate your movements so that all parts of your body are now vibrating together.

Watch the vibrations, amplify them, and relax into them, allowing yourself to be carried by the current. Let yourself "be vibrated" by the energy. Feel the pleasure of the shaking—the impression that every cell in your body is electrified, dancing, merging with every other cell as it shakes off tensions and toxins.

You can tell that streaming is beginning to happen when you feel a sense of heat in your muscles. This occurs in different places with different people. It often starts around the legs because this is where the most tension is and then moves upward. Another sign is when small, quick vibrations come spontaneously from within, replacing the larger shaking movements.

When the streaming reaches your head, you will have the feeling that you are shaking loose your thoughts, worries, and concerns. Your head is becoming loose and your mind clear and at ease.

Then visualize the energy traveling back down through your body to your feet. Regrounding the energy is important; otherwise you may suffer from headaches caused by too much energy in your head.

When you feel it's time to end the practice, let the streaming soften, take a few deep breaths, and slow down until your body is almost motionless. You may have the feeling that you are internalizing the streaming and that this sensation is becoming increasingly subtle.

Then become completely still. Stay in tune with the experience, and let it remain as a background—an underground stream—for the remaining two exercises. If you feel ready, go directly to the next practice. If not, end with a dance and then relax.

Pointers

When you begin this practice, you may fear losing your balance. If you feel insecure, it helps to open your eyes for a while and focus on some object in front of you. It also helps to breathe deeply all the way down to your belly, making the sighing sound "Aaaah" as you exhale.

This is a delicate exercise and may provoke performance anxieties about whether you are doing it right or concern that nothing is happening. The distinction between voluntary and involuntary shaking is elusive, so don't judge yourself for not being swamped with involuntary sensations. You can assist the involuntary vibrations by imagining that you are a spectator at a show, an observer sitting in a ringside seat, watching all that is happening to your body and relaxing into it.

For several sessions the involuntary streaming sensation may remain localized in one part of the body, and you may need to use voluntary movements and visualizations to help it to spread. If parts of your body feel very stiff, you may benefit from a few deep massage sessions. This will facilitate the Streaming Process. Encourage yourself by asking, "How would it be if this wavelike motion in my legs went on by itself? Where would it go next?" Look for the place where the vibration would spread, and expect it to happen.

Be patient. You may need to practice the Streaming Process ten or twenty times to get the hang of it. Eventually, if you totally involve yourself in the practice, your whole body will relax into involuntary streaming. The switch to involuntary vibration will happen if you remember the initial instructions: maintain the Basic Stance, keep your spine and neck straight and relaxed, and breathe through your mouth.

When you do make the transition to involuntary streaming, this becomes a very restful and pleasant experience. The energy no longer comes in spurts, like water from a hose, but evenly, as if you are dissolving into an internal river of energy. The river may be moving slowly, but it has deep currents. You may also feel that you are tapping into a previously unknown source of energy, more and more of which is becoming available.

Let go of your desire to control your body with your mind. You may also have to let go of a fear of falling or a fear of shaking out of control. Tightness in the muscles often has its origins in these two fears. If you are really anxious about falling, you can do the exercise with your eyes open. Remember, the shaking can do you no harm; it is regulated by your body, which has its own wisdom, so you can safely hand over control to it.

Sometimes people begin to experience involuntary vibrations in a particular part of the body and then feel frightened and cut off the sensation, stopping their breathing and contracting their muscles in a sudden spasm. This reaction is probably the result of some deep emotion—anger, fear, grief, neediness—that has been locked in the affected area. For example, you may feel tears coming as a result of an energy block being opened in the chest. Let the emotions be released and expressed. If you have cut short the exercise, begin again, and allow the vibrations to move up through your body to the point where they stopped. Soon you will be able to move through the block and allow the vibrating energy to rise higher.

Sometimes people are their own worst critics, chastising their bodies for not being more responsive. If such thoughts arise, focus on your breathing, and allow them to pass through your mind like traffic on a highway. Don't pay much attention to them. This practice gives you a tremendous opportunity to become an impartial observer. When you lose the vibrations, simply start over. You get as many chances as you need.

ADVANCED STREAMING. When you are proficient at the Streaming Process, do it while visualizing the Inner Flute. Imagine that your Inner Flute is a channel through which you can direct your energy like a current that flows between the two poles—the genitals and the brain—streaming continuously between them.

Depending on where you focus the energy, you can change the quality of your experience, moving from orgasm to ecstasy as the flavor of the streaming changes from being intense and chaotic to becoming increasingly subtle, deep, and expanded. Further development of this advanced stage will be explained in chapter 12.

THE BUTTERFLY

In this exercise you internalize the streaming and focus the sensations in your pelvis and genitals, sharing your sexual feelings with your partner in an intimate way.

Purpose and Benefits

Most people have difficulty experiencing genital arousal while simultaneously letting go of control. In 101 ways, some subtle, some obvious, we try to stay in control of our sexual responses, holding our breath, stopping pelvic movements, interrupting the arousal phase because we feel undeserving of so much pleasure.

In this exercise you will learn how to surrender while feeling aroused. This requires you to trust your partner, because letting go of control makes you feel open and vulnerable. You are not, however, surrendering to a particular person. In this practice your partner is acting as a door through which you give yourself permission to surrender to intense feelings of arousal in your own body that may otherwise seem too threatening. So in a way, you are surrendering more deeply to yourself.

The Butterfly also establishes a bond of intimacy between you and your partner. As genital arousal develops, you can experiment with allowing yourself to share it and show it. For many people this is not easy. As you will see, it can be quite challenging to feel aroused, to show it, and to keep looking in your partner's eyes, only inches away from your own. But this will give you a chance to move quickly through any guilt, shame, or distrust that you may still have about sexual pleasure and satisfaction.

If you have shared the self-pleasuring rituals of chapter 7, this practice should be easy. In my experience, however, the Butterfly can still be an unexpected challenge because here you are in a more vulnerable position.

Preparations

This exercise is best done immediately after the Streaming Process so that your body has a strong energy charge that will intensify your feelings when you move into the Butterfly.

Create your Sacred Space.

Both partners should be naked.

The Butterfly position. Your partner is acting as a doorway through which you give yourself permission to surrender more deeply to yourself.

Allow 20 minutes for this practice.

You can choose either soft, sensual music at low volume, or silence.

Practice

Partner A, the woman, is the receptive partner. She lies down on her back, the soles of her feet flat on the floor, knees bent, feet together.

Partner B, the man, is the active supporter. He sits behind her head, with his legs spread apart so that her head is between his thighs, close to his crotch. His legs can be outstretched or bent at the knee. He can also be in the Opening Lotus position, with legs crossed. For comfort, see whether Partner A needs a small cushion behind her neck and whether Partner B needs to sit on a cushion.

Partner A, hold your partner's hands. To avoid muscle tensions in your arms, raise your forearms, with your elbows resting on the floor, and let your hands fall gently back against Partner B's legs, holding his hands in this restful position.

Close your eyes. Make sure your pelvis is relaxed. Focus your attention inside your own body on the feelings you experienced in the Streaming Process. Recall the small streamings that were running through your body, and allow yourself to experience them again.

Begin breathing through your mouth. Relax your body, especially your pelvis, and feel your weight sinking into the floor. Exhale slowly with a sigh or small sound, and let your thighs fall outward. Feel that you are opening yourself, giving yourself, showing yourself to your partner.

Inhale slowly, bringing your thighs back together, feeling that you are taking your energy back into yourself. Let your inhaling and exhaling be even and continuous, with no pause between them.

To encourage streaming in your pelvis and thighs, let your thighs fall outward gently and slowly but not completely. Stop them at a point just before full relaxation, maintaining a slight tension around your hip joints. You can also encourage streaming through your genitals by using the PC Pump.

As you feel energy beginning to stream, stimulate it further by focusing your breathing in that area and relaxing it. Continue like this, with your eyes closed, until you can perceive the sensations inside. As you open your thighs, allow yourself to feel childlike, vulnerable, and open. This is a gesture of surrender, but it is also arousing and exciting.

Partner B, you are in charge, much like a parent with a small child—caring, supportive, attentive, loving. Your partner is going to be very vulnerable and will need your complete support at all times. Keep looking into Partner A's eyes throughout the exercise. You can also synchronize your breathing pattern with hers. Move from neutral support to warm encouragement by giving a loving smile or making sounds in harmony with her. Avoid speaking.

Partner A, when you are familiar with the movement of your thighs, opening on the exhale, closing on the inhale, open your eyes and look into your partner's. His face is inches away, and you are opening your legs, exposing your genitals. This may be threatening at first. You may feel intruded upon because you are so open and revealing deep sexual feelings. See if you can accept this uncertainty. If there is fear or resistance, allow it, continuing the same movement pattern and deepening your breathing. Eventually, if you keep going, the constriction will transform itself into a relaxed flow as you give expression to your feelings.

Begin to say, *"Yes,"* each time you exhale and open your thighs. Say nothing on the inhale. This simple *yes* expresses many things: "Yes, I am exposing myself to you; I am letting you in. Yes, this is my pleasure, my energy, my vibration. Yes, I am showing myself to you because I trust you." Tune into these feelings as you say, "Yes," opening your legs and looking at your partner.

Continue like this for ten minutes. You may feel like a baby; you may feel needy. Tears of gratitude may start to flow, or feelings of shame may well up from within. This exercise helps you experience all these emotions and helps you move through them.

Play with your "yes." Find different sounds that express what you are going through—a soft whisper, a giggle, or a loud "yah!" Let yourself pass through all the moods this exercise provokes, and sound them.

After ten to fifteen minutes, slow down the leg movement, bring your legs together, become still, close your eyes, and internalize the experience, becoming aware of small vibrations deep within your body. Without doing anything, observe what is happening inside.

Partner B, after letting your partner rest for a few minutes, you may feel like placing one hand on her genitals and the other on her head or heart. Or you may wish to lie down beside your partner, hold her close, and whisper in her ear, "Thank you for what you have given me."

End with a Heart Salutation and Melting Hug.

Exchange roles. Partner A, the woman, now plays the supportive role, and Partner B, the man, is the active partner.

Pointers

You may have moments when you are doing the active part of this exercise mechanically, not feeling anything. Or you may feel uncomfortable about being so exposed. You may hesitate and experience self-doubt. Don't worry. Accept these fluctuations in mood, let them be there, and keep going. It is important not to interrupt the exercise, so you have the chance to experience opening your heart to your partner. When you do, you may feel as though your chest is opening and you are falling deeply into an inner sense of acceptance and surrender.

If at some point you feel it is really too difficult to continue eye contact, close your eyes and come back to yourself. Whenever you are ready, open your eyes and continue the exercise with eye contact.

In this exercise it's very easy to feel shame, embarrassment, or a sense of inadequacy because most people are not accustomed to showing strong sexual feelings in this intimate and revealing way. Usually they close their eyes in such "private" moments. But muster your courage and keep showing yourself to your partner. Fear can be a good teacher. If you can confront it and move through it, you will take a quantum leap toward self-acceptance and self-esteem.

After lying down and relaxing together for some minutes at the end of the Butterfly, ask yourselves if you are ready to explore more deeply your feelings of surrendering to each other. If your answer is yes, move on to the Bonding Relaxation.

THE BONDING RELAXATION

In the previous exercises you learned how to build up an energy charge, focus it in the genital area, and show your sexual feelings to your partner. In the Bonding Relaxation you and your partner will learn how to relax deeply and diffuse sexual energy throughout your bodies.

Understanding that you don't have to do anything about feeling sexual is an important step in High Sex. I use the term *bonding* because the experience approximates the state of fusion between the mother and infant or between the mystic and the universal life force—a state in which one experiences a dissolution of boundaries between subject and object, knower and known.

Purpose and Benefits

Research conducted by Dr. Rudolf von Urban, a distinguished American physician and pioneering sexologist who in 1949 wrote the book, *Sex Perfection and Marital Happiness,* has shown that when lovers relax deeply together, a resonance effect, called entrainment, begins to take place between their energy fields that brings profound healing to both. According to von Urban, when a man and woman are bonded in deep relaxation, they can enjoy a long-lasting, whole-body orgasm. Of those fortunate enough to have experienced this, many regard it as more deeply satisfying than the conventional genital climax.

Alternating between high arousal and relaxation, and having a full experience of each state, you will naturally be able to combine both simultaneously. The Bonding Relaxation facilitates this merger and is also important because it is the first step toward the experience of the "Valley Orgasm" that we will explore in chapter 12.

Preparations

At first glance this practice may seem incredibly simple—just two people lying together—but the Bonding Relaxation is very important as a stepping stone to ecstasy. It requires careful preparation. You need to have become proficient at the preceding exercises so that you can do Shaking Loose, the Streaming Process, the Butterfly, and then move directly into the Bonding Relaxation. In this way your bodies will be fully charged with energy, and you will be able to follow the subtle currents that flow between you. If this amount of preparation seems too arduous, you can do Shaking Loose and then take a relaxing bath before proceeding directly to the Bonding Relaxation.

Choose a comfortable, soft place to lie together, such as a bed, a thick carpet, a moss-covered patch in the forest, or a waterbed.

Play soft, relaxing music.

Enjoy the Bonding Relaxation for 20 to 30 minutes.

The Spoon position. Move the pelvis gently backward and forward, following your breathing.

Practice

Begin with a Heart Salutation.

Lie close together in any of the following bonding positions:

☐ Both partners lie on their right sides, in the "spoon position," with one partner's back touching the other partner's front. Make sure you both have adequate pillow support under your necks to avoid muscle tension. Take your time to become really comfortable.

   The advantage of this position is that the pelvis can move freely, and both partners, although very close to each other, can move independently. This allows a lot of subtle exploration in which the pelvis can move gently backward and forward, following the breathing. Finding a common rhythm with your partner in this manner is easy and exciting.

☐ The lighter partner lies on top of the heavier one. Before you start, make sure there is a pillow *next* to the head of the partner lying on the floor, so the partner who is above can have enough head support to avoid neck tension. This position can be tricky in the beginning, but it's delicious when you get the hang of it. The partner on top may worry that he or she is too heavy, but this is seldom the case. The more you allow yourself to relax, the lighter you will feel to your partner. It is only when you try to hold yourself up by staying tense that you feel heavy. When both partners really relax—in most cases, after five to ten minutes—a melting effect takes place, and the question of weight vanishes.

☐ If you are both accustomed to another position of lying close while being relaxed, you can also choose that. Try to have as many parts of your bodies as possible in contact with each other, especially the chest.

When you have found the right position, imagine that any leftover tensions or fears are being expelled through the current of your exhalation. Watch your breathing: Is it relaxed, yet deep? How is your partner's breathing rhythm? Is it slower or faster than yours? Can you adjust your rhythms together? Be aware of other small details—your partner's warmth, the softness of his skin, the curvature of her shoulder, the tender feeling of protection, the sensual caress of a hand on your back.

Let any unexpressed feelings, such as resentments and worries, be released fully as you exhale. No disappointment remains, no anger, no expectations. Your heart is simply open. Feel the relief, the tranquillity. Feel yourself becoming lighter each time you exhale. It's a beautiful feeling to allow yourself so much trust that you can simply lie there and let the other person in.

As you relax, enter the realm of feelings. Allow the music to flow into your chest as you inhale. Let it fill your chest, your whole back, your neck and throat. Relax your face, especially the muscles around your eyes

Position for bonding relaxation. When both partners relax deeply for ten to twenty minutes, a melting effect takes place, and the question of weight vanishes.

293

and mouth. Let your tongue float inside your mouth without touching any part of the mouth cavity. This has a deeply relaxing effect. Feel as if the space inside your head is expanding.

As you exhale, release any need to think and analyze. Feel your spirit becoming broad and wide. As the music penetrates your whole body, from your feet to your head, imagine you are simply floating on the notes. Say softly to yourself, "I am present, alive, receptive."

The more sensitive and transparent you become, the more you begin to feel formless, entering a new reality where doing and not doing are one, where gentleness and subtlety give expression to your softness and vulnerability. Let each part of your body relax more and more deeply, as if each time you exhale, you are letting yourself fall through the air, knowing a parachute is about to open. You can let go, it is quite safe, and you are welcoming each other more and more as you relax.

As you feel the connection between your warmth, energy currents, and heartbeats, the boundaries between your bodies will begin to merge and dissolve. Usually this takes about 15 to 20 minutes, sometimes up to half an hour.

You may wish to harmonize your breathing rhythms fully, inhaling and exhaling together effortlessly.

If it feels right, you may also wish to explore inverted breathing: When one exhales, the other inhales simultaneously. Let this exploration be completely effortless. Let yourself tune in to other dimensions you would like to share with this being. Can your heart welcome him or her deeply and openly? Can your spirits connect? Can you flow together toward unknown realms of ecstasy? As you feel a *yes* arising in your heart, you move farther along the path to High Sex.

Pointers

Some people feel they should remain in the same position in the Bonding Relaxation, even when they begin to feel uncomfortable, because they don't want to disturb their partner. It is contrary to the very idea of relaxation to remain in a position that doesn't feel right, however, even if your partner seems to enjoy it. Do not hesitate to readjust your position or to tell each other if you need to move during this exploration. But remember: Any movement has to be slow and gentle. As the relaxation deepens, one partner may have the experience of "floating" beyond the boundaries of the body, and it can be quite a shock if the other person moves abruptly.

Avoid the trap of expecting cosmic ecstasy after five minutes. You may feel disappointed if nothing special happens at first. Each new step needs to be repeated several times before you get the hang of it.

When you have explored the Bonding Relaxation together in this effortless manner, you can go a step farther and apply it to your love-making.

THE SEXUAL BONDING RELAXATION

In the final practice in this chapter, you prolong this relaxation technique and integrate it into your lovemaking.

Purpose and Benefits

This exercise is particularly beneficial when you feel tired—with no energy for sexual athletics—yet you are in a tender mood and would like to be joined. It teaches you how to integrate feelings of trust, merging, and melting into your lovemaking.

Sexual Bonding is extremely relaxing and healing. Dr. von Urban prescribed this method to hundreds of patients and did extensive research showing that it improved marital relationships and lessened insomnia, high blood pressure, irritability, ulcers, and other health problems. He attributed this healing effect to streams of bioelectrical energy that were stimulated by lovers in each other's bodies. Moreover, he discovered that when the lovers had been lying together for 20 to 30 minutes, the two streams melted and merged, creating a unified energy field. Love, says von Urban, enhances bioelectrical conductivity and allows the streams to flow freely. Negative emotions such as fear, anger, and resentment block the flow.

Preparations

This practice is best done as a continuation of the Streaming Process, the Butterfly, and the Bonding Relaxation.

Allow from 30 minutes to an indefinite period.

The sex organs become quiet, satisfied, demagnetized, as perfectly as by the orgasm, while the rest of the body of each partner glows with a wonderful vigor and conscious joy, or else with a deep, sweet contentment . . . tending to irradiate the whole being with romantic love; and always with an after-feeling of health, purity and well-being.

—J. William Lloyd

295

Play soft, sensual music such as *The Way Home* by Kevin Braheny, or *Light of the World* by Constance Demby.

Practice

Begin kissing and caressing very slowly, and notice how your erotic sensations seem close to the surface of the skin after the previous exercises, because of the energy charge you have built up. As your energies are aroused, gentle kissing and caressing will help them to flow throughout your body.

At first the aroused energy is likely to flow toward the genitals, creating a localized tension that would usually be released through genital orgasm. If this happens and you feel the sexual tension becoming too strong, discontinue kissing and caressing, remain motionless, and relax into the flow of inner sensations you have built up during the period of arousal. This will diffuse the energy away from the genitals. Let the energy flow through the entire body as you relax into it, breathe into it.

Then, when you feel the energy has been diffused, unite sexually in a comfortable position that allows you both to remain relaxed. One of the best is the "scissors" position, with the man lying on his right side.

There is no need for the man to have an erection or to penetrate his partner's vagina completely. It is enough if half the penis is inserted in the vagina. Let this penetration be very gentle and nondemanding. Rather than seeing it in terms of the man penetrating the woman, have the feeling that you are penetrating each other, merging together not only physically but also emotionally, mentally, and spiritually. After insertion, continue to breathe and relax together, diffusing the wave of excitement that may have accompanied the penetration.

Inhale, focusing on your genitals, anus, and the pelvic floor. Exhale fully, relaxing the pelvis, the buttocks, and the muscles around the genitals and anus.

As you inhale, feel as if your partner's energy is flowing into your sex center. Let the music help this flowing-in sensation. As you exhale, feel that any discomfort, longing, pain, or tension—located inside the vagina, cervix, uterus, penis, testicles, or prostate—is leaving your body. Allow these secret areas to relax and open like flowers in the morning sun.

You are always relaxing, relaxing, falling back into the heart. Effortless awareness is the key. All your energies will be drawn upward, diffused throughout the body, and absorbed into increasingly more exalted energy centers. As this takes place, lustful tendencies will be transmuted into feelings of love and the need for conventional orgasm will lessen.

—James N. Powell
Energy and Eros

The Scissors position.

You may want to practice the PC Pump at this point to enhance the contact of the vaginal walls with the penis and intensify your mutual arousal.

Surrender to the flow of warmth and tingling that you may experience at this stage. Merge into it, and let it radiate to your beloved. As you relax into these sensations, you may feel your hearts dissolving, your breathing becoming one. Explore this subtle, internalized way of lovemaking in which erotic excitement can be generated by small movements of the woman's internal genital muscles and subtle shifts in breathing rather than by the dynamic pumping of ordinary lovemaking.

Whenever you feel the need for more stimulation, return to a stronger movement and friction between the genitals, but rather than cresting into orgasm, relax once again into the excitement, and feel the aroused energy stream through your body—into your heart and head as well as your pelvis and genitals. Proceed as in the Bonding Relaxation, relaxing, merging, melting, becoming one, allowing your energies to dance by themselves.

If no attempt is made to induce the orgasm by bodily motion, the interpenetration of the sexual centers becomes a channel of the most vivid psychic interchange. While neither partner is working to make anything happen, both surrender themselves completely to whatever the process itself may feel like doing.

—Alan Watts
Nature, Man and Woman

297

After 20 to 30 minutes, your bodies may begin to vibrate spontaneously. Allow these vibrations to expand, accept them, let them dance through you. They manifest the awakening of the Ecstatic Response. When this dance of energy inside your body and heart subsides, remain united for as long as you wish, or even let yourselves fall asleep while still joined sexually. For days following this event you may feel alive and relaxed, even luminous.

Pointers

Do not expect the normal arousal and peak of genital excitement in this practice. This is truly a meditation; you simply allow the flow of energy to follow its own course, without interfering. If, however, you do experience genital orgasm and ejaculation, don't suddenly break off the practice or blame yourself. Just allow the climax to happen. It is a continuation of previous sexual habits. Stay in a bonded embrace for 20 to 30 minutes afterward, enjoying the postorgasmic state of sleepy relaxation.

If you feel sexual energy or tension accumulating in the genital area, practice the PC Pump and use the Inner Flute to help circulate the energy away from the genitals.

You may have the feeling that nothing is happening, and compare Sexual Bonding unfavorably with the excitement of genital stimulation and release. This, too, may be a reflection of previous sexual habits. Be aware that you have a choice between your familiar sexual patterns and this new experiment. You don't have to feel compelled by your arousal to move into genital sex. You are training yourself to become accustomed to containing more and more orgasmic energy without immediate release. Nor does the mind need to feel bored by inactivity. It has a natural capacity to maintain a relaxed awareness and enjoy inner stillness if you present it with a method that is appealing. The more you enjoy Sexual Bonding, the deeper the experience will become.

After 20 to 30 minutes of deep relaxation inside each other, some people may be shaken by jolts of energy shooting through the body. This experience can be disconcerting at first. It is an instinctive way of cutting off the unfamiliar sense of formlessness and bringing oneself back to ordinary reality—"into the body." If this happens, simply relax and allow the feeling of boundlessness to reemerge.

This meditation often induces a loss of ego boundaries and opens the doors of transpersonal perception into a feeling of unity with the whole of existence. Sometimes, after being joined sexually for 20 to 30 minutes, you and your partner's energies may start their own dance, often in the form of shaking and vibrating together, while you are doing nothing; it is happening by itself.

After practicing the Sexual Bonding Relaxation as part of the training in High Sex, Johanna, a therapist in her thirties, said, "It's like being totally surrounded by a feeling of peace, calm, ecstasy—like moving through timeless space, totally connected with yourself and with your partner."

∿

In this chapter you explored some of the subtlest and most complex practices offered up to now. With perseverance and focused relaxation, you gained glimpses of the ecstasy that becomes available in High Sex.

First you learned to loosen up your body with the Shaking Loose exercise, preparing yourself for the experience of energy streaming.

Then, in the Streaming Process, you experienced the essential component of nongenital orgasm: energy streaming through the whole body. Relaxing into this energy, you also discovered the involuntary phase of this practice, allowing the streaming to carry you beyond conscious control into the Ecstatic Response.

In the Butterfly you learned how to focus this intense excitement in the pelvis and genitals, sharing your sensual excitement with your partner. Then you explored relaxing deeply with each other, learning the art of connecting sexual arousal with the whole body, particularly the heart, in the Bonding Relaxation.

Finally, in Sexual Bonding, you discovered that when you are sexually joined and completely relaxed together, a new level of intimacy and trust develops that in turn carries you into a mutual experience of ecstasy.

In chapter 10, Expanding Orgasm, you will focus on orgasm as a sexual phenomenon. This chapter teaches you about your sexual geography and proposes a radical approach to healing tensions and traumas stored in the genital area, opening the way for joyful release through full genital orgasm.

☙

EXPANDING ORGASM

In contrast to what you have just learned, this chapter offers new ways to inspire you to experience a wild, joyful, and complete genital orgasm. This may surprise you. After all, you have been concentrating on moving your focus away from the genitals in order to experience orgasm independent of the sexual context. Now I am going to tell you to drop any idea of transforming energy and center your total attention on your genitals so that you can experience a complete sexual orgasm of release.

There is good reason for this seeming paradox: Without understanding and experiencing the arousal, containment, and circulation of energy in your body, as you did in chapter 9, the pleasures of full genital orgasm often remain incomplete. Of course, almost everyone is familiar with having orgasms in their genitals, but the point here is to be able to experience these powerful events in their ultimate depth, potency, and beauty. Many clients who come to work with me realize that their genital experience falls far below its full potential. They notice that the usual cycle of sexual foreplay, arousal, peak, discharge, and relaxation brings short-lived satisfaction, momentary relief from tension and little else. As you will discover in this chapter, genital orgasm offers much more. It can be an ecstatic experience that shakes you to the very roots of your being.

The ability to experience full release through genital orgasm is an essential part of High Sex. Genital orgasm is the most natural, primordial expression of life energy. We cannot consciously expand and transform this energy if we are not also capable of accepting and enjoying it. To ignore the genital experience in favor of the so-called transcendental joys of ecstasy, as many teachings advocate, is a subtle form of condemnation, and as I said at the beginning of this book, in High Sex nothing is to

Many men and women mistakenly believe that if they experience their sexual energy, they must do something about it—they must perform, act it out, discharge it. Since having sexual energy is simply a function of being alive, all they need to do with it is experience it. They can learn to contain it and to allow it to spread out to the whole body rather than to express it genitally.

—Jack Lee Rosenberg
Body, Self, and Soul

be denied, including the animal nature of our sexuality. High Sex teaches that the instinctual part of your nature is not separate from the transcendental. The animal is not separate from the angel. Because they are two aspects of the same energy, a full exploration of sexual loving and genital orgasm can open the door to ecstasy.

The first questions that come to mind when engaging in this exploration are What is orgasm? What has been discovered about it? How have our attitudes about orgasm limited our potential to be orgasmic? We need to place the orgasmic experience within its historical context to help put High Sex in perspective.

Having established your own perspective on sexual orgasm, you may wonder how it actually happens. What is the role of my genitals in my experience of orgasm? Does the quality of the orgasmic experience depend on the relative sizes of the penis and the vagina? These questions lead us to the next issue, which is of utmost importance in High Sex: the nature of our genital geography and its influence on our ability to experience pleasure. The more you understand your own sexual geography and that of your partner—the way your sexual organs match—the more opportunities you will have to improve the intensity of erotic stimulation and the quality of your lovemaking. This chapter offers suggestions that may inspire you to find your own unique ways to establish genital compatibility.

In High Sex, however, even if you are well-matched, you need to develop optimum sensory awareness at the genital level. Can you feel and enjoy every inch of your partner's genitals during lovemaking? If not, your sexual organs may have been affected by the body-armoring process that I described in chapter 5. As I will explain in this chapter, the genital organs are as prone to body armoring as any other part of your body, resulting in genital insensitivity that prevents people from feeling deeply what is happening to them during lovemaking. To experience sexual orgasm fully, you may need to restore sensitivity to your sex organs, healing the tensions incurred during past negative sexual experiences and transforming them, step by step, into pleasurable sensations.

The methods that I present in this chapter for sensitizing these areas are radical and revolutionary. To my knowledge, they have not been presented elsewhere in the literature of either ancient Tantra or modern sexology. These methods may feel unsettling to you at first. They have, however, been practiced successfully by hundreds of people in the advanced phase of the Love and Ecstasy Training and have yielded dramatically effective results. They have expanded people's orgasmic potential and at times have even healed deep traumas in the genital area that for years prevented people from experiencing orgasm.

Note here that contrary to most authorities on sexuality, my purpose is not to give you new lovemaking techniques, but rather to prepare you for a natural, spontaneous erotic flow that can carry you beyond all techniques into a state that the Tantrikas called *lila*—the playful enjoyment of sexual loving according to your own nature.

HISTORY OF THE ORGASM

Having given you an overview of this chapter, I would like to give you a brief description of our sexual history. In the past, limited information about the nature of orgasm has effectively limited sexual potential. Today research has brought much new information, and as a result, our possibilities have greatly expanded. We know that much more is possible. Yet many people still believe that a man can have only one kind of orgasm, usually termed the "penile orgasm," located in the penis and testicles, and woman two kinds, either clitoral or vaginal. In reality, both men and women can enjoy many different kinds of sexual orgasms, opening up a tremendous range of possibilities for experiencing pleasure.

To illustrate my point, let me mention some discoveries about the orgasmic response that I will discuss in more detail later in this chapter:

- □ During sexual orgasm, women can ejaculate as well as men.
- □ Genital orgasm in men and women can happen independent of ejaculation.
- □ In lovemaking both women and men can experience multiple orgasms.
- □ A full genital orgasm can open the door to altered states of consciousness.

Even though these discoveries have been well-documented in numerous research programs and have been known for some time, they still come as a surprise for many people. Yet my impression is that if one person can do it, we can all do it!

The word *orgasm* carries with it a great promise of fulfillment. It originates from two Greek words: *orgasmos,* meaning to grow ripe, swell,

303

and be lustful, and *orge,* meaning impulse. It also has roots in the Sanskrit word *urj,* meaning nourishment, power, and strength. If we had adhered to these definitions, we would, no doubt, have avoided much of the trouble that has accompanied the limited interpretations given to the orgasmic experience down through the ages.

Until recently, rigid distinctions were made between male and female orgasms and between different types of female orgasms. Sigmund Freud, for example, asserted that any woman who did not switch from experiencing clitoral orgasms to deeper vaginal orgasms at puberty remained sexually and psychologically immature. He also regarded the clitoris as a kind of atrophied penis, giving credence to the idea that the female genitals are by nature an inferior copy of the male organs. In 1920, Freud explained in *A General Introduction to Psychoanalysis:*

> Of little girls we know that they feel themselves heavily handicapped by the absence of a large visible penis and envy the boy's possession of it; from this source primarily springs the wish to be a man. The clitoris in the girl, moreover, is a region of especial excitability in which auto-erotic satisfaction is achieved. The transition to womanhood very much depends upon the early and complete relegation of this sensitivity from the clitoris over to the vaginal orifice.

Freud's assumption intensified the polarization between the sexes, perhaps causing untold distress to thousands of women who may have considered themselves to be inadequate and immature when they failed to achieve vaginal orgasm. It was not until 1953 that Alfred C. Kinsey destroyed the myth of clitoral versus vaginal orgasm when he published *Sexual Behavior in the Human Female,* reporting that almost half the 2700 American women he studied achieved orgasm through the clitoris, and that there was no evidence to indicate that these woman were any less mature than those experiencing vaginal orgasms. Kinsey declared that the supposed transfer of sensitivity from the clitoris to the vagina was a "biological impossibility."

As early as 1948, Kinsey also discovered that orgasm and ejaculation in the male can be two distinct and separate occurrences—a very important factor in High Sex and an integral aspect of the ancient Tantric teachings of the East. Kinsey wrote, "Orgasm may occur without the emission of semen. It also occurs among male adults who deliberately constrict their genital muscles in the technique known as coitus reservatus.

These males experience real orgasm which they have no difficulty in recognizing even if it is without ejaculation."

Meanwhile, Wilhelm Reich, in his ground-breaking book *The Function of the Orgasm,* published in the 1940s, broadened the definition of orgasm by becoming the first sexologist to describe it as an event involving the whole body, not just the genitals. Reich believed that a person's emotional health was related to his or her capacity to experience complete, whole-body orgasmic release in the sexual act. He felt that a full orgiastic discharge was one of the most healing experiences, both physically and emotionally, that a person could have. He was also the first Western sexologist to consider that healthy sexual functioning is connected with an ability to experience higher states of consciousness.

Contrary to the whole-body approach of Reich, William Masters and Virginia Johnson studied the human orgasmic response in isolation, observing it as a measurable and quantifiable process. They were the first researchers to make the study of sex an empirical science, carefully measuring 700 people's physiological responses during orgasm in a series of laboratory studies conducted between 1954 and 1965. Masters and Johnson helped to dissolve the distinctions between male and female sexual responses, reporting striking similarities that included parallel sensitivities in the penis and clitoris, mutual flushing of the chest during the "plateau" phase of sex, and identical rhythmic contractions of the anal sphincter during orgasm. They also asserted that female sexual sensations occur primarily through the stimulation of the clitoris, not the vagina.

In 1982, Alice Ladas, Beverly Whipple, and John Perry offered a new perspective on orgasm, summarized in their book *The G Spot,* asserting that the sexual responses of men and women match in almost every detail. Their approach helped to break through the gender gap and the polarization of the sexes fostered by Freud, revealing a sense of mutual and complementary sexual responses between men and women. The most exciting and widely reviewed aspect of their sexual research was their discovery that vaginal orgasm happens through the stimulation of the "G spot," a small pleasure point located about two inches deep on the upper part of the vaginal channel. When properly stimulated, the area swells, becoming firm, distinctly different from the rest of the vagina, and leading to orgasm in many women. Equally important was their assertion that during orgasm women can experience a release of clear fluid that is different from urine or vaginal lubrication and is equivalent to an internal ejaculation. There has been considerable argument about the existence of the G spot and female ejaculation. Many doctors deny both. In my opinion this attitude is the continuation of a male-dominant perspective that is slowly becoming obsolete. The fact is that the G spot *does* exist. Research reported in *The G Spot* and later in *Eve's Secrets: A New Theory of Female Sexuality,* by Josephine Lowndes Sevely, gives ample scientific evidence.

I personally experienced both the G spot and female ejaculation long before it came to the attention of scientific research. At that time no male doctor or sexologist could give me any explanation about these matters. The ancient Tantric texts, however, mentioned the existence of female ejaculation thousands of years ago. In the Kama Sutra of Vatsyayana, an ancient Indian treatise on the art of lovemaking, it is written, "The semen of women continues to fall from the beginning of the sexual union to its end, in the same way as that of the male."

In extensive research published in *Eve's Secrets,* which appeared in 1987, Sevely contributed further to the melting of sexual distinctions between men and women by stating that the genital anatomy of the female is "homologous" to that of the male—meaning that the sexual responses of men and women match in almost every detail and complement each other. Sevely defines orgasm as "the capacity for both men and women to experience a sequence of sexual sensations that bring about complete gratification." This can happen *with or without ejaculation* on the part of the man and the woman, and *with or without penile penetration.* In my experience, Sevely's definition is correct, properly suggesting that orgasm is an all-encompassing event that involves a variety of ongoing reactions between the mind and body, the brain and genitals. It does not emphasize the "how you get there" aspect of orgasm. Rather, it is open-ended, which respects individual uniqueness and differences in response-ability.

The next breakthrough in research into the human orgasm brings us very close to the perspective of High Sex. In their acclaimed book, *ESO* (Extended Sexual Orgasm), Dr. Alan Brauer and his wife, Donna, demonstrate that genital orgasm is not merely a set of reflex responses that last an average of 12 seconds, but an experience that can, through training, be extended to 30 minutes or longer. They note that during this extended sexual orgasm, there is a drop in the body's level of arousal. In other words, your heartbeat and breathing slow down, your blood pressure drops, and you generally "cool off," even though you are experiencing

During a lengthy period of perfect control, the whole being of each is merged into the other, and an exquisite exultation experienced . . . the interchange becomes satisfactory and complete without emission . . . In the course of an hour the physical tension subsides, the spiritual exaltation increases, and not uncommonly visions of a transcendent life are seen and consciousness of new powers experienced.

—Alice Stockham

increasingly intense levels of pleasure. This confirms one of the secrets of High Sex: staying relaxed in high states of arousal.

Although the Brauers focus mostly on genital orgasm followed by ejaculation, their recognition of the subjective ecstatic component of sexual orgasm as an altered state of consciousness brings modern Western sexology close to the Tantric perspective. They do not, however, complete the journey from orgasm to ecstasy in which the aroused energy is redirected instead of being released in an extended "blow-off." It is as if the Brauers rediscovered the coastal plain of a vast continent already mapped by Tantra but declined the offer to go inland and explore further.

Julian Davidson of Stanford University undertook to prove the theory that orgasm occurs in the mind as well as in the body and is an altered state of consciousness. His hypothesis confirmed that of the American neurologist Robert J. Heath of Tulane University, who found that certain areas of the brain produce sensations of sexual pleasure when directly stimulated by means of electrodes. Dr. Gilbert Tordjman, a French sexologist, made the relationship between the sexual organs and the brain even clearer by describing the brain as "our primary sexual organ" and proposing a "sexual three-stage rocket" through which orgasmic sensations in the genitals are relayed to the brain. According to his theory, these sensations pass through the following series of three hierarchically organized centers that refine the experience into higher and higher levels of consciousness:

Stage One: The medullary reflex system at the base of the spine that produces sexual responses such as erection of the penis, vaginal lubrication, and ejaculation.

Stage Two: The diencephalolimbic system, the so-called archaic brain, a centralized network located between the two hemispheres. Sexual impulses traveling up from the base of the spine are processed here by the pituitary gland and the secretions of the endocrine glands and are experienced as pleasure.

Stage Three: The neocortical system, the two hemispheres, the so-called higher or modern brain, where the orgasmic energy is refined into the Tantralike experience of altered states of consciousness.

In Western sexology acknowledgment of the ecstatic component of orgasm is becoming increasingly common, heralding a new direction in

The pleasure in sex is described by Freud and others as the reduction of tension; in eros, on the contrary, we wish not to be released from the excitement but rather to hang onto it, to bask in it, and even to increase it.

—Rollo May
Love and Will

the study of human sexuality: a meeting between the scientific and the spiritual, the objective and the subjective aspects of sexual loving.

I hope that this brief survey of the latest discoveries in the study of human sexuality has helped to prove another important point: that the struggle to compare male and female sexual responses—and to assert the dominance or superiority of one over the other—is obsolete. Scientific research confirms what I have personally experienced working with thousands of people for the past 12 years—namely, that it is not only meaningless to make such value judgments but also harmful, because it perpetuates the dominance of one gender over another and robs each one of its creative power and its contribution to the other.

Rather than separating the male and female responses—for example, by asserting that men ejaculate and women do not, or that women are multiorgasmic while men are not—we can look at them as mirrors of each other, complementing each other. Rather than setting one type of orgasm against another—for example, by claiming that a woman's vaginal orgasm is superior to a clitoral orgasm—we can value them as uniquely personal expressions of pleasure. Rather than pitting scientific fact against subjective experience, we can see that both can support each other in the quest for sexual fulfillment.

We can, therefore, move forward from a point of equality between the sexes. We can focus on equal training, equal preparation, and equal potential. This supports the oriental concept of Yin and Yang—the female and male principles—in which the Yang element is part of the Yin and vice versa. There is no "top dog"; neither is inherently more valuable or important than the other. They are two complementary sides of the same coin, helping to sustain and nourish each other.

EXPANDED ORGASMIC POTENTIAL

In exploring the realm of High Sex, you come to know that there are as many kinds of orgasms as there are stars in the sky, and each promises an infinity of possibilities for pleasure. The following list is by no means exhaustive, but will serve as an indication of the body's orgasmic potential:

☐ The penile orgasm in men
☐ The prostatic orgasm in men, which I will discuss in more detail later in this chapter

☐ A blended orgasm, resulting from simultaneous stimulation of the penis and the prostate

☐ The clitoral orgasm in women

☐ The vaginal orgasm in women

☐ A blended orgasm, resulting from simultaneous stimulation of the clitoris and the G spot

☐ The anal orgasm in both sexes

☐ Local orgasms of the breast, throat, and lower spine, in both men and women. These can happen during peak stimulation of a certain area of the body.

☐ Orgasm with ejaculation in both men and women

☐ Orgasm without ejaculation in both men and women

☐ A mixture of both: beginning with orgasm without ejaculation and ending in full release

☐ Multiple orgasms in women. These usually happen when a woman's partner can stimulate and love her for at least 30 minutes to an hour.

☐ Multiple orgasms in men

Within this range of experiences, I distinguish between two basic types of orgasms: the *explosive* orgasm of outward release, and the *implosive* orgasm of inward expansion. Both of these can happen to the man and to the woman, because both sexes have equivalent and complementary physiological and genital configurations.

The explosive orgasm corresponds to the normal genital response through the stimulation of the penis or clitoris and vagina. There is a build-up of arousal and then a sudden, involuntary reflex response in which the tension of arousal is released or "thrown out" through ejaculation.

The implosive orgasm is deeper, slower, and subtler. It takes longer to emerge and happens primarily through the stimulation of the prostate in the male and the G spot in the woman. In men this type of orgasm also can include the prostate, perineum, anus, and lower spine. In women it involves the G spot, cervix, uterus, and lower spine. In the implosive orgasm the energy of arousal is contained in the body and redirected upward through the Inner Flute. In the advanced stages, a full-body orgasm is experienced without ejaculation. In High Sex you can, with training, personally discover the reality and pleasure of the implosive orgasm.

GENITAL GEOGRAPHY

In addition to expanding your ideas about the nature and scope of orgasm, it will also be helpful to deepen your understanding of the variety of physical shapes and sizes of the genitals—what I call sexual or genital geography—and the important role this information plays in your ability to experience orgasmic pleasure. This vital information has been missing from sex education, and its lack causes unnecessary anxiety and misunderstandings.

Many people, especially women, worry about being unable to achieve orgasm. They tell me they don't feel sufficiently aroused during sex with their partners; they don't realize that correcting the problem often is only a question of adjusting the physical position in order to adapt to differences in sexual anatomy. Any couple's style of sexual intercourse needs to take this into account, yet we tend to get locked into one conventional style, pattern, or position—sometimes precisely the one that is not going to stimulate the internal pleasure trigger points.

The Kama Sutra and other ancient scriptures on sacred sexuality offer timeless information on genital types and their needs. For example, in some women the clitoris is located three to four finger widths from the entrance to the vagina and their G spot is deeply set. It is unlikely that these women will be able to be sufficiently aroused to experience orgasm while making love in the conventional missionary position, with the man on top. Their clitoris is too far from the entrance of the vagina to make easy contact with the penis, and they will require direct clitoral stimulation during penetration. They also will need to find positions that will enable the penis to reach the G spot, possibly using a pillow under the small of the back, or crouching on all fours and being penetrated from behind.

In other women the clitoris is right next to the entrance of the vagina, almost a part of it, and the G spot is close to the opening of the vagina—about half-a-finger deep. They will be able to reach orgasm quite quickly in the man-on-top position without manual stimulation, because their clitoris will be in contact with the penis.

In other women the clitoris is long and hooded, and is farther away from the vaginal entrance. Their G spot is also located fairly deep. Their preferred positions in lovemaking are on top of the man, being taken from behind on all fours with bowed back, or lying down side-by-side with the man's legs between her own (see "the scissors position" in chapter 12).

Others have a fleshy vagina with a clitoris that is covered by a thick hood with many folds. The vagina is wide and shallow, and the G spot is located halfway back. In lovemaking they like good contact between the genitals. Deep penetration will be uncomfortable because of the shallow vagina, so they prefer lying in the spoon position (on her side, with his front to her back) or lying flat on the belly with their legs together while being penetrated from behind.

In the Kama Sutra, types of penises are distinguished by length and thickness, while types of vaginas are classified according to depth or shallowness. The most compatible matches happen between genitals of corresponding sizes. For instance, a long, thick penis is a compatible match for a deeply set, fairly wide vagina. A short, thin penis is best suited to match a shallow, narrow vagina. Other unions are possible, however, depending on the lovers' skills. High Sex teaches the skills we need to counteract differences in genital geography. This information can be a revelation for couples who previously believed they could not achieve satisfaction with each other.

Even if the sizes of your sexual organs are different, lovemaking can still be a joy when you know which styles to adopt in accordance with your genital geography.

Once you have followed the practice section of this chapter, you will also know much more about the pleasure spots or orgasmic trigger points that are available in lovemaking, and how to arouse them. This will benefit everyone, regardless of genital shape and size. Before you come to the practice, however, you need to move from outer to inner geography, so that you can better understand what you will be touching in each other's bodies.

The Vagina: A Female Road Map

A good working knowledge of the male and female genitals is essential in High Sex. In particular, you must come to know your own physical geography intimately; otherwise you will not be able to apply this understanding to your lovemaking. In my seminars I have found that after an initial period of embarrassment about exploring their own sexual organs, people quickly grasp the benefits of this form of improved self-knowledge, especially at the genital level, as a necessary step to

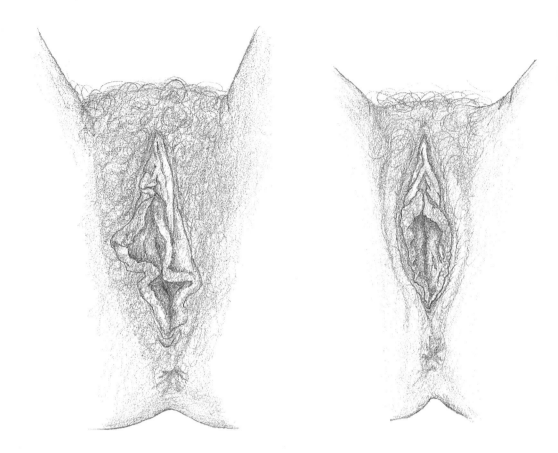

Varieties of female genital geography.

becoming better lovers. As you will see in the practice section of this chapter, this knowledge is especially important when healing the genitals of the negative effects of body armoring. Healing can only take place when you have a good feeling for the area and understand how your genitals function.

I will begin with a description of the vagina. Women, you can treat this section as an exercise if you like, sitting down in front of a mirror—a hand mirror will also be useful—and following me on a tour of your "garden." Men, please follow this section closely. The more you understand your partner's sex organs, the better your lovemaking will be. If you wish, you can also follow the tour with your partner as she examines herself.

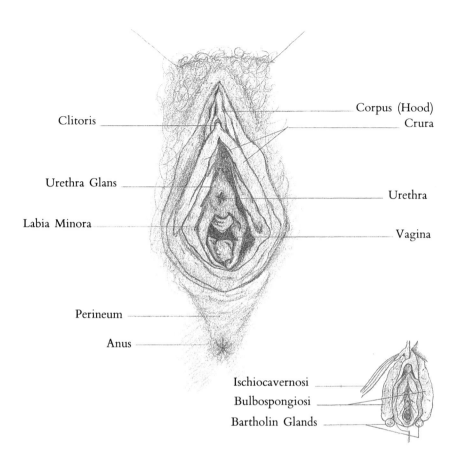

The vagina: a female road map.

Clitoris

Corpus (Hood)

Crura

Urethra Glans

Urethra

Labia Minora

Vagina

Perineum

Anus

Ischiocavernosi

Bulbospongiosi

Bartholin Glands

When you spread the minor labia apart, you can see the mouth of the vagina, which leads through the vaginal channel to the cervix and uterus. Immediately above the mouth is the entrance to the urethra, which leads to the bladder. Above it, at the interconnection of the minor lips, or sometimes higher, is the clitoris under its protective cover or hood.

The clitoris continues in the form of two leglike parts that run along the lower part of the pubic bones on either side of the vaginal channel. The clitoris is composed of the crown (tip), corpus (body), and crura (legs). The crown can be seen when the covering folds of the hood are drawn back. It is highly sensitive to stimulation. The corpus and crura, which are not visible, can be felt with the fingertips, just under the surface of the skin. The entrance to the urethra is surrounded by an acorn-shaped

313

protruding edge called the glans. Like the clitoris, it is richly endowed with nerve endings that render the area exquisitely sensitive to touch. During coitus the glans is pressed between the pubic bone of the woman and the penis of the man and has the potential to develop a painful or pleasurable response, depending on the quality and sensitivity of your lovemaking.

A spongy tissue called, aptly enough, the spongiosum surrounds the urethra, and the same kind of erectile tissue can be found between the vaginal lining and the legs of the clitoris. These are highly sensitive areas that swell during arousal.

Along the floor of the urethral channel—the "ceiling" of the vaginal channel—lie the Bartholin ducts, also called the female prostatic glands. They can be felt by a gentle stroke of a finger, inside the top of the vaginal opening. The area feels ridged, whereas the side walls of the vagina are smooth. This area has become known as the G spot. G is the initial of its discoverer, a German physician named von Grafenberg. During sexual arousal it swells to the size of a pea, a round protuberance that presses against the vaginal wall during lovemaking, enabling the woman to tighten her grip on the penis.

When a woman has been highly stimulated, perhaps having had several orgasms, she may experience a full orgasmic release that is accompanied by expulsion of a clear fluid from the G spot—in other words, an ejaculation. Female ejaculate is made of several fluids: vaginal lubrication, cervical mucus, fluids from the uterus, secretions from the Bartholin ducts and from the G spot itself. According to Sevely, "All women normally ejaculate sexual fluids from the prostatic glands." Some women can do so rather quickly, but from my experience most take 30 minutes or longer, even up to an hour. Research has confirmed that women in their sixties, seventies, and eighties experience and enjoy ejaculation. It is important to note here that a woman can experience a completely fulfilling orgasm without ejaculation. So there is no need to think *If I don't ejaculate, I'm not a real woman!* Experiencing pleasure is far more important than whether or not you ejaculate.

The deepest part of the vaginal channel surrounds the cervix. Located near the sacral nerves, this area, when stimulated, sometimes has an effect like electricity shooting or streaming up the spine in strong, wavelike pulsations. The cervix opens into the uterus, the walls of which become a living network of muscle fibers that contract and expand during deeply felt orgasms. There are connections between the nipples and the

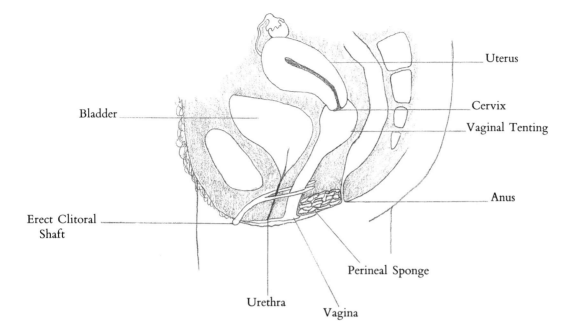

uterus and also between the nipples and the clitoris that allow some women to feel excitement in these lower areas through stimulation of the nipples alone.

In the space between the vagina and the anus is the perineum. This area is very delicate and extremely important in High Sex. I call it the "Gate Keeper" because when you press on the perineum or contract the perineal muscles, it helps transform orgasm into an implosive energy that is recirculated upward through the Inner Flute. Unfortunately, this area is often damaged by difficult childbirth. It is cut to enlarge the vaginal passage through which the baby must pass, and thus becomes the seat of much fear and pain that needs to be healed before some women can enjoy intense sexual pleasure.

The vagina is supported by the pelvic floor muscles, which are shaped like a figure-eight around the vagina, urethra, and anus. The biggest muscle is the pubococcygeus, or PC muscle, which connects the front of the pelvis to the lower spine and which you learned about in chapter 6. These muscles contract and expand during lovemaking, stroking the penis and sending pleasure signals to the brain via the nervous system. During orgasm the contractions intensify to a series of involuntary, very pleasurable spasms.

Anatomy of a female orgasm. At the onset of orgasm the vagina enlarges around the cervix area, an effect called *tenting*. With repeated or prolonged orgasm, the upper part of the vagina, near the cervix, goes through push-out contractions.

315

In terms of your subjective experience, all these subtle and infinitely complex parts work harmoniously together during sexual arousal, sending messages to the spinal cord that are speedily passed on to the brain, telling it, "Yes! You are experiencing pleasure and moving toward ecstasy."

As you deepen your knowledge of the vagina and its responses during lovemaking, you will also become more aware of what happens in this area during orgasm:

☐ An engorgement, tumescence, or "erection" of the vaginal lips, clitoris, and vaginal walls as the tissues fill with blood
☐ A bearing-down from the upper part of the vagina through the descent of the uterus and cervix
☐ A clasping, caressing action, as the muscles around the middle and front of the vagina rhythmically expand and contract
☐ Rhythmic contractions of the PC muscle

A Road Map for the Penis

Now that we have explored the woman's "secret garden," it is equally important to develop a good knowledge of the man's organ of love so that you can appreciate its beauty and understand, in the practices, how to bring healing to this area. Women, please follow this section closely. If you wish, you can also follow the tour with your partner as he examines himself. This, too, is part of expanding your potential as a wonderful lover.

The penis is as simple as the vagina is complex. It has no bones and no muscles. The main internal feature of the penis is the urethra, which expels urine from the bladder. This tube is surrounded by spongy tissue, and during sexual arousal this tissue fills with blood, causing the glans and shaft of the penis to swell to several times their unaroused state. This is what causes erection—a man's first response to sexual stimulation.

Below the penis is the scrotum, which houses the two testicles, in which sperm is produced and stored in the two epididymides—adjacent to the testicles. From the epididymis, sperm travels up and out of the scrotum via the two vas deferens tubes. Each tube passes into the seminal vesicles, which make their own contribution to the composition of seminal fluid, or semen. The seminal vesicles connect to the prostate, a gland the size of a chestnut that surrounds the urethra, which is located

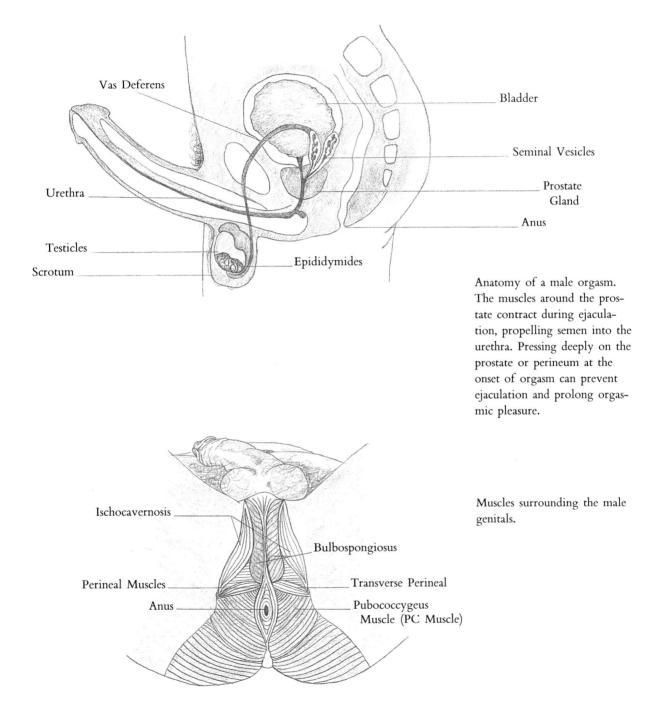

Vas Deferens

Bladder

Seminal Vesicles

Urethra

Prostate
Gland

Anus

Testicles

Scrotum

Epididymides

Anatomy of a male orgasm.
The muscles around the prostate contract during ejaculation, propelling semen into the
urethra. Pressing deeply on the
prostate or perineum at the
onset of orgasm can prevent
ejaculation and prolong orgasmic pleasure.

Ischocavernosis

Bulbospongiosus

Perineal Muscles

Transverse Perineal

Anus

Pubococcygeus
Muscle (PC Muscle)

Muscles surrounding the male
genitals.

directly in front of the bladder, sitting above the anus. The prostate secretes prostatic fluid, the major component of semen.

The muscles around the prostate contract during ejaculation, propelling semen along the urethra and out of the penis. As with the female G spot, the male prostate can be highly sensitive to sexual-erotic stimulation, especially when the penis is erect and the man close to orgasm. In fact, this form of stimulation can play a key role in expanding a man's capacity to experience sexual pleasure and is of essential importance in High Sex, yet is overlooked in most studies of male sexuality.

The genitals are anchored to the pelvic floor by a set of muscles that enhance sexual responsiveness—the ischio cavernosis, the bulbo spongiosus, the perineal muscles, and the PC muscle. These muscles are responsible for the involuntary movements of the pelvis during lovemaking. Male orgasm begins with the pleasurable contraction of these muscles.

Having examined the anatomy of the male and female sexual organs, becoming more aware of how they look and feel, we are ready to move toward a better understanding of body armoring in the genitals and how to remedy the loss of sensitivity.

HEALING YOUR GENITAL ARMORING

As I said in chapter 5, body armoring is a process whereby past traumatic experiences are stored in the body's muscle tissues. What happens is that the body's tissues harden, creating tension and blocking energy in the area that has been traumatized. By armoring itself, the body's intention is to reduce its vulnerability to pain. But this process has the parallel effect of reducing our capacity for feeling pleasure.

In this regard the male and female sex organs are as prone to armoring as the rest of the body and can function at a reduced level of sensitivity. In fact, because the sexual organs have been subjected to vigorous condemnation from childhood onward, the genital area has become a major storehouse of negative imprints, greatly reducing our capacity for sexual pleasure and preventing full enjoyment of orgasmic release. Think about it for a moment. Traces of the emotional content of every unsatisfactory sexual experience have been recorded in the muscular tissues of your genitals, building up tension in the area so slowly that you did not even suspect that it was happening.

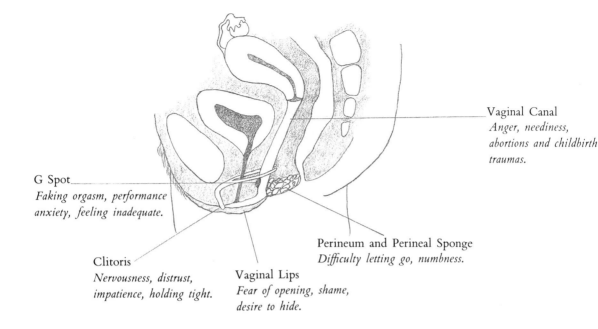

G Spot
*Faking orgasm, performance
anxiety, feeling inadequate.*

Vaginal Canal
*Anger, neediness,
abortions and childbirth
traumas.*

Clitoris
*Nervousness, distrust,
impatience, holding tight.*

Vaginal Lips
*Fear of opening, shame,
desire to hide.*

Perineum and Perineal Sponge
Difficulty letting go, numbness.

In men, circumcision, early experiences of guilt and fear associated with masturbation, clumsy prostatic examinations, and a compulsion to demonstrate "masculinity" by being forceful and thrusting in lovemaking all contribute to genital armoring. This armoring can manifest itself as a hardening of the penis, causing penile insensitivity that requires extremely strong stimulation in order to achieve arousal or, by contrast, it can result in an oversensitivity and fragility of the foreskin that translates into the attitude, "Don't touch me!" Armoring in men also manifests itself in the form of chronic tension in the anal sphincter muscles, involuntary erections, and an attitude of sexual greed—the need for repeated genital stimulation.

In women, armoring can be caused by guilty masturbation, forceful male fingering, sexual intercourse without sufficient foreplay, making love when you don't feel like it, failing to reach orgasm, having an abortion, or undergoing a caesarian birth or a hysterectomy. These contribute to the buildup of insensitivity in tissues around the vagina and pelvis. This tension manifests itself most commonly as a subtle tightness or stiffness in a vagina that never fully relaxes, even during intercourse. As a result, it is only narrowly receptive to the male organ.

Through working with many women, I have been able to create an

Map of body armoring in and around the vagina.

"armoring map" of the vagina, showing how certain types of fears are related to specific areas of the female sex organs.

☐ *Vaginal lips:* fear of opening, shame, desire to hide, a feeling of "I can't do this!"
☐ *Clitoris:* nervousness, distrust, impatience, holding tight, like clenching your fists or teeth when you don't want to express your anger
☐ *Perineum and perineal sponge:* difficulty letting go into pleasure, numbness
☐ *G spot:* sexual frustration as a result of faking orgasm, performance anxiety, feeling inadequate, pushing for orgasm and not getting it
☐ *Vaginal canal around cervix:* anger, expecting the worst, neediness, feeling like a victim, abortions, and childbirth traumas

If you are not sure whether genital armoring applies to you, try answering these questions. Think about them slowly rather than giving a reflex response:

Women: Were you forced into sexual intercourse or sexual manipulation at an early age, before you were ready?

Have you ever made love because your partner was turned on, even though you didn't feel like it?

Have you ever felt your partner left you "hanging in midair" while he was already "over the edge"?

Have you ever faked an orgasm?

Men: Have you ever made love as a performance, even though you had no enthusiasm for it?

Have you ever found yourself so busy giving pleasure to your woman that you forgot about your own pleasure?

Both: During sex have you ever found to your dismay that you couldn't feel anything "down there"?

Have you ever made love as way of avoiding confrontation with your partner or covering up your anger?

Have you ever believed that everyone else was sexual and orgasmic, while you were lagging way behind, feeling just a trickle of a sensation?

If you answered yes to any of these questions, you probably have some body armoring in your genitals. This armoring also translates into psychological attitudes—for instance, feeling uncomfortable talking about your sexuality or your genitals, or feeling discomfort when your lover examines your genitals. Working with hundreds of people, I have

Penetration. During lovemaking, shallow thrusts allow friction of the glans against the G spot, which can be highly arousing for both partners. Alternate the shallow thrusts with deep penetration of the penis inside the vagina. When the penis is healed, it can remain flexible and relaxed even inside the vagina.

found that armoring seriously inhibits sexual sensitivity and therefore blocks deeper pleasure. I have also found that it is difficult for people to be open to the ecstasy of High Sex until the whole genital and anal area has been cleaned of imprints left by negative sexual experiences. Only through direct, hands-on, loving massage around and inside the genital area can we effectively heal these past wounds and transform pain into pleasure. To do this we need to direct our full attention and acceptance to the way our genitals feel.

When the penis is healed, it becomes flexible, warm, and vibrantly alive when erect. In addition to the stimulation provided by vigorous sexual intercourse, this increased sensitivity enables the man to receive pleasure by resting his penis in the vagina in a gentle, relaxed, nondemanding way. Prior to healing, he may not have been able to feel anything without continued stimulation.

When the vagina is healed, it becomes naturally yielding, soft, and welcoming, allowing a sense of trust and playfulness in lovemaking. The vaginal muscles are elastic and respond to the penis by massaging it naturally.

Love and acceptance are the key ingredients for healing. That is why we need to understand the meaning of loving ourselves and our bodies before we can even think of making love with another person. Only then are we fully ready and available for the joys of ecstatic lovemaking.

Veronique, a busy executive secretary, attended one of my European seminars and told the following story of her own sexual healing. "I had fallen into a lovemaking pattern that permitted men to penetrate me before I was fully ready to receive them," she explained. "This habit developed during a long relationship I had in my twenties and continued for many years afterward. Then, at the age of 36, I began a beautiful love affair with Roland, a French dancer. We quickly became very intimate and tender with each other. Lovemaking became a slow, unhurried affair in which foreplay was as intriguing as intercourse.

"One day, Roland suggested that I lie on my back, relax, and close my eyes. He said he wanted to give me a vaginal massage. I accepted, although I was a little apprehensive. He spent a long time caressing and stimulating my clitoris without conveying any need for penetration. He also caressed my whole body and suggested I breathe deeply whenever I felt pleasure. When I was very aroused, he penetrated my vagina with his fingers. Very slowly, he started circling with his fingertips, gradually going deeper. Suddenly he came to a place that triggered an unusual sort of electric, erotic sensation in me. At first I was scared and began to tense up. It was almost too much. But he kept telling me to breathe and relax. I could feel his love, his caring touch, and the electric sensation started spreading to the rest of my vagina. Eventually, Roland penetrated me from behind, allowing his penis to touch that spot inside me again. As he made love to me, he caressed my clitoris with his hand. We got into a strong, steady rhythmic movement, and at the apex of excitement, I had an intense orgasm, feeling at the same time a warm liquid gush forth inside my vagina. The sensation of pleasure was so overwhelming that I burst into tears! It gave me such a sense of release and contentment. I realized how much pleasure I had been denying myself and how my genitals were only then awakening from a long period of insensitivity.

They needed healing, love, and gentle caresses from a patient partner. After that, it was like being a teenager again—starting my sexual education from the beginning. My love life has never been the same since. It is so much more relaxed and pleasurable than before."

As Veronique discovered, when the genitals are healed, there is no fear, no identification with past traumas, and therefore no habitual tendency to contract. Your male or female organs are free to enjoy their instinctual ability to experience ecstatic lovemaking. When you experience union between your healed sexual organs, you will have an impression that they have a loving perceptiveness—an intelligence of their own—that can guide you to the most exquisite and pleasurable experiences. This will enable you to surrender mental control in lovemaking more readily, and this in turn will bring you maximum enjoyment of your orgasmic feelings.

The exercises you are about to do will heal your sexual organs through a form of deep tissue massage, continuing the process begun in chapter 7 with the Sexual Dialogue between Vajra and Yoni, bringing recognition, love, and acceptance to your genitals. We are about to begin delicate practices that may feel threatening to you. But if you follow the instructions carefully, you and your partner will gain intimacy and depth within your relationship. The result will be more love between you and more sensitivity during lovemaking.

HEALING THE YONI

In this practice you will learn how to heal the vagina, sensitizing tissues and expanding their potential for orgasmic sensations.

Purpose and Benefits

For the male partner, this practice is an opportunity to relax and purify the Yoni, the "sacred ground" of his pleasure, to show his respect, care, and tenderness and to build up a deep level of intimacy with his partner. For the woman it is an opportunity to guide her partner into her most intimate area and to describe precisely how it feels and what she needs. This will give her strength and self-confidence. It will also open both partners to a relationship in which they become willing to be each other's student and teacher, building an equal partnership in sex. In the following instructions I assume that the Healing of the Yoni is given by a man, although it can also be given by a woman.

Preparations

The lotus represents the perfection of beauty and symmetry. The yoni is likened to the lotus in the early stage of its opening and in its fully open form. Like the lotus which is not saturated by the water that it rests upon, any more than its flowers are soiled by mud, the yoni remains perpetually pure and is not soiled by any action.

—Ajit Mookerjee
Kali

I first discovered the following massage practices working with Jack Painter, the founder of Postural Integration. Later I adapted them to the Tantric perspective of High Sex.

Before and during these massages, you will need to draw on all the skills you have learned so far. Here are some reminders:

☐ On the emotional level, remember the importance of laughter and playfulness. Keep it light. You may encounter many fears that can be healed with the support and tenderness of both partners.
☐ Tune into each other. It's helpful to look into each other's eyes and maintain eye contact as much as possible during this practice.
☐ Check the physical exercises in chapters 4 and 5 for building up a strong energy charge in the body. The receiving partner needs to build up an energy charge prior to beginning the massage. Do the grounding exercises, such as dancing, jumping, and shouting, to bring aliveness into the pelvic area. Use the Three Keys of movement, breathing, and vocal expression to maintain this high-energy state while receiving the massage. This can be done even while the receiving partner is lying down.
☐ The Pelvic Curl (chapter 5) is particularly important here because it enhances the pelvic response during the massage. The PC Pump (chapter 6) will also be useful; make repeated sucking movements with the vagina and anus throughout the practice.
☐ Use the Butterfly exercise (chapter 9) to bring a sense of openness and trust to your sexual feelings.
☐ If you feel fear and resistance at the outset, go into the Vajra-Yoni dialogue (chapter 7), and give a voice to your genitals.
☐ During the practice open your Inner Flute (chapter 6). This is the best way to direct the released energy through all the organs in the body.
☐ During the massage, each partner has a distinctive role. The man who is giving the massage has responsibility as guide and facilitator. The giver should not impose his views about the progress of the

session, however. He should listen and guide according to the feelings of the receiver.

HYGIENE. Because the next three practices involve touching the vagina, penis, and anal areas with deep massage, hygiene is of great importance. Cut your fingernails very short, and file down any sharp edges so that you do not hurt the delicate tissues of these parts. Wash your hands thoroughly with soap and water before each exercise, and keep a bottle containing alcohol nearby so that you can disinfect your hands as soon as you have finished Healing the Yoni.

Review the section on safe sex in the appendix. If you are with a new partner, use latex gloves. This applies to all types of exchanges: male-female, male-male, female-female. If you follow these instructions carefully, there will be no problems of infection or disease.

Use plenty of lubricant with these massages. Water-soluble ones are best because oil-base lubricants tend to clog the pores of the soft tissues and prevent natural lubrication.

When you have finished, throw the gloves away, and disinfect your hands before doing anything else. As an extra precaution, do not touch your partner's eyes or mouth—or your own—with the hand that has been in contact with the genitals before you have disinfected it.

If you are a woman menstruating, follow what feels right for you personally. Some women are more sensitive and their potential for arousal greater at this time of their cycle, so they may enjoy doing the practice while menstruating. But your partner should use latex gloves. Done properly, combined with slow breathing and deep relaxation, this practice can heal premenstrual cramping and symptoms of contraction and pain. If, however, you feel it is unaesthetic or uncomfortable, wait until your period is over.

Before you start, make sure you go to the toilet and empty your bladder and bowels, and then douche vaginally and anally. Avoid chemical germicide substances. Use filtered water and a few drops of lemon juice, or water mixed with three drops of *pure* essential oil of lavender (natural nonabrasive germicide).

If you are the partner who gives, you may wish to create the Sacred Space around your partner. Bring flowers, crystals, aesthetic or personal power objects, feathers to tickle with, perfume, essences, and a beautiful bowl filled with water on which a red flower is floating.

Make sure the room is well-heated, as the receiver will relax and be naked. Also be sure that you have plenty of time. This session may take up to an hour-and-a-half, especially the first time. Later, an hour will be enough.

Soothing music will help, possibly with positive subliminal suggestions, such as *Releasing Natural Healing Forces* or *Releasing Fear and Worry* by Jonathan Parker's Gateways Insitute (see Appendix II).

Practice

In Healing the Yoni, Partner A is the woman, the receiver. Partner B is the man. If you decide to begin with the man as receiver, you should proceed directly to the next exercise, Healing the Vajra, and then return to Healing the Yoni.

After Partner A has built up a strong energy charge in her body, begin with a Heart Salutation and Melting Hug.

Partner A, lie down with your back resting against one or several thick pillows, knees up, legs apart.

Partner B, sit or kneel between her thighs.

Partner B, begin by holding a bowl of water (with a red flower floating in it). Sit in front of your partner, offering the bowl and bending forward in salutation to the Yoni.

Partner B says, "I offer you this flower and water as a sign of my love. May they capture and dissolve any tensions that have kept the gate shut. I am honored to be allowed into the garden as your healer." If this statement feels awkward, you can make up your own salutation, or simply give a Heart Salutation to the Yoni.

Partner B, begin to massage Partner A's pelvic area and inner thighs, gradually approaching the vaginal lips. Lubricate your hands well, and lightly stimulate the clitoris. Watch Partner A's responses to see if she is ready to allow you in. She may move her pelvis toward you, rotate her hips, and make sounds of pleasure when she is. Before sliding your fingers in, lovingly ask her permission.

Partner A can use the PC Pump at this point, so there is a feeling that Partner B's finger is being sucked inside her Yoni. Check with your partner if she requires one finger or two. Some women may have better sensations with two fingers for the purpose of this exercise. Partner B, encourage Partner A to use the Three Keys and PC Pump to maintain a high energy charge in her body.

Healing the Yoni: As you massage the vaginal wall, vibrate the finger to promote relaxation in the tissue. At the same time, the receiving partner should practice the PC Pump and Sexual Breathing.

Once inside, crook your finger like a beckoning sign. Begin by pressing just inside the vagina, at the top, behind the ridge of the pubic bone. Rotate slowly to the left, then slowly to the right. Go very, very slowly, and encourage Partner A to breathe, make sounds, curl her pelvis, and continue the PC Pump while you massage her.

If Partner A encounters pain or tension, Partner B may feel a kind of hard nodule in the tissue, or a grainy sensation. Stop massaging, let your finger rest on the spot with the same steady pressure, and breathe together with your partner.

When the tension starts to be released, both partners may feel an impression of heat—even burning. This can continue for one to four minutes. Wait until the heat has gone, and then move on.

Partner B, when you touch any of these places, Partner A may feel sadness or have flashbacks to moments of sexual aggression, abortions, difficult childbirths, or incomplete sex. Encourage her to express these feelings and to give them a voice, as if she has returned to the scene.

Partner B, ask Partner A for guidance during this process, so that you know when to stop and when to go on. Partner A can give directions such as, "Please stay on that spot a little longer; I don't feel it's finished. . . . Okay, now you can move on."

When you've gone around the first ring—the band of tissue directly behind the entrance to the vagina—it's time to move deeper. Touch the

Healing the Yoni: Partner B, help partner A to keep the channels of energy open between her vagina and the rest of her body by making caressing movements and blowing air gently from her pelvis to her face.

area in the middle of the vaginal channel. Repeat the movement with your crooked finger, pressing as deep as your partner allows and encouraging her to breathe deeply the entire time.

Keep pressing until Partner A clearly feels where your finger is touching her vagina, but don't make any sudden, jabbing movements. Unhurried slowness and firmness are the keys to effective healing here.

Partner B, help Partner A keep the channels of energy open between her vagina and the rest of her body by making caressing movements with your free hand from her pelvis to her heart and head and by blowing air gently from her pelvis to her face.

At this stage of the massage, you can alternate between a crooked finger and a straight finger. Press firmly against the walls of the vagina, all the way around, using a stiff, straight finger.

At the bottom of the vagina, you will feel the soft tissue that separates the vagina from the anus. Through this membrane you can feel the tailbone and sacrum. Press gently and deeply against these bones, using a zigzag movement with straight fingers. Ask frequently if your movements are acceptable. Ask your partner to express the excitement, anger, joy, or grief that may be related to this area.

In the upward and middle part of the vaginal channel, you will be working with a soft, spongy tissue called the urethral sponge. You will also massage the G spot—an area the size of your fingertip. The spot can be located between half an inch and two inches inside the opening, on the upper (belly) side of the vaginal chamber. Normally the G spot is not so easily apparent to the touch unless Partner A is aroused, which is probably not the case at this point. So ask Partner A to guide you.

Discovering the exact location of the G spot is a training in itself. In the beginning many women don't feel it. When they do begin to feel it, they may also feel a burning sensation or a sudden need to urinate, or they may wish to pull away from your finger. When this happens, both partners should take a few deep breaths and relax completely, not moving. Stay on the same spot until your partner's tissues can accommodate and integrate this new sensation.

In my experience this is often an area where a great deal of pain and tension has gathered. Every time a woman doesn't experience full orgasm, there is a kind of yearning mingled with disappointment—a feeling of wanting and not getting—that creates armoring in the tissues here. This is your chance to heal these wounds, so be patient and tell each other what is going on. Partner B, help Partner A to maintain her energy charge during this delicate exploration, using the Three Keys.

When you are ready, move to the third and last area—the deepest part of the vagina. Here you will also encounter traumas related to the pain of an abortion or difficult childbirth or forceful sex. Just before you reach the cervix, there is an archlike space. Push against the tissue here with the side of your stiffened finger—not on the cervix directly, but all around it. Press as strongly as your partner will let you. Here you will encounter the muscle attachment to the hip bone.

Remember to stop whenever Partner A encounters tension. The more tension she feels, the more she will feel a burning sensation or a sudden desire to urinate or want to move away because fears are surfacing.

Tell Partner A, "Describe the sensation. Is there an image, a scene, a memory, a color? Breathe into my finger. Move your pelvis around my finger as you wish. Make sounds. I'm here with you to support you."

Healing the Yoni: Just before you reach the cervix, there is an archlike space. Push against the tissue here with the side of your stiffened finger—not on the cervix directly but all around it.

If there is a lot of pain in this area, don't push your partner beyond her limitations. It may take more than one session to heal the vagina, but a time will come when the contact of Partner B's finger will feel more and more pleasurable. This is a sign that the Yoni is healing and ready to be pleasured.

When you feel it is time to finish the session, keep your finger in Partner A's vagina, and invite her to start self-pleasuring her clitoris. Use this session to unfold the sensitivity of the G spot, giving Partner A the possibility of a blended orgasm with the clitoris and the G spot.

Partner B, you will need to find the correct rhythm and point of contact on the G spot. When Partner A confirms that you have got it right, stay with the same rhythm and stroke. You are allowing Partner A to build up arousal, and her confidence and trust will develop through your steady, rhythmic motion (about one stroke per second is usually right). In the beginning it is easy to lose the point. Don't get discouraged or impatient. Keep communication open and clear.

At the onset of orgasm, Partner A may feel her vaginal muscles squeezing rhythmically, followed by a ballooning effect, as the upper part of the vagina opens up. If the orgasm goes deeper, she may experience a feeling of bearing down—an impression that the uterus and cervix are pressing down into the vagina. Many Tantric and Taoist teachers regard these signs as an indication that the woman is ready to explore new heights of arousal, so you should both feel free to continue stimulation if this feels appropriate.

It is important for both partners to understand that a woman's orgasm is composed of many mini-orgasms and that she may need 30 minutes to reach a full orgasm involving deep vaginal contractions. She may need an hour or more to reach higher levels involving blended orgasms, such as clitoral-vaginal or vaginal-uterine. To do this she needs to be encouraged to allow more and more pleasure, moving from the clitoris to the vagina to the whole body.

For his part, the man needs to be able to sustain the rhythmic movement and timing that the woman needs to be satisfied. Otherwise, the tension that has been removed from her body may return. This responsibility can be taken negatively by the man as performance pressure, but it can also be seen as a challenge to his willingness to be open and to learn new ways of giving pleasure to the woman he loves. The rewards for satisfying a woman are not small. What you get in return is the woman's full capacity for love, joy, and nurturing.

Partner B, when this session is complete, ask your partner whether she is ready for your fingers to leave her "enchanted garden." She may ask you to wait a bit longer. Do so, maintaining eye contact with her, then remove your fingers very gently and disinfect your hands immediately. Partner A will probably need some time to be still, relax, and integrate the new sensations and discoveries. Ask her what she needs: a glass of fruit juice, different music, a sheet to cover her body, or for you to lie close and hold her.

End with a Heart Salutation and Melting Hug.

Pointers

In this exercise and the ones that follow, many people feel simultaneously frightened and attracted. Before they begin, some of my clients imagine they will never be able to do these practices. But once they have, they report deep satisfaction.

The first time you do this massage, don't worry too much about how well you are following the instructions; otherwise you may exhaust yourself. Be loving and supportive—that is far more important. Doing the practice a second or third time, you will naturally learn to be more precise. In my experience it is better to forget about technique and learn as you go along. The real teaching here is that you need to be receptive and sensitive to each other.

It is quite normal for the receiving partner to express hesitation, doubt, resistance, or fear at some stage during this massage. Don't take this as a sign to stop the session or as a sign of your inadequacy as the giver. Stop, breathe, wait, and allow the moment of tension to pass. If the receiver tells you very clearly, "I can't go any further," then gently ask her permission to leave the vagina, removing your finger in a slow, soft manner.

Men, be aware that, in this session, your partner is giving you a precious gift at a deep level, the gift of her trust in you as a healer. Be sensitive. Do not criticize or make any negative comments, for this will destroy the whole purpose of the session. As the giver, remember to change your position often. Take care not to get so lost in your partner that you forget about yourself and become tired.

For maximum benefit, do this session once every two months for a year. It took me about six to ten sessions to heal completely the pain and armoring in all parts of my Yoni. Lovemaking after that became much easier and more joyful.

You may want to exchange the roles right away or reserve the next session for another time.

HEALING THE VAJRA

This massage heals body armoring and sensitizes the penis. It also loosens the pelvic floor muscles, allowing more mobility during lovemaking.

Purpose and Benefits

We have already covered the massage of the penis in chapter 7. What is important here is to focus on the attachments of the penis and the scrotum to the pelvic floor, and on the network of muscles in this area. When body armoring is present, these muscles are chronically contracted, often impairing erection and ejaculation control. Healing the Vajra will help to correct these problems.

As in the Healing of the Yoni, the tenderness and attention of the giving partner, this time the woman, will help to build up intimacy between both of you.

Preparations

Create the Sacred Space.

Proceed in the same way as for preparations for the vaginal massage described above. Partner B, the man, needs to build up an energy charge in his body before this practice begins.

In this massage it is important to use plenty of lubrication with natural substances like olive or almond oil. The tissues around the penis and scrotum are delicate and can be easily irritated. Partner A, make sure that your nails are clipped and filed for smoothness.

Allow an hour-and-a-half for the first time you do this massage. Later you can shorten it to an hour.

In the previous massage the man was in his customary role of being active and in command. In the next two practices, however, he will be the receiver, handing over control to the female partner, and he is therefore likely to feel more vulnerable and insecure. The giver, the woman, should provide a lot of support to help him relax into his new role, maintaining eye contact and offering words of encouragement.

Play soothing music, as indicated in the previous exercise.

Practice

Begin with a Heart Salutation and Melting Hug.

Partner B, as the receiver, you should lie on your back, feet on the floor, knees raised, thighs spread apart.

Partner A, sit cross-legged in front of your partner's genitals and make the offering of a bowl containing a flower floating in water. Say, "I offer you this flower as a sign of my love. May it capture and dissolve any tensions that have kept Vajra away from his power. I am honored to be Vajra's healer."

Partner B, apply the Pelvic Curl and PC Pump. Partner A, encourage him to use the Three Keys and to breathe all the way down to his genitals.

Partner A, stroke the front of Partner B's body, loosening the neck

"I offer you this flower as a sign of my love. I am honored to be Vajra's healer."

muscles and any obvious places of tightness before approaching the genital area.

The genitals lie in a hollow, almond-shaped space between the pubic bone in front and the sitting bones at the back. They are attached to these bones by the pelvic floor muscles, and these are the muscles we are going to heal in this massage.

Work like a sculptor, finding the grooves between the muscle tissues and the bones, opening and cleansing these places, using the rounded tips of your fingers, not the nails, as a wedge. Using both hands, press against the edge of the bone, between the scrotum and the thighs. At this point, Partner B, the receiver, should rotate his feet out and in very slowly, permitting Partner A to massage more deeply into the muscular structure. Follow the edge of the bone, from the pubic bone all the way around to the perineum.

334

Healing the Vajra: Follow the edge of the bone between the scrotum and the thighs, massaging deeply into the muscular structure.

Healing the Vajra: Massage the perineum area.

To work on the perineum, tell your partner to do the PC Pump, and feel his muscles and scrotum lifting up. Meanwhile, press down on the perineum. Both of you should be breathing strongly. As Partner B relaxes, continue the pressure, but with less force. Repeat this rhythm several times, cleaning the whole area.

Do not press on the scrotum itself.

Partner B will appreciate it if you occasionally stimulate his penis, because this will create a balance between pleasure and release of tension.

At the base of the penis—between the penis and the scrotum—you will find a little muscle called the corpus spongiosum. Explore and massage it.

Then move to the scrotum and testicles. Massage the testicles, pinching them lightly and making small circles around them. Avoid using a lubricant because you need a strong grip. If you feel tension or pain, massage around the area slowly, breathing deeply until it has dissolved.

Bring the massage to a close by lightly caressing the whole area.

End with a Heart Salutation and Melting Hug.

THE ANAL HEALING MASSAGE

Next we come to the most delicate part of this work: the healing of the anus. The anus is considered a taboo area. It is kept in the dark, rarely looked at, hardly ever touched except by toilet tissue, and is given little attention, even though this part of the body has great orgasmic potential and can play a key role in High Sex.

Purpose and Benefits

Our first anal traumas are usually associated with toilet-training—being taught either to "push it out" or to "hold it in" when we were young. This learned reflex is carried over into adult life, in which we automatically keep a tight anus, especially when under emotional stress. In addition, the area around the anus was often the prime target whenever we were punished by hitting or spanking when we were children, creating more traumatic memories and insensitivity. Moreover, many people in my workshops have reported painful memories of receiving a prostate exam by a doctor who rammed a finger in without any sensitivity. This is why most adults learn to associate fear with tensing the anal area, and also why uptight people earn the derogatory label "tight-ass."

One more thing: The style of lovemaking most favored by Western culture—the thrusting, "I'm-in-charge" performance—may look good in the movies, but in real life it wreaks havoc with the man's buttocks, closing up the anus and the back part of the pelvis. In the long run, anal tension becomes chronic, and the perineal muscles become permanently contracted. As a result, sexual sensations are greatly diminished, as is a man's ability to enjoy prolonged lovemaking without ejaculating.

Many men are afraid that contact in the anal area may be a sign of latent homosexual tendencies. I see it differently. In my work, I've noticed that when a man has healed this area of his body, he does not change his sexual preference but can make love for longer periods, relax more, maintain his erection longer, and reward himself with increased sensitivity in his Vajra. Research and experience have proved overwhelmingly that the orgasmic potential of the anus in men *and* women exists independent of any homosexual tendencies.

I've also noticed that when the buttocks and anus are relaxed, the man doesn't feel preoccupied with having an erection all the time. This brings him closer to the High Sex approach, in which making love is celebrated as a delightful activity without any preconceived ideas about whether or not the man's penis should be continuously erect.

After experiencing the Anal Healing Massage, one client told me, "When we started, I was extremely scared, and my anus was completely tense. I realized that I had never allowed anybody to see my "emotional shit"—my sorrow, my anxiety, my fears. There was a deep longing to allow someone in. The preliminary preparations gave me a lot of trust. For the first time I could allow myself to open up, let things happen, be receptive. For the first time, too, I could experience pain as chronic tension and transform it into pleasure when I consciously relaxed the anus."

One of the main reasons why I have taken the rather daring step of introducing the Anal Healing Massage in this book is that it includes direct contact with the prostate gland, which is critically important in heightening and intensifying orgasmic experiences in men. When the prostate has been healed and is stimulated, many men can experience an implosive type of orgasm. Because this type of orgasm happens through penetration—by the fingers of the woman—it can open a man to the more feminine, receptive apects of his nature, generating a deep, subtle, whole-body orgasm. As a result, men need no longer feel they are being left on the "outer rim" of sex. As their female partners move deeper from the clitoral to the vaginal orgasm, men can move from the penile orgasm to a deeper, subtler implosive type of orgasm involving both the penis and stimulation of the prostate.

By denying and hiding the
sensuous/sexual function of the
prostate, the male of the species is
kept from realizing the essentially
androgynous aspects of his being,
which would make him less aggressive, more contemplative and
nurturant. The cultural conspir-
acy against the pleasurable utili-
zation of the prostate appears
designed to foster macho attitudes
and characteristics and to maintain and foster the male's aggressive stance.

—Herb Otto
New Orgasm Options

There is another benefit: When they become familiar with the
location of the prostate, men can prevent ejaculation by reaching around
behind the buttocks with one hand—just prior to the point of no return—and pressing hard against the perineum point. In his book *The Tao
of Sexology,* Dr. Stephen Chang explains, "During ordinary orgasm and
ejaculation, the prostate contracts and expands, pumping its secretions
into the urethra. Pressing the perineum point controls and decreases the
rate at which the prostate is emptied. Instead of the few seconds it usually
takes during ordinary orgasm, it may take as long as five minutes to
empty the prostate. This results in a five-minute-long orgasm!"

Many sexologists acknowledge the benefits of this kind of massage, but few are willing to guide people on how to do it safely and
effectively. I cannot accept this dual attitude. Either it is beneficial, or
it is not. And because it is extremely beneficial, I am sharing it with
you. If you find the whole idea of anal massage too scary or distasteful,
consider it optional. But discuss your reasons for doing so with your
partner, and find constructive alternatives, such as external massage of
the perineal area. You can experience High Sex without the Anal Healing Massage. But I will be perfectly frank: It is the most powerful
shortcut I know to orgasm enhancement, and I have observed its unde-
niable healing effects on hundreds of men. Moreover, exchanging this
massage requires so much sensitivity and care that it builds up a deep
bond between partners.

Do not judge yourself for not wanting to participate in an anal
massage. Trust your own feelings. This is the limit you have set for
yourself, and there must be a good reason for it.

Preparations

For this exercise the partner who gives the massage should use surgical
latex gloves. When you have finished, immediately dispose of the gloves
and disinfect your hands with alcohol. The anus is a natural receptacle
for bacteria—that is why hygiene precautions are required—but it
doesn't have to be thought of as "dirty" in the sense of revulsion and
disgust.

For additional cleanliness, the receiver should have an anal douche
beforehand; the anus will then become very soft and gentle to the touch,
feeling to some degree like a woman's vagina. The receiver should also
be sure to urinate before the practice.

The relationship between the giver and the receiver should be exactly the same as in Healing the Yoni. The giver needs to be supportive and gentle, and the receiver should be explicit in guiding the massage. Maintain clear communication throughout.

Remember, it is the change in psychological attitude that contributes most to sexual enhancement, not technical expertise in locating and massaging each specific point that I identify. If this exercise is done with a lot of tenderness and love, it can be wonderfully intimate and fun and can help you build up deep trust in each other—in itself a powerfully transforming factor.

The Anal Healing Massage is beneficial to both men and women, and the same procedures apply to both, the only exception being the absence of the prostate gland in women. Men should avoid receiving this kind of massage if they have a history of inflammation or infection of the prostate, because it might reawaken the symptoms. In this case it is best to refrain or consult your physician.

Create the Sacred Space.

Allow one to two hours for this practice.

Play the sensual music that was suggested for Healing the Yoni.

In the following practice I recommend that the man begin as the receiver because he usually has more tensions in the anal area. If he experiences the healing nature of this massage, he will be a much better giver when his turn comes.

Partner A is the woman and the giver. Partner B is the man and the receiver.

Practice

Exchange a Heart Salutation and Melting Hug.

Partner B, charge up your energy by dancing, jumping, shouting, and using the Three Keys. The aim here is to ground yourself, becoming aware of the connection between your pelvic area, your legs, and the earth.

When Partner B's body feels warm and vibrant and his breathing is deep and unconstricted, he lies down on his back in the same position as the previous massages. Another possibility is for him to lie on his stomach. This is more convenient as far as easy access to the anus is concerned. Lying on one's back, however, allows good eye contact and a greater sense of intimacy.

Partner A, make the salutation to the anus, offering a flower floating in water and saying, "I offer you this flower as a sign of my love. May it transform any tensions that have gathered in the lower gate. I am honored to bring you healing and pleasure."

Partner A, the giver, begins by lightly massaging Partner B's chest. While you're doing this, tenderly tickle him or crack a joke, so you can bring humor to this loaded situation. Help your partner to maintain an energy charge through the methods previously mentioned: deep breathing, alternating with shallow, panting breaths; Pelvic Curl; PC Pump; and the expression of feelings through sounds. Keep the excitement at a high level.

After massaging his body and coming close to his anus, put on a latex glove, and lubricate the area around the anus itself. Tickle the rim of the anus without going in.

After asking permission, enter slowly with one finger (index or middle finger, with the nail trimmed so that there are no sharp corners). As you start the penetration, let your partner contract the anal muscle around your finger, inhaling as he does so, and then relaxing and exhaling. Repeat this several times. Let him sigh as he exhales to help release tension.

At first, do not enter more than a quarter of an inch. Then stop so your partner can assimilate this new sensation. Continue when you feel the anus relax and when the receiving partner feels it is not an invasion but a "friendly expedition." Again, encourage deep breathing at this point.

A good way to move farther into the anus is to let your finger vibrate slightly. This also helps to melt away tension. You can repeat this procedure anytime you encounter an area of tension, pain, or fear.

When your finger is slightly inserted, you can work inside the anal ring, pushing against the anal muscle with a straight finger. Move very slowly all around the ring, while jointly encouraging your partner to do the PC Pump and deep breathing.

Once you feel that the first anal ring has relaxed, you can move inward to the second sphincter muscle at the entrance to the rectum proper. Curl your finger at the upper joint as in a hooking gesture. Use the flat end of the finger, below the nail part. Turn slowly in a rotating movement, and push rhythmically against the tissue. Be slow and gentle because the tissue here is delicate.

As in the vaginal massage, constantly ask your partner for feedback.

The Anal Healing Massage: Let your finger vibrate, while pushing against the anal ring to melt away tension. Contract and relax the anus in short successive pulsations.

Partner B, the receiver, is encountering new sensations. He may at first assume they are uncomfortable and wish to pull away. Ask him, "Is this new feeling uncomfortable or just different?" Leaving your finger inside, encourage your partner to describe what these new sensations are like.

Keep going, and whenever there is tension, stop, maintain steady pressure, breathe deeply together, and wait. Encourage Partner A to vocalize.

Sometimes negative emotions are held in this area—repressed energies that are turned against oneself, such as "I'm not good enough," or "I can't do that." Ask him about images and memories that may be coming up. Encourage a dialogue, perhaps with a parent about toilet training or with a doctor who performed a rough examination.

Partner A, the giver, may encounter tensions in the form of nodules in the tissue and burning sensations. This is normal and can be felt by both the giver and receiver. If you stay in the position, pressing gently on the painful spot and breathing together, the burning sensation will disappear after two to five minutes as the tension is released. Partner B should remain still and breathe deeply to assimilate whatever is happening.

As you move deeper into the rectum, you can massage the coccyx, or "tail bone"—the last bone in the spine. Then you can move farther in and press against the sacrum bone in a slow, zigzagging movement.

While you are doing this movement inside, it is helpful to let your other hand slide under the sacrum, supporting the area from outside. This two-handed massage creates a pleasant sensation of support and safety for Partner B, the receiver.

Then turn your finger from up to down and work the internal area of the perineum. You can also press with your thumb on the outside of the perineum, holding the perineal base between finger (inside) and thumb (outside).

You are now ready to work on the prostate. Move your finger back up to the twelve o'clock position. It is now directed deeply toward the pubic bone. At first the prostate may seem hidden in the surrounding tissue. Slowly, carefully, go deeper. You will eventually feel a round surface the size of a chestnut. Spend time getting to know this area and becoming sensitive to it.

Massage the surface of the prostate, applying as much pressure as your partner allows, while he practices deep breathing, expression of sound, and gentle pelvic curling movements. It is helpful to vibrate your finger on the prostate. Stay in the area for up to ten minutes. Move all around the prostate, vibrating your finger and encouraging Partner A to describe his sensations to give you precise guidance about where to apply pressure.

At this point Partner B may get the impression that his bladder is full and he needs to urinate. Usually this is not the case, and you can both appreciate the illusory nature of this sensation more easily if he remem-

The Anal Healing Massage: The prostate feels like a round surface the size of a chestnut. Massage all around it in a zig-zag fashion. Vibrate your finger gently. Encourage your partner to breathe deeply and practice the PC Pump. This can induce a deep, implosive orgasm.

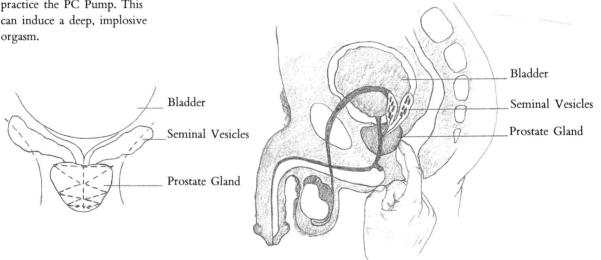

Bladder

Seminal Vesicles

Prostate Gland

Bladder

Seminal Vesicles

Prostate Gland

bered to urinate before the session starts. If it feels irresistible, however, he shouldn't strain himself unnecessarily. Very slowly and gradually disengage so that Partner B can relieve himself. Then begin again. Work through feelings of discomfort until a clean, clear feeling of pleasure begins to emerge.

To terminate the session, ask your partner if it is appropriate to remove your finger. Do so very, very slowly and gently while he performs the PC Pump.

Partner A should go to the bathroom immediately, remove the surgical latex gloves, and wash her hands abundantly in cold water while exhaling deeply, helping any tensions in her fingers to flow away. She should then disinfect her hands with alcohol.

Allow at least 15 minutes for both of you to remain silent and relax lying down, listening to soothing music.

End with a Heart Salutation.

Complete the practice with a light and loving discussion, focusing on the following points: the most difficult moment, the best moment, and what each partner learned from this exchange.

Exchange roles. Partner A now receives the Anal Healing Massage from Partner B.

Pointers

When you have received this massage for the first time, you may feel very open and vulnerable for several hours afterward, so make sure you have plenty of time to rest in a comfortable, nonthreatening environment.

During this massage accumulated anger—even rage—may suddenly surface. This happened to me once when I was the receiver. Up to that moment I felt the whole internal structure of my anus was completely smooth and relaxed. Then my partner hit one spot, and immediately I began to see red and flew into a rage.

Pictures came into my mind; memories of men who had been insensitive to me suddenly resurfaced as if they had just happened. I felt overwhelmed by feelings of distrust toward all men and wanted to fight back with all my anger and strength. It was an irrational, deep-seated emotion that had to be expressed.

In resolving these feelings, I was greatly helped by the vivid memory of the ceremony that my partner did just before we started. He had offered a salutation with a rose in water, saying, "May the anger stored in your Dark Cavern be allowed to flow and to be transformed into power." This gave me the permission I needed to go into a full release. With my partner's finger still in my anus, I sat up, looked into his eyes, and became a wild lion, roaring with all the power in my guts. My partner, in the fashion of a supportive facilitator, roared back. We had a confrontation for 20 minutes like two enraged animals, and when it subsided I could feel how the walls of my anus had completely relaxed. There was no more pain.

This may be an extreme example. I am not suggesting that you should do the same. But I *am* suggesting that you *not* follow the usual, conditioned reaction of suppressing these kinds of emotions. Find creative ways to release them that seem easy and helpful to you.

Don't make love for at least 24 hours after the massage has taken place. You have to give your body time to integrate what has happened.

When you do make love for the first time, start slowly, using the Three Keys. Build up the charge until you feel the full, erotic, joyful, instinctual drive expressed in genital sex. Go for it until you can allow full conscious release. If the massage was done well, you will notice a profound enhancement of sensations in the whole genital area. Some men report being able to feel every inch of the vaginal wall with the Vajra. Women report sensations they never had before.

Women, when your male partner reaches the stage in the Anal Healing Massage where it becomes painless and pleasurable, you can try this exciting experiment: Ask him to self-pleasure his Vajra while you simultaneously stimulate his prostate. Eventually he may experience a blended orgasm in which both areas reach a peak of pleasure. The interesting point here, as far as High Sex is concerned, is that it is easier to experience orgasm without ejaculation. The involuntary contractions of the prostate are delayed or even stopped, preventing the expulsion of seminal fluid through the penis without diminishing the sensation of extreme pleasure.

At the onset of orgasm in many men, there is a tendency to exaggerate the thrusting forward of the pelvis and the tightening of the anus in order to feel contact with the Vajra. A man may fear that he will lose pleasurable sensations in his Vajra by letting go of this tightness.

With this practice, however, a man can easily develop the experience of being relaxed and open in the anus while maintaining a pleasing erection in front—resulting in an ecstatic balance between assertion and receptivity. This balance between the masculine and feminine sides of his nature greatly enhances his orgasmic potential. He becomes more focused in the present moment and less goal-oriented, feeling less compelled to run after ejaculation in order to relieve tension.

Some people are afraid that they will encounter the partner's stool during this massage. It is useful to know that even a minor anal douche—one or two cups of water at the most—will prevent this, because the anus and rectum do not usually hold stool. Normally, it is kept higher in the intestine.

When you have familiarized yourselves with the vaginal and anal massage, the man can give simultaneous massages to the woman in both her vagina and her anus. If you choose to do this, however, be aware that the hand that is massaging inside the anus should not be used to massage inside the vagina. And for men, it can sometimes be more powerful to receive the Anal Healing Massage before receiving the Healing the Vajra massage.

A word about blended orgasms: as I have indicated, this is one of the most pleasurable activities. During the first few sessions, however, it may feel awkward for the woman to stimulate her clitoris while the man is massaging deeply inside her vagina, or for the man to stimulate his penis while the woman is massaging his prostate. Be patient. Many new sensations have to be assimilated. Take your time and introduce blended stimulation only when you both feel ready.

As I have explained, it may take several sessions to complete this healing process. When it is completed, you will notice a transition from pain to pleasure, from tension and anxiety to vitality and expansion. As you come closer to this transition, you become more confident and more willing to transform negative sensations into pleasure.

If you have a good collaboration between giver and receiver, you will notice the precise moments when negative sensations give way to more elasticity and more vitality in the body areas being massaged. The interplay between the touch of the giver and the tissues of the receiver becomes an innocent, exquisite dance. You will be surprised by how pleasurable the genital massage becomes. Ultimately your arousal builds up to an experience of streaming sensations running through the entire area, as there is much less body armor in the musculature and tissues of the pelvic floor.

🙟

In this chapter you learned about the different types of orgasmic experiences that are available to you in the context of the latest findings in sexology. Through this you learned that there is an immense variety of orgasmic experiences and that it is limiting to choose one type. You also learned that you and your lover can deepen your orgasmic experiences if you develop positions and lovemaking styles that are compatible with your genital sizes.

Through the Healing the Yoni massage, women discovered how to heal body armoring inside the vagina through deep tissue massage, thus freeing the sexual organ to be more responsive and sensitive in lovemaking. You also learned how to find and sensitize the G spot, thereby exploring the possibility of female ejaculation.

Men discovered, through the Healing the Vajra massage, how to heal body armoring in the penis and the muscles that connect the penis and scrotum to the pelvic floor, so that genital sensitivity may be increased.

Men and women, through the Anal Healing Massage, both learned how to relax and bring loving attention to the anus through deep tissue massage, helping to heighten sensitivity in this area and also to transform related psychological attitudes—feeling uptight, holding on to objects or people, hiding one's feelings, wanting to be in control—into a natural state of self-acceptance.

Next we move from the explosive orgasm to the subtler delights of the implosive orgasm.

❧

CHAPTER 11

FROM ORGASM TO ECSTASY

One of the most exciting aspects of High Sex is that it stretches your limits and presents you with the unexpected. While the orientation of chapter 10 was to encourage you to explore fully the pleasures of genital orgasm, this chapter proposes the opposite. It presents you with a paradoxical idea: In order to experience the timeless joy of ecstasy, you have to be willing to move beyond your natural attraction to genital orgasm and give up, at least temporarily, the intoxication of explosive release. This is of critical importance in High Sex. Every teacher in the field of transpersonal sexuality advocates diminishing the frequency with which you ejaculate. Without this ability the experience of sexual ecstasy is likely to elude you.

Most of the teachings on sacred sexuality in the Taoist and Tantric traditions advocate withholding ejaculation for men, while advising women to do the opposite—that is to say, encouraging women to develop their ability to be multiorgasmic and also to ejaculate. These teachings correspond to a modern attitude that also encourages the woman to explore her full orgasmic potential while requiring the man to assist his female partner lovingly by controlling or delaying his own ejaculation.

My approach differs from the traditional teachings. If women wish to use their sexual energy as a means of experiencing ecstasy, it follows that their energy, too, has to be contained, redirected, and refined and not released in genital orgasm. In my experience women as well as men can benefit tremendously from learning how to contain aroused sexual energy and move it upward through the body to higher energy centers. Women do not, however, have to concern themselves with whether or not they

The average orgasm is only ten seconds long. The average frequency of intercourse is once or twice a week. That's twenty seconds a week, about one and a half minutes a month, about eighteen minutes a year. In fifty years, that's about fifteen hours. For fifteen hours of ecstasy we devote how many thousands and thousands of hours to thinking about sex, worrying about sex, daydreaming about sex, wishing for sex, planning for sex?

—Alan P. Brauer, M.D., and
Donna J. Brauer
ESO

ejaculate, because—again, from my experience—female ejaculation does not result in a depletion of energy.

In High Sex the goal of redirecting sexual arousal also applies to men. To do this, men must take the additional step of mastering the urge to ejaculate. This means developing the art of withholding ejaculation until it becomes easy and pleasurable for them to contain the energy and direct it upward in the same way their female partners do. Therefore, when I talk in this chapter about withholding ejaculation, I am addressing men.

Often this question of withholding genital orgasm is misinterpreted as an ascetic discipline that denies sensuality and pleasure. This is a misunderstanding. I am not talking about giving up orgasm. I am pointing to a way to transform the energy that is normally consumed in short-lived genital release in order to achieve a much more ecstatic and psychedelic form of orgasm. And I use the word *psychedelic* here in its true meaning: *psyche-delos,* "mind-manifesting," showing forth the true dimensions of the self-spirit—that is, revealing a liberating, prolonged, even timeless form of orgasm involving your body, heart, mind, and spirit.

You may be asking yourself why I have waited almost to the end of this book to emphasize withholding ejaculation. It is because this book is about enjoyment, about learning how to enjoy your natural sexuality before proceeding to ecstatic experiences beyond genital release. I want to avoid contributing to the destructive attitude, prevalent in many esoteric teachings, that sex is a "lower" activity that spiritually ambitious people should transcend in their thirst for higher states of consciousness. Such judgments have no place in High Sex.

At this point in my training, there is a subtle trap. Having succeeded in heightening the pleasures of genital sex, many people will be tempted to remain at this level of experience. Having realized that they were previously loving at 10 percent of their potential, they will want to catch up on the other 90 percent and simply enjoy lovemaking in a wild, abandoned, playful manner. If that is what you wish to do, please go ahead. Joyful, spontaneous lovemaking is indeed a healing and highly pleasurable experience.

This is not the end of the road to High Sex, however, and if you choose to remain at this level of sexuality, you will eventually notice a sense of dissatisfaction setting in. The joy of ejaculatory orgasm is fleeting—a momentary experience that one is forever trying to recapture,

The conventional orgasm is genital discharge. It is a form of bodily elimination. It is sexuality lived after the model provided by the organs of digestion and elimination. It empties us. It is a form of reactivity or recoil. It separates us from others and from Life. . . . It reinforces attachment to subjectivity, inwardness, obsessive thinking, reactive or negative emotions, bodily contraction, and self-possession.

—Da Love-Ananda
Love of the Two-Armed Form

until one begins to wonder, "There must be more to orgasm than this!" Yes, there is much more, but, as you have done before in this book, you need to be willing to go through the insecurity of a transition to the new and the unknown, trusting that the outcome will transform your lovemaking. Once again, let me reassure you that I am proposing an *alternative* to the sexual style you already enjoy, not a *denial* of it.

Do not expel your semen needlessly. Do not expel your semen forcefully, as if dashing something down from the heights. You'll upset the five main bodily organs, injure the life-energy channels and give rise to every kind of ailment as a consequence.

—Ishimpo

MALE ATTACHMENT TO EJACULATION

In our culture ejaculation has long been regarded as the ultimate expression of male sexual power and virility. Young boys often learn to masturbate together and compare who can shoot his semen the farthest. And women think that when a man can make love and ejaculate several times in a night, he is *really* a man. So switching the emphasis from explosive ejaculation to implosive orgasm may be a tricky matter in the beginning.

Male ejaculation is a two-part reflex. In the emission phase the prostate gland contracts and empties semen into the urethra. In the expulsion phase a rhythmic, wavelike muscle contraction in the pelvis propels the semen down the urethra and out the penis. The pleasure experienced as a result of these involuntary contractions makes up the genital orgasm.

In chapter 7 we explored ways for men to contain or delay ejaculation by pressing on the perineum point, just before the emission phase of the orgasm, which is felt as "the point of no return." This pressure prevents the semen from entering the penis. Instead, it remains in the prostate, where it is reabsorbed into the bloodstream and carried to the rest of the body. If you, as a man, have become familiar with this practice, as well as with the PC Pump, introduced in chapter 6, you may have already developed the ability to experience "dry orgasm," the orgasmic experience of the expulsion phase—the vibrations of the pelvic muscles—without any emission of semen.

Before lovemaking many men decide they will stop before the point of no return. But in the heat of sex, their female partner gets so excited that the man receives no support from her to resist the "final rush." Or he becomes so desirous for release himself that he forgets his intentions and thinks, *Ah, I'll do it next time; this feels too good!*

In my trainings this issue comes up again and again. Many men want to satisfy their female partners and move toward High Sex, yet they express difficulty in restraining themselves from "coming." In dealing with this, I usually point out how we have been brought up to assume that sex requires a sharp focus on the genitals. Apart from reproduction, we believe that the whole point of making love is to reach the most intense orgasm of genital release. Furthermore, we think that this kind of orgasm is good because it releases tensions that may otherwise build up into stress.

I have found that this is a limited perspective. In male ejaculation the energy is not sustained but discharged and is followed by a sense of depletion. The pleasure is short-lived, usually lasting no more than a few seconds, and it rarely feels completely fulfilling. Because a woman's energy is not depleted by her sexual climax—for her, depletion happens more through menstruation than through ejaculation—she is ready for more lovemaking, while the man typically is not. Male ejaculation often cuts off the communion between partners, as if the man has suddenly turned off the TV while his female partner is still watching the show.

I believe this difference is one of the major reasons for unhappiness in intimacy between men and women. There is nothing worse for a woman than to have a man ejaculate after a short while without finding out in advance whether the timing is right for her. She feels deserted and dissatisfied. And it's not much fun for the man either. He often feels tired, empty, and remote afterward. He abruptly loses interest in his lover and wants to turn over and go to sleep.

Even today, after the publication of hundreds of books and thousands of magazine articles on the subject, statistical research indicates that between 30 and 70 percent of American women don't experience fulfilling orgasm during intercourse. I think this is often due to their partner's focus on ejaculation. In a recent survey of 100,000 women, Shere Hite discovered that only 30 percent experience orgasm during intercourse. She concluded that intercourse "was never meant to stimulate women to orgasm."

Such reports foster the belief, deep-seated in many women, that it's impossible to get satisfaction from a man—a belief that fuels the distrust and hostility between the sexes. My feeling is that such attitudes arise because men tend to equate orgasm with ejaculation and because both men and women usually remain unaware of the ecstatic orgasmic experi-

A man's semen, or vital essence, or "ching" is the driving force in a man's love for his woman. Once he has ejaculated, it is like letting the air out of a balloon—he feels flat, especially so when he ejaculates frequently.

—Jolan Chang
Tao of Loving

ences that are available when the focus of lovemaking shifts away from the genitals to flooding the whole body with loving, relaxed energy.

The perspective of High Sex is based on the understanding that a man and woman *can* achieve fulfillment through each other in lovemaking. When they shift the focus of their pleasure beyond the need for the explosive release of the genital orgasm, they gradually learn to contain the energy. As they relax into it, they become fluid and flowing, like the wave falling back into the ocean. At that level the rewards and the enjoyment are so great that the man no longer needs to ejaculate. This is the way to ecstasy.

BEYOND EJACULATION

There are many advantages to making love without ejaculation. For men, you can enjoy making love more often, and you will not feel depleted. When you *do* ejaculate after containing your energy longer, your orgasm is stronger. Because you will maintain an erection for a longer time, you can satisfy a woman more completely, bringing her through several intense orgasms. This will allow her to trust you more fully. She will feel your heartfelt desire to fulfill her. In return, you are sure to receive her unconditional love and experience a more harmonious relationship.

Some men resist the idea of nonejaculatory sex because they think that it is unhealthy to hold in the sperm, but the Taoists argue that the contrary is true. They believe that withholding ejaculation is of considerable psychological and physical benefit to men and cite everything from increased self-confidence to the easing of chronic back pain. They also advocate a precise timetable of ejaculation that varies with a man's age: A 23-year-old man should not ejaculate more than once every four to five days if he wishes to avoid depleting his energy reserves, and a 40-year-old man should not ejaculate more than once every eight days.

My work with clients seems to indicate that the Taoists are right. If ejaculation is avoided for a prolonged period, the vital elements that contribute to the manufacture of sperm will gradually be reabsorbed into the body through the blood and will contribute to maintaining a youthful, vigorous, healthy male body, with strong bones, clarity of mind, and sexual potency. The whole nervous system and the glands and organs are energized by this process. After experimenting with withholding ejaculation, many of my male clients report seeing more clearly and feeling more alive, sprightly, and self-confident.

Carlo, a 29-year-old chiropractor from Sacramento, had a personal experience of this phenomenon. He and his wife, Elizabeth, had just completed the second cycle of my year-long training. "Eli and I had arranged to go on a skiing vacation in a little cabin in Lake Tahoe," he explained. "When we arrived, the weather got very bad. It was snowing so hard, we couldn't go anywhere. So we were cooped up like rabbits. That was fine with us, because after the training we were so turned on to each other that it felt as if we had just fallen in love. We spent almost the whole time in bed and made love several times a day. Our attraction for each other was so intense that we put side all thoughts of containing and redirecting our sexual energy. It was what you could call totally wild sex. I ejaculated each time we made love, and we had intense and wonderful orgasms. The weather remained bad, so we continued like this for three or four days. Then I noticed a gradual shift in our energies and mood. We were getting tired, slightly impatient with each other, a bit depressed and nervous. Also, my back was beginning to feel sore. Finally it reached a peak in a fierce quarrel about some ridiculously minor event—who should do the dishes. All of a sudden, it felt as if we had lost our trust in each other. We realized that this was probably linked with the way we had been making love. Our energy was spent, and we felt empty.

"We decided that from then on, we would practice what we had learned about High Sex and, while enjoying lovemaking, redirect the energy through the chakras together. I did not ejaculate for some days. The weather did not clear up, but we did! The results were wonderful. We held each other very close during lovemaking, stopped before the point of no return, visualizing that we were carrying the orgasmic energy to our hearts and then to the third eye. Gradually we began to experience a deep, melting, meditative feeling of being joined in body and soul. We rediscovered our love for each other, a sense of delight, mutual acceptance, trust, and generosity. There were no more quarrels. We could both see very clearly the different effects of the two styles of lovemaking: throwing the energy out or keeping it and transforming it."

Please don't let Carlo's story mislead you into thinking that ejaculation is bad and High Sex is good. That is not the point. Both approaches can be right, depending on the circumstances. It is, however, good to be aware that you have a choice about which direction to take.

In the following exercises you learn how to kindle the fire of desire as a catalyst to carry your spirit higher. It is a delicate art, because you will constantly be tempted to release the buildup of sexual arousal in the form of an explosive genital orgasm. Instead, you will redirect this aroused energy up through the body to the head, allowing it to carry you toward higher levels of experience. Some ancient Taoists called this practice "Riding the Tiger." In one form or another, this method of transforming orgasmic energy has been central to all the great traditions of sacred sexuality. In some Taoist literature it is also referred to as the "Small Heavenly Cycle" or the "Life Wheel of the Seven Glands." In the Tantric tradition a similar practice was called "Contemplating the Inner Moon." I have borrowed the expression "Riding the Tiger" for my own development of this practice because it is indeed a powerful energy on which you will be riding.

The ancient teachers also talked about remaining desireless in the height of sexual arousal. They mean that in lovemaking both men and women are typically filled with an agenda of desires—for orgasm, for release, for possessing the beloved. They carry in their minds images of these goals, aim for them, and in this way are incapable of directing their total attention to what is happening in the present moment. Remaining desireless at the height of passion, you are not concerned with the next moment. You have no thought of the future. You are then capable of directly feeling and enjoying all the erotic sensations that are happening to you in the present, while simultaneously remaining slightly aloof as a neutral observer. This "witnessing" becomes possible only when you remain focused on the unfolding love play. You do not know where it is taking you, what will happen, or when it will end. You don't imagine, anticipate, or direct the show. You simply wait, watch, observe, and "ride" the energy. This is the ultimate discipline, the highest meditation.

We dis-identify by observing. Instead of being absorbed by sensations, feelings, desires, thoughts, we observe them objectively without judging them, without wanting to change them, without interfering with them in any way. We see them as distinct from us, as if we were looking at a landscape. We calmly observe those psychic arabesques from a detached viewpoint.

—Piero Ferrucci
What We May Be

MASTERING THE PRACTICES

If you wish to reap the full benefits from such advanced practices as Riding the Tiger, you will need a solid grounding in the previous steps of the training. So if you feel the need to polish up any specific prior exercise, this is the time. You may particularly want to review chapter 5, Honoring the Body Ecstatic, so that you can enhance sensory awareness; chapter 6, Opening the Inner Flute, because you will now be learning an advanced stage of this practice; or chapter 7, Self-Pleasuring Rituals, which introduces men to ways of withholding ejaculation, a skill that is also required in this chapter.

If you have had a positive experience with these previous exercises and have moved from practice to enjoyment, you should have the skills you need to proceed. If this is the case, at this point you deserve to congratulate yourself and your partner for your interest and curiosity, as well as your perseverance and thoroughness, all of which have helped to bring you this far in your journey.

In a sense, this training is like that of a mountaineer who didn't know much when he started out on his climbing adventure but who acquired his skills along the way as he encountered each challenging step. These skills have gone more deeply than you may be aware, activating new pathways within your nervous system and refining your body's responses to pleasure. Now you are ready to climb the remaining distance to the mountain's peak, where you can enjoy the rarified atmosphere—the brightness, clarity, and sense of aliveness offered by High Sex. I invite you to climb up to the very top, and naturally this means leaving the plateau where you are now standing. I'm not saying that you have to give up good sex—not at all. I'm saying, "It is beautiful here, but it is extraordinary up there!"

RIDING THE TIGER ALONE

We have already worked with generating sexual arousal and bringing it up through the Inner Flute to the heart center (chapter 7). Next we are going to bring that work to its completion by moving energy all the way to the brain.

Reading the following instructions on paper may sound dry because we are talking about ecstasy, not experiencing it. But don't be deceived by appearances. These practices are a real treasure. Reading won't do, however. A direct experience of them will provide you with true understanding.

Purpose and Benefits

The purpose of this practice is to bring warm, healing vitality and awareness to each of the "stations" on the pathway of the Inner Flute—

the energy centers, or chakras. You will begin at the sex center and work upward toward the crown chakra at the top of the head. You can learn to bring orgasmic energy to each of the centers, thus experiencing the different qualities of orgasm that are available and facilitating the transformation of orgasmic energy as described in chapters 6 and 7. And you can sensitize these areas so that it will be easier to establish a direct connection between the sex center, the third eye, and the crown chakra.

One of the effects of the following exercise will be to stimulate the glands that regulate the flow of vital energy in your body and also affect your awareness of how your energy moves. For example, by bringing energy to the brain, you will be stimulating the pineal gland, a small cone-shaped organ near the pituitary gland and the hypothalamus. Today some scientists believe that it is the regulator of regulators—a modulator of the activity of other endocrine glands as well as brain functions. Recent research has shown that in response to light that reaches it indirectly from the eyes, it secretes hormones that affect sexual activity. It also has a calming effect on the central nervous system that has led many modern mystics to connect it with meditation. Some researchers also believe it may be responsible for inner visions of light attributed to the energy center known as the "third eye." The pineal and pituitary glands together play a major role in refining information that flows from the sensory organs to the brain, supporting the High Sex view that sexual energy can gradually be transformed into higher states of consciousness.

In the following practice you will see that I have linked each gland with a specific chakra or energy center in the body. In my experience the visualization of each energy center with the corresponding endocrine gland in the body can greatly assist people in transforming the quality of their orgasmic energy as it moves through the chakras. Rather than adhering to the biological functions of these glands, I will focus on the subjective effect of this practice, encouraging you to experience how the flow of energy through your body can revitalize each gland.

Preparations

In this practice you will be visualizing a spiraling light inside your body. You may wish to keep a burning candle in front of you during this exercise and, whenever you feel the need, look at the flame for a while to help you maintain a strong mental image of the moving light within. After looking at the flame, close your eyes and feel as if you are taking

Riding the Tiger Alone: To help you visualize a spiraling light inside your body, you may wish to keep a burning candle in front of you. Look at the flame to maintain a strong mental image of the moving light within.

356

the light of the candle inside your body. It may be an idea or a mental picture. Focus on the visualized light in a relaxed, gentle way. Do not strive too hard, or this may hinder the process. To refresh your memory on how to visualize, check the Dancing Gods practice in chapter 4.

Create the Sacred Space.

Do this exercise in silence when you learn it for the first time. Later you can play gentle, sensual music.

Wear loose clothing made of natural fibers, open in front.

For maximum effect, you need to do all the following exercises on an empty stomach.

Let the room be warm and comfortable.

Make sure there will be no interruptions. This is important. If you break off this exercise before it is completed, you may experience negative effects such as dizziness and headaches.

This exercise should be done alone at first and then with your partner. You can do it sitting or lying down. Set aside 30 minutes.

Light . . . light, visible reminder of invisible light.

—T. S. Eliot

Practice

Open the Inner Flute, using the PC Pump and Sexual Breathing. Remember to continue these throughout the exercise.

Rub your hands together vigorously to energize them. Bring heat through your hands to the parts of the body you will be touching.

EXPANDING THE SEX AND NAVEL CENTERS. In this first step you will flood the two lowest centers—the genitals and the navel—with sexual energy.

Women, stimulate your breasts, massaging them with outward, circular movements, starting at the center of the chest, between the nipples, and moving outward and upward around the breasts, then inward and downward to the starting point. Massage them for about three minutes. This will activate the glands.

Stimulate the nipples, pressing and turning them between your index finger and thumb, breathing deeply and moving your chest to help the sensations spread through your breasts.

Then move your hands down and massage your belly and navel area in circles. Follow the movements that feel right for you.

Go to the vagina, massaging the area between the inner and outer vaginal lips in a circular fashion.

Men, make circular movements around your chest and belly in the same manner as the women for three to five minutes.

Then move your hands to your scrotum and begin to massage the perineum area, then your testicles, gently pulling them up, pressing them against the pubic bone, then pulling them down while you breathe and use the PC Pump.

You can choose to do this with two hands or with one hand while you stimulate your penis or rub your belly with the other. You're not doing the Self-Pleasuring Ritual, so don't stimulate yourself to the point of no return. It is enough to generate warmth, aliveness, a tingling sensation around the genitals and perineum.

Once the sexual energy is aroused and the "cauldron" is burning, both men and women should inhale deeply through the nose, filling the chest, lungs, and belly. Inhale all the way down to your genitals. Holding your breath, relax the muscles of your body as much as possible. This is the same procedure that you followed in Moving Pleasure Energy to the Heart in chapter 7. With practice you will be able to hold your breath without tensing and thus avoid blocking the flow of energy.

Learning how to hold your breath while remaining relaxed is very important. In the moment between your inhalation and your exhalation—known in medical terms as "apnea"—you may suddenly find yourself transported beyond normal thought processes into a feeling of lightness and emptiness, enhancing your inner experience of ecstasy.

At the same time you hold your inhalation, tighten the muscles around your anus and perineum, using the PC Pump. Feel the energy throbbing in the genitals, anus, and lower belly. Feel the entire pelvic area and lower belly filling with warmth. To intensify the sensation, take another short, quick inhalation—as if you are topping off a gas tank—and tighten the PC muscle as you do so. Remember to keep the rest of your body as relaxed as possible while holding the breath. You will feel an expansive, outward movement in your belly—it will feel round, like an inflated balloon—as the air in your lungs presses down on it.

At the same time, the contraction of the PC muscles will be pulling upward and inward against this downward pressure, creating a subtle friction that intensifies the energy. For some people this also creates a preorgasmic sense of erotic pleasure.

Practice this inhalation several times until you clearly feel energized in the pelvic area and lower belly. Then inhale, hold your breath, and visualize a glowing, radiant, and warm light spiraling throughout the pelvic and lower belly area. The aim here is to feel your whole pelvis

Riding the Tiger Alone: While you keep the body relaxed, inhale deeply through the nose. Fill the lungs, chest, and solar plexus with air. Hold for one second. Then inhale further and fill the lower belly with air. Hold the inhalation while you let the belly expand and practice the PC Pump.

filled with its radiance, touching the sacrum at the back and the walls of the belly in front.

To help this visualization, think of a shooting star or a golden ball spiraling inside you. The light is revitalizing and healing all the organs and glands in this area—the prostate and testicles in men, the perineal gland and ovaries in women, and the kidneys and adrenals in both sexes. Visualize these glands, letting the light and warmth surround them.

Try to hold your breath for 30 seconds. If this is difficult, then charge up the area by panting with short breaths in quick succession. With practice, you will be able to hold your breath for longer and longer periods, even up to a minute.

When you can't hold your breath any longer, exhale slowly through your nose, totally relaxing your genital and anal muscles. Imagine, as you did in Opening the Inner Flute in chapter 6, that the energy and light are flowing out through your sex center as you exhale.

Repeat the exercise.

Inhale, tighten your pelvic muscles, relax the rest of your body, hold the air, feel the warmth, the spiraling light, the tingling in this area. Exhale through your nose, feeling the warmth and light streaming out through your sex center.

Do this three to six times. You will know the exercise is effective when you start feeling a tingling sensation in the genitals and perineal area. Each person responds differently, however. Some people "see" or "feel" a light in the area. Others feel warmth, throbbing, or pulsation. People who are fully relaxed and sensitized may experience miniorgasmic sensations, especially as they exhale slowly.

EXPANDING THE POWER CENTER. The next step is to move the energy up to the third chakra—the solar plexus or power center—located just beneath the rib cage.

Make sure there is a feeling of stimulation in your genitals. Throughout this practice you need to keep a fire of arousal burning in your sex organs. Again, massage your breasts and belly and caress your genitals, breathing deeply, while rocking your pelvis gently.

Inhale deeply, tighten your anal and sex muscles as before, doing the PC Pump. As you inhale, imagine you are sucking the fire of your arousal through the Inner Flute to your solar plexus. Hold your breath, relax your body—except for the genital and anal muscles—and feel the pressure of air pressing out against the power center.

Feel this area filling with warm energy, throbbing and radiating with spiraling light. Imagine that the light is revitalizing your pancreas, the gland that controls digestive processes and helps you feel inner harmony and balance and a sense of well-being in your body.

Hold the breath as long as you can, then relax. Exhaling slowly through your nose, allow the energy to flow back down the Inner Flute and out through your genitals. Do this three to six times.

EXPANDING THE HEART CENTER. Check to see if you have a pleasant feeling of arousal in your genitals. If you feel they are still sensitized from the previous step, you can continue without further stimulation. If necessary, stimulate your breasts, belly, and genitals once again.

Inhale deeply, filling your chest, feeling the energy moving up to the heart center, at a point between your nipples in the middle of the

Riding the Tiger Alone: Spiraling the light and healing energy through each center.

Pineal
Pituitary

Thyroid

Thymus

Adrenals

Pancreas

Ovaries (Female)
Testes (Male)

chest. Hold the breath, relax your body, and feel your lungs and chest expanding under the pressure. Do the PC Pump, tightening your anal and genital muscles.

Concentrate on the center of your chest. Feel the warmth spreading, the light spiraling, as if the sun is shining from inside, radiating its warm rays from your heart.

Feel this radiance energizing your thymus gland, the center for rejuvenation and the guardian of the immune system, which brings a sense of gratitude to you for the gift of life.

Slowly release the breath, exhaling through your nose, feeling that the warm energy is trickling back down the Inner Flute and out your genitals. Repeat three to six times.

EXPANDING THE THROAT CENTER. Maintain a sense of arousal in your sexual organs.

Inhale deeply, pulling the energy to your throat—the center of your expression—and imagining that your throat is being filled with air. Hold the breath. Keep the muscles of your body relaxed.

Do the PC Pump. Focus on your throat, and "listen" to any sensations there.

Now imagine light spiraling in this area, spreading from the back of your neck to the front of your throat, healing your thyroid gland and vocal chords. The thyroid regulates the body's growth and metabolism; it also relays and transforms energy between the sex center and the brain.

Exhale slowly through your nose, allowing the energy to move down through the Inner Flute and out through the genitals. Repeat three to six times.

EXPANDING THE THIRD EYE CENTER. Stimulate your breasts, belly, and genitals once again. This time you are going to pull the energy to a point in the center of your head, behind your third eye.

Inhale, pulling the energy up. As you do so, gently roll your eyes upward, without effort, behind closed eyelids, as if to accompany the direction of the energy, helping to lift it up. It is as if you are looking up and in, to a point at the very center of your head.

Hold your breath and focus on this area, with your PC muscle contracted and the rest of your body relaxed.

The energy is spreading through the middle of your head. Your brain is being revitalized by the light that is spiraling in this area. Imagine that your pituitary and pineal glands are being flooded with light.

Spiraling the light out the head.

You may experience many different sensations—a tingling, a clap-ping sound, an impression of shimmering light, a blue light that is waxing and waning in the third eye. Or you may not have any visual impressions, but you may feel a sense of peace, an impression of lightness and expansion. Repeat three to six times.

After sufficient practice a kind of magnetic effect is created that automatically attracts energy, making meditation easy and enjoyable.

EXPANDING THE CROWN CENTER. Again, stimulate your breasts, belly, and genitals. Inhale, pulling the energy all the way to the crown of your head—the center that traditionally is described as the place in your body from which you may experience ecstasy. If you need to find the crown center, draw an imaginary line across the top of your head between your ears, and another from your nose to the top of your head. Your crown point is located where these two lines meet.

As you hold the breath, spiral the light in your crown center at the top of your head. Then imagine that there is an opening like a funnel coming out through your crown and that you are shooting the energy out through this opening like a fountain, giving your energy to the universe.

Exhale, visualizing the energy returning from the universe, through your crown, and send it down the Inner Flute and out through your genitals. Repeat three to six times.

End the practice by simply sitting or lying in a comfortable position and observing your breath moving in and out through the Inner Flute.

Pointers

Some centers in the body can feel less sensitive than others. This means there is too little energy in those organs and glands, and they need to be charged more strongly. Focus especially on these centers. Massage them in a spiraling fashion with Tiger Balm—a stimulating cream composed of eucalyptus and menthol, which is available in oriental import shops. Make extra spirals of light inside. Do the stretching exercises in chapter 5, or yoga postures, or stretch out on the floor—do anything you feel is helpful in bringing aliveness to the area you are trying to sensitize.

You can greatly assist this process by concentrating on the area throughout the day, continuously sending healing energy and love to it. You can also enhance sensations in each energy center by applying in a circular fashion the following specific essences to each center:

> *Perineum:* Ylang-ylang
> *Navel:* Sage
> *Solar plexus:* Tiger Balm
> *Heart:* Rose
> *Throat:* Eucalyptus
> *Third eye:* Mint
> *Crown:* Lavender or rose

There also may be places that hurt. This means the glands and organs are inflamed or overcharged, and the energy isn't moving through them very well. Massage them gently, imagining that you are releasing, diffusing, and emptying the energy from these areas. A few sessions of deep massage may help release tensions in these areas.

In this practice if nothing is happening immediately, you may feel discouraged and doubtful. If this happens, remain focused on your breathing and use positive affirmations that support your practice, such as, "I am healing myself," or "I am opening the way for new orgasmic experiences."

After practicing Riding the Tiger for a while, you will find it is easy to move directly from the genitals to the third eye or the crown. This is because you have sensitized and healed all the glands and chakras that lie in the path of the Inner Flute, and the channel is open. It is important to go step by step, however. If you shoot the energy straight from the genitals to the head without opening the other centers, it is unlikely that you will feel anything.

At first when your energy moves to the center of your head, you may feel dizzy or "spaced out." Don't worry. You are gradually tuning your brain and nervous system to accommodate more energy. This sensation will subside within an hour at most. You may also feel a pressure at the top of your head. In this case imagine that your energy is shooting out from the crown of your head into the sky, like a ray of light at sunrise. This visualization will relieve the pressure.

As I said at the beginning, it's not good to stop the exercise halfway, with the energy arrested in the heart or throat or other center. Make sure you complete the whole cycle. And after pulling the energy up on each inhalation, it is very important to return the energy back down through the Inner Flute and out through the sex center as you exhale. Otherwise you may get headaches and other unpleasant side effects.

When you have learned how to Ride the Tiger alone, you are ready to do it together.

RIDING THE TIGER TOGETHER

Purpose and Benefits

The purpose of this exercise is to move energy step by step through the Inner Flute with a partner, energizing each chakra in unison until you both feel the energy meeting and merging between you at each center. You will be learning a new alphabet that expresses energy in terms of rhythms, colors, light, and electricity rather than the verbal language of ideas. It is important for you to concentrate on your perceptions—for example, "I am feeling warmth and a tickle of excitement in my belly"—rather than paying attention to mental concerns about what is happening, such as "I wonder what my partner is feeling." The more you can remain focused on your own sensations of energy, the more you will perceive the rhythms that you share with your partner: your heartbeats and breathing, and tiny movements in your bodies. Gradually these rhythms will take on a reality of their own. You may feel them as electrical sensations or "see" them as internal patterns of color and light.

Riding the Tiger together, you will learn to play your Inner Flutes together as a way of directing orgasmic sensations to any point in the body during lovemaking and modulating their quality and intensity. This is how orgasm is transformed into ecstasy.

All real living is meeting.

—Martin Buber

Preparations

Create the Sacred Space.
Allow 30 to 40 minutes for this practice.

Practice

Begin with a Heart Salutation and Melting Hug.
Slowly and erotically stimulate each other, taking turns giving and receiving. The receiver—for example, the man—can massage his own chest while the woman gently massages his scrotum.
Then exchange roles. The man can massage the woman's vagina, while she massages her breasts, or vice versa.
When you feel aroused and open to further exploration, lie down in one of the Bonding Relaxation positions. Another option is to do this exercise sitting on a chair, with the woman sitting on her partner's lap. It is important to have the front parts of your bodies in close contact.
Men, when Vajra is ready to knock at the door, ask permission to enter the Yoni. Women, if the answer is yes, let him in gently while doing an active PC Pump, conveying the feeling that you are sucking Vajra into your garden. Once Vajra is inside, you can maintain stimulation and arousal by applying the Pelvic Curl, combined with the PC Pump and Sexual Breathing.
Keep your external movements to a minimum. The energy should be generated by the subtler, inner types of movements that we have been

Riding the Tiger Together: Pulling your vital sexual energy up through the Inner Flute together. Hold your breath and visualize the light spiraling through each center.

367

practicing in previous chapters. If you feel that you are coming close to orgasm through these subtleties, make sure you don't pass the trigger point! On the other hand, if at any time in the following practice you feel you are losing sexual stimulation, break off the exercise and focus on lovemaking until you have restored a sense of mutual arousal. Then take up the practice again where you left off.

Harmonize your breathing, inhaling and exhaling together. Take time to find a common rhythm. Concentrating on your breathing will amplify your sensations and keep you from "spacing out" into thoughts and fantasies.

When you are both ready, begin by revitalizing the sexual and navel centers, following the steps of the previous exercise. Inhale together, tightening the genital muscles. As you do so, imagine that you are "drinking" the energy of your partner, mixing it with your own energy and drawing it up your Inner Flute. Feel this energy expanding through your sexual organs, your pelvis, lower belly, and the area around your navel. Exhale, allowing the energy to fall back down the Inner Flute and out through your genitals. Practice this rhythm of inhaling and exhaling together until you feel energized in the entire pelvic area.

Then, when you are ready, inhale together, pull the energy up the Inner Flute, hold your breath, and visualize the light spiraling in your pelvis, filling the area with a healing warmth. Gradually expand the spirals of light so that they encompass the sex and navel centers of your partner. Imagine that your energies are beginning to melt and merge in this area. Some teachers of sacred sexuality call this practice "chakra merging."

Each time you exhale together, be sure to send the energy and light down the Inner Flute and out through your genitals. Do this together three to six times. As with Riding the Tiger Alone, you will know that this part of the practice is working when you start to feel warmth and a tingling sensation in your genitals and lower belly.

Then move to the solar plexus. One partner can signal when he or she is ready to move to the next center by pressing firmly on the shoulder of the other partner. Inhale together, tighten the PC muscle, and draw your energy, mixed with your partner's, up the Inner Flute to your solar plexus. Hold your breath, spiral the light, and expand it to include both your own power center and that of your partner. Exhale, sending the energy and light down the Inner Flute and out through your genitals. Do this three to six times.

Taking your time, move step by step to the heart, throat, third eye, and crown centers. Follow the instructions for Riding the Tiger Alone. Repeat the sequence of inhaling, drawing the energy up the Inner Flute, holding your breath, spiraling the light, and sending the energy back down the Inner Flute on the exhalation three to six times in each center.

Remember to end the session by bringing the energy back down through the Inner Flute to the sexual center. Then rest and relax inside each other for ten to fifteen minutes. Observe how you feel connected now. Is there a difference from the way you felt at the beginning of the practice?

Finally, when you feel it is the right time, separate gently, sit face to face, and do a Heart Salutation. Communicate to each other what you experienced, how you feel, and what you learned.

Do this exercise many times together over a period of several weeks, until you develop a good sense of harmony together and an awareness of each other's subtle rhythms, and can clearly feel an energy flow between each other's centers as you move through them.

Pointers

Make sure that you are in a good mood before you begin the exercise so that you remain relaxed and light about it. In the beginning you may get impatient or feel discouraged because you are not feeling much. Try to complete the whole cycle of the exercise anyway. The mind has a natural tendency to question, judge, and wander. Rather than following it, stay focused on the practice.

At first while you are trying to synchronize your breathing and visualizations, you may feel a little clumsy, but with practice it will get easier. Remember to have fun! If things don't flow easily, don't push. Take a break, drink a glass of champagne, review earlier practices in the book—for instance, self-pleasuring in front of each other—and come back to this practice when you are ready.

If you have difficulty moving through the seven centers together in harmony, focus at first on three: the sex, heart, and third eye. Repeat this shortened method until you have established an easy rhythm together, and then expand it to include the other four centers.

Don't feel constricted by technique or the particular pattern in which the technique is taught. Allow spontaneity to take over if you feel that your needs or the needs of your partner are carrying you in that direction. Make sure you complete the cycle, however, remembering to return the energy to the sex center each time.

SHOOTING TO THE CROWN TOGETHER

When you feel that both of you have mastered Riding the Tiger—to the point where it feels really good—you can shorten and refine it by shooting the energy together from the genitals up the Inner Flute directly to the crown chakra or the third eye chakra. Please remember what I said earlier, however, about not skipping over the practices that include all seven centers before you try this direct method.

Purpose and Benefits

In this practice you will develop a really strong sensation of the Inner Flute, feeling a direct connection between the genitals and the third eye or crown through breathing. This method will help you strengthen your perception of the inner channel.

It is up to you both to experiment and decide whether you prefer to shoot energy to the crown or to the third eye. When energy is shot directly to the third eye, it will often release color patterns behind your closed eyes. Later the mind feels crisp and clear, and thinking becomes sharp and easy. Moving energy to the third eye has another advantage: It can give you an almost instant impression of being lifted up and away from problems and stress into a new inner space, much as a plane shoots through the clouds until it bursts out above them into the pure blue sky. The third eye is a doorway to instant meditation.

When energy is shot directly to the crown chakra, you may visualize that you are sending it out into the universe and, in this way, expanding your energy and awareness beyond your body. You may feel at one with your partner and the whole of existence, experiencing a dimension greater than the normal limitations of self. This is why, in the traditions of sacred sexuality, this center is often represented by the thousand-petaled lotus—the energy expands and radiates in a thousand different directions. Simultaneously, universal energy can be received through the opened crown chakra.

Oceanic *or* Apollonian ecstasy *. . . is characterized by extreme peace, tranquility, serenity, and radiant joy. The individual involved . . . experiences a blissful, tension-free state, a loss of ego boundaries and an absolute sense of oneness with nature, with the cosmic order, and with God. A deep intuitive understanding of existence and a flood of various specific insights of cosmic relevance are characteristic for this condition.*

—Stanislav Grof
Beyond the Brain

Preparations

You can move directly from the previous practice into this phase, or take a break. If you decide to take a break and then go on, start with a Heart Salutation when you come back, and resume lovemaking in a playful, spontaneous way, until you both feel as though your bodies are vibrating with erotic sensations.

Allow 30 minutes for this practice.

Practice

Begin with a Heart Salutation.

Adopt the Bonding Relaxation position. One partner, most likely the one on top, lies with his mouth next to the other partner's ear. Comfort is a priority. If this position doesn't feel good, try it with the man sitting on a chair and the woman in his lap.

Synchronize your breathing, inhaling and exhaling together. When you have found an easy rhythm, invert the breathing pattern so that one partner is exhaling while the other is inhaling. The inverted breathing should be deep and slow. Take time to harmonize depth and rhythm. One partner may have a quicker rhythm or perhaps a shallower breathing pattern. Play with these rhythms for five to ten minutes, until you adjust to each other in an easy flow.

When inverted breathing becomes easy and flowing, switch to mouth-to-mouth breathing. To make the experience more erotic, begin by titillating each other's lips, then move into a real "deep throat" French kiss, exploring the entire mouth with your tongue. Next, staying in the same basic position, bring your mouths very close to each other. Your lips are touching loosely so that a little outside air is incorporated into the exchange of air.

Continue the inverted exchange, feeling the warm current of air as you inhale your partner's exhalation all the way down to your sex center. Imagine that you are not only exchanging breath but also energy, light, colors, sounds, rhythms, and heat. Let these images come effortlessly as you switch off your thought process and focus on the breathing.

When the man exhales, he imagines that he is giving his energy through his penis into the woman's vagina. When the women inhales, she should drink this energy in, as if through her vagina, mixing it with her

Hold your breath and pull the energy into your head and out into the universe.

own energy, mingling the Yang and Yin essences, and pulling it up through her Inner Flute to the third eye and crown.

Exhaling, the woman brings the energy back down the Inner Flute to her sex center and gives it to her partner. The man, inhaling, then sucks in her energy through his Vajra, mixes it with his own energy, and draws it up through the Inner Flute all the way to his crown.

Men, you can enjoy rocking your pelvis to stimulate arousal, but remain below the point of no return, avoiding ejaculation.

Then combine all the elements. As you inhale, tighten your anus and add the PC Pump. At the end of the inhalation, roll your eyes upward. As you exhale and come down, remember to visualize the Inner Flute, relax the genital muscles, and feel your energy going out through your sex center to your partner.

Women, you can use imagery to help you relax and fall in time with this rhythmic practice. For example, it may inspire you to compare the opening and closing movement of the Yoni to the gentle movement of a sea anemone responding to the movement of the tides.

As you breathe, develop the impression that you are "touching" the genitals with the power of your breath. It is as if your breath is picking up the genital arousal from within the Inner Flute and carrying it to the higher centers, where it is transformed. This visualization will enhance the erotic sensations of pleasure in your genitals.

When you have mastered this practice, focus your attention on the third eye or crown chakra. Pull the energy all the way up, hold the breath, and feel that you are spiraling the golden point of light in the middle of your head. Let it shoot out the crown into the universe before you exhale and bring it back down.

Move your energy up and down the Inner Flute in this manner for five to ten minutes or as long as you feel comfortable.

End with a Heart Salutation.

Pointers

This is a subtle and sophisticated practice. It can be very ecstatic, but you may have to confront a few difficulties before you get there. One of the most common is a feeling that you are suffocating. If this happens, stop the inverted breathing, and take time to breathe deeply and easily on your own. Don't feel you have to force yourself to follow a common breathing pattern with your partner until you faint! Another way to avoid this feeling of suffocation—without breaking off the practice—is to slow down your breathing rhythms and allow extra air in through the side of your mouth.

Whenever you feel frustrated, drop your goal orientation. Take the steps one at a time. Be patient and willing to continue after taking a break. Communicate what is happening to you in a positive sense. Avoid such phrases as, "You are breathing too fast." Instead, say something like, "I feel it is difficult for me to follow your breathing rhythm. Could you slow down?" Stay with the level that is enjoyable and easy, until you are relaxed and ready to move ahead to the next part of the practice.

In the beginning some people complain of too much pressure in the head or tensions in the neck when they inhale and pull the energy up toward the third eye or crown. If this happens to you, visualize the energy shooting out through the crown, and this will relieve the pressure.

Remember to end this cycle by bringing the energy back down the Inner Flute and out through your genitals.

A word on hygiene: Some people feel shy about exchanging each other's breath, especially if one is a smoker and one is not, or if one has a cold. Make sure you have brushed your teeth and have clean breath. Don't do this exercise if you are feeling sick or if you have just eaten.

Keep your body relaxed, even when you are doing the PC Pump and rolling your eyes upward. If you don't relax your body, the energy will not shoot up through the Inner Flute easily.

When you become familiar with this exploration, you may enjoy the feeling that your energy is shooting from your genitals up the Inner Flute to your brain, where you experience an ecstatic, slow-motion sensation of stepping out of time and space. Or you may feel as if you are in a glider, soaring in the sky.

CHARGING OTHER AREAS OF THE BODY

As a variation on the previous practice, you can try using different amplitudes and rhythms of breathing to charge specific areas of the body. For example, together you and your partner can charge the chest area by breathing very dynamically and strongly, using shallow, panting breaths. Remember to stay synchronized, using kissing and mouth-to-mouth inverted breathing. A warm, expanding glow in the chest will tell you that you have succeeded.

You may want to do the same in the belly. Play with different speeds. If you go slowly and deeply, this will help you to become aware of the sex center and the sensations there. When you go slowly, it's also easier to follow the whole flow of energy. So take your time until you have thoroughly visualized the movement of energy up and down the Inner Flute. If you go quickly in the inverted breathing, you won't have such a strong sense of connection with the two poles—the sex center and the head—but this is a good way to make the Inner Flute more open.

THE VALLEY ORGASM: LEVEL ONE

The practices I have described as Riding the Tiger Alone and Together, Shooting to the Crown, and Charging Other Areas of the Body can be included in the broad category of "Yang" practices. They are all forms of "doing," involving physical techniques and mental visualizations. In them you consciously try to create a certain effect.

The other option at this stage of the journey to High Sex is to explore the "Yin" approach, in which you forget technique and create a mood of innocence and spontaneity.

Purpose and Benefits

This practice allows the energy of sexual arousal to find its own pathway to higher levels of ecstatic experience.

Preparations

Create the Sacred Space.

Before you make love, enter into the spirit of play with your partner, using any of the methods in this book: dancing and stretching together, giving each other a massage, leading each other into the Streaming Process, until you feel that tensions, problems, and a goal-orientation have been dropped. You are exploring ways to slip into a spontaneous flow, learning how to be present in the moment so totally that you don't think about what the next moment will bring.

When you live in this flow, you become just like two children coming together to play, inventing new games, relating in different ways until you feel you can trust each other. You are becoming friends with

375

your partner on a deeply intimate level, feeling respect and devotion and accepting the other without judgment.

The Yin approach requires a good sense of humor, so create a relaxed, supportive context for the practice. Welcome your partner completely, without reservations, without expectations that he or she must perform in any particular way.

Play soothing, relaxing music (see Appendix II).

This practice lasts at least 30 minutes.

Practice

Proceed with a Melting Hug and a Heart Salutation. Recall the spirit of the Tantric salutation "I salute you as an aspect of myself."

Begin to make love naturally and effortlessly. Let this be a continuation of your play together, almost as if you don't notice when you finish playing and when you start making love.

In this mood you can do whatever turns you on. When you both feel ready, make love in a strong, active way, until your energies are fully aroused. Then, when you reach the edge of orgasm, stop and completely relax.

Use one of the positions you adopted in the Bonding Relaxation: the scissors position, the missionary position, the spoon position, the man sitting on a chair with the woman on his lap.

Remain motionless, consciously relaxing your whole body. Let your breathing and your partner's breathing rhythms harmonize. Gradually allow the boundaries between your bodies to melt and merge as you become one breath, one warmth, one blended energy flow. Focus your awareness on subtle internal sensations. This is a "feeling awareness"— you are contemplating the energy inside without doing or directing anything.

Focus on the sexual and navel chakras. Feel what is happening there. The warmth of the aroused energy may be spreading slowly through this area. It may be felt as a tingling, a sensation of light, or a vibration being exchanged and shared with your partner. You are dwelling in the energy, letting yourself be, enjoying doing nothing, going nowhere. If you have been thorough in following the practices in earlier chapters, the energy will take its own course. You are facilitating the delicate transition from the activity of the mind, which wants to direct, push, and control, to a mindless state that allows the body to take over with its own wisdom.

The orgasm is spontaneous when it happens of itself and in its own time, and when the rest of the body moves in response to it. Given the open attitude of mind and senses, sexual love in this spirit is a revelation. Long before the male orgasm begins, the sexual impulse manifests itself as what can only be described, psychologically, as a melting warmth between the partners so that they seem veritably to flow into each other. To put it in another way, "physical lust" transforms itself into the most considerate and tender form of love imaginable.

—Alan Watts
Nature, Man and Woman

376

A magnetized current moves between your foreheads.

After five to ten minutes, the man may start losing his erection, or the fire of arousal may begin to fade. If you feel like it, take time to generate more arousal. Start undulating against each other's bodies, playing like two dolphins and rekindling the fire. Again, make love in your own unique way, whatever comes naturally. When you attain a high level of excitement, stop, relax completely, and allow yourself to focus on the heart center. Maintain a feeling awareness of how the energy is moving in this center. Is there a pulsing? Do you feel your heartbeat? Is there a warmth radiating out from your partner's heart, merging with your own warmth? Do you feel the gratitude of receiving your partner's love? Remember, you are not looking for anything specific. Use your feeling awareness and ask yourself, "How does my sexual fire feel when I dwell in this area?"

When you feel it's time, maybe after five to ten minutes, make love again in a playful, active way. Use any methods that will help—PC Pump, Sexual Breathing—to stimulate the sexual fire until you come to another peak.

Again, relax totally, and this time focus your feeling awareness on the area in the middle of your brain, behind the third eye. Maybe you want your foreheads to touch at this stage, but keep your neck relaxed.

In receptivity we are capable of opening to radiant gardens of energy. Love is not like a building that we make or construct, but like a tree that grows, shaping itself from within and according to the laws of its own being.

—James N. Powell
Energy and Eros

377

Is there a sense of magnetized energy moving between your two foreheads? Is the sexual current tingling all the way to this point? Do you sense that you are becoming quiet and meditative, or experiencing a kind of clarity and peace?

To amplify the experience, you may wish to open your eyes while your foreheads are touching, so that you are looking into each other's eyes from close up. The two eyes in front of you will eventually blend into one eye that is located exactly in the position of your partner's third eye. It is as if your own eyes are attracted like a magnet to that point. You are going cross-eyed without doing it voluntarily, as if your eyes are being pulled into a vortex. It is a very powerful sensation.

Steadily looking at this eye, you may feel as if you are falling into each other. You are letting go at deeper and deeper levels, and finally you fall so completely that the other becomes you and you become the other. There are no more separations, but an exhilarating feeling of boundless, limitless space all around, within and without. Beyond the mind, you are tasting the void of no mind—the great emptiness of pure consciousness that, containing nothing, reflects everything.

When you are ready, let your eyes close again, and come back to yourself. Reconnect with the rest of your body and relax. You may end this session with deep relaxation for another five to ten minutes, or continue to make love. But if you wish to move directly from this practice to Valley Orgasm: Level Two, it is very important for the male partner not to ejaculate so you may build up the energy for the next level. When it feels right, tenderly ask each other whether this is the moment to separate.

End with a Heart Salutation.

Take a break, have a glass of wine, put more logs on the fire, but stay in the nonverbal mode of relating for another 15 minutes after separating. Afterward, sit down facing each other and have a gentle conversation about what you experienced, asking, "What was the most difficult point for you in this journey? What was the best moment? What did you learn? How can you bring this into your everyday life?" Take a few minutes for each partner to ask and answer these questions. Let one speak while the other listens without interruption or comment.

Pointers

This exercise has different effects on different people. Some experience burning energy shooting up to the head; others feel a lot of energy

The health of sex and sensuality lies in the personal, in that ancient, ever-new feeling of unselfish bonding that can create a new relationship, a new life, or a new society.

—George Leonard

diffusing through the body, without a buildup in any particular center. Others feel a much stronger sensation in one center than in others. Finally, for some people, nothing may happen at all.

Remember, you are not striving for a goal. Stay in touch with the spirit of mutual support and exploration. Subtle processes are taking place within you. New pathways for your energy are emerging as a natural response to these practices. They will be revealed consciously, in their own time, with renewed exploration.

Again, if you feel dizzy, or tense in your neck, you can relieve it by imagining that the energy is flowing out through the crown of your head. The dizziness will subside after 30 to 40 minutes and even more quickly if you take a bath in which you have sprinkled four drops of essential oil of mint.

THE VALLEY ORGASM: LEVEL TWO

Purpose and Benefits

Now you can explore even more deeply the art of doing nothing and letting go in lovemaking. This is an opportunity to have the ultimate experience of the Yin aspect of High Sex. It can be extremely cleansing and restful to allow yourself to go into lovemaking without any questions, goals, visions, or worries, or without the need to achieve anything—simply to be. And it is encouraging to feel, after ten to twenty minutes, that the energy within you does flow and dance and vibrate by itself, even when you do not direct it.

Preparations

Level Two is an addition to Level One and should be done as a continuation of the previous experience.

Practice

Begin making love, moving together toward a peak of arousal. Use the Three Keys—breathing, movement, and sound—and be totally absorbed in your pleasure. The higher your peak of excitement, the deeper you will be able to enter this level of High Sex.

Let your lovemaking be wildly erotic and playful. As you approach the peak—just before the point of no return—stop and completely relax with each other. There is no need to focus on any particular center. There is no need to do anything except to be totally present and relaxed in this moment, in the here-and-now, open to everything, expecting nothing. Enter into total "non-doing." Let yourselves be.

The alchemy of your mutual arousal is like throwing a stone into still waters. The ripples will continue on their own.

At this moment you need to relax and trust the process that is going on inside both of you. Your two energies are dancing by themselves, merging and moving as if there is a melt-down going on between you. They will weave their own dance, and this can manifest itself at many different levels. You may see color patterns, as in a kaleidoscope. You may feel taken over by a tide of vibrations or currents. You may fall into a blissful state between half-waking and half-sleeping that leaves you wondering where you went and why you suddenly feel so refreshed when you come out of it.

Allow space for the mysterious to unfold: something will happen by itself in about ten to twenty minutes. In the ancient texts it is said that it will take as long as 30 minutes. But don't break off to look at the clock! Trust that something is happening whether you feel it or not and that you don't need to do anything about it.

Pointers

Don't try to synchronize anything at this stage. Either it will happen by itself, or it won't. Don't try to make it happen.

People who are very dynamic and active in their lives sometimes experience difficulty in this practice when crossing the threshold from doing to non-doing, because their minds are telling them that nothing is happening. Pay no attention to the impatient chatter of your mind. Focus on your inner sensations, relax, and eventually you will be rewarded.

What becomes apparent in the experience of the Valley Orgasm is that ecstasy is effortless.

This chapter was particularly difficult to write because the ecstatic experience is such a personal, intangible, and ineffable experience that words feel clumsy. The most important point to remember is that you are really tracing your own path. These methods are a support. When you have embodied the different approaches of Yin and Yang, you can blend the two according to your own inclinations.

Just as a gourmet cook will use the best recipes as a springboard for new and creative inventions, so you can use this chapter as an inspiration to follow your own road to ecstasy. The best learning is practice, and the best results come when you least expect them.

During my explorations I have had sessions that were completely flat, in which I was extremely grateful for my sense of humor, or I would have been devastated. Other sessions that began unpromisingly opened out unexpectedly into ecstatic journeys beyond description.

In this chapter you learned, through Riding the Tiger Alone, how to revitalize and sensitize the chakras and glands to facilitate the movement of energy through the Inner Flute. Through Riding the Tiger Together, you discovered ways to transform orgasmic energy in unison with your partner as you establish a connection between each other's chakras. A deep connection between your genital sensations and your higher chakras through inverted mouth-to-mouth breathing was explored in Shooting to the Crown Together. Charging Other Areas of the Body taught you how to apply the principle of shooting energy to the crown chakra while changing your breathing patterns. Finally, through The Valley Orgasm, you learned how to make love and relax together in a deep letting-go, allowing your merged energies to follow their own dance as you remained bonded inside each other.

In the next and final chapter, you will discover how to Ride the Wave of Bliss. This ecstatic approach to Tantric lovemaking is the subtlest and most complete of all the practices in this book.

CHAPTER 12

❦

RIDING THE WAVE OF BLISS

W hen I was living in Paris, I became friends with a man named Rampal who was acclaimed as a great psychotherapist and a gifted "magician" in the science of Tantra.

Rampal was hardly a sex symbol in the ordinary sense. During the war, while working in the Resistance, he suffered a wound to his lower spine. Nerves had been severed. Doctors told him that would never be able to walk again. The government gave him a 100 percent disability pension.

But he refused to remain a cripple. Instead he turned to the Tantric traditions in an attempt to heal himself, using ancient visualization and meditation techniques to project the image of an "energy body" parallel to his physical form that healed his shattered nervous system. He succeeded. After some years he was able to walk with only a slight limp and, confounding medical opinion that his wounds had rendered him permanently impotent, began to make love normally and fathered two sons.

On hearing that I was studying the Tantric scriptures, Rampal invited me to his home for a practical demonstration. When I arrived, the first thing I noticed was a Tibetan painting, a *tanka,* hanging in the waiting room, depicting an awesome deity sitting with crossed legs in the lotus position. Sitting on his lap, with her legs wrapped around him, was a very sexy woman. They were naked and clearly in a state of ecstasy. The painting aroused my curiosity. If this was a meditation, I thought, I wanted to learn it.

Rampal welcomed me into his study. He had an appearance of effortless elegance and nobility, wearing a casual pale yellow silk shirt and navy pants. Although it was in the middle of the city, the room felt quiet

When you come to be sensibly touched, the scales will fall from your eyes; and by the penetrating eyes of love you will discern that which your other eyes will never see.

—François Fénelon

383

The Buddha Vajrasattva and his consort, the Dakini Great Dignity, in blissful union are dancing in the sky. This represents the logo of, and is copyrighted by, the SkyDancing Institute founded by the author.

and protected. As we spoke, I told him that I wanted to experience the secrets he had learned. In response he asked me to try a simple experiment: to stand across the room, opposite him, with my feet parallel—about 18 inches apart—to bend my knees slightly, let my mouth fall open, and begin to breathe deeply.

"As you continue to breathe deeply, let your genital muscles relax," he said in a low voice that seemed to come from his belly. Rampal announced no goal and offered no theory about what he was doing. Even though his instructions were intimate, his tone was casual. Nobody had talked to me that way before.

"Now let the connection between us intensify through the eyes," he told me. His eyes were an intense, luminescent green.

Soon I was inhaling fully, exhaling deeply and evenly, keeping my mouth open, and bending my knees while relaxing the rest of my body and gazing at him. What would he ask me to do next?

"As you inhale, rock your pelvis gently back," said Rampal. "As you exhale, let it rock forward, as if you were giving yourself to me."

384

I did so and felt a surge of energy combined with vulnerability, such as one may feel in the presence of a new lover. Despite the physical distance between us, a sense of intimacy was growing through our steady gaze. I felt deeply connected to him, yet independent and grounded in myself.

Rampal next suggested that as I inhaled and rocked back, I should become aware of the energy that was developing in my pelvis and let it move up, as if it were rising through my body in a tube—the Inner Flute. Upon exhaling, I should reverse the flow, letting the energy descend as my pelvis rocked forward. I did as he instructed and began to feel highly aroused, even though we had not touched.

Rampal then asked me to walk slowly toward him while continuing the exercise. I felt like a tightrope walker about to have an orgasm while poised above a canyon. When I reached him, he gently touched points in my shoulders and back, as if to adjust my posture.

Even though I felt a little awkward and inexperienced, I sensed his acceptance of me and was able to relax even further. As I exhaled, I felt a strong vibrancy, like an electrical current, stream through my body. Then Rampal sat down cross-legged on the floor and placed a small pillow on his lap. He invited me to sit on the pillow with my legs around him.

We were both fully dressed. His manner was not at all seductive. Instead I felt as if we were both paying homage to the energy that I was experiencing, as if we were celebrating the power that we shared.

As I sat on his lap, he told me that Buddhists call this position *yab yum*—the union of mother and father. I recalled the painting I had seen in Rampal's waiting room and felt excited to find myself imitating the woman's pose, as if I were being initiated into an ancient mystery.

Rampal was behaving in an ordinary and matter-of-fact manner. I wanted to move and express my excitement, but he kept saying in his deep, quiet voice, "Keep the energy inside; breathe into it softly. Stay focused on it; relax into it."

We sat breathing together for some minutes. After a while, he said, "Now that you are relaxed, tighten your genital muscles as you inhale. Tighten them as a dancer would tighten her thigh muscles before springing into the air. Inhale deeply and tighten. Feel the energy moving up the spine as you do so." I did it. "Now," he went on, "gently relax the genital muscles as you exhale. Let go. Let yourself fly."

As we sat there, breathing and rocking and gazing together, I was learning to "hold my horses" while relaxing into their stride. After a while we fell into a subtle rhythm. I had a sense of being lifted up, independent of my will—of floating. I was not "doing" it—it was happening to me naturally. "Let it continue," Rampal whispered. "Breathe through the mouth, more deeply now, all the way down to your sex center."

I felt as if my lungs had become a bellows stoking my inner fire. Rampal was breathing with me, moving with me, as if he were inside me. I felt tremendously excited. Some part of me rebelled against the control, the waiting that this practice imposed on my arousal. Why hold back? Surely there was much to be said in defense of wild, spontaneous lovemaking. But I already knew that way. I had experienced it many times.

As if reading my thoughts, Rampal suggested, "Instead of keeping the excitement and energy in your sexual center, allow it to move upward as you inhale, toward your brain. Feel, as you inhale, that you are drinking me in, taking my energy into you, inhaling my soul."

I felt that my energy was a growing sphere, pushing against the limits of my physical body, then expanding beyond it.

"As you exhale, relax the genitals," I heard Rampal say. "Feel that you are opening your gates. Offer your energy; offer your spirit. . . . Yes, that's it." The energy was subtle yet so vibrant that it was almost tangible, as if I were being enveloped in a luminous egg that had existed unnoticed within my body and that was expanding and surrounding us as we breathed and gazed into each other's eyes.

Looking at him so intensely was threatening at first. Would he not see the ragged edges of my soul, the secret fears and self-doubt? But as I opened myself to Rampal's love and surrendered to his gentle guidance, our energies blended and went aflame. It was as if a protective filter between us had been removed, a filter that I ordinarily used to keep things under control and to protect my sense of separateness.

Now, surrounded by the egg of light, Rampal also seemed luminous. On some level of reality, this man was no longer Rampal and I was no longer Margo. We had become a delicious dance between breath, energy, and light.

After this initiation our friendship deepened. Through the sessions that followed, I came to appreciate his skill in revealing and enhancing my own Tantric abilities, and I began to understand the hidden meaning of the Tantric painting in his waiting room. Through sexual union the divine couple acts out a larger union of universal untapped energies. They ride a wave of bliss that takes them higher and higher, blending sexual energy and spiritual awareness in a bid to touch the highest experience available to human beings. This is the very secret of High Sex—this union of sex and spirit, matter and consciousness, earth and sky.

My experience with Rampal provided the seed for this chapter. Recognizing that the *yab yum* position was the ultimate form of Tantric union, I experimented with different methods of practicing this classic posture. I was fascinated by it, knowing that it held the key to ecstatic lovemaking.

In my continuing exploration of sexual ecstasy over the years, I tested every breathing technique, every body position, every exercise and visualization method for its effectiveness in facilitating the experience of ecstasy in the *yab yum* position. Those that passed the test I absorbed into my training and shared with others. I experimented, too, with different ways of refining the position itself and ultimately developed the following practice, which I call Riding the Wave of Bliss (for brevity's sake I will refer to it as the Wave Of Bliss, or simply the Wave).

The Wave of Bliss brings together all the previous practices of this book. To me this is the most exquisite practice, but it is also the most unpredictable. Some people click into it right away. Others take much longer. It is a sophisticated posture, so some people get serious and approach it as a yoga lesson. Then the erotic, playful, and spontaneous elements are lost, and with them disappears the relaxed attitude that maximizes your chances of experiencing ecstasy. That's why I am going to advise you to begin with other postures of lovemaking, as preparations for your experience of the Wave of Bliss. So be sure to contain the orgasmic energy and not be tempted into genital release.

THE BASIC POSTURES OF LOVE

Many books have been written about the various postures of lovemaking, so I will not go into great detail here. I have made classifications that embrace the basic postures, but don't become preoccupied with technique. What's important here is to remember the Inner Flute as you experiment with each position, and to keep visualizing the movement of energy through this channel.

I encourage you to begin your experiments with these positions while still dressed, as this will remove any tensions that may be present in a sexual context. Find the positions in which you both feel most comfortable. Learn which muscles are employed in which posture, how your body sizes fit together best, what postures are best for relaxed lovemaking, who feels more comfortable on top, and so on. Then you can experiment with these positions while naked and, if it feels good to you, try lovemaking while shifting from one position to another.

Purpose and Benefits

Enjoy these postures as playful gymnastics—just rolling around on the floor, experimenting innocently. Treat them as warmup exercises, much like ballet dancers perform before they leap onto the stage for their *pas de deux.*

Moving from one position to another, you will learn the art of varying your posture several times during a single lovemaking session. This will loosen old patterns, keep your body alive and vital, and prepare you for the position used in the Wave of Bliss. Keep playing until you have established a flow of movements and moods that encompass several different positions of your choice.

Preparations

Create the Sacred Space.

Use plenty of cushions and pillows to support your neck and stay relaxed during lovemaking; otherwise the circulation of energy is cut off, and you may wake up with a stiff neck the next morning. When lying on your back, a pillow under the kidneys provides good support and allows deep, comfortable genital penetration, especially for the woman.

It is better to do these practices on an empty stomach, so avoid eating beforehand.

Practice

As you move into the following postures, try to experiment with maintaining eye contact whenever possible—something that we don't usually do in lovemaking. Feel how locked eyes can intensify your feeling of intimacy, trust, and opening up to each other in many of the positions that follow.

When you need to enhance feeling sensations in the genitals in any of the positions, experiment with Pelvic Rocking, the PC Pump, and Sexual Breathing. Integrate the skills you have learned, such as the Butterfly and the Bonding Relaxation, while you experiment with the postures of love.

During lovemaking you can push the soles of your feet against a wall or some firm surface. This grounding facilitates the expansion of orgasmic pulsations from the pelvis down to the feet.

"Make love anywhere except in bed!" said one of my teachers. We need to take lovemaking out of the bedroom and into nature, into the open air, the water, the forest. This can be regenerating and exciting and adds the zest of the forbidden.

THE MAN ON TOP POSITION. This is the classic "missionary" position, in which the woman lies on her back, with the man on top. This is a good one to start with because, according to the Taoists, it respects the woman's innate nature—her qualities of water, coolness, and slow rhythm. The posture allows the woman to be passive at first, giving her time to unfold, receive, open, and slowly change from water to fire.

Man on top.

The missionary position is a good way, too, for the man to feel his power and strength. It promotes intimacy between partners because lips, hearts, and genitals can touch.

This is not a good position, however, for men who tend to climax quickly, because it promotes speedy ejaculation. Also, if a man is tired, he will not enjoy the athletic movements this position requires of him. When the Vajra is long and big and the Yoni is shallow and small, penetration in this position may be too deep and may bruise the cervix. And if a woman is independent-minded, she may feel trapped in a dependent role in this position.

VARIATION OF THE MAN ON TOP POSITION: MORNING AND EVENING TUNING. The Taoists call this variation the "morning and evening prayer" because it is beautiful to do upon awakening or just before going to sleep. In the man on top position close your eyes, and lock mouths, legs, and arms. The man does not ejaculate but uses just enough movement to maintain his erection. This state is close to the Sexual Bonding Relaxation and brings harmony to the Yin-Yang balance of both partners.

Morning and Evening Tuning.

The Rolling Tickle.

VARIATION OF THE MAN ON TOP POSITION: THE ROLLING TICKLE. While remaining inside the woman, the man sits or kneels. The woman continues to lie on her back, with her knees pulled up to her chest. The man can either rest his hands on her thighs or slide them under her buttocks to move her up and down.

The man moves in and out while the woman rolls her thighs up and down. This can be especially exciting because the Vajra can touch the G spot precisely. It may also give a sense of power to a man and a sweet taste of surrender to a woman.

The Push-Pull position.

VARIATION OF THE MAN ON TOP POSITION: THE PUSH-PULL. Not many people know this position, which requires a lot of suppleness in the pelvis and thighs. The man is in the same position as in the Rolling Tickle. The woman lies on her back, her feet against the man's chest, her arms gripping the man's waist as she reaches through between her thighs. She has mobility, control over their movements, and a good sense of grounding. This position gives her the capacity to roll her pelvis up and down, and she can regulate the depth at which her partner's penis penetrates her vagina. The Push-Pull position favors the release of playful aggression, especially when accompanied by deep sighs or growling sounds from the belly.

THE WOMAN ON TOP, OR SHAKTI POSITION. This is the reverse position, with the woman on top. Now she has the power. She is the initiator—the man can take a back seat and relax. He can more easily channel and circulate his energy up through his body, for he is the one who is receiving and relaxing.

The woman is free to move. She can lean back, resting her hands on the floor behind her; she can sit upright; or she can lean forward and rest her hands on the floor on either side of the man's torso. With this

Woman on top: Shakti position.

Woman on top: Variation of
Shakti position.

freedom she can shift the angle of penetration of the Vajra and help it
to touch inside her Yoni at exactly the right points. This can cure
menstrual cramping. It is a natural sequel to the previous posture.

VARIATION OF THE WOMAN ON TOP: SWOOPING SHAKTI. The woman squats
and slowly lowers herself onto the erect penis. She moves up and down,
keeping the penetration shallow—with the penis at the entrance to her
Yoni—for several strokes, then lowers herself so the Vajra penetrates
deeply and touches her cervix. Mastering the Squatting Together exercise
in chapter 5 is good preparation for the woman.

Swooping Shakti.

THE ART OF SEXUAL ECSTASY

She is milking and sucking the Vajra, as a child would be drinking from its mother's breast. Strong, deep breathing is very arousing for the woman during this practice. A strong PC muscle greatly facilitates the woman's ability to grip the Vajra firmly, giving enhanced pleasure to both herself and the man in this position.

For the man it can be extremely arousing if the woman reproduces the strong thrusting movements that he usually initiates when approaching orgasm. In this way he can experience the same thrusts while remaining passive. If the man practices the PC Pump, he can strengthen his erection inside the Yoni and respond to her movements in a palpable way.

VARIATION OF THE WOMAN ON TOP: EROTIC SHAKTI. This is a great one for both partners to practice enhancing their awareness of internal erotic sensations. The woman sits still, with the Vajra fully penetrated in her Yoni. The two partners lock their gaze, and the woman practices internal

The Erotic Shakti position.

sexual arousal by doing the Pelvic Curl, combined with Sexual Breathing and the PC Pump.

The man responds with Sexual Breathing and the PC Pump, receiving her movements and feeling the pressure of her vaginal walls rhythmically gripping his Vajra.

THE SCISSORS POSITION. This is advantageous when you wish to join in lovemaking but are too lazy for sexual acrobatics. It offers great freedom of movement for both the man and the woman, particularly spinal and pelvic movement. The man lies on his right side, with the woman lying next to him on her back. Her right leg is between his thighs, and her left leg is on top.

The woman can stimulate her clitoris manually—or the man can do it for her—while she is being penetrated. This facilitates the experience of a blended orgasm of the clitoris and the vagina.

The position is also good for practicing synchronized and inverted breathing. It allows you to start making love in a very relaxed, meditative fashion, bringing awareness to the tiniest movements, pulsations, and breathing rhythms.

The woman can easily vary the angle and degree of penetration. For example, by gripping the man's thigh resting between her legs and slowly moving her head and torso away from him—almost to a 90-degree angle—both partners can enjoy an exciting feeling of sexual traction. The woman can enjoy total control of the degree of penetration by pulling on the man's thigh. The man can feel the different ways in which his Vajra is being held and gripped, and the different sensations available in the front, middle, and rear of the vagina.

This position is also recommended for lovemaking during the last months of a woman's pregnancy.

THE SPOON POSITION. This position is beneficial for developing free movement of the pelvis, because no weight is pressing down on either partner.

Both partners lie on their sides. The man is behind the woman and holds her tight, penetrating her from behind. This can give the woman a strong sensation of energy moving up the Inner Flute, as her spine is being warmed and stimulated by the man's chest and belly.

Focus on sensations that are created through the action of thigh and pelvic muscles by practicing the Pelvic Curl, Pelvic Breathing, and the PC Pump.

Hiding in the Crevice.

THE HIDING IN THE CREVICE POSITION. The woman lies outstretched on her belly, with the man lying on top. She may need a pillow under her belly. This position is particularly good when the Yoni is shallow and the Vajra is long, because as the Vajra enters from behind, the woman can clench her buttocks and give the man the impression that the length of her vagina is extended. This enables the man to make deep strokes with his Vajra that would otherwise be painful for the woman.

When the Yoni is broad, the woman can tighten the vaginal channel with the PC Pump and provide both herself and her partner with more sensations. In addition, the pressure of the woman's buttocks against the man's pubis and upper thighs extends the pleasure zone for him.

THE PIERCING TIGER POSITION. The woman crouches on all fours with buttocks raised, while the man kneels behind her, holding her waist and hips. He alternates shallow thrusts with deep penetration. The man should take care not to make his deep thrusts too vigorous, or he will hit the woman's cervix, which may cause her discomfort.

The woman feels especially vulnerable in this position, but the animalistic quality of it can be very exciting. You can enhance the pleasure and sensuality of this position by making sounds like animals in heat. If you are used to silent sex, this may seem odd at first, but such sounds are merely a variation of the Three Keys that you have used

The Piercing Tiger.

throughout this book. Try making the mewing and hissing cries of a cat, or the growling and snarling of a dog. These sounds will be particularly beneficial if you use them to express the sensations you are feeling in your sexual region.

THE STANDING SHIVA POSITION. This is one of the best positions to make contact with the G spot. The woman lies on her back on a table and the man stands between her thighs. She spreads her legs, brings her Yoni to the edge of the table, and rests her thighs against his torso. Raising her legs, she hooks her knees over his shoulders, giving her leverage to move her pelvis up and down and thereby adjusting the positions of the Vajra

399

The Standing Shiva.

inside her. In this way she can find the best position to bring the Vajra
in contact with her G spot. The man alternates between shallow and deep
strokes.

ORAL LOVING

Oral loving can play a major role in High Sex, but it is not essential to
experience ecstasy. It depends on your personal preference whether or not
you choose to integrate it into your practices. Throughout this book my
primary concern has been to prepare you on an energy level, helping you
to develop greater sensitivity and scope so that your preferred methods

of lovemaking can become more and more pleasurable, opening the way for higher, subtler levels of experience. So in the same way that I do not recommend specific "how to" techniques of lovemaking, I neither encourage nor discourage people to move into oral sex.

In my personal experience, however, there are benefits to reap from the unusual energy circuitry that oral lovemaking brings into play. For instance, when the mouth of one partner connects with the genitals of the other, energy will flow in a different way than when their genitals are connecting. By using these different circuits, the two partners can help to balance their inner male and female polarities. When the male partner is kissing the female partner's breast, for example, he is adopting a male, or Yang, role. He is the doer, the active one, and the woman is Yin. But when the woman's breast becomes very aroused through his kissing and fondling, it sometimes produces small amounts of a thin white liquid—sweet to taste, but not the same as milk—that the man can then drink. In this way he becomes the receiver, and the roles are subtly reversed. In

There is a subtle channel that connects the lips, nipples, and clitoris. When the links in this channel are hooked up through loving erotic contact, while you stimulate one area, you also stimulate the others.

401

the sacred Taoist traditions, the mixing of love juices—such as female breast fluids and male saliva—contributes to the harmonization of Yin and Yang in both partners.

Another aspect of oral loving is that when you use your lips on your partner's mouth, breast, genitals, or any other part of the body, a chain of associations may be triggered that links your lovemaking to the oral gratification you received as a baby from your mother's breast. It is a very pleasant form of regression, a sudden feeling of being projected back in time to one's early childhood, reexperiencing life from that perspective. Evoking these deep, early, primal experiences can be a very soothing and liberating experience. This kind of regression is especially likely when the man sucks on the woman's breast. He may have a very strong feeling of being a baby again, sucking on his mother's nipple, and this sensation may give him an image of his partner as mother-goddess, nurturer, provider. When the woman's mouth kisses the man's Vajra, it can feel as if she, too, is again a little baby, sucking on her mother's breast. Since the shape, sensitivity, and lubrication of the mouth corresponds to that of the Yoni, she can also have the sensation that she is being penetrated. This combined feeling of being both a baby and adult can be an extremely erotic experience.

When lovers have sensitized their bodies through the High Sex practices that I have outlined, they gradually discover a whole network of subtle and sophisticated energy connections that link different erogenous zones, heightening the sense of gratification that oral lovemaking can bring. In women a correspondence can be felt between the nipple and the clitoris and between the midpoint of the upper lip and the clitoris. In men there is a correspondence between the tongue and the Vajra. And there are many more connections that you can discover and explore for yourself.

If you enjoy oral lovemaking, it is good preparation for the following practice, the Wave of Bliss, which is very subtle and requires a lot of preliminary erotic stimulation in order to be fully effective.

She should have him suck her Lotus and show his pleasure. Inhaling the odor, he should enter with his tongue, searching for the Red and White secretions. Then she should say to him, "Eat my essence! Drink the Waters of Release! O Son, be a slave as well as a father and lover!"

—Chandamaharosana Tantra

RIDING THE WAVE OF BLISS

Having explored the various positions of lovemaking and the added dimension of oral gratification, we come to the ultimate lovemaking posture in High Sex: Riding the Wave of Bliss.

Purpose and Benefits

In the Wave of Bliss, the man sits in the Opening Lotus position with the woman sitting in his lap, her legs wrapped around his waist. Their mouths are touching, and the man's Vajra is inside the woman's Yoni. Erotic arousal in this position happens internally, with no external movements of the body. It's all going on inside, with muscle contractions and breathing.

Riding the Wave of Bliss:
Uniting the male and female,
the Inner Man and Inner
Woman.

404

This position is very powerful. It allows partners to generate sexual arousal while containing this energy within their bodies. This contained energy triggers the Streaming Reflex, and as the energy streams upward through the Inner Flute, it awakens the Ecstatic Response. The fact that the two partners are sitting, not lying down, promotes the upward movement of energy.

No other lovemaking position described in this book contains the energy in such a complete way, because in this position all the usual avenues through which energy escapes from the body are closed. In the terminology of High Sex, all the body's "gates" are "locked."

- The sexual gate is locked, because the two partners are inside each other.
- The anal gate is shut—both partners are rhythmically tightening their anal muscles through the PC Pump.
- At the other end of the Inner Flute, the gate of the mouth is locked because the partners' mouths are firmly pressed together, as they are doing inverted breathing.
- Energy that normally escapes through the eyes is recirculated by gazing into each other's eyes.
- Energy that might otherwise be dissipated in strenuous, athletic lovemaking is contained, because arousal is achieved through subtle internal movements of the genital muscles, harmonized with the breathing.

Riding the Wave of Bliss unites all the polarities: male and female, positive and negative, sexual and spiritual. The union of the male and female elements happens not only between two partners but within each partner. In the essential spirit of the Tantric tradition, the outer partner becomes a doorway for you to experience an internal union of your Inner Man and your Inner Woman.

This position is also extremely healing for the heart. It promotes a deep intimacy, because you are so close to each other, completely inter-twined, chest to chest. This facilitates a sense of surrender, like a child in the mother's arms—a feeling of letting go, protecting each other, trusting. These qualities in turn generate a sense of love and caring that carries on as a subtle mood throughout your daily life.

In the Tantric tradition the Wave of Bliss is used to open the higher levels of the Inner Flute, triggering powerful experiences of bliss. For example, this poetic quotation from Satchakra-Nirupana, an ancient Tantric scripture, describes how channeled energy is experienced when it flowers in the crown chakra: "She is beautiful, like a chain of lightning, and fine, like a lotus fiber, and shines in the minds of the sages. She is extremely subtle, the awakener of pure knowledge, the embodiment of all bliss, whose true nature is pure consciousness."

It really can happen this way. Riding the Wave of Bliss, you can "see" your inner light and feel the wisdom of all-encompassing consciousness.

Preparations

Don't let yourself be discouraged by the seemingly complex picture that this practice presents. Remember, there are many skills in your life for which you may have had to train in a more strenuous manner than you are doing here. Think of a surfer, training himself to ride the waves—it's exactly the same. The surfer needs balance, courage, perseverance, a fit body, and a joy for what he's doing, even if he falls off his board for days on end before mastering his sport.

In order to enjoy the Wave of Bliss in an effortless way, you need to have fully integrated the following parts of this book:

- ☐ You need to remain playful and relaxed—don't take this seriously as a dutiful practice. Try the Inner Smile in chapter 4.
- ☐ Make sure there is no unexpressed resentment between you and your partner. Resolve any contradictions through Moving beyond Resistance in chapter 3.
- ☐ You need to tune in on a deep level with each other's spirits through Soul Gazing (chapter 4).
- ☐ To be comfortable in the position, you need to open and stretch the pelvis, so your body can stay relaxed. Practice the exercises in chapter 5.
- ☐ To strengthen the mobility of the pelvis while making love in the Wave of Bliss position, practice the Pelvic Curl in chapter 5 and Pelvic Rocking in chapter 6.
- ☐ To experience the whole range of possibilities that the Wave offers, you need to be able to circulate the energy up and down the Inner Flute. Practice Opening the Inner Flute in chapter 6.

We learn orgasm. Orgasm is itself a form of adaptation that we learn at an early stage of life, even earlier than we become genitally active. We learn orgasm in being sustained, in nursing. We learn it in the pleasurable bodily states that we may realize early in life, and we associate those acquired pleasurable states with a continual connection to Life. . . . We identify it at the most rudimentary level, just as we identify the pleasure of nursing as an infant. It is a solution to the dilemma of life, to the sense of emptiness, of needing to be fed, of feeling that we are not inherently one with infinite pleasure or Bliss.

—Da Love-Ananda
Love of the Two-Armed Form

☐ In order to ensure that the sexual energy aroused by this exercise can flow while you stay relaxed, you need to practice the Streaming Process, the Butterfly, and the Bonding Relaxation as explained in chapter 9.

☐ To maximize the subtle sensations in the genitals that are required for the Wave, you need to have healed and sensitized the genital tissues, as described in Expanding Orgasm in chapter 10.

☐ You need to be able to use your breath to channel the energy through the Inner Flute, which you learned in chapter 11.

Familiarizing yourself with Riding the Wave of Bliss can be very enjoyable. For example, you don't have to give up normal lovemaking in order to practice the Wave. All you need to do is integrate it, perhaps for ten minutes, each time you make love, so that it adds a new dimension. Make love normally, then switch to the Wave for as long as it feels comfortable. Keep alternating until the Wave becomes so ecstatic that you're not interested in anything else. This *does* happen. There is so much bliss available in the Wave that you may come to feel that normal lovemaking is dull in comparison. The more you practice, the better it gets.

When getting into this position for the first time, many women think, *My God, I'm going to be too heavy!* But this is usually more fear than fact. My advice to the woman is that as you lower yourself onto your partner, think of yourself as light and relaxed, without either slumping down or getting tense. Let the soles of your feet touch behind the man's lower back, giving you good grounding and support during the practice. You'll be able to rest on your feet, and this will give you upward mobility and leverage—another way of not being too heavy. Men should be sure you tell their partners when they need a break from taking their weight. You aren't out to break any endurance records.

In this practice the man may need a small pillow under his buttocks, and the woman can sit directly on his lap. If that's uncomfortable, the woman can put a pillow under her buttocks—resting on the man's thighs, between his crotch and his ankles.

Before moving into the practice, I'm going to give you two alternative positions that allow you to move from the Opening Lotus—relieving any strain that has built up—without interrupting your connection with each other.

The Crouching Shakti.

THE CROUCHING SHAKTI. The man sits in the Opening Lotus, while the woman squats on him, with her feet resting on the floor on either side of his hips. This alleviates the weight problem and gives her additional leverage. This posture is also good when the man starts to lose his erection, because the woman is free to move up and down on the Vajra while doing the PC Pump.

THE RECLINING LOVERS. Both partners lean back, taking the weight of their bodies on their arms, with their chests apart, unlocking their legs. Moving gently back and forth in a rocking motion, they can use this position to stimulate arousal again. Further stimulation can be added by doing the PC Pump and gazing in each other's eyes.

When you are thoroughly familiar and comfortable with the practices mentioned above, create the Sacred Space, and put on music that sounds like the waves of the sea or like a snake charmer's flute. Have some dynamic dance music ready to play at a moment's notice.

Approach the Wave of Bliss not only as an exercise but as a meditation. Nothing should be done hurriedly or mechanically. Take every step slowly and consciously, watching what is happening.

You need to be naked or to wear a loose kimono or robe that is open in front. My favorite way of dressing for this practice is just to tie a scarf or shawl around my hips in the Balinese fashion. My partner does the same.

There should be a bowl of scented massage oil within easy reach. You will need a large towel for both of you to sit on so that the floor is protected from the oil.

Allow 30 to 90 minutes for this practice.

You will be learning the Wave of Bliss in seven steps. If at any point you feel the need to stop, do so. You do not have to complete all seven steps in one practice session. You can take a break, switch to normal lovemaking, and move into other postures. Ultimately, however, your goal is to move smoothly through all seven steps.

Practice

Begin with a Melting Hug.

Do a special Heart Salutation for this practice. The woman says, "I salute you, Shiva [or his real name], as an aspect of myself." The man says, "I salute you, Shakti [or her real name], as an aspect of myself."

Roll around and try the basic postures that I have described, and include some variations of your own, just as a game and a playful way of stretching the body. Then, after a massage or a glass of wine, begin to feel turned on and make love normally, the way you like, staying on the brink of genital orgasm without going beyond the point of no return. When you have reached a peak of arousal, switch gears, and adopt the Wave of Bliss position. Slowly bring the focus of your attention away from your partner and inside yourself.

Play with this transition. Go back to normal lovemaking, then

The Reclining Lovers.

switch to the Wave. Alternate between the two. With practice you will eventually be able to adopt the Wave for hours on end.

When you have practiced these transitions for a while, separate and allow a short cooling-off period. Then you are ready to move into the seven steps of the Wave of Bliss.

STEP ONE: PELVIC ROCKING. Kneel down, facing each other, not touching. Each partner straddles a *zafu* or hard pillow. Close your eyes. This will allow you to focus more fully on the inner sensations. Put aside any thoughts of how complicated this practice may seem to you, and take it one step at a time. You are going to begin with the basic movement of Pelvic Rocking.

Begin to rock your pelvis backward and forward, in the way I described in chapter 6. Make sure the area between your genitals and anus rubs firmly against the cushion. Feel how this rocking creates a tingling in your genitals. Do this for about five minutes.

STEP TWO: CULTIVATING AROUSAL. In the same position, keeping your eyes closed, continue the Pelvic Rocking, and emphasize sensations in your genitals by adding the PC Pump, again as described in chapter 6.

As you rock backward, tighten the genital muscles. As you rock forward, relax them. Continue for about five minutes until you feel warmth and tingling in your genitals and pelvis.

STEP THREE: OPENING THE INNER FLUTE TOGETHER. Open your eyes and look at each other, synchronizing your rocking rhythms. This is the Dual Pelvic Rocking exercise described in chapter 6. Continue to use the PC Pump. Be aware of your genital sensations while at the same time connecting with your partner through your eyes.

After a while add the Sexual Breathing, also described in chapter 6. As you rock your pelvis backward and tighten the genital muscles, inhale deeply, imagining that you are pulling the sexual energy up the Inner Flute all the way to the third eye. As you rock your pelvis forward, relax the genital muscles and exhale, imagining the energy coming down the Inner Flute and out through your genitals.

Imagine that you are connecting the earth with the sky through your breathing. As you inhale through your genitals, you are picking up the energy from the roots, the earth, symbolized by the sex center. Continuing the same inhalation, you are sending this energy up to the sky, symbolized by the third eye or crown. As you exhale, you bring the energy back down from the sky, down through your body, and out into the earth.

Keep looking in each other's eyes, stay relaxed, and gradually let yourselves tune in to a common rhythm. Try it fast, then try it slow, until you find a pace that feels easy and natural.

After a few minutes, play with the possibility of inverting your breathing. When one exhales, rocking forward with the pelvis, the other is inhaling and rocking the pelvis back.

Feel that you are "kissing through the breathing." Even though your lips are not touching, the partner who inhales is drinking the exhaled breath of the other partner. Feel the subtlety of this delicate exchange at a distance.

STEP FOUR: THE PLAYFUL WAVE. The concentration required in practicing these steps may draw you into a serious mood. This next step is designed to introduce playful spontaneity.

Maintaining eye contact and remaining seated on your cushions, switch on the dynamic dance music. Slowly reach out toward each other with your hands, and touch your palms. Begin a hand dance with each other. Let your hands be like antennae that follow the rhythms of the music. Let your breathing be deep, through the mouth.

Still sitting in the Opening Lotus position, facing each other, bring your whole body into the dance, moving your arms, upper torso, and pelvis in harmony with the pressure and counterpressure of the hands as they dance against each other.

Take the opportunity to explore various moods. Make wild, expansive movements, then slow down and be soft and subtle, with smaller movements. Make vertical movements, then circular ones. Spread your hands wide apart, with your arms sideways, then bring them close together.

Let your breathing carry the movement, as if the movement is an extension of the energy that your breathing generates.

Be aware of who is leading and who is following, who is pushing and who is yielding, how the energy is flowing between you. Switch roles. Feel the difference between the times when you are allowing yourself to be guided and the times when you provide the impulse for a new movement.

As the lead and response of good dancers appears to be almost simultaneous, as if they were a single entity, there comes a moment when more intimate sexual contact occurs with an extraordinary mutuality. The man does not lead and the woman follow; the man-and-woman relationship acts of itself. His "advance" and her "response" seems to be the same movement.

—Alan Watts
Nature, Man and Woman

The Playful Wave.

As you play, see if you can incorporate Pelvic Rocking and Sexual Breathing, maybe breathing out to your partner as you push forward and then sucking in your partner's breath as you surrender to his or her counterpressure. After five to ten minutes, finish the hand dance by delicately sliding the robes off each other's shoulders, or untying the cloths around each other's hips.

Sit naked, facing each other, and bring the bowl of massage oil between you. One partner receives, and the other covers him or her with oil. Cover your partner generously and sensuously, oiling the torso, breasts, arms, genitals, perineum, and thighs. Make it a sliding, sensuous

413

experience. Feel the sensuality of your hands sliding smoothly over the skin. Apply generous amounts of oil because soon you will be gliding against each other in a very erotic way.

When you oil the genitals, slide your hand under your partner's perineum, at the bottom of the pelvis. As you oil this area and caress it, look in your partner's eyes and use tender names, expressing your feelings of excitement and enjoyment. During this massage continue the slow dance of your bodies, rocking your pelvises in harmony with each other.

When you have thoroughly oiled each other, laughing and playing like two kids, notice how you feel more relaxed about this practice.

When you feel playful and ready to move on, return to the snake charmer or ocean music.

414

Approach each other, assuming the position of the Wave. Feel the delicious contact of oiled skin as the woman sensuously lowers herself onto the man, while he guides his Vajra into her Yoni. If the male partner does not have an erection, the exercise can be just as efficient without it, providing the genitals are in contact and the Vajra is turned upward— resting between the belly of the man and the clitoris of the woman. You may wish to penetrate later, whenever you feel it is appropriate.

STEP FIVE: CONNECTING BREATH TO BREATH. I will describe the remaining steps of the Wave as if the Vajra is inside the woman, but as I have said, this need not be the case. Take the time to feel each other, with the man in the Opening Lotus, and the woman sitting on him with her legs wrapped around him. Make yourselves comfortable. Before going into formal practice, move around, circle the pelvis, and try the two alternative positions I mentioned earlier, the Crouching Shakti and the Reclining Lovers.

Experiment with the use of pillows both for the man and woman. When the position feels comfortable, take a few minutes to relax against each other's chests, with the woman's mouth against her partner's ear.

Then, in a very tender and gentle way, start the Pelvic Rocking, PC Pump, and Sexual Breathing. Take time to learn how to adapt to this new position. Move against each other, harmonizing your rhythms. Pick up the tingle in the genitals, and begin to move it up and down through the Inner Flute, inhaling and exhaling together.

When you feel that you have integrated all these steps inside yourself and in harmony with your partner, look into each other's eyes, maintaining the rocking, PC Pump, and breathing. Make sure that your shoulders, neck, and spine remain relaxed.

When you're ready, exchange a kiss, mouth to mouth, and begin the inverted breathing. As your partner exhales through the mouth, inhale the warm current of air through your own mouth, and imagine that it travels all the way down to your genitals. If this seems difficult at first, you can allow a small amount of fresh air to enter by leaving small gaps at the sides of your joined mouths. As you become more familiar with this practice, seal your two mouths together completely so you are drinking and exchanging the same breath.

Integrate the inverted breathing with the Pelvic Rocking and PC Pump. When the woman rocks her pelvis forward, exhaling, she gives her energy to her partner. The energy passes out through her vagina, into her partner's penis. Inhaling, the man does the PC Pump, rocks his pelvis

415

back, and sucks the woman's energy through his penis, mingles it with his own, and sends it all the way up the Inner Flute to his third eye.

Then the man exhales, sending the energy down his Inner Flute and out through his penis, relaxing his genital muscles, and giving it to his partner, who is inhaling and drawing his energy in through her Yoni. She mixes his energy with her own and sends it up her Inner Flute to her third eye.

If you find that your breathing rhythms are different, forget about the PC Pump for a while, and focus totally on the breathing. Make quick, shallow breaths while maintaining mouth-to-mouth contact. This opens and expands the chest and lungs. When you are ready, return to a slower pace of breathing. You may now be able to harmonize your breathing rhythms and return to the practice.

At first this step may seem complicated because you have to integrate so many elements. Don't worry. Continue to be playful, and try different amplitudes, different rhythms of breathing. If one of you notices that the other is getting too serious, be sure to lighten the mood with tickles, humor, and other playful activities.

STEP SIX: OPENING TO YOUR INNER LIGHT. This step is the key to moving orgasmic energy from the genitals and transforming it into an ecstatic and meditative experience.

Continue the mouth-to-mouth inverted breathing. Close your eyes. As you end the inhalation, roll your eyes slightly upward and focus them on the third eye. Feel as you do so that you are bringing the pleasure, the orgasm, the ecstasy of both yourself and your partner to this point. Use whatever muscles help further this image of drawing all this energy upward. For example, in addition to contracting the PC muscle, you may wish to tighten your stomach muscles slightly, rock your pelvis back, and lift and expand your chest.

Once you have "arrived" at the third eye, hold your breath. Keep the genital muscles contracted, keep your eyes rolled up—this locks the two gates—and then relax the rest of your body. The more you can relax your whole body, the more you will experience how the energy shoots up the Inner Flute and expands into the area behind your forehead.

After a while, you may have the feeling of an explosion of light or a shooting star or fireworks. You may have the impression that your energy is becoming subtler and subtler, like a gentle wind, expanding

The pins and needles that started in my head were now spreading down through my body, at the same time I felt I was being drawn upwards and in a great and wonderful rush of power that rose eventually to a crescendo and bathed me through and through with glorious burning, embracing Light. Then slowly, gently, I came back . . .

—Vanora Goodhart

Opening to Inner Light.

beyond the boundaries of your body, becoming part of the sounds around you, part of existence itself. This all happens in a short moment.

Remember that you have been doing inverted breathing, so while you have been inhaling, your partner has been exhaling. While you have been holding your breath on the inhalation, he or she has been keeping the lungs empty.

Maintain this gap between breaths as long as is comfortable. When you let go and begin to exhale, try to do so *slowly* and consciously, sending the energy down the Inner Flute. Several things can happen. You may feel that the energy is awakening the Streaming Reflex and feel ripples and vibrations up and down your spine. You may also have the impression that light is raining down on your body—little particles of light, or golden rain.

While you have been exhaling, your partner has begun to inhale, drawing your energy in through the genitals, mixing it with his or her own energy, and sending it up the Inner Flute to the third eye. As you hold your breath while you exhale, your partner holds it while inhaling. Then the cycle is repeated as your partner slowly exhales and you begin to inhale.

Repeat this step until you feel you are moving from practice to enjoyment, and it becomes an effortless dance between you and your partner.

Always end the visualization by bringing the energy down from the third eye to the genitals, grounding it close to the earth. Otherwise you may feel disoriented.

STEP SEVEN: THE INFINITE CYCLE. In this final step you will create a continuous, circular flow of energy as it passes up through the woman and down through the man. The female partner inhales, drawing the energy from her sex center up the Inner Flute to her mouth, not to her third eye. Then she exhales into her partner's mouth and throat, visualizing that the energy is passing into his Inner Flute and down through his Inner Flute to his genitals, completing one cycle. On the next inhalation, the female partner again picks up the energy at her own sex center, sucking the energy from her partner, and again draws it up the Inner Flute to her mouth. Exhaling, she passes it to her male partner, repeating the cyclical movement of energy.

The male partner visualizes the movement of energy in the same way as the woman. Inhaling, he receives the breath and energy of his female partner through his mouth and sends it *down* his Inner Flute—not up, as he is accustomed—all the way to his genitals. Exhaling, he imagines the energy passing out through his Vajra into the woman's Yoni and then up her Inner Flute to her mouth.

In this way a closed or infinite cycle is created. You are not holding the breath at any moment. It is a rhythmic cycle with relaxed, ongoing breathing. Find a pace and rhythm with which you can be relaxed.

If it feels more comfortable, you can reverse the direction of this infinite cycle, visualizing it passing up through the man and down through the woman. The man exhales, sending the energy into the woman's mouth and down her Inner Flute to her genitals. As he begins

The Infinite Cycle.

to inhale, he sucks the energy in through his genitals and up his Inner Flute to his mouth where, on exhaling, he again passes it to the woman.

The female partner holds the same visualization: As she inhales, she receives the energy through her mouth and allows it to flow down her Inner Flute to her genitals. As she exhales, she imagines that it is passing into the man, up his Inner Flute and out through his mouth.

419

The Advanced Infinite Cycle.

Try both methods. Be sure to practice one fully before switching to the other. One important point to remember here is that the partner who is inhaling while visualizing the energy moving down through his or her body should avoid doing the PC Pump. This will keep the pelvic floor relaxed and allow the energy to move easily out through the genitals.

THE ADVANCED INFINITE CYCLE. When you have practiced the infinite cycle until it becomes effortless, you are ready to experiment with the advanced stage of this practice. Here you and your partner will be doing visualizations that are different but parallel.

Maintain the inverted breathing.

As the woman inhales, she visualizes that she is drawing the energy in through her genitals and up her Inner Flute to her mouth. She exhales, imagining that she is sending the energy into her partner's mouth and down through her partner's Inner Flute to his genitals.

As the man inhales, he imagines that he is sucking the energy in through his genitals and up his Inner Flute to his mouth. He exhales, imagining that he is sending it into the mouth of the woman and down her Inner Flute to her genitals, where he begins to pick it up again on his next inhale.

Both partners are visualizing an infinite cycle of energy, but they are visualizing it moving in opposite directions. This may seem confusing at first, but actually it is very simple. If you feel perplexed, my advice is not to try to work out what your partner is doing with his or her visualization. Maintain a clear image of how you are moving the energy, and maintain a steady rhythm of inverted breathing.

Gradually a feeling of harmony will arise. You will lose your ideas of "doing" and fall into a Yin mood of receptivity. The practice is simply happening by itself. You are in the middle point between Yin and Yang. There is such a balance that nobody is leading or following. It is an empty point between the two—the void.

If you can find this point of deep relaxation, the physical body, gender, and personality begin to disappear. Instead of two individuals, you become a flow and rhythm of energy, mirroring the impersonal flow of energy in the universe itself.

This can become extremely ecstatic. There is a kind of "ping-pong" dynamic operating between the sexual and spiritual poles within you, each one activating the other. The sexual sensation in the genitals gets transmuted into a feeling of light in the brain, and this in turn gets transformed back and channeled into the sexual feeling, which again gets stimulated.

Eventually you get the impression that you have become one breath, one energy, one flute, one organism—even that the man has the Yoni and the woman has the Vajra. You don't know who is the male and who is the female.

For me this exercise is the very best of High Sex. When the Inner Flute is really open, the woman can have the impression that the tip of the man's Vajra is reaching all the way to the third eye and tickling her in that place, and that her whole body has become a vulva.

The same applies to the man. Ramakrishna, the Indian sage, described this sensation in one of his advanced meditations, saying that the male and female had united inside him, and every pore of his skin felt as if it had become a genital organ.

When you feel ready to end this exchange, slow down and be still while remaining inside each other. Stay like this for five to ten minutes. Then you may wish to move back into normal lovemaking or to slowly disengage, making a Heart Salutation and sitting for a while in meditation or lying together without speaking. After 15 to 20 minutes, talk to each other about your experiences in the usual way—one listens while the other speaks.

Pointers

In this practice I have asked you to draw up energy to the third eye. If you find it easier and more effective to visualize energy moving to the crown, however, feel free to use that center instead.

In step seven of the Wave, I gave you a method that sends energy down through the man and up through the woman. This practice reflects the ancient Tantric perception of the man as a "sky being," with a natural ability to channel energy through his body in a downward direction from the sky to the earth. The woman is perceived as an "earth being," with a natural ability to channel energy in an upward direction from the earth toward the sky. As I have pointed out, however, you are free to reverse the direction of the cycle if you find it more harmonious and effective.

Riding the Wave of Bliss is a subtle practice. In the beginning you may feel rather like a do-it-yourself electronics engineer sitting amid a pile of circuit boards, wires, and silicon chips that the instructions say will fit together to create a fabulous computer. Follow the instructions, but don't be obsessed with technical details. The mind has a natural tendency to seize hold of techniques, anticipating that their correct application will produce immediate results. Tantra, however, rewards those who take technique lightly, who practice sincerely but nonseriously. It rewards those who are patient with themselves and with others. It offers method only as a means of going beyond all methods, taking you to a place of such ease and familiarity with the practices of High Sex that you can respond moment to moment to whatever your lovemaking requires.

Although the ultimate flowering of the Wave of Bliss comes in loving union with a partner, you can use almost all its elements to generate ecstatic states either by yourself or with a partner who is not yet skilled in High Sex. Using Pelvic Rocking, the PC Pump, and Sexual Breathing to arouse your energy, moving the energy up the Inner Flute to the third eye and then expanding it beyond the body is something that you can do independently. In other words, the gift of High Sex is yours alone. Of course, it is wonderful to share this gift with your beloved in the Wave position, but it is liberating to know that you are not dependent on the other person for your sexual fulfillment.

In its essence High Sex is not technique but love, not a method but a deep relaxation into the heart. It is a state of being. All methods lead to this understanding: that a point is reached when the ecstasy for which you have been seeking and searching suddenly overwhelms you, floods through your body, consumes you. That is the moment when you abandon the method, abandon all attempts to manipulate, rationalize, or categorize the experience. In that moment you allow yourself to move beyond the control of the mind and let yourself be possessed by something bigger than you, carrying you into a timeless experience of ecstatic loving. Then you have truly experienced High Sex. Then there are no longer two people involved, but one. In fact, there is not even one. There is only the experience of ecstasy. There is only bliss. What can you do in such moments? You cannot say anything. You can only sing, dance, or play a song with your beloved in deepest gratitude. Never think for a moment that you can possess ecstasy. For the truth is, you can only be possessed by it. This book is a preparation. It helps you prepare for something that comes as a gift—and leaves the moment you try to grasp it.

INTEGRATING HIGH SEX INTO DAILY LIFE

Having encouraged you to explore the heights of ecstasy, I would like to end this book on a down-to-earth note: You can apply the elements of the Tantric attitude—self-love, spontaneity, pleasure, and relaxation—in your life as a whole. You can expand your newly found sensuality and aliveness to include not only your beloved but also your family, your place of work, and your environment. The pleasure that you experience in lovemaking need not be an isolated or unusual event. The enjoyment you experience in your Sacred Space need not be unconnected to how you are feeling at the office. High Sex offers you a whole new way of life. You can feel sensual while brushing your teeth, eating your breakfast, or walking down the street. You can feel vibrantly alive while driving a car. The Tantra vision, remember, includes everything, not just your sexuality.

The first place to begin is at home with your family. As you know, many of the practices in this book involve opening the heart, becoming more intimate and honest, and these qualities are bound to affect other people who are close to you. Children especially are very receptive to the changes in mood that these practices provoke. Some fathers and mothers have told me that, when they practice High Sex, their children immediately notice the difference and respond by being more joyful, trusting, and relaxed themselves.

Through the vision of High Sex, you recognize that your children, too, are dancing gods. And the chances are that as you become more playful, you can more fully enjoy the naturally playful spirit of children. One participant in my seminars decided to explore this spirit by following his five-year-old child on all fours around the house, doing exactly what he did, touching the things he touched, rolling and jumping with him. He commented, "It was a beautiful way to experience being totally involved in the present moment, a secret of High Sex that children already know."

You can also create rituals with your family, devising special feasts and sensory-awakening games. You can take turns being the one who offers objects for the senses, while the others receive, or you can invent a family version of the Yin-Yang Game.

Your experience of High Sex also may inspire you to reduce the gap that usually exists between work and play. Your training in High

Sex will have given you a clearer idea of what nourishes you, and this in turn may encourage you to choose work that helps you to grow and flower. You will learn the secret of creating quality time, because you set aside an evening each week to practice High Sex. Perhaps you can see ways of slowly adding periods of quality time to your schedule, creating more and more moments that you enjoy: a break in your routine, a stroll in the fresh air, an interval for meditation, a special lunch date with your beloved.

High Sex gives you a taste of your personal sensuality, and this is not something you need to leave behind when you go to work. You can dress in clothes that allow you to maintain that quality throughout the day. You can arrange to receive a massage once a week, practice your favorite sport, move your body in ways that stimulate your newly opened energy channels. You can remember to breathe deeply, relax, and stay centered, and this will help you not to get involved in situations of unnecessary stress.

What I am proposing is a gradual, step-by-step transition toward a lifestyle that brings you pleasure and joy in all dimensions. You have transformed your love life—why not the whole of your life? The challenge to change is an exciting one, and it can succeed. I have seen the benefits of High Sex manifest themselves in many people's lives: They work in a more creative way, enjoy their work more, make more money, and are more willing to choose jobs and environments that are nourishing to them and to shift away from a negative experience of work as drudgery.

Often I find that I am having "sex" merely by being in the presence of certain people. It no longer matters whether they are male or female, what they look like, how they live, what they do. . . . I am always "making love" with those around me in accordance with their capacity to enter energetic rapport. It does not require words, or even knowing one another.

—Richard Moss
The Black Butterfly

CREATING A SUPPORT GROUP

One of the most beneficial things that you can do to integrate the spirit of High Sex into your lifestyle is to create a support group. This will provide you with a network of people interested in enhancing pleasure in their lives, enabling you to share what you have learned and helping you to maintain the practices that have given you a taste of sexual ecstasy.

To start a support group, I recommend that you choose friends who are close to you, whom you trust, whom you feel are creative, open-minded, and attractive. Invite a group of four to ten of them for an evening. Keep the group fairly small and intimate.

Tell your friends about your experience of High Sex—what it has given you, how it has helped you. Then ask if they are interested in exploring ways to bring more ecstasy into their love lives. If you receive a positive response, propose an agenda for the group, stating your goals and vision. Explain that the group requires a commitment to develop the art of enjoying oneself and that its aim is to transform attitudes that stop people from doing this. Ask each of your friends to tell the group which areas in their relationships and lovemaking they feel happy with and which they would like to change. Make sure everyone gives concrete and practical examples from their lives. Get participants to look at those areas where they could bring in more sensuality and enjoyment.

Make sure that people do not spend the whole time talking about their problems. Many people find this easier than to accept the fact that it is possible to become more ecstatic.

Introduce a ritual or game that will be enjoyable and pleasing for the group, such as the Sensory Awakening Ritual or the Moving beyond Resistance practice. Choose any of the appropriate structures offered in this book. End this structure with a Heart Salutation and a Melting Hug.

If you receive the support of your friends in organizing the group on a regular basis, decide to meet at least one evening a week, if possible, or one weekend each month. Decide what topic you will focus on at the next meeting. You may want to suggest that they read this book and find the practices that seem especially relevant to their situations.

Suggest forms of exploration in High Sex that each member of the group can do between now and the next meeting. Ask all participants to keep a journal so that they can report back to the group. Begin each new session with feedback from people about their experiences with the practices. Make sure each meeting is clearly structured, with a beginning, middle, and end. Keep track of time, and stay in touch with group members by phone. You may want to select a different group member as coordinator of each session on a rotating basis.

The theme of your meetings need not be sexual at first. Rather, you should look for ways to connect people in their hearts and spirits, through dance and ritual. It may take a little daring on your part to challenge the beliefs that your friends have about the way love can work in their lives. But by giving them support and encouragement, you will grow and expand as you offer them new possibilities.

I would like you to join me in creating a new context for sexual loving, by giving back to sexuality the sacredness that it enjoyed in the ancient Taoist and Tantric traditions. To do so, we have to start in the simplest way, in our daily lives, cultivating what we enjoy and sharing it with others.

In the words of the ecstatic Sufi mystic, Jallaludin Rumi, "Let yourself be loved, O Beloved, in the One. And from this One move out into the world, carrying within you the great potent energies of life to green your world, to create planets, suns, stars, stones, waves, oceans, to create new forms of life and expression—whether a friendship, a feeling, or a new form of vocation."

May your life be the reflection of the Ecstatic One within.
May this Ecstatic One be the instrument of love without end.

❦

SAFE SEX

One of the reasons why the High Sex approach to lovemaking is so appropriate for our times is that it inspires a new awareness of sexual attitudes and relationships that offers the best possible protection against sexually transmitted diseases (STDs). In the age of AIDS and other STDs, training in High Sex enables you to protect yourself fully because it places so much emphasis on building intimacy and trust between partners before sexual intercourse, and on breaking through sexual taboos that might otherwise inhibit you from taking hygienic precautions. High Sex offers a step-by-step preparation that enables both partners to be fully ready and safely prepared when the time comes for lovemaking. It also teaches you how to be orgasmic independent of the sexual context, so that with practice you can lie safely in your lover's arms and experience a full-body orgasm without sexual penetration, thereby relieving you of the longing that sexual desire can create. With High Sex you don't have to be genitally sexual to be satisfied, and when you do move into sex, you can be ecstatic and hygienic at the same time.

The sexual training in this book calls for a very clear understanding of the current situation concerning the AIDS epidemic and other STDs. According to the statistics given by the American Social Health Association, 27,000 Americans, male and female, contract some form of sexually transmitted disease every day. One in every four Americans contracts a sexually transmitted disease between the ages of 15 and 50. Up to 10 million people are currently suffering from STDs in this country.

Included in these statistics are carriers of the AIDS virus. In 1988, estimates of the number of Americans infected with the AIDS virus varied from an "official" figure of 1.5 million—accepted by most experts—to the doubled estimate of 3 million that has been projected by Masters and Johnson in their controversial book about AIDS, *Crisis: Heterosexual*

Behavior in the Age of AIDS. In this book Masters and Johnson issued an urgent warning to America's heterosexual population about the AIDS threat, saying that the vast majority of people still believe that the virus is largely confined to high-risk groups such as homosexuals, bisexual males, and intravenous drug users, whereas in reality it is steadily spreading into the heterosexual community. They further assert that heterosexuals have a 1-in-400 chance of contracting AIDS during unprotected vaginal intercourse when making love for the first time with someone who is carrying the virus, whereas other researchers argue that the risk is only 1 in 1000 or less.

My point is this: Whoever is right and however long the odds, you need only contract the AIDS virus once to commit a fatal mistake, because as of this writing, there is no known cure. The data is constantly changing, but at this time it is generally accepted that after a period of three months to five years, the infection develops into a fully symptomatic case of AIDS that is virtually always fatal.

The AIDS virus is transmitted through the exchange of bodily fluids. The most common form of sexual transmission of the virus until now has been from man to man or man to woman, through semen that enters the bloodstream of a passive sexual partner via small tears or lesions in the tissues of the vagina or anus. Women also can give the virus to men, however, and, conceivably, to other women.

Once you become aware of these risks, you know that you cannot rely on anyone else to protect you from AIDS and other STDs. You have to do it yourself. If you have not already done so, you have to take full responsibility for your safety, relying on your own intelligence and intuition. From this moment on, if you are not in a long-term monogamous relationship, you need to start changing your whole way of approaching sexual relationships. The first thing to do is to take a good look at your own attitudes, setting up your own standards of what you consider to be safe. You need to establish your boundaries. The sexually liberated approach of jumping into bed with unfamiliar partners won't work anymore. Nor will the belief that if you "think positively," you will not be affected by the AIDS virus. But there is no need, either, to take the puritanical view that the current STD epidemic is punishment for our sins. You do not have to renounce the natural desires of the flesh to be safe. In fact, the STD threat provides each of us with a great incentive to look honestly and directly at the issue of sexuality, recognizing that neither denial nor indulgence can provide us with effective answers to the problem. High Sex, however, can give us a solution.

In dealing with Safe Sex in the context of High Sex, I make a distinction between new partners and long-term partners. In this context safe sex refers only to preventing the communication of sexual diseases, not to preventing pregnancy.

SAFE SEX FOR NEW PARTNERS

In this section I will apply the attitudes of High Sex to the situation that arises when two people who do not know each other feel a sexual attraction. In doing so, I am not simply addressing people who are looking for partners with whom to practice this training. I want to apply the attitudes of High Sex in a wider context, to illustrate their general value.

First of all, the safest approach is to take your time in getting to know someone before having sexual intercourse. This fits well with the High Sex view that a sense of intimacy is essential to satisfying lovemaking. Take time to feel at ease and comfortable with each other so that you can discuss your sexual histories and determine the level of risk involved in sexual contact. One of the greatest barriers to this kind of openness and honesty is the common tendency to avoid acknowledging the sexual attraction verbally. Many people feel embarrassed talking about sex and would rather move directly into intercourse than raise the subject with a new partner. The closer they come to the actual moment of sexual penetration, the more delicate the situation becomes and the less willing they are to interrupt the flow of events with such questions as, "I'd like to talk about safe sex for a moment. How do you feel about it?" or "Are you okay about using condoms?" or "Have you been tested for AIDS?" This reluctance is particularly true for the man, who is prone to performance anxieties and who tends to move toward lovemaking through a series of carefully orchestrated moves designed simultaneously to arouse the woman and to minimize the chances of losing his erection.

The safest and most direct way of dealing with the issue is to acknowledge mutual sexual attraction at the moment when it arises. Raising the issue of sex may embarrass your partner, and you may face some resistance—"Condoms turn me off," or "This isn't the right time to talk about this stuff." This is a challenging moment, for you need to be strongly in touch with your own standards of safety and not to compromise. The risk of missing out on one sexual encounter is a small price to pay for your life. This delicate moment is also an opportunity to be supportive and sensitive. The best approach here is to reassure your partner that you are genuinely interested in lovemaking, explaining that certain precautions have to be dealt with first.

Many of the guidelines and practices in the opening chapters of this book are useful at this stage, especially those that aim at establishing clear communication and an honest exchange of information. These chapters also offer a number of ways in which two people can experience intimacy and arousal without the risk of intercourse. In fact, all the High Sex practices up to and including chapter 8 can be enjoyed without sexual intercourse and make a beautiful preparation for safe sex. Thus, the sexual attraction felt by two people is not put on hold, but acknowledged and enjoyed, including many kinds of hugging, caressing, and touching, while avoiding the exchange of bodily fluids. These forms of extended foreplay can sometimes be far more arousing than intercourse itself.

This is the time to get to know your new partner's sexual history, and it is important to maintain a healthy skepticism, not idealizing your partner because you are ready to fall in love and want to believe every word he or she tells you. Express your vision of safe sexuality, listen to your partner's, and see if they are compatible. If you decide that it is safe to make love, make it clear that condoms will have to be used. There is simply no alternative. They are a necessity because they prevent the exchange of bodily fluid, but they are not necessarily an unfortunate necessity. Once you understand how to use them properly, they can become a kind of second skin rather than an uncomfortable barrier. Just as you make an art out of sexual loving in High Sex, you also can make an art out of using condoms. Learn about the different kinds; find out which are the safest brands; select your favorites. Don't opt for fancy colors and shapes over brand reliability. Then practice putting them on. If you are a man, you can practice with yourself. If you are a woman, you can practice either with an intimate male friend or on a suitable object like a zucchini. Become so proficient that when the time comes for lovemaking, you can easily maintain sexual arousal and body contact with your partner while reaching for the packet, opening it, removing the condom, and rolling it on the penis. Women need to become skilled at helping a man maintain his arousal while slipping a condom on his penis. The old-fashioned style of lying back, eyes closed, and pretending not to notice as the man fumbles around in his pockets for the package is inappropriate for safe sex. The self-pleasuring rituals in chapter 7 will be particularly helpful here to maintain arousal. If the man seems inexperienced, you can softly inquire, "Do you want to put it on, or shall I?" Or, if you sense that the man's awkwardness is due to your presence, you can tactfully disappear into the bathroom while he pleasures himself to maintain his erection and rolls on the condom.

In my opinion, everyone who is sexually active should carry a "sexual safety kit" that includes a variety of condoms and lubricants. Lubricants are very helpful in maintaining sexual sensitivity and also prevent sore spots from developing in the vagina as a result of friction with the latex. It is tempting to add lubricant to the penis before fitting a condom on it, but this could result in the condom sliding off the penis during lovemaking, so it is best for the man to wear prelubricated condoms, using additional lubricant only in the vagina. Make sure your lubricant is waterbased, because oil-based lubricants tend to break up the latex. I recommend either KY Jelly or Astroglide. There is one brand of spermicide, nonoxynol-9, that provides additional protection because it destroys the AIDS virus.

If you feel a strong resistance to using condoms, ask yourself two questions:

"Do I respect myself enough to protect myself from any risk?"

"Do I respect my partner enough to protect him or her from any risk?"

Using a condom is a "yes" response to these questions. Don't be lulled into unsafe practices by such attitudes as, "I've been tested for AIDS—I'm safe, so there's no need to bother."

When you have the condom in place, you can make love. But if your lovemaking is strong and passionate, you need to check once in a while to see that the condom is still there and not broken. Again, use plenty of lubrication. If the condom comes off or breaks, stop making love so that both partners can urinate, wash their genitals, and apply nonoxynol-9. Some experts recommend that women do *not* douche in this situation because this can create small lesions in the vaginal tissues that may admit the AIDS virus.

Once the man has ejaculated, be aware that he must withdraw his penis from the vagina fairly soon, because when the penis shrinks, it can slip out of the condom. As the man withdraws, hold the base of the condom against his penis so that it stays in place until fully outside the vagina. Throw the condom away immediately. Avoid contact of genital fluids with the hands. If there has been any manual contact with sexual fluids, then wash your hands. If you have a cut finger, make sure that it is sealed with a bandage, and be especially careful to avoid contact with sexual fluids.

The fact that condoms tend to desensitize the penis can actually be an advantage, helping men to make love for longer periods without ejaculating. The reduction of sensitivity in the genitals also supports the High Sex perspective of turning the whole body into an erogenous zone, helping sexual partners to expand their repertoire of sensual moves and stimulating caresses. The ultimate step in this whole-body expansion of sensitivity is to experience an orgasm independent of the genital context—a skill that you can learn in this book.

To maintain an erection with a condom, you may need to develop a strong, dynamic style of lovemaking because the penis requires additional stimulation. This can be fun. With practice you can become so skilled at building sexual arousal that you no longer notice the condom's presence.

During a first sexual encounter, I would recommend avoiding oral sex, unless you do it on a penis covered with a condom. A good trick is to begin by placing a drop of lubricant on the penis directly before putting on the condom. The condom can then slide over the skin of the penis easily, and this can be very exciting. Remember, however, not to move from this form of oral intercourse into vaginal intercourse, because the condom is likely to come off.

With anal intercourse, the big risk is that the walls of the rectum are highly absorbant and will allow a virus to pass through much more easily than the walls of the vagina. For this reason, I discourage anal sex, even with the use of condoms.

Researchers are still debating whether the AIDS virus can be communicated through the exchange of saliva in kissing. The virus has been found in saliva in small quantities. Personally, I recommend avoiding deep French kissing except with a long-term partner.

SAFE SEX WITH A LONG-TERM PARTNER

When it becomes apparent that the connection between you and your partner is developing into a longer relationship, then you should consider taking the additional precaution of an AIDS test. Until quite recently it was thought unnecessary for the general heterosexual population to be tested, but now more and more experts are recommending widespread testing as a way of controlling the spread of the virus. If you both test negative, continue to use condoms for three months and remain monogamous, then get tested again. If again the result is negative, you may consider dropping the use of condoms, but bear in mind the fact that the virus can remain undetected for much longer periods.

In debating whether to drop condoms, your judgment will be influenced by the sexual histories of you and your partner. You must also take into consideration whether or not you trust each other to be responsible about other sexual contacts. Hidden love affairs on the side represent a threat to safe sex unless you honestly discuss this issue. One good way to proceed is to commit yourselves to an agreement that you will both use condoms and other precautions in sex outside the relationship, while not using condoms with each other. If either of you encounters an unsafe situation outside your relationship—for example, in which a condom has broken during intercourse—you need to tell each other immediately. You may want to reintroduce condoms into your relationship for a while.

FURTHER READING

I recommend further reading on the subject so that you can fully protect yourself against AIDS and STDs. These two books are a good place to start:

The Complete Guide to Safe Sex from the Institute for Advanced Study of Human Sexuality (Specific Press).

Safe Encounters by Beverly Whipple and Gina Ogden (McGraw-Hill).

APPENDIX II

✿

MUSICAL SELECTIONS

The following listings are suggestions drawn from my favorite music used during the seminars as well as privately. I have divided the listings into five categories:

I: Music for Relaxation and Meditation
II: Music for Sensual and Erotic Play
III: Music for Movement and Dance
IV: Music for Opening the Heart
V: Special Music for Processes in this Book

Wherever address or source is not provided, music titles can be purchased at most large record stores. All the titles listed can be found at the distributors listed at the end of this section. Wherever an address is provided, you can order the title by mail.

I: Music for Relaxation and Meditation

Guru Ram Dass, Kim Robertson, Invincible Records, Box 13054, AZ 85002

SkyDancing Chakra Chants, Margo Naslednikov, Bauer Verlag, 2 Kronenstr. D- 7800 Freiburg, West Germany

The Ecstasy of Peace: Transcendence and The Alpha Experience by Brother Charles, M.S.H. Association, Rt. 1, Box 192-B, Faber, VI 22938

The Way Home by Kevin Braheny, Music from the Hearts of Space, Backroads Distributors, 417 Tamal Plazza, Corte Madera, CA 94925

This! Commentaries of the Bamboos, Music from the World of Bhagwan, distributed by Chidvilas, Box 17550, Dept. F9B, Boulder, CO 80308

Tibetan Bells II by Henry Wolf and Nancy Hemings. Celestial Harmonies 006

The Fairy Ring, Mike Rowland. Sona Gaia Productions, 1845 N. Farwell Ave., Milwaukee, WI 53202

Environment 1/Ocean Tambura, Anugama, Nightingale Records

Rainbow, Ariel Kalma, Nightingale Records

Music to Disappear In, Raphael, Hearts of Space

Inside the Great Pyramid (and others titles) by Paul Horn

Skies above Skies, Constance Demby, Sound Currents, Box 5044, Mill Valley, CA 94942

II: *Music for Sensual and Erotic Play*

I Love to Love You, Baby by Donna Summers

Oxygene by Jean-Michel Jarre

The Tibetan Book of the Dead, TMT Music Productions, D-8000 Munich 40, West Germany

Silk Road by Kitaro

Ecstasy by Chaitanya Hari Deuter. Kuckuck 044

Love Me Love Me, Jimmy Cliff

Dare Me, Pointer Sisters

Jumpstart My Heart by Natalie Cole

Rejoice by Tutare, Box 2855, San Anselmo, CA 94960

Turn of the Tide, Barclay James Harvest

Fragrances of a Dream, Kobialka

Dervish Symphony by AL Greiner Khan

Antarctica by Vangelis

White Winds by Andreas Vollenweider

III: *Music for Movement and Dance*

Totem by Gabrielle Roth, The Moving Center, Box 2034, Red Bank, NJ 07701

Exotic Dance by Anugama and Sebastiano, Nightingale Records

Bad by Michael Jackson

Spiral by Vangelis

Midnight Express (film soundtrack)

3rd World Child by Johnny Clegg and Savuka, Capitol Records

Drums of Passion, Olatunji. Columbia CS 8210

Open Mind, Jean-Luc Ponty, Atlantic Records (especially the first cut)

Hot Stuff, Donna Summers

IV: Music for Opening the Heart

Three cassettes: (1) *Journey into Love,* (2) *Shine!,* (3) *Hidden Waters/Sacred Ground* by Sophia, Box 1207, Carmel Valley, CA 93924

Allelujah by Raphael (same address as above for *Sophia*)

Novus Magnificat, Constance Demby (see address above)

Hello My Baby, Lady Smith Black Mozambo

Yes to the River, Music from the World of Bhagwan, distributed by Chidvillas

On Wings of Song: Many Blessings, distributed by Philo Records, USA

Tears of the Moon, by Coyote Oldman, distributed by Michael Graham Allen, 434 Chautauqua Ave., Norman, OK 73069

I Am Your Man (one song by this title), by Leonard Cohen

Wings to My Heart by Rosie Lovejoy, Hearts of Space

ENYA by Enya

Odes by Vangelis and Irene Pappas, Polydor 2473 109

Missa Gaia, Paul Winter and Consort, Living Music LC 0002

V: Special Music for Processes in this Book

SkyDancing: The Love and Ecstasy Training by Margo Anand and Steven Halpern. Margo's voice and Steven's musical guidance will help you integrate what you've learned in this book. Available from Sound Rx and the SkyDancing Institute.

Rajneesh Kundalini Meditation (for the Streaming Process in chapter 9)

Einstein on the Beach by Phil Glass (for the Streaming Process in chapter 9)

Sacred Space Music by Constance Demby (for Creating Your Sacred Space in chapter 3)

(1) *Releasing Natural Healing Forces* and (2) *Releasing Fear and Worry*. Subliminal music tapes by Jonathan Parker's Gateways Institute, Box 1778, Ojai, CA 93023 (for Healing the Yoni, Healing the Vajra, and Healing the Anus massages in chapter 10)

Open like a Flute, Ariel Kalma (for the processes in chapter 9 and Riding the Wave of Bliss in chapter 12)

Mail Order Sources for the Music

You can find Steven Halpern's music and Margo's cassettes at Sound Rx, Box 151439, San Rafael, CA 94915, 1-800-72-NEW AG or 415-453-9800 in California.

You can find all the above-quoted titles that do not have their own special references at Backroads Distributors, 417 Tamal Plazza, Corte Madera, CA 94925, 1-800-825-4848.

All Rajnessh-related music and meditation tapes are distributed by Chidvillas, Box 17550, Dept. F9B, Boulder CO 80308.

Nightingale Records is distributed by Meistersinger Musikproduiktion, Bamberger Str. 4, 8550 Forchheim, West Germany, telephone number 091 91/80808.

Visual Guidance

"Riding the Wave of Bliss" one-hour video tape teaching you steps of SkyDancing Training for Ecstasy and Love offered in this book. Write to: SkyDancing Institute, 20 Sunnyside Avenue, Suite A219, Mill Valley, CA 94941, USA.

꙳

RESOURCES

After reading this book, you may wonder about the possibility of participating in a seminar that teaches the principles of Sacred Sexuality. For many people, working together with others enhances their ability to learn new practices. The boost given by the energy and support of the group encourages them to abandon old habit patterns, deepens their commitment, intensifies their experiences, and speeds up the momentum of the training. However, some people tend to avoid such seminars because they believe they are nothing more than orgies.

I would like to say that, in most cases, these fears are unfounded. In the study of High Sex there is no need for lovemaking in a group context, and I know of no good teachers who encourage it. In my seminars there is no lovemaking during group sessions, no nudity, and participants are not pushed beyond the limit at which they feel comfortable. The seminars vary in length from a few days to a series that extends over the course of a year. They are available to anyone who feels inspired to explore his or her High Sex potential, to awaken the Inner Lover, to join in deep communion with a beloved, and to experience the ultimate sense of oneness that ecstasy brings.

The Love and Ecstasy Trainings are taught through the SkyDancing Institute. For any information regarding trainings in the USA, contact:

SkyDancing Institute
20 Sunnyside Avenue, Suite A219
Mill Valley, CA 94941   1–415–381–0844.

and in Europe to:

SkyDancing Institute
Postfach 3326
8049 Zurich, Switzerland

❧

ACKNOWLEDGMENTS

I have, in the years it took to complete this work, been given tremendous inspiration, help, and encouragement from many exceptional people in Europe, India, and the U.S.A.

Among those who inspired me on my path, my deepest gratitude goes to Osho Rajneesh. His unique vision of Tantra emphasizes qualities like spontaneity, transcending guilt about sexuality, and bringing into it an attitude of innocence and playfulness. From him I learned to integrate sexuality, love, and meditation. His spiritual teachings on Tantra, Yoga, and Zen have been widely acknowledged to be in the great mystical traditions of the East and to offer effective means of awakening and growth. As a Tantric master, he certainly fits perfectly into the Tantra tradition of crazy wisdom and rebellious mystics. I am indebted to his teachings as expressed in *The Tantra Vision*, published in 1979 by the Rajneesh Foundation, 17 Koregaon Park, Poona 411001, India. Some of the ideas expressed in Chapter One have been inspired by this book as well as the story of Mulla Nasruddin on page 237, which is excerpted from the book.

Thanks also to Michel Sokoloff, who showed me the tao of sacred sexuality; to Kaveesha, who nurtured the wisdom of the High Priestess; to Swami Satchidananda, who initiated me into Integral Yoga; and to Bob Hoffman, who opened the door to personal freedom through the Hoffman Quandrinity Process.

I am most grateful to my publisher, Jeremy Tarcher, who shared my vision and supported it through many occasions when I was feeling discouraged. Without his encouragement and understanding, his careful supervision and revision of the manuscript, this book would never be what it is today.

Next my grateful appreciation goes to Subhuti, one of the fastest, brightest, and most professional writers I have worked with. Just at the

443

moment when he was needed, he jumped into the project and helped me write, rewrite, and revise until we had a final manuscript. His speed, inspiration, and reliability helped the vision of this book come to life.

My thanks also to Craig Comstock for helping me to get started through his patient and enthusiastic support, his coaching and editorial supervision of the first stage of the book. Thanks to John Loudon for his organization of the material, and to my editor, Connie Zweig, for her intelligent and empathic editing.

I would like to acknowledge my partner and coteacher, Aman P. Schroeter, who, through his love and support during the last 10 years, has inspired me to develop and teach many of the structures of the Love and Ecstasy Training. Thanks to Martin Kremer, Dieter Schmidt, and Helga Koppler, founders and directors of Forum International, for their love and their sense of Tantric celebration. Also, my thanks to Carlo Kosha Pati for being such an inspired playmate in the exploration of SkyDancing. To Suwanna Gauntlett, for her enthusiasm and encouragement when I needed it most. My appreciation to Jack Painter for the contribution of his own work and teachings, and to Wulfing von Rohr for his dedication and humor in guiding me through the intricacies of international publication. I am grateful to be part of a global family of celebration partners in Tantra: Sunito Plesse and Bijo St. Clair, Ariel and Ama Kalma, Bhakfa and Azul, Anne Pierard, Rashma and Siddhartha, Stephen A. Vasey, Christian and Jenny Combescure, Mimi Steiglitz, Lori Grace, Rainbow, Emerald, Kutira.

My thanks also to Leandra Hussey for her elegant artwork. Finally, last but not least, I give honor and thanks to Boris and Quinette Naslednikov, my parents and friends, for their unconditional, nonjudgmental, humorous support on my path.

INDEX

Alan, Woody, 35
Anal Healing Massage (exercise),
    336–345
Anus, 153, 309
    healing massage (exercise), 336–345
Arousal, 36
    gender gap in, 200–201
    of men, guidance in, 230–232
    of women, guidance in, 226–229
Awakening Your Inner Lover (exercise),
    10, 55–59

Basic Stance (exercise), 134–136
Bioenergetic therapy, 152, 197, 274
Body
    conscious recognition of (exercise),
      136–139
    dissolving blocks in, 275–279
    learning to love, 124–129
    purification ritual (exercise), 132–134
Body armoring, 128, 129. *See also*
      Genital armoring
    anal area, 336–345
    deep breathing and, 131
    genital, 318–338
Body image, 123–125
Bonding, 291–299
    exercises, 290–299
    integrating into lovemaking, 295–299
    positions for, 292–293
    sexual, 295–299
Bonding Relaxation (exercise), 290–294
Brain, and orgasm, 307
Brauer, Alan and Donna, 29, 306–307
Breath/breathing, 385–386
    awareness of, 50–51

awareness of (exercise), 52–55
    deep, 51, 130–131
    inverted exchange of, 190–191, 370,
      371–374, 415–419, 420–421
    sexual (exercise), 179–183
    streaming and, 288–289
Butterfly (exercise), 286, 288–290

Centers of energy. *See* Chakras; Third
    eye
Ceremony of Recognition of the Body
    (exercise), 11, 136–139
Chakras, 168–175
    bringing awareness to (exercises),
      354–374
    sensations related to, 169–170
Chang, Stephen, 213, 338
Children, 424
Clitoris, 313, 314, 320
    orgasm through, 304, 305
    stimulating, 205, 206, 226–227, 228
Coming Together: Pleasuring Each
    Other (exercise), 224–234
Conscious Breathing: Following the
    Breath (exercise), 52–55
Core Energetics (Pierrakos), 168
Creating Your Sacred Space (exercise),
    11, 71–78
Crown chakra, 174, 370, 363–364
    shooting energy to (exercise),
      370–374

Dancing Gods (exercise), 11, 105–113
    Dance of Shakti and Shiva, 112–113
    Dance of Shiva, 111–112
Dialogue, sexual, 214–219

Diary, 14–15
Dodson, Betty, 198–199
Dual Pelvic Rocking (exercise),
    188–191
  with inverted breathing, 190–191

Ecstasy, sexual. *See also* Ecstatic
    Response; High Sex
  defined, 273
  energy charge and, 3–4, 41
  through expanded orgasm, 272–276
  relaxation and, 28, 29
  three-step process in generating,
    28–33
Ecstatic Response, 26, 29–30, 275
  awakening, 271–299
  awakening (exercise), 282–285
  beginning of, 274
  development of, 273–299
Ejaculation. *See also* Orgasm
  delaying, 211–213, 232, 349–350, 351
  explosive, 349, 350–351
  female, 305–306, 314, 347, 348
  orgasm versus, 37
  premature, 200
  withholding, 347–354
  withholding (exercise), 375–379
Endocrine glands, 166, 355
Energy, sexual
  building up, 271–299
  containing during lovemaking, 405
  directing to crown chakra (exercise),
    370–374
  generating (exercises), 174–191
  infinite cycle of, 418–419, 421–423
  internalizing, 164–165
  redirecting to brain (exercises),
    353–375
  releasing, 128–129, 152
  sending to genitals, 414, 416
  sending to third eye, 370–371,
    373–374, 416–418, 421–422
  Tantra on, 41–42
Erotic Touching (exercise), 11, 139–142
ESO (Brauer and Brauer), 29, 306
Eve's Secrets (Lowndes), 306

Eye(s), 378
  receptive, 118
  rolling upward, 182, 362

Fantasies, sexual, describing, 86–91
Fears, sexual, 24–25, 32, 83–84
Female polarity, 39–40
Fingertip Stroking (exercise), 142–144
Focusing, 21, 23, 44
Forehead chakra, 173–174, 362–363. *See
    also* Third eye
Freud, Sigmund, 304

G spot, 228, 305–306, 309, 314, 320
  ejaculation from, 314, 322, 330
  locating, 228, 329
  massaging, 228, 329, 330
  orgasm and, 309, 330
G Spot, The (Ladas, Whipple, and
    Perry), 305–306
Gender identity, 238–246
Gender stereotypes, 238–239, 253
Genital armoring
  female, 318, 319–320
  healing, 318–338
  healing exercises, 321–346
  male, 318–319
  recognizing, 320
Goal orientation, giving up, 44,
    46
Greer, Germaine, 35
Guilt, eliminating, 43

Healing, sexual, 33
Healing the Vajra (exercise), 332–336
Healing the Yoni (exercise), 323–332
Hearing, awakening sense of,
    100–101
Heart chakra, 172–173, 360, 362
Heart Salutation (exercise), 59–62
High Sex, 3, 4, 7, 172, 199, 347–349,
    422, 423
  approach to practices, 14–26
  integrating into daily life, 424
  methods of, 8
  overview of training, 10–13

practices *(see names of individual exercises)*

Hugging exercise, 78–82

Ichazo, Oscar, 5, 116
Inner Flute, 163–192, 285, 359, 364, 368, 385, 419, 421
    discovering, 164, 166–175
    opening, 11–12, 178, 180–183
    orgasm and, 164–165
    pathway of, 163–164, 166
    in Riding the Wave of Bliss, 405–406, 411–412, 416, 418–419, 421
Inner Lover, 47–63. *See also* Awakening Your Inner Lover (exercise)
Inner Man/Inner Woman. *See* Masculine/feminine components of personality
Inner Smile (exercise), 114–115
Intimacy, enhancing, 93–120
    Butterfly exercise and, 286
    exercises, 96–120
    Yin-Yang game and, 258, 261
Iyengar, B. K. S., 168

Jung, Carl G., 240

Kinsey, Alfred, 197, 304–305
Kundalini energy, 26, 275. *See also* Ecstatic Response

Laing, R. D., 4
Liberating Masturbation (Dodson), 198
Light
    inner, 406, 416, 418, 422
    visualizing, 361, 362, 363, 364
Lowen, Alexander, 168, 197, 274
Lower belly chakra, 171–172, 357–359
Lubrication, 201, 204, 206, 226, 325, 333

Masculine/feminine components of personality (Inner Man/Inner Woman), 39–40, 239–257
    recognition of, 239–245

in Riding the Wave of Bliss, 403, 405
    stereotypes, 238–239
    visualization of (exercises), 247–253
Maslow, Abraham, 273
Massage, 126, 364–365, 413–415
    of anus, 336–343
    of G spot, 228, 329, 330
    of perineum, 207, 334–335
    of prostate, 342–343
    Slipping and Sliding (exercise), 144–145
    of vagina, 322, 323–326
Masters, William and Virginia Johnson, 304
Masturbation. *See* Self-pleasuring
Meditation, 44, 51, 371
    masturbation as, 198–199
Melting Hug (exercise), 78–82
Men
    genital geography of, 316–318
    guide to arousing women, 226–229
    guide to self-pleasuring, 206–207
Movement, 131
Music, 26, 100, 101, 102, 104, 146, 280, 291, 326
Myths about sexuality, 33–38

Oils, 134, 144, 202, 409, 413–414
Opening Lotus (exercise), 159–162
Opening Lotus position, 403, 408
Oral loving, 400–403
Orgasm. *See also* Ejaculation; Peak sexual experiences
    blended, 309, 330–331
    brain and, 307
    clitoral, 309
    delaying, 211–214, 229
    diffused, 272
    discoveries about, 303–308
    dry, 304–305, 349
    versus ejaculation, 37, 304–305
    expanded, 272–276
    explosive, 309
    extended, 29, 309
    full-body, 29–30, 35, 36, 309, 337

Orgasm, *continued*
  genital, 29, 30, 273–274, 301–306,
    308–309
  implosive, 309, 337, 349
  kinds of, 304, 308–309
  nongenital, 271–273
  prostatic, 308, 309, 314
  spiritual enlightenment and, 41–42
  vaginal, 308, 309, 315, 316

Painter, Jack, 153
Partner, practicing with, 18–21
PC muscle. *See* Pubococcygeus muscle
PC Pump (exercise), 175–178
Peak sexual experiences
  describing to partner, 88–91
  energy charge and, 3–4
  relaxation and, 2–3
Pelvic Curl (exercise), 152–159
Pelvic Rocking (exercise), 184–188
  with partner, 188–191
  with PC Pump and Sexual Breathing,
    187–188
  in Riding the Wave of Bliss, 411
Pelvis
  charging with energy, 154–159
  increasing flexibility of (exercise),
    152–159
  opening up (exercises), 146–159
  rocking (exercises), 184–191
Penis
  anatomy of, 316–318
  healing massage (exercise), 321–322,
    332–336
  manual stimulation of, 230–232
  self-pleasuring, 206–207
  special names for, 215–216
  squeezing to delay ejaculation, 212
Perfumes, 134
Perineum, 153, 315, 320
  massaging, 207, 334–335
  pressing on, 212, 225, 229, 232, 315,
    335, 338, 349
Pierrakos, John, 168–169
Playfulness, 25, 93, 113–114
  exercise, 114–115

Pleasure, cultivating, 43–44
Pleasuring Each Other (exercise),
  224–234
Positions. *See* Postures of lovemaking
Postural Integration, 153
Postures of lovemaking, 387–403
  Erotic Kali, 396–397
  Hiding in the Crevice, 398
  Kali, 393–394
  Missionary, 389–390
  Morning and Evening Tuning, 390
  Piercing Tiger, 398–399
  Reclining Devas, 408–409
  Riding the Wave of Bliss, 387, 403,
    407–409
  Rolling Tickle, 392
  Scissors, 397
  Spoon, 397
  Standing Shiva, 399–400
  Swooping Kali, 394, 396
  vertical, 405
  yah yum, 383, 385, 387
Practicing, 15, 17–20
  alone, 18
  with partner, 18–19
  with partner of same sex, 19–20
  patience in, 17–18
Prostate, 207, 309, 316, 318, 337, 338
  massage of, 342–343
  orgasm and, 308, 309, 314
Pubococcygeus (PC) muscle, 175, 176
  development of, 178–179
  pumping (exercise), 175–179

Reich, Wilhelm, 152, 197, 275, 305
Relaxation, 19
  bonding and, 290–299
  breathing and, 386
  extended orgasm and, 29, 291
  of genital muscles, 384–386
  during high state of arousal, 2–3,
    28–29, 272, 307–308
  during intercourse, 378, 380
  massage and, 126
Repression, sexual, 37
Resistance, 22–25

moving beyond (exercise), 82–91
moving through, 24–25
overcoming, 22–24
suspension of present beliefs and, 24
Riding the Tiger Alone (exercise),
354–355, 357–364
Riding the Tiger Together (exercise),
365–366, 368–370
Riding the Wave of Bliss (exercise), 13,
31–33, 403, 405–423
Inner Flute in, 411–412, 416, 417,
418, 421
positions, 403, 405, 407–408, 415
steps, 411–422
Ritual of Purification (exercise),
132–136
Role-Playing Each Other (exercise),
253–256

Sacred, sense of, and sexual union, 40
Sacred Space, defined, 68
Safe sex, 21, 325
Sanctuary (Sacred Space)
creating, 60, 68–78
exercise, 75–78
Sanella, Lee, 275
Saraha, 6
Satchitananda, Swami, 5
Self-love, 42, 47–50
exercise, 55–59
Self-pleasuring, 193–235
exercises, 200–234
for men, 206–207, 211–213
moving energy to heart, 207–209
moving energy to third eye, 209–210
overcoming guilt about, 194–196
with partner (exercises), 214–224
for women, 204–207
Self-Pleasuring in Front of Each Other
(exercise), 223–224
Self-Pleasuring Ritual (exercises),
200–214
Discovering the Magic Wand,
206–207
Exploring the Forbidden Fruit,
204–206

Moving Pleasure to the Heart,
207–209
Sending Energy to the Third Eye,
209–210
Spreading the Sexual Fire, 207–208
Self-Pleasuring Under the Eyes of Your
Beloved (exercise), 219–223
Sense of flow, 2
Senses, awakening, 96
exercise, 11, 96–105
Sensitivity, 36
armoring and, 321
heightening, 131, 199–200
Sensory Awakening Ritual (exercise),
11, 96–105
Sensory deprivation experiment, 27,
28
Sensuality, expanding, 424, 425
Sevely, Josephine Lowndes, 306, 314
Sex chakra, 170, 357
Sex drive, and energy, 41
Sex Perfection and Marital Happiness
(von Urban), 291
Sexual Behavior in the Human Male
(Kinsey), 196
Sexual Bonding Relaxation (exercise),
295–299
Sexual Breathing (exercise), 179–182
Sexual desire, lack of, 238
Sexual Dialogue (exercise), 214–219
Sexual ecstasy. *See* Ecstasy, sexual
Sexual energy. *See* Energy, sexual
Sexual Solutions (Castleman), 213
Shaking Loose (exercise), 276–279
Shakti, 5, 106
Shiva, 5, 106
Shooting to the Crown Together
(exercise), 370–371, 373–374
Sight, enhancing sense of, 104–105
Slipping and Sliding (exercise), 144–148
Solar plexis chakra, 172, 360
Soul Gazing (exercise), 11, 116–120
Sounds, 131
Spontaneity, enjoyment of, 43
Squatting Together (exercise), 148–152
Stance, basic (exercise), 134–136

Streaming Meditation (exercise), 279–285
   Inner Flute and, 285
Streaming sensations, 12, 28, 31, 274–275
   breathing and, 288–289
   exercises, 279–290, 417
   involuntary, 274–275, 282–285
Stretching exercises, 146–152
Support group, creating, 425–426
Surrender during arousal, 46, 289–290, 405

Tantra, 5–7
   perspective of, 8, 10, 38–42, 425
Tantric attitude, 6, 42–44, 46
Tantric tradition, 6, 37–46, 49, 123, 241, 347, 405
Tao of Sexology, The (Chang), 213, 338
Taste, enhancing sense of, 101–102
Third eye, 209–210, 229, 352, 370. See also Forehead chakra
   sending energy to, 370–371, 373–374, 415–419, 420–422
Three Keys (to build up and discharge energy), 130–132, 174, 213, 234
Three-step process, 28–33
Throat chakra, 173, 362
Tibetan Yoga and Secret Doctrines (Wentz), 166
Tordjman, Gilbert, 307
Touch, enhancing sense of, 102–104
Touching, erotic, 139–146
   exercises, 140–145

Vagina
   anatomy of, 311–316
   armoring of, 319, 320

healing through massage (exercise), 322, 323–326
   manual stimulation of, 227–229
   special names for, 215–216
Vajra. See Penis
Valley Orgasm (exercises)
   Level One, 375–379
   Level Two, 379–380
Vibrations, 274
   generating (exercises), 276–299
Visualization, 179, 181, 224, 355, 357, 359, 361
   of Inner Flute, 166–167, 180–182
   of Inner Man/Inner Woman (exercises), 247–253
   in Riding the Wave of Bliss, 416–419, 421
Visualizing Your Inner Man and Inner Woman (exercise), 12, 247–252
von Urban, Rudolf, 291

Watts, Alan, 257–258
Women
   genital geography of, 311–316
   guide to arousing men, 230–232
   guide to self-pleasuring, 204–206

Yah yum position, 383, 385, 387
Yin and Yang, 39–40, 118, 243, 269, 401–402, 421
Yin-Yang Game (exercise), 257–269, 424
Yoni. See Vagina

Zafu (meditation cushion), for pelvic rocking, 160, 185, 411